EMILY POST'S POCKET BOOK OF ETIQUETTE is an abridgment, containing the essence of the most recent revised edition of Emily Post's ETIQUETTE, published by Funk & Wagna... Digest, Inc.

D1444242

EMILY POST'S
POCKET BOOK OF
Etiquette

Elizabeth L. Post

PUBLISHED BY POCKET BOOKS NEW YORK

EMILY POST'S POCKET BOOK OF ETIQUETTE

Funk & Wagnalls edition published April, 1965

A *Pocket Book* edition
1st printing......September, 1967

This *Pocket Book* edition is printed from brand-new plates made
from completely reset, clear, easy-to-read type. *Pocket Book*
editions are published by Pocket Books, a division of Simon & Schuster,
Inc., 630 Fifth Avenue, New York, N.Y. 10020. Trademarks registered
in the United States and other countries.

L

PREFACE

to the Eleventh Edition

When my husband and I became engaged, one of the first things he wanted to do was to take to me to Edgartown, Massachusetts, and introduce me to his grandmother, Emily Post. In spite of his reassurances, and obvious devotion to her, I had all the natural reservations about meeting the famous First Lady of Etiquette, and I was a very nervous young lady when we arrived at her lovely island home that day in June, 1944. And I remained nervous for at least five minutes! In that space of time, I found that the supposedly unapproachable authority on all our manners and behavior was the sweetest, most natural, warmhearted, unaffected person I had ever met. From that day on, we were as close as two people separated by a span of some years can be, and I was never once made uncomfortable or self-conscious in her presence. That, to me, is the proof of the value of etiquette. To practice perfect manners without appearing to be "stiff" and at the same time to let those about you feel that *they* are equally well-mannered is a goal that can be achieved only by making consideration and unselfishness an integral part of your behavior.

My husband and I, and our children, spent a great deal of time with "Grandmama," as we always called her, and the children loved her as much as we did. Even they felt the gracious atmosphere that radiated from her and were almost invariably at their best in her presence, not because they had to be, but because they wanted to be.

We often discussed etiquette in those years, both the subject itself and the book she wrote about it. Emily Post was thoroughly aware of the changing pattern of modern living and made a point of keeping in constant touch with the changes both through her correspondence with readers and through the activities of the members of her own family. Furthermore, she fully realized that the time would come when etiquette would necessarily be affected by these changes. She herself eliminated and changed parts of her original work in frequent revisions over the years, and she foresaw that one day still other parts would no longer be applicable. And, conversely, she recognized that new aspects of modern life, nonexistent then and therefore unmentioned in earlier editions, would need to be considered.

As a result, Emily Post founded—in 1946—the Emily Post Institute. The purpose of the Institute was, and is, to perpetuate the traditions of gracious living by making available the most recent information on etiquette today. The staff of the Institute worked closely with Mrs. Post herself, and she actively supervised all phases of the work until her recent death. She insisted from the beginning that I take an active part, and it is for this reason that I have undertaken this revision of *Etiquette*.

All of us connected with this project have constantly kept in mind the need to maintain the high standards set by Emily Post, although in the less formal life that most of us lead today, some of the rules may seem more stringent than ever. If we have succeeded in making this revision of her book a useful, readable, and practical guide on all questions of etiquette for young and old alike, then we will know that we have carried on the work started by Emily Post as she would have wished.

ELIZABETH L. POST

CONTENTS

CONTENTS

PART ONE

THE ART OF CONVERSATION

1

Introductions, greetings, farewells

The words we say as we meet or take leave of someone can create an impression with far-reaching consequences. Therefore, the forms we use on such occasions may be of considerable importance. Automatic familiarity with them leaves our minds free for the more complicated arts of conversation and gracious listening.

UNBREAKABLE RULES OF INTRODUCTION

Though rules for introductions have become much less rigid in recent years, certain forms must be followed. A younger person is presented to an older person. A gentleman is always presented to a lady, even though she is no older than eighteen. No woman is ever presented to a man, with the following exceptions: (1) the President of the United States; (2) the recognized head of another country; (3) a member of a royal family; (4) a cardinal or other high church dignitary.

THE USUAL FORMS OF INTRODUCTION

The simplest introduction, suitable whenever two individuals are introduced, is the mere pronouncing of the two names: "Mrs. Woodman—Mrs. Norman." A man is also introduced:

"Mrs. Woodman—Mr. Norman." A mother introducing a man to her married daughter says, "Mr. Brown, I would like to introduce you to my daughter, Mary Smartlington."

To refer to one's husband as "Mr. Smith" or to one's daughter as "Miss Smith" is discourteous. But if the daughter has a different name, it may be said with a pause between that makes a parenthesis: "My daughter [pause] Mrs. Smartlington." The same pause may be used when introducing a stepparent and an acquaintance. To avoid confusion, if your names are likely to be thought the same, you say, "Mrs. Brown— my stepfather," then, after a pause, "Mr. Jones." This sounds much more pleasant than "Mrs. Brown—my mother's husband."

The name of the older or more notable person is said first. A woman's name is said before a man's, unless the preposition "to" is used before the lady's name. If, for instance, you find yourself saying Mr. Norman's name first, you can turn this slip into a polite gesture by saying, "Mr. Norman, may I introduce you to Mrs. Maddox?"

Formally, a man introduces another man to his wife: "Mr. Brown, I should like to introduce you to my wife." To a good friend, a husband would say, "Jim, I want you to meet my wife" (never "the wife"). Then, as though in parentheses, he says to his wife, "Mary, Jim Buyer" or "Mr. Buyer." Or if they are all young, he probably says, "Mary, this is Bob Ace."

A lady introduces her husband to friends as "John" and to acquaintances as "my husband." The two names of safety are "my husband" and "my wife" because they are proper no matter to whom you are talking. With other than friends, acquaintances and business associates, "Mr. Brown" and "Mrs. Brown" are quite correct.

An introduction prefaced by the phrase "This is," said with an enthusiastic inflection, expresses warmth and charm. London *Punch* once had a drawing of a small boy approaching his mother, holding an abashed small girl by the hand and radiantly explaining, "Mummy! THIS IS HER!" In the same way, a child would introduce a beloved teacher enthusiastically, "Mother, *this* is Miss Brown," or "Miss Brown, *this* is my mother!"—in the sense of "Behold! this is she—my mother."

Relatives-in-law:

A lady formally introduces her son's wife to acquaintances as "my daughter-in-law," but with friends she uses the less formal "Mary, Dick's wife." The warmth of voice is important. By tone alone, the same words may convey every shade of feeling from cool indifference to adoration. To introduce a parent-in-law as simply "Father" or "Mother" may be confusing. "This is my mother-in-law" is preferable, or "my husband's sister" and "my brother John's wife" (or "Jim's sister" and "John's wife" to one who knows who Jim and John are). Such identifications are clearer than "my sister-in-law."

Teen-agers and young adults:

Informality is the rule among young adults and teen-agers. Muriel Manners, for example, taking a friend to a country club, greets a group of friends with "Hello, everybody. This is Sally Stranger." Everyone then calls Sally by her first name and further introductions are made in the same way: "Sally Stranger, Lucy and Bob Gilding." Or, "Lucy, this is Sally Stranger"; then to Sally, "That is Bob Gilding, and that is Tom Brown," for a man is always introduced to a girl. The newcomer waits to be called by her first name before calling others by theirs. A younger person never calls an older person by his or her first name unless he is asked to; the choice lies with the older person.

Other permissible forms:

Other forms of introduction might be called conversational introductions. For example: "Mrs. Parker, you know Mrs. Robinson, don't you?" or "Mrs. Robinson, have you met Mrs. Parker?" Sometimes a few words of explanation make the introduction of a stranger pleasantly smooth. "Mrs. Worldly— Miss Jenkins. She writes as Grace Gotham." Or, "Mr. Neighbor, I should like you to meet Mr. Tennis. He has just won the tournament at Forest Hills." These explanations can be overdone, however, and may create the effect of trying to impress one's acquaintance with another's importance.

Forms to avoid:

Never say, "Mr. Jones, shake hands with Mr. Smith," or "Mrs. Jones, I want to make you acquainted with Mrs. Smith." In introducing one person to another, do not call one of them "my friend." You may say "my aunt" or "my sister" or "my cousin," but to pick out one person as "my friend" implies that the other person is not. "Mrs. Smith, I want you to meet Mrs. Jones" is correct, but never "Mrs. Smith, meet Mrs. Jones." The last phrase lacks friendliness and courtesy. Do not repeat "Mrs. Jones—Mrs. Smith. Mrs. Smith—Mrs. Jones," unless the name is foreign or difficult to pronounce. Then repeating the name a second time slowly is helpful.

To say "What is your name?" is abrupt and unflattering. If giving your own name doesn't elicit the information, find a third person later and ask, "Who was the lady with the gray feather in her hat?" The next time you see her, you will be able to say, "How do you do, Mrs. Green?"

FORMAL AND CEREMONIAL FORMS OF INTRODUCTION

The most ceremonious introduction possible is: "Mrs. Distinguished, may I present Mr. Traveler?" or "Mrs. Young, may I present Professor Gray?" "Present" is more formal than "introduce," but "may I introduce" is equally proper.

To the President of the United States:

The correct introduction of either a man or woman is: "Mr. President, I have the honor to present Mrs. [or Mr.] Williams" —or "Mrs. Williams of Chicago," if further identification is necessary. Mrs. (or Mr.) Williams simply bows. If, as is customary, the President offers his hand, Mrs. Williams takes it, but she does not offer hers first.

To a reigning sovereign:

Because one's name has been put on a presentation list beforehand, at the actual presentation the "accepted" name is repeated from one functionary to another and nothing is said to the king or queen except "Mrs. [or Mr.] Williams." Mrs. Williams curtsies. If the king offers to shake hands, she curtsies again as she gives him her hand. (If she objects to curtsying, she must not ask to be presented to the sovereign.) Mr. Williams follows the same procedure, bowing instead of curtsying.

On less formal occasions, a woman is presented to any member of a reigning family, "Your Royal Highness [or whatever the title], may I present Mrs. Williams?"

To a church dignitary:

To a cardinal, one says, "Your Eminence [or in England, "Your Grace"], may I present Mrs. Williams?" One who is not a Catholic behaves as he would to a king, but a Roman Catholic drops on the right knee, places the right hand, palm down, under the cardinal's extended hand and kisses his ring. A woman is always presented to archbishops, bishops, monsignors and priests. Mrs. Williams replies by saying to the archbishop or bishop, "How do you do, Your Excellency?" and to the monsignor, "How do you do, Monsignor Ryan?" To a priest she says either "Father Kelly" or simply "Father."

To other distinguished persons:

With the exception of state and high church dignitaries, distinguished persons are all presented *to* a woman by their proper titles. A foreign ambassador is presented, "Your Excellency, may I present you to Mrs. Williams?" —or a senator, "Mrs. Williams, may I present Senator Davis?" A senator is always "Senator Davis," even when he is no longer in office. But the President of the United States, once out of office, becomes "Mister."

Former governors and ambassadors are "The Honorable." On ceremonial occasions, you would present "The Honorable John Jones, former governor of the State of Blank." Among friends he may be introduced simply as "Mr. Jones."

Doctors and judges are introduced and addressed by their titles. Protestant clergymen are "Mister" unless they hold the title of doctor, dean or canon, in which case the surname is added to the proper title. A Catholic priest, however, is "Father Kelly," whatever his other titles may be.

If the one making the introduction has neglected to use a title, the safest thing to say is "How do you do?" After that you may address any gentleman as "Sir." In fact, to avoid repetition of long titles like "Your Royal Highness" or "Mr. President," it is preferable to say "M'am" or "Sir" occasionally.

(For a chart of titles used in addressing and introducing important persons, see Chapter 5.)

WHEN TO INTRODUCE

Receiving lines:

When a large, formal party is given in honor of someone unknown to most of the people invited, the hostess receives with the special guest. People are presented to her as they arrive: "Mrs. Eminent, this is Mrs. Neighbor." Mrs. Eminent offers her hand. At a smaller, friendly party given for someone known to the majority of the guests, the guest of honor does not receive with the hostess, but sits or stands in a convenient place so that others can go up and talk with her. (If you should happen to arrive after the receiving line has dispersed, you must look for the guest of honor and present yourself; otherwise you will appear very rude.)

Formal dinners:

At a formal dinner all the people seated at the same table talk to each other, with or without a formal introduction. Strangers sitting next to each other usually introduce themselves. A gentleman says, "I'm Arthur Robinson." An older lady replies, "I'm Mrs. Hunter Jones," but a younger one says, "I'm Mary Brown," and perhaps adds, "Bob Brown's wife." When a young woman finds herself next to an unknown man at a dinner party, she may talk to him without telling him her name. But if he introduces himself to her as "John Blank," she says, "I'm Mary Smith"—not "Miss Smith."

One person to a group:

On formal occasions, one person is not introduced to each and every person already present. An arrival may be introduced to one or two people, or he may be left to talk with those nearby without exchanging names. But at a small lunch, for instance, let us suppose you are the hostess. Your position is not necessarily by the door, but near it. Mrs. King and Mrs. Lawrence are sitting close to you and Miss Robinson and Miss Brown farther away. Mrs. Jones enters. You go to her, shake hands, then you stand aside, as it were, to see whether Mrs. Jones goes to speak to anyone. If she apparently knows no one, you say, "Mrs. King—Mrs. Jones." Mrs. King, if she is younger, rises, shakes hands with Mrs. Jones, then sits down; or if she is about the same age as Mrs. Jones she merely extends her hand and remains seated. Without repeating Mrs. Jones's name you turn to the other lady sitting nearby saying, "Mrs. Lawrence." You look across the room and continue, "Miss Robinson, Miss Brown—Mrs. Jones." The two nod and smile but do not rise. Then the hostess seats Mrs. Jones next to one or more of the earlier arrivals and they all enter into conversation. When you are making such introductions, it is a good idea to say the name of the person already present first in order to get her attention, since she may be busily engaged in conversation.

Sometimes a hostess at a large party leads a guest on a tour around the room to make sure that he—or more especially she —is introduced to everyone. This results in the poor stranger being hopelessly confused by too many names. The better procedure is, as described above, to introduce her to a nearby group and let her sit down with them. They will make her feel comfortable and introduce her to others.

INTRODUCING ONESELF

At all informal gatherings, the roof of a friend serves as an introduction and everyone there *always* talks to those near them. But at a large party (a dance or a wedding reception), you are not required to speak with those whom you do not know unless you and another guest find yourselves apart from the others. Then you may comment on the beauty of the bride or on the weather. If you wish, you may introduce yourself with an identifying remark: "I am Sally's cousin," or "I am a neighbor of the groom." To talk or not to talk depends on mutual willingness. When you have a good reason for knowing someone, then you introduce yourself. For instance: "Mrs. Worldly, aren't you a friend of my mother? I am Jane, Mrs. John Smith's daughter." Mrs. Worldly says, "I am indeed. I'm so glad you spoke to me."

(For information on announcing oneself in business situations, see Chapter 2.)

WHEN NOT TO INTRODUCE

We all know introduction enthusiasts who cannot let one person pass another without insisting that they stop to be introduced. At a small "get-together," this is quite all right, but at a wedding reception or any general gathering, it is a mistake. A newly arrived visitor is not introduced to someone who is taking leave. Nor is an animated conversation between two persons interrupted—especially one between a young man and a young woman—to introduce a third.

INTRODUCING EMPLOYEES IN A HOME

There are occasions when a halfway introduction seems most appropriate. Suppose you wish to make a domestic employee known to a guest. "Olga, would you please take Mrs. Jones's bag to her room?" Or you might say to your guest, "Mary, this is Hilda, who will be glad to take your bag for you." Or in the case of a loved and respected servant, a young man might say to his new fiancée, "Mary, this is Lizzy Smith who has brought me up," and to Lizzy, "Lizzy, I know you will love Mary as much as I do."

Often one domestic helps in so many ways that she becomes almost a member of the family and rightfully expects to be treated as such. The thoughtful employer might say to a house guest, "Mary, this is Sally Jones, whom we couldn't manage without. Sally, this is my oldest friend, Mrs. Charles."

WHAT TO DO WHEN INTRODUCED
What to say:

If, in answering an introduction, you have not heard the new name clearly, it is perfectly correct to say simply, "How do you do?" But adding the name of the person you have met is the warmest, most polite response, and helps in committing it to memory. For example, when Mrs. Worldly had been introduced to Mr. Struthers, she replies, "How do you do, Mr. Struthers?" He simply nods, or he may say, "I'm very glad to meet you." If Mr. Struthers is someone whom she has long wanted to meet, Mrs. Worldly may go on to say, "John Brown speaks of you all the time"—or whatever may be the reason for her special interest.

When and how to shake hands:

Gentlemen always shake hands when they are introduced to each other even if they have to cross a room to do so. Ladies may do as they wish. When a gentleman is introduced to a lady, she generally smiles, nods, and says, "How do you do?" But if he should extend his hand, she gives him hers.

As to whether or not to shake hands on parting, there is no fixed rule. You are more likely to shake hands with someone whom you find sympathetic, but you can be courteously polite and at the same time reserved to someone who does not appeal to you.

Everyone dislikes to shake a "boneless" hand extended as though it were a wet rag or to have one's hand shaken violently. What woman does not wince at the viselike grasp that cuts her rings into her flesh and temporarily paralyzes her fingers? The proper handshake is made briefly, with a feeling of strength and warmth. At the same time one looks into the face of the person whose hand one takes. In giving her hand to a foreigner, a married woman relaxes her arm and fingers, as it is still customary in some Latin countries for him to lift her hand to his lips. Younger women usually offer their hand to the older; otherwise, women merely clasp hands, give them a dropping movement rather than a shake, and let go.

When to rise:

On formal occasions, the hostess always stands at the door and the host nearby. Both shake hands with each arrival. On informal occasions, they both rise and go forward to greet each guest. The children in the family rise for every grown person who enters the room and stand until the older person is seated. Grown as well as half-grown members of the family other than the host and hostess rise to greet guests, but do not necessarily shake hands.

A woman guest does not stand when being introduced to someone at a distance, nor when shaking hands with anyone, unless that person is much older. Should an elderly lady enter the room in which many other ladies are seated, only the members of the family rise, since seven or eight all getting up produces an effect of confusion.

Every gentleman stands as long as his hostess or any other lady near him does. Nor does he sit if any other gentleman with whom he is talking remains standing. Furthermore, a man always rises when a woman comes into a room. In public places, a man does not jump up for every woman who is a stranger to him if she happens to approach him, but if she addresses a remark to him, he stands as he answers her.

When a woman goes to a man's office on business, he stands up to receive her, offers her a chair and remains standing until she is seated. When she rises to leave, he gets up instantly, stands for as long as she remains, then goes with her to the door, which he holds open for her.

In a restaurant, when a lady greets him, a gentleman merely makes the gesture of rising slightly from his chair and nodding. *(For additional details, see Chapter 9.)*

The young greet the old:

It is rude for young people not to go and shake hands with an older person of their acquaintance when they meet away from home, especially someone to whose house they have often gone. There is no need for them to enter into a long conversation. The older person should avoid detaining the young person with endless questions on his health and activities or those of his family.

NAME "BLACKOUTS"

When you are talking with someone whose name you are struggling to remember and are joined by a friend who looks inquiringly from you to the nameless person, all you can do is to introduce your friend to the stranger by saying to the latter, "Oh, don't you know Mrs. Neighbor?" The tactful stranger then announces her own name. If she says nothing, however, and Mrs. Neighbor makes matters worse by saying, "You didn't tell me your friend's name," the only solution is to be completely frank, admit you do not remember the name, throw yourself on their mercy and then ask them to complete the introduction themselves.

When meeting someone who may have forgotten you, never say, "You don't remember me, do you?" Unless the person you speak to greets you by name, say at once, "I'm Mrs. Brown, or Mary Brown," and then, if this does not bring a sign of recognition, "We met at the Roberts'."

INFORMAL GREETINGS

"Hello," the universal form of greeting in America, is acceptable in any situation except after a formal introduction. Even comparative strangers say "Hello" in passing, and among young people it is considered friendly after a first-name introduction. "Sally, I'd like you to meet Joan," and Sally says, "Hello, I'm glad to meet you, Joan."

In the business world, "Good morning" is the usual greeting before the lunch hour. After lunch, the somewhat stilted "Good afternoon" has been largely replaced by "Hello"; but it is still used as a phrase of dismissal, indicating an interview is ended, a class is dismissed, etc. Among friends or business acquaintances who know each other personally, "Good-bye" or "Good night" is said on parting.

GREETINGS IN PUBLIC

In Europe a gentleman bows to a lady first. In the United States a lady is supposed to greet a gentleman first, but today few people observe this formality. When one passes a casual acquaintance, a tipping or slight raising of the hat by the man and a smiling nod from the woman is all that is necessary.

In theaters, restaurants, shops or almost any public place, people speak to acquaintances as long as the greeting does not create a situation that may disturb others around them, as it would in the middle of a play. If they are too far apart to speak without shouting, they simply smile and wave.

Unless one has a good memory for people, it is always better to nod to someone whose face is familiar than to run the risk of ignoring an acquaintance. It is often difficult to recognize people whom one has met, when they are wearing a different type of dress or hat. One must be careful not to confuse such unintended rudeness as shortsightedness or absentmindedness with an intentional cut. A "cut," the direct stare of blank denial, insulting to its victim and embarrassing to every witness, is, happily, a rare occurrence.

THE ANSWER TO "HOW ARE YOU?"

Normally, the correct and conventional answer is "Fine, thank you" or "Very well, thank you." To one who is a chronic invalid or is in great sorrow or anxiety, a gay "Hello, Mrs. Jones! How *are* you? You look fine!" is tactless and unkind.

TAKING LEAVE

When a visitor is ready to leave, he or she merely stands. To one with whom he has been talking he says, "Good-bye, I hope I shall see you again soon," or, simply, "I'm glad to have met you." To the first, the other answers, "Thank you, I hope so too"; or to both, merely, "Thank you." In taking leave of a group of strangers—whether you have been introduced or merely included in their conversation—you nod and smile a "Good-bye" to anyone who happens to be looking at you, but you do not attempt to attract the attention of those who are unaware that you are leaving. When leaving a party early, you find your hostess and say good-bye without attracting any more attention than is necessary, in order to avoid being the cause of breaking up the party prematurely.

2

Names and titles

USE OF FIRST NAMES

In general, first names should indicate that people have met more than once. If, however, during the first meeting one person finds she is drawn to another by common interests or mutual friends, it is perfectly correct for her to say, "Please call me Sally." At any informal party in the home of friends, it is customary to use first names after having responded correctly to the introductions. If you don't, you will be thought stiff and unfriendly.

(For what to do when introduced, see Chapter 1.)

Many people of middle age and older think that being called "Sally" or "Jack" by Doris Sophomore and Bobby Freshman puts them on the same age level, suggesting a camaraderie which often does not exist. But if Mrs. Autumn and Mr. Sere prefer to be "Sally" and "Jack," no one else has a right to object.

CHILDREN AND OLDER PEOPLE

Parents:

Unfortunately, in America today respect for older people is not as prevalent as it was a few generations ago. Nevertheless one of the areas in which a parent should still insist on respect is in the way they permit their children to address them. *It is a flagrant violation of good manners for children to call their natural parents by their first names.*

Stepparents:

Because circumstances vary there can be no set rule about what children should call their stepparents. It depends only on what seems to be best in each case. Children should never be forced to call a stepparent "Mother" or "Father" or any nickname having that meaning, especially if their own parent is living. If they *choose* to do so, it is a compliment to the stepparent and should be encouraged.

If a child goes to live with a stepparent at a very young age, and if his own parent is dead or if the child is not and probably never will be acquainted with that parent, then he would consider his stepparent as his own and say "Mother" or "Father," particularly if he hears stepbrothers or stepsisters using those names. If the child is older when one parent remarries, the situation is quite different. If he has known the stepparent for some time, he may call him (or her) by a nickname or even by his first name. Actually, an appropriate nickname seems to be the best solution, provided it is not a derivative of "Mother" or "Father."

Names for parents-in-law:

A bride may call her parents-in-law by whatever names she chooses. Usually, and naturally, parents-in-law are called by names that mean mother and father but are not the names that the bride uses for her own parents. The ban against "Mother" and "Father" results from consideration for one's own parents who are not often happy to hear their own special names bestowed elsewhere. The less intimate relationships of aunts, uncles and even grandparents never come into question because the bride calls all such relatives of her husband's exactly what he does, and he does the same in speaking of hers.

Other adults:

A child or young person may call an older person by his first name *only* when that person has specifically asked that he do so. As long as the child understands that it is done at the request of the grown-up, it is quite acceptable. For example, some adults dislike being called "Aunt" or "Uncle" or "Cousin." Intimate friends, devoted to the children, may also feel that "Mr. (or Mrs.) Surname" does not express the close relationship they desire and suggest nicknames for themselves. Otherwise, a child addresses all friends of his parents as "Mr. (or Mrs.) Surname."

REFERRING TO HER HUSBAND OR HIS WIFE

Correctly a lady says "my husband" when speaking of him to an acquaintance. But to a friend or to the friend of a friend she speaks of him as "John." This does not give anyone else the privilege of calling him "John" unless asked to do so.

In the same way, Mr. Worldly speaks of "Edith" to intimate masculine friends and to every woman whom they both know socially, whether they themselves call her "Edith" or "Mrs. Worldly." But to a man not an intimate friend and to a woman who is a stranger, he speaks of her as "my wife." In most business situations, if he has occasion to speak of her, he would say, "Mrs. Worldly thinks thus or so . . ." Thus, when the Duke of Edinburgh, accompanying Queen Elizabeth II, was hailed by a former shipmate in the British Navy, he correctly introduced him to "my wife."

ANNOUNCING ONESELF

Arriving at the door:

When an adult member of the family comes to the door in answer to your ring, you never call yourself "Mr." or "Mrs." or "Miss" but announce yourself as "John Grant" or "Sally Smythe" and explain the purpose of your visit. If he obviously does not recognize you, you further identify yourself by a sentence or two: "I'm a friend of Jim's at the office" or "Susan and I met at the Barrys' cocktail party." If a child answers the door, you say, "I'm Mr. Grant [or Mrs. Smythe]. Would you please call your mother for me, if she is at home?"

If the door is answered by a maid who does not know you

and if you are not expected, you announce yourself as "Mr. John Grant." If you are expected, you merely say, "Mr. Grant."

The businessman announces himself:

When you enter an unfamiliar office, say to the receptionist, "Good morning. My name is Rodger Salecurve. I have a ten o'clock appointment with Mr. Byre." At this point, you offer your business card (if you carry one)—it will help the receptionist to give your name correctly to the person you wish to see. If you do not have a specific appointment, you may add a little information about your business. "Good afternoon, I am Rodger Salecurve of the Schmid Corporation. I would like to see Mr. Byre about our line of lubricants."

On the telephone:

When the title "Doctor" indicates a degree required for the practice of a profession, as in medicine, surgery or dentistry, it is used instead of "Mister" at all times. But a title stemming from a degree in law, philosophy, literature, science, etc., is used mainly in professional work. In private life, a man may continue to call himself "Mister" and usually uses "Mr." or no title at all on visiting cards or social directories. Friends and acquaintances may wish to call him "Doctor" in courtesy.

NAMES LEGALLY CHANGED

Whenever a name by which one has been known is changed, social and business associates should always be notified of the change quickly. The simplest way is to send out formal announcements in this form:

Mr. and Mrs. John Original Name
Announce that by Permission of the Court
They and Their Children
Have Taken the Family Name of
Miller

3

The good conversationalist

A practical rule for a conversation is: STOP, LOOK, LISTEN. "Stop" means not to rush recklessly forward; "Look" means pay attention to the expression of the person with whom you are talking; and "Listen" is the best advice possible, because the person whom most people love to sit next to is a sympathetic listener who really listens. A fixed expression of sympathy while your mind wanders elsewhere won't do. It never fools anyone.

PLEASANT TALK

Humor is the rarest of gifts. If you know anyone who is gay, beguiling and amusing, do all you can to make him prefer your house and table to any other, for where he is, there is the successful party. But beware of the forced wit; he is always a bore.

Fishing for topics:

If we want to be thought sympathetic, intelligent or agreeable, we must "go fishing." In talking to a person whom you have just met and about whom you are in complete ignorance, try one topic after another, just as a fisherman searches for the right fly. "Are you fond of the theater?" you ask. If the answer is "yes," you talk theater. When that subject runs down, you talk of something *you* have been doing—planting a garden, contemplating a vacation, or similar safe and natural topics. Do not snatch at a period of silence. Let it go for a little while. Conversation is not a race that must be continued at breakneck pace.

Introducing oneself is sometimes the most practical way to begin a conversation. You might say, "I'm Betty James. My husband and I live in the country, but we often come to town to go to the theater." The stranger may reply that he lives in the city, but his favorite occupations are golf and fishing. Talk of these leads to other things. It's really very simple.

Another helpful gamble, especially if you are a woman, is to ask advice. "We are planning to drive through the South. Do you know the roads?" Or "I'm thinking of buying a television set. Which make do you think is best?" It is safe to ask his opinion on almost anything: politics, sports, the stock market, the current fad. If you are a man talking to a young woman, ask her what she thinks about work, young people, amusements. If she is an older woman, she will probably talk to *you!*

Avoid criticism of a religious creed or disagreement with another's political convictions. Also be careful not to let amiable discussion turn into argument. A 'tactful person says, "It seems to me thus and so," but never "That's not so!" If another's opinion seems unreasonable, you quickly find a more pleasant subject. If you care so intensely about a subject that you can only lecture about your fixed point of view, don't mention that subject. But if you are able to listen with an open mind, you probably need put no barriers on any topic. Argument between cool-headed, skillful opponents can be a delightful, amusing game, but it is very dangerous for those who may become hot-headed and ill-tempered.

The tactless blunder:

Examples of tactlessness include the means-to-be agreeable elderly man who says to an old acquaintance, "Twenty years ago you were the prettiest girl in Philadelphia." Or to a mother whose only son has just married, "Why is it, do you suppose, that young wives so often dislike their mothers-in-law?"

Personal remarks:

It is always pleasant to hear something appreciative about something one has done. "Your speech was splendid!" "What a delicious dinner you gave us." "I've never seen such beautiful flowers." But it is bad taste to comment on physical attributes or ask about expense or other money matters. "What a lovely dress! How much did it cost?" is exceedingly rude.

The sympathetic listener:

The person who is seemingly eager for your news or enthralled with your conversation, who looks at you with a kindling of the face and gives you spontaneous and undivided attention, is the one to whom the "orchid" for the art of conversation would undoubtedly be awarded.

UNPLEASANT TYPES

The bore:

A bore might be described as one who insists on telling you at length something that you don't want to hear about at all. He insists that you hear him out to the bitter end in spite of your plainly shown disinterest. His constant repetition is deadly dull. But the most delightful people are those who refuse to be bored. One way out is to try being agreeable yourself; that helps and may break the stream of monotonous conversation. Boredom often comes with laziness, an unwillingness to shift one's point of view. So if you find yourself sitting in the hedgerow with nothing but weeds, don't shut your eyes and see nothing; instead find what beauty you may in the weeds.

The wailer:

Too many people use as the staples of their conversational subject matter misfortunes, sickness and other unpleasantness. Don't dwell on your own problems. Your audience has them, too, and won't be entertained by yours. Only your nearest and dearest care how many times you have been to the operating room.

The cutting wit:

Sharp wit tends to produce a feeling of mistrust even while it stimulates. Furthermore, the applause that follows a witty sally tends to make well-intentioned people more and more sharp-tongued; in the end it makes others uneasy and one's self unpopular.

"I'd say it to her face!":

A good resolve to make and keep, if you would keep your friends, is never to speak of anyone without, in imagination, having him or her overhear what you say. One often hears the exclamation "I would say it to her face!" Be very sure that this is true and then—nine times out of ten—think better of it and refrain. Preaching is all very well in a textbook, schoolroom or pulpit, but it has no place in society. Society is supposed to be a pleasant place; telling people disagreeable things to their faces or talking behind their backs is not a pleasant occupation.

For those who talk too much:

Regrets are generally for what you said rather than for what you left unsaid. "Better to keep your mouth closed and be thought a fool than open it and remove all doubt." Don't pretend to know more than you do. To try to discourse learnedly about something you know very little about is to make others look on you as a half-wit. No person of real intelligence hesitates to say, "I don't know." Above all, stop and *think* what you are saying. This is really the most important rule. Know when to listen to others, but know also when it is your turn to carry the conversation. Then remember that nothing holds the interest of the listener when it is too long dwelt upon or told too often.

PART TWO

CORRESPONDENCE AND GREETING CARDS

4

The appearance and style of your letters

The letter you write is a mirror that reflects your appearance, taste and character. You can, with practice, make yourself write neatly and legibly. Observe straight lines and regular margins on both the left and right sides of the sheet—the left-hand margin is usually a little wider than the right. It is perfectly correct to type letters to friends if you wish. All business letters—from home as well as office—should be typed if possible, but some forms of correspondence must always be written by hand.

Never type an invitation, an acceptance or a regret.

Never type letters of congratulation or thanks.

Never type letters or notes of condolence.

STATIONERY

A person whose handwriting is large should pick a larger size paper than someone whose writing is small. Low, spread-out writing looks better on a square sheet of paper, tall pointed writing on high and narrow paper. Rough or smooth paper is a matter of personal choice—but let the quality be good, the shape and color conservative. Do not use scented or oddly shaped paper and avoid excessive ornamentation.

The flap of the envelope should be plain and the point neither skimpy nor unduly long. When the paper is thin, use envelopes with colored linings so that the writing cannot be read through the envelope. Linings of unrestrained masses of red and gold, swirls of purple and green or other striking colors are not in good taste—though linings for Christmas card envelopes may be as gay as the ornaments that decorate a Christmas tree. Oblong envelopes are excellent for business, but those more nearly square are smartest for personal use.

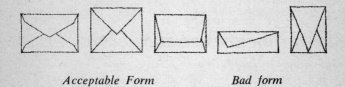

Acceptable Form   *Bad form*

Deckle-edged paper or clean-cut edges is a matter of personal choice. Both are correct.

Paper for a man:

A man's writing paper should always be conservative: plain white or cream, gray or granite, single sheet 7 or 7¼ by 10 or 10½ inches and engraved (or printed) at the top in black, dark gray or navy blue. His *business* stationery is engraved (or printed) in plain block letters with his name (without title), his address and, if he wishes, his telephone number. For his *social* correspondence, he uses paper of the same color and size, but he may use initials instead of his name, or a crest if he has one. The single sheet in each case is folded in threes to fit into a 7¼ or 7½ by 4-inch envelope. This stationery is correct for both typed and handwritten letters. Writing ink should be dark blue or black.

Paper for a woman:

White, cream, all blues, grays and, more recently, greens are in best taste. Paper should be of small or medium size, single or double sheets, plain or with colored border. It may be engraved (or printed) with either a monogram or initials. It may have only the address or it may have both monogram or initials and address. The color of the lettering must match the border. Writing ink should be black or blue or green to match the color of the paper. A married woman's name is written "Mrs. William Frost," not "Mrs. Mary Frost" or "Mary Frost." An unmarried woman uses "Miss" only on the envelope.

Paper for everyone in the family:

A paper suitable for the use of all the members of a family has the address engraved or printed in plain letters at the top of the first page. Frequently the telephone number is put in small letters under the address. Or it may be put in the upper left-hand corner, with or without a small telephone device, and the address in the center.

> 350 Chestnut Street
> Philadelphia 11, Pennsylvania
> TELEPHONE ORMOND 4-7572

> 18 Walnut Road
> Peoria, Illinois

For the young correspondent:

A young teen-ager may use his or her name—Peter Frost or Elizabeth Jones—or a simple monogram. A young girl may also use only her first name—Elizabeth (in full) or Betty if she prefers. Or her stationery may be decorated with a spray of flowers or other pretty design in the upper left-hand corner (this is never suitable for use by an older woman, however). A very young child—boy or girl—may use a drawing of a kitten or a puppy or some other animal.

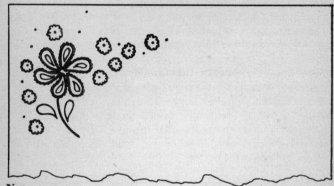

Note paper:

For short notes or invitations, acceptances or regrets, a supply of fold-over note paper, half the size of a single sheet of a lady's writing paper, is invaluable. It may be of any color appropriate to the household, and engraved or printed with initials or with the owner's name and address and possibly with the telephone number.

Paper for a country house:

Paper for a country house may be less rigid in form. When the telephone exchange, mailing address and station or airport are located in different towns or areas, a little symbol for each is stamped or printed in the left-hand corner.

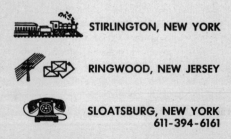

STIRLINGTON, NEW YORK

RINGWOOD, NEW JERSEY

SLOATSBURG, NEW YORK
611-394-6161

Printing or engraving:

Paper upon which one's full name and address are printed has become indispensable to everyone who must write many letters. Therefore printed paper for informal social correspondence and for business letters is generally accepted as entirely correct. You may wish to have in addition a small supply of engraved paper, though no one will think any the worse of you if you do not.

Crests:

When an old family has used their family arms continuously since they brought the device—and their right to it as certified by the colleges of heraldry—from Europe to America, its use is proper, although, at the present time, somewhat conspicuous. The crest is the exclusive property of male members of a family, although it may be used jointly by husband and wife on some occasions. It never appears on the paper of a widow or spinster—a heraldic rule apparently unknown to most Americans. A widow may use the device on the shield of her husband's coat of arms, transferred to a diamond-shaped device called a lozenge. She may also, if she chooses, divide the lozenge perpendicularly into two parts and crowd the device from her husband's shield into the left half and the device from her father's shield into the right half. A spinster uses her paternal arms on a lozenge without crest or motto.

Your home address and the date:

If your stationery is not marked with your address, let your correspondent know where to reply by putting your address either on the upper right side of the first page of your letter, or, especially on a short note, at the far left, just below the level of your signature. Whether or not your stationery is already printed, the date goes either at the upper right-hand side of the first page of a letter or at the end and to the far left of the signature of a note.

Sincerely,
Mary Swenson
(Mrs. John Swenson)

45 Barton Street
Racine, Wisconsin
May 5, 1967

Recipient's address:

On business letters the address of the receiver is put at the left, below the level of the date and directly above the salutation, exactly as it appears on the envelope.

June 7, 1967

Mr. James Johnson
Smith, Johnson & Company
New York, New York (and the zip code number)

Dear Mr. Johnson:

Personal letters and notes, however, have the address of the receiver *only* on the envelope itself.

The salutation:

For business letters, the salutation "Dear Sir" or "Dear Sirs" is better than "Gentlemen" (never "Messieurs").

June 7, 1967

Smith, Johnson & Company
20 Broadway
New York, New York (and the zip code number)

Dear Sirs:

If a firm or organization is composed of women, the salutation is "Dear Madams" (never "Mesdames").

An impersonal business letter to a woman begins:

Mrs. Richard Worldly
500 Fifth Avenue
New York, New York (and the zip code number)

Dear Madam:

A business letter from a man to a woman customer or client he knows personally begins with the same address form as above, but instead of "Dear Madam" the salutation is "My dear Mrs. Worldly" or "Dear Mrs. Worldly."

The most formal beginning of a social letter to a woman is "My dear Mrs. Smith." Increasingly intimate are: "Dear Mrs. Smith," "Dear Sally," "Sally, dear," and "Dearest Sally." A man is always addressed "Dear Bob" when something less formal than "Dear Mr. Smith" is desired.

(For forms used in addressing distinguished persons or those in special categories, see Chapter 5.)

The closing:

The best ending to a formal social note is "Sincerely," "Sincerely yours," "Very sincerely," or "Very sincerely yours." "I remain, dear madam," is no longer in use, but "Believe me" is still correct when a degree of formality is to be expressed in the close of a note.

> Believe me
> Very sincerely yours,

The close of a business letter is "Yours truly" or "Yours very truly." "Faithfully" or "Faithfully yours" is appropriate for a man when he is writing to a woman or for any noncommercial correspondence, such as a letter to the President of the United States, a member of the cabinet, an ambassador, a clergyman, etc. "Respectfully" is used only by a tradesman to a customer or by an employee to an employer.

"Sincerely" in formal notes and "Affectionately" or "Love" in intimate notes are the most used today, though "Cordially" is also widely used. "Yours in haste" or "Hastily yours" is allowable only if the communication indicates necessary haste. "Gratefully" is used only when a benefit has been received: to a lawyer who has skillfully handled a case or, possibly, to a friend who has gone to unusual trouble to do you a favor. In an ordinary letter of thanks, the signature is "Sincerely," "Affectionately," "Devotedly"—whatever your usual close may be.

(For forms used in letters to distinguished persons or those in special categories, see Chapter 5.)

The signature:

In America, John Hunter Titherington Smith, finding his name too much of a penful, chooses J. H. T. Smith for letters and documents, or perhaps at the end of personal letters, John H. T. Smith. Of course, if the letter is to a business associate whom he knows personally he may simply sign "Jack" over the typed "J. H. T. Smith." Mail is addressed to him in the typed form (or the printed form, if the letterhead carries his full name).

A married woman always signs a letter to a stranger, a bank, a business firm, etc., with her legal name. If her stationery is marked with her full married name and address, her signature —Mary Jones Mathews—needs no further explanation. Otherwise, she gives her married name (to which the reply will be sent) in one of several ways. When she writes by hand, she adds her married name in parentheses, beneath her signature, thus:

> *Very truly yours,*
> *Mary Jones Mathews*
> (*Mrs. John Mathews*)

When the letter is typed, her married name is typed beneath the space left for her signature, though not necessarily enclosed in parentheses.

> Very truly yours,
> *Mary Jones Mathews*
> Mrs. John Mathews

A woman uses "Mrs." in her signature only on a hotel register, on a business telegram or on an order letter to a tradesman thus: "Mrs. John Smith." To a servant in her employ it is "Mrs. Smith."

An unmarried woman uses much the same form in a typed letter:

> Sincerely,
> *Mary Jones*
> Miss Mary Jones

When she writes by hand, she may use this style:

> *Sincerely,*
> (*Miss*) *Mary Jones*

A professional woman whose professional name differs from either her married, (or her unmarried name) uses her own name in her *social* correspondence. For example: if in private life she is married (Mrs. John Mathews) or single (Mary Jones) she follows the forms prescribed above. But, if in her professional life she uses the name Mary Cotton, then in her *business* letters, she signs Mary Cotton only, and under it types "Miss Mary Cotton":

> Very truly yours,
> *Mary Cotton*
> Miss Mary Cotton

If the letter is handwritten, she may simply sign it "(Miss) Mary Cotton."

Folding a letter:

After signing a letter the paper is folded once for an envelope that is as deep as half the length of the paper, and twice for an envelope that is a third as deep. Paper that must be folded into thirds is used only as personal stationery for men or for business purposes. Note paper is the same size as the envelope and goes into it flat with only the original fold.

THE OUTSIDE ADDRESSES

Write the name and address on the envelope legibly, including the zip code number, using a straight margin on the left:

> *Mr. Harvey S. Simpson*
> *4 Hillside Lane*
> *Clinton*
> *Ohio* (and the zip code number)

Correct use of "Esq.":

"Esq." is seldom used today in the United States except by conservative members of the older generation, by lawyers and by justices of the peace. It may be used on handwritten invitations and personal letters. However, on any formally engraved invitation and its envelope Esq. should not be used.

A widow or divorcée:

Never address a note or social letter to a married woman—even if she is a widow—as Mrs. Mary Town. A widow always keeps her husband's name. If her son's wife should have the same name, she becomes Mrs. James Town, senior, or simply, Mrs. Town, if she is the only one in her community with that name. A divorced woman usually takes her own surname in place of her ex-husband's Christian name. If she was Mary

Simpson before her marriage, she correctly calls herself Mrs. Simpson Johnson. However, to avoid confusion, some divorceés prefer to use "Miss (or Mrs.) Mary Johnson"; if they do, you must address them in that way.

Daughters, sons and children:

Formerly, the eldest daughter was correctly Miss Taylor, her younger sister, Miss Jane Taylor. Today Miss Alice Taylor and Miss Jane Taylor are invariably used. Envelopes to children are addressed to Miss Katherine Taylor and to Robert Taylor, the latter with no title. Little boys under ten years of age are addressed as "Master"; at college-age they are called "Mr." In between, they are addressed with no title. "The Messrs. Brown" is correct only for unmarried brothers, never for a father and son.

"Personality" and "Please Forward":

If you are writing to someone at his home address, never write "Personal" on it. But on a social note to a friend's business address it is entirely correct. "Please forward" is correct if you know only a former address but not the current one, or if the person to whom it is addressed is traveling and you are not sure the letter will reach him before he leaves the last address you have.

Return address:

Customarily, a return address is put on the face of a business envelope at the top left-hand corner. On a personal letter, it used to be put on the flap—this was and still is particularly true on personal *printed* stationery. But today (in response to requests made by the United States Post Office) it is permissible and advisable on a handwritten envelope to put the return address on the face. The handwriting should be small and include the zip code number.

Unsealed letters:

Best form dictates that any letter given to a person (other than a commercial messenger) for delivery by hand be unsealed unless it has a valuable enclosure. If the envelope is sealed beforehand it is polite to explain why. Though not obligatory, customarily the person carrying it seals it immediately in the presence of the writer.

5

Addressing important persons

The following chart has been prepared to cover as many as possible of the situations likely to occur in the ordinary course of events—and some not so ordinary. Special attention has been given to the official and formal occasion; naturally Governor Marvin's friends will continue to call him Joe at purely friendly functions and their wives will continue to address their dinner and luncheon invitations to the Governor's wife. Only when a wedding or other formal invitation would be sent to both husband and wife is it necessary to use the special forms included below in the "Social Correspondence" column.

Federal custom in the United States bestows the title "Honorable," first officially and then by courtesy for life, on the following: the President, Vice President, United States Senators, United States Congressmen, members of the cabinet, all federal judges, ministers plenipotentiary, ambassadors and governors of all states. But this title is not used by the person himself on his visiting card or letterhead or in his signature. The people of the state address their state senators as "The Honorable Lawrence Hamilton, State Senator," as a courtesy title only. Best usage dictates that "The Honorable" (spelled out in full) appear on a separate line, as shown in the chart in this chapter, and that his wife, when she is included, have a line to herself below his name and slightly indented.

The correct forms for addressing representatives of other countries who are living in the United States are firmly fixed by governmental protocol. But whether their wives are addressed as Mrs., Madame, Señora or some other title depends upon the

Personage	ENVELOPE ADDRESS	SOCIAL CORRESPONDENCE	INFORMAL BEGINNING OF LETTER
THE PRESIDENT	The President The White House Washington, D.C.	The President and Mrs. Washington The White House Washington, D.C.	My dear Mr. President:
THE VICE PRESIDENT	The Vice President United States Senate Washington, D.C.	The Vice President and Mrs. Hope Home address	My dear Mr. Vice President:
CHIEF JUSTICE, SUPREME COURT	The Chief Justice The Supreme Court Washington, D.C.	The Chief Justice and Mrs. Page Home address	My dear Mr. Chief Justice:
ASSOCIATE JUSTICE, SUPREME COURT	Mr. Justice Katsaros The Supreme Court Washington, D.C.	Mr. Justice Katsaros and Mrs. Katsaros Home address	My dear Mr. Justice Katsaros:
CABINET MEMBER	The Honorable Gary George Gussin The Secretary of the Treasury or The Attorney General or The Postmaster General Washington, D.C.	The Honorable The Secretary of the Treasury and Mrs. Gussin Home address or *(for a woman cabinet member)* Mr. and Mrs. Henry Leo Woods	My dear Mr. Secretary: or My dear Mr. Attorney General: or My dear Mr. Postmaster General or Madam Secretary:
FORMER PRESIDENT	The Honorable Alfred Edward Work Office address	The Honorable Alfred Edward Work and Mrs. Work Home address	My dear Mr. Work:
UNITED STATES SENATOR	The Honorable John Wandzilak United States Senate Washington, D.C.	The Honorable John Wandzilak and Mrs. Wandzilak Home address or *(for a woman senator)* Mr. and Mrs. John Row Doe	My dear Senator Wandzilak:
THE SPEAKER OF THE HOUSE OF REPRESENTATIVES	The Honorable Walter James Grevesmuhl The Speaker of the House of Representatives Washington, D.C.	The Speaker and Mrs. Grevesmuhl Home address	My dear Mr. Speaker:
MEMBER OF THE UNITED STATES HOUSE OF REPRESENTATIVES	The Honorable Henry Cobb Wellcome United States House of Representatives Washington, D.C.	The Honorable Henry Cobb Wellcome and Mrs. Wellcome Home address or *(for a woman member)* Mr. and Mrs. John Knox Jones	My dear Mr. Wellcome:
AMBASSADOR OF THE UNITED STATES	The Honorable John Wilson Smith The Ambassador of the United States American Embassy London, England	The Honorable John Wilson Smith and Mrs. Smith Home address or *(for a woman ambassador)* Mr. and Mrs. Leeds Walker Home address	My dear Mr. Ambassador: or My dear Madam Ambassador:

FORMAL BEGINNING OF LETTER	INFORMAL CLOSE OF LETTER	FORMAL CLOSE OF LETTER	IN CONVERSATION	TITLE OF INTRODUCTION
Sir:	Very respectfully yours,	I have the honor to remain, Most respectfully yours,	Mr. President or Sir	*Only the name of the person being introduced is spoken*
Sir:	Sincerely yours, or Faithfully yours,	Very truly yours,	Mr. Vice President or Sir	The Vice President
Sir:	*Same as above*	*Same as above*	Mr. Chief Justice or Sir	The Chief Justice
Sir:	Sincerely yours,	*Same as above*	Mr. Justice or Mr. Justice Katsaros or Sir	Mr. Justice Katsaros
Sir: or Dear Sir: or Madam:	*Same as above*	*Same as above*	Mr. Secretary or Mr. Attorney General or Mr. Postmaster General or Sir or Madam Secretary	The Secretary of the Treasury or The Attorney General or The Postmaster General
Sir:	*Same as above*	*Same as above*	Mr. Work or Sir	The Honorable Alfred Edward Work
Sir: or Madam:	*Same as above*	*Same as above*	Senator or Senator Wandzilak or Sir or Madam	Senator Wandzilak of Alaska
Sir:	*Same as above*	*Same as above*	Mr. Speaker or Sir	The Speaker of the House of Representatives
Sir: or Madam:	*Same as above*	*Same as above*	Mr. Wellcome or Mrs. Jones or Sir or Madam	Representative Wellcome of Nebraska
Sir: or Madam:	*Same as above*	*Same as above*	Mr. Ambassador or Madam Ambassador or Sir or Madam	The American Ambassador or (*if necessary*) Our Ambassador to England

Personage	ENVELOPE ADDRESS	SOCIAL CORRESPONDENCE	INFORMAL BEGINNING OF LETTER
MINISTER PLENIPOTENTIARY OF THE UNITED STATES	The Honorable James Lee Row The Minister of the United States American Legation Oslo, Norway	The Honorable James Lee Row and Mrs. Row Home address *or (for a woman minister)* Mr. and Mrs. Arthur Johnson Home address	My dear Mr. Minister: or My dear Madam Minister:
CONSUL OF THE UNITED STATES	Mr. John Smith American Consul Rue de Quelque Chose Paris, France	Mr. and Mrs. John Smith Home address	Dear Mr. Smith:
AMBASSADOR OF A FOREIGN COUNTRY	His Excellency Juan Luis Ortega The Ambassador of Mexico Washington, D.C.	His Excellency The Ambassador of Mexico and Señora Ortega Home address	My dear Mr. Ambassador:
MINISTER OF A FOREIGN COUNTRY	The Honorable Carluh Matti The Minister of Kezeah Washington, D.C.	The Honorable Carluh Matti and Mrs. Matti Home address	My dear Mr. Minister:
GOVERNOR OF A STATE	The Honorable Joseph L. Marvin Governor of Idaho Boise, Idaho	The Honorable Joseph L. Marvin and Mrs. Marvin Home address	Dear Governor Marvin:

State Senators and Representatives are addressed like U.S. Senators and Representatives, with appropriate addresses

MAYOR	His [or Her] Honor the Mayor City Hall Easton, Maryland	His Honor the Mayor and Mrs. Lake Home address *or (for a woman mayor)* Mr. and Mrs. L. T. Wayne Home address	Dear Mayor Lake:
JUDGE	The Honorable Carson Little Justice, Appellate Division Supreme Court of the State of New York Albany, New York	The Honorable Carson Little and Mrs. Little Home address	Dear Judge Little:
BISHOP, PROTESTANT	The Right Reverend John S. Bowman Bishop of Rhode Island Providence, Rhode Island	The Right Reverend John S. Bowman and Mrs. Bowman Home address	My dear Bishop Bowman:
CLERGYMAN, PROTESTANT	The Reverend David Dekker Address of his church *or (if he holds the degree)* The Reverend David Dekker, D.D. Address of his church	The Reverend David Dekker and Mrs. Dekker Home address	Dear Mr. [or Doctor] Dekker:
RABBI	Rabbi Paul Aaron Fine Address of his synagogue *or (if he holds the degree)* Paul Aaron Fine, D.D. Address of his synagogue	Rabbi [or Doctor] and Mrs. Paul Aaron Fine Home address	Dear Rabbi [or Doctor] Fine

FORMAL BEGINNING OF LETTER	INFORMAL CLOSE OF LETTER	FORMAL CLOSE OF LETTER	IN CONVERSATION	TITLE OF INTRODUCTION
Sir: *or* Madam:	*Same as above*	*Same as above*	Mr. Row *or* Mrs. Johnson	Mr. Row, the American Minister *or (if necessary)* Mrs. Johnson, the American Minister to Denmark
Sir: *or* My dear Sir:	*Same as above*	Sincerely yours,	Mr. Smith	Mr. Smith
Excellency:	Sincerely yours, *or* Faithfully yours,	Very truly yours,	Mr. Ambassador *or* Excellency *or* Sir	The Ambassador of Mexico
Sir:	Sincerely yours,	*Same as above*	Mr. Minister *or* Sir	The Minister of Kezeah
Sir:	*Same as above*	*Same as above*	Governor Marvin *or* Sir	The Governor *or (if necessary)* The Governor of Idaho
Sir: *or* Madam:	Sincerely yours,	Very truly yours,	Mr. Mayor *or* Madam Mayor	Mayor Lake
Sir:	*Same as above*	*Same as above*	Mr. Justice	The Honorable Carson Little, Judge of the Appellate Division of the Supreme Court
Right Reverend Sir:	Faithfully yours, *or* Sincerely yours,	Respectfully yours,	Bishop Bowman	Bishop Bowman
Sir: *or* My dear Sir:	Sincerely yours,	Sincerely yours, *or* Faithfully yours,	Mr. [or Doctor] Dekker	Mr. [or Doctor] Dekker
Dear Sir:	*Same as above*	Sincerely yours,	Rabbi [or Doctor] Fine	Rabbi [or Doctor] Fine

Personage	ENVELOPE ADDRESS	SOCIAL CORRESPONDENCE	INFORMAL BEGINNING OF LETTER
THE POPE	His Holiness Pope Paul VI *or* His Holiness the Pope Vatican City		
CARDINAL	His Eminence Alberto Cardinal Vezzetti Archbishop of Baltimore Baltimore, Maryland		
ARCHBISHOP, ROMAN CATHOLIC	The Most Reverend Preston Lowen Archbishop of San Francisco San Francisco, California		Most Reverend and dear Sir:
BISHOP, ROMAN CATHOLIC	The Most Reverend Matthew S. Borden Address of his church		My dear Bishop Borden:
MONSIGNOR	The Right Reverend Monsignor Ryan Address of his church		Reverend and dear Monsignor Ryan:
PRIEST	The Reverend John Matthews [*and the initials of his order*] Address of his church		Dear Father Matthews:
MEMBER OF RELIGIOUS ORDER	Sister Angelica [*and initials of order*] *or* Brother James [*and initials*] Address		Dear Sister Angelica: *or* Dear Brother James:
UNIVERSITY PROFESSOR	Professor Robert Knowles Office address *or (if he holds the degree)* Dr. Robert Knowles *or* Mr. Robert Knowles	Professor [*or* Doctor *or* Mr.] and Mrs. Robert Knowles Home address	Dear Professor [*or* Doctor *or* M Knowles:
PHYSICIAN	William L. Barnes, M.D. Office address	Doctor and Mrs. William L. Barnes Home address	Dear Doctor Barnes:

FORMAL BEGINNING OF LETTER	INFORMAL CLOSE OF LETTER	FORMAL CLOSE OF LETTER	IN CONVERSATION	TITLE OF INTRODUCTION
Your Holiness:		Your Holiness' most humble servant,	*See Chapter 21*	*See Chapter 21*
Your Eminence:		I have the honor to remain, Your Eminence's humble servant,	Your Eminence	*One is presented to* His Eminence, Cardinal Vezzetti
Your Excellency: or Most Reverend Sir:	*Same as formal close*	I have the honor to remain, Your Excellency's humble servant,	Your Excellency	*One is presented to* The Most Reverend, The Archbishop of San Francisco
Most Reverend Sir:	Faithfully yours,	I have the honor to remain, Your obedient servant,	Your Excellency	Bishop Borden
Right Reverend and dear Monsignor Ryan:	Respectfully yours,	Respectfully yours,	Monsignor Ryan	Monsignor Ryan
Reverend Father:	Faithfully yours,	I remain, Reverend Father, Yours faithfully,	Father or Father Matthews or Your Reverence	The Reverend Father Matthews
My dear Sister: or My dear Brother:	Faithfully yours,	Respectfully yours,	Sister Angelica or Brother James	Sister Angelica, [or Brother James,] may I present Mrs. Jones
Dear Sir:	Sincerely yours,	Very truly yours,	Professor [or Doctor] Knowles *(within the college)* Mr. Knowles *(elsewhere)*	Professor [or Doctor] Knowles
Dear Sir:	*Same as above*	*Same as above*	Doctor Barnes	Doctor Barnes

usage of the particular country (that is, the wife of the Mexican ambassador is Señora Ortega), but sometimes, especially when a difficult or little known language is involved, she uses Mrs. or Madame.

In this age of international travel, we may need information about the important personages of countries other than our own. Customs vary and no general rules can be made for the more than one hundred nations in the world. Should you find yourself about to leave for Ghana or Japan or Finland, try the consulate nearest you or the embassy in Washington or the mission to the United Nations in New York where information officers stand ready to facilitate your communication with their homelands. Of course, when you arrive in a foreign land, any American embassy or consulate is usually equipped to help traveling Americans in such matters.

6

Personal letters

THE LETTER EVERYONE LIKES TO RECEIVE

The letter we all like to receive carries so much of the writer's personality that he or she seems to be talking to us. Here are suggestions to make your letters reflect your personality.

Don't stop too long to think of *how* to say it. Decide what you want to say, then write it as quickly as possible as if you were talking to your friend. Use the same colloquial, informal language you do when you speak. The clever use of punctuation adds interest and variety, much as the change in tone of a speaker's voice can. Underlining a word, if done in moderation, or using an exclamation point after a phrase or sentence gives emphasis where you want it. A dash instead of a grammatical phrase can be effective: "We went to a dance last night—what a party!" Contractions are also useful: "I don't know" instead of "I do not know." For a personal touch, occasionally use the name of the person to whom you are writing.

LETTERS THAT SHOULDN'T BE WRITTEN

Letters of gloomy apprehension:

Don't write needlessly of misfortune or unhappiness, yours or another's, even to members of your immediate family. Chronic calamity writers who luxuriate in pouring out all their troubles and their fears of trouble-to-come on paper to their friends are both a bore and a menace. "My little Betty has been feeling miserable. I am worried to death. The doctor keeps insisting there is nothing to worry about, but doctors don't seem to appreciate what anxiety means to a mother," etc., etc.

The dangerous letter:

Avoid writing a letter to anyone—no matter whom—that would embarrass you were you to see it in a newspaper above your signature. Every day letters that should never have been written are put in evidence in courtrooms where they sound quite different from what was innocently intended. If you are determined to write an emotional letter either in affection or anger, at least put it away overnight in order to reread it and make sure that you have said nothing that may sound different from what you intended to say. A gentleman never writes a letter that can be construed as damaging to any woman's good name.

Spoken remarks that would amuse can pique and even insult their subject when written. Without the interpretation of the voice, gaiety becomes levity, raillery, accusation, and words that should be of a passing moment are made to stand forever. Angry words in a letter always sound stronger and are more permanent than the spoken word. Admonitions from parents to their children are quite proper in a letter—they are meant to endure and be remembered—but momentary annoyance should be expressed briefly. The habit of writing in an irritable or faultfinding tone to children insures that these letters will not be read by their recipients.

THE DIFFICULTY IN BEGINNING

For most people the difficult parts of a letter are the beginning and the closing. Here are a few helpful suggestions.

Such beginnings are: "I know I ought to have written sooner, but I haven't had anything to write about," or "I suppose you have been thinking me very neglectful, but you know how I hate to write letters," are most ungracious. Instead of slamming the door in your friend's face, why not hold it open? "Do you think I have forgotten you entirely? You don't know, Ann, how many letters I have planned to write you." Or "Time and time again I have wanted to write you, but each moment that I saved for myself was always interrupted by—something."

It is much easier to begin a letter in answer to one that has just been received. The news contained in it is fresh and the impulse to reply needs no prodding. For example: "Your letter was the most welcome thing the postman has brought for ages," or "Your letter from Capri brought all the allure of Italy back to me." Then you take up the various subjects in Ann's letter, which will probably launch you without difficulty upon topics of your own. Always answer specific questions—it is maddening to have them completely overlooked.

ON ENDING A LETTER

Just as the beginning of a letter should give the reader an impression of greeting, so should its ending express friendly or affectionate leave-taking. Never seem to scratch helplessly around in the air for an idea that will effect your escape. "Well, I guess you've read enough of this" or "You're probably bored by now so I'd better close" are stupid. When you leave the house of a member of your family, you don't have to think up any special sentence in order to say good-bye. Leave-taking in a letter is the same. In personal letters to friends, instead of the standard forms of closing, try something like this:

Will write again in a day or two.

Martin

Lunch was announced half a page ago! So good-bye for today.

Nancy

Counting the hours 'til next weekend!

Betsy

THANK-YOU LETTERS

In the following examples of letters from young persons, such expressions as "divine," "awfully," "too wonderful" are purposely inserted. Stilted phrases such as "pleased with," "very," "most kind" lose all the flavor of youth. Even the letters of older persons, although more restrained than those of youth, should avoid smugness or affectation.

Letters of thanks for wedding presents:

All wedding presents are sent to the bride, but her letters of thanks are written as though the gifts had been sent to both the bride and the groom. For example:

Dear Mrs. Beck,
To think of your sending us all this wonderful glass! It is simply divine! Jim and I both thank you a thousand times.
The presents are, of course, to be shown on the day of the wedding, but do come in Tuesday morning for a cup of coffee and an earlier view.
Thanking you again, and with love from us both.

Affectionately,
Joan

For a present received after the wedding, she might say,

Dear Mrs. Chatterton,
The mirror you sent us is going over our living room mantel as soon as we can hang it up! It is exactly what we most needed, and we both thank you ever so much.
Please come in soon to see how becoming it will be to the room.

Yours affectionately,
Mary Smith Smartlington

Thanks for Christmas and other presents:

Dearest Lucy,
It was wonderful of you to send us the gorgeous armchair. Jack says I'll never get a chance to sit in it if he gets

there first. In fact, Lucy, we both thank you ever and ever so much.

With much love,
Sally

Dear Kate,
I am fascinated with my utility box—it is too unusual for words! You are the cleverest one anyway for finding what no one else can! And you certainly were sweet to think of me. Thank you ever so much.

Love,
Ethel

Thanks for a baby present:

Dear Mrs. Cooper,
Thank you ever so much for the lovely blanket you sent the baby. It is so pretty and soft and it keeps him cozy on the coldest days!

Do come in and see him, won't you? We both love visitors, any day between 4 and 5:30!

Affectionately always,
Lucy

BREAD-AND-BUTTER LETTERS

When you have been staying overnight, or for a longer time, at someone's house, a letter of thanks to your hostess *within a few days after the visit* is absolutely necessary.

Bread-and-butter letters are difficult for many people to write. You have been visiting a friend and must write to her mother, whom you scarcely know. You begin "Dear Mrs. Town" at the top of a page, then the forbidding memory of Mrs. Town stops you. It would be easy enough to write to Pauline, the daughter. Very well, write to Pauline then—on a piece of scrap paper—about what a good time you had, how nice it was to be with her. Then copy the note you composed to Pauline and on the page beginning "Dear Mrs. Town," add "Love to Pauline, and thank you again for asking me," end it "Affectionately"—and there you are! Even if you cannot write a letter easily, the most awkward note is better than none—for to write none is the height of rudeness.

After a house-party weekend:

Dear Franny,

There is no house to which I always go with so much pleasure—and leave on Monday morning with so much regret—as yours.

Your party over this last weekend was simply wonderful! Thank you ever so much for having included me.

With much love to you all,

Betty

Dear Mrs. Oldname,

Thank you more than I can tell you for a wonderful week. I enjoyed every minute of it and think you were very kind to include me in such a delightful house party.

Very sincerely,

John Huntington Smith

From a bride to her new relatives-in-law:

A letter written by a bride after a first visit to her husband's aunt and uncle won the love of the whole family. This is the letter:

Dear Aunt Abigail,

Now that it is all over, I have a confession to make! Do you know that when Dick drove me up to your front door and I saw you and Uncle Bob standing on the top step—I was simply paralyzed with fright!

"Suppose they don't like me" was all that I could think. My knees were actually knocking together! And then you were both so marvelous to me—you made me feel as though I had always been your niece—and not just the wife of your nephew.

I loved every minute of our being with you, just as much as Dick did, and we hope you are going to let us come again soon.

With best love from us both,

Your affectionate niece,

Eloise

After visiting a close friend:

Dear Ellen,

    It was dull and stuffy in town this morning after the fresh coolness of Strandholm and the beauty of your place. It was so good being with you and I enjoyed every moment.

With love,

Caroline

Dearest Bett,

    We both had a wonderful time!

    You were very good to ask us so soon again, and we thank you very, very much.

Yours,

Mary

To an acquaintance:

After a visit to an acquaintance or to someone who has shown you special hospitality in a city where you are a stranger:

My dear Mrs. Duluth,

    It was more than good of you to give my husband and me so much of your time. We enjoyed and appreciated all your kindness to us more than we can say.

    We hope that you and Mr. Duluth may be coming East before long and that we may then have the pleasure of seeing you at Strandholm.

    In the meanwhile, thank you for your generous hospitality. Our kindest regards to you both.

Sincerely,

Katherine Hill Starkweather

LETTERS OF CONGRATULATION

On an engagement:

Dear Stella,

    We are both delighted to hear the good news. Ted's family and ours are very close, as you know, and we have always been especially devoted to him. He is one of the finest—and now luckiest—of young men, and we send you both every good wish for all possible happiness.

Affectionately,

Nancy Johnson

Dear Ted,
   Just a line to tell you how glad we all are to hear of your happiness. Stella is everything that is lovely. Of course, from our point of view, we think she too has made an excellent choice! Every good wish to you from your old friends,
                                        Arthur and Nancy Jackson

Dear Bob,
   So you've landed her! Wonderful! I know how crazy you've always been about her—and she's worth being crazy about. In short, I think it's great, and send every wish for happiness to you both.
                                                        George

Letter from a mother to her son's fiancée:

When a mother cannot, perhaps because she lives too far away, visit her son's new fiancée, a letter goes to her, giving the reason. The general outline is:

Dear Mary,
   John has just told us of his great happiness, which, of course, brings joy to us. How we wish we were near enough [or whatever the reason is] *to immediately welcome you in person.*
   We send you our love and the hope that we shall meet very soon.
                                        Sincerely and affectionately,
                                                    Martha Jones

On the birth of a baby:
Dear Sue,
   We were so delighted to hear the news of Jonathan Junior's birth. Congratulations to all three of you! I can just see big John bursting his buttons with pride.
   May I come to see you and the baby the first time that I am in town? I will call and let you know when that will be.
                                                    Much love,
                                                        Helen

Other letters of congratulation:

Dear Mrs. Steele,

We are so glad to hear the good news of David's success; it was a splendid accomplishment and we are all so proud of him and happy for you. Our love and congratulations to both of you.

Affectionately,
Mildred Bowen

Dear Michael,

We all rejoice with you in the confirmation of your appointment. The state needs such men as you—if we had more of your sort, the ordinary citizen would have less to worry about. Our best congratulations!

James Bowen

THE LETTER OF INTRODUCTION

A letter of business introduction can be more freely given than a letter of social introduction. For the former, the persons introduced need only have business interests in common; social compatibility is a necessary requisite for the latter. It is, of course, proper to give your personal representative a letter of introduction to anyone to whom you send him.

For letters of social introduction there is one chief rule: never *ask* for such letters of introduction, and be very sparing in your offers to write them, because a letter of social introduction demands unequivocally that the recipient immediately give liberally of his time, interest and hospitality to the bearer of the letter.

When you have a friend who is going to a city where you have other friends and when you believe that it will be a mutual pleasure for them to meet, a letter of introduction is proper. But sent to a casual acquaintance—no matter how attractive or distinguished the person to be introduced—it is a gross presumption.

The more formal note of introduction:

Dear Mrs. Miller:

Julian Gibbs is going to Buffalo on January tenth to deliver a lecture on his Polar expedition, and I am giving him

*this note of introduction to you. He is a great friend of ours
and I think that perhaps you and Mr. Miller will enjoy meeting him as much as I know he would enjoy knowing you.*

With kindest regards, in which Arthur joins,

Very sincerely,
Ethel Norman

If Mr. Norman wishes to introduce one man to another, he
gives his card to the visitor, inscribed as follows:

Introducing Julian Gibbs

Mr. Arthur Less Norman

Mr. Norman also sends a private letter by mail, telling his
friend that Mr. Gibbs is coming.

Dear Jack,

*I am giving Julian Gibbs a card of introduction to you
when he goes to Buffalo on the tenth to lecture. He is de-
lightfully entertaining and a great friend of ours. I feel sure
that Mrs. Miller would enjoy meeting him. If you can conveniently ask him to your house, I know he would appreciate
it; if not, perhaps you could put him up for a day or two at a
club or arrange for a reservation in a good hotel.*

Faithfully,
Arthur Norman

Informal letter of introduction:

My dear Ruth,

*I am giving this letter to George Perrin, a great friend of
ours, who is going to be in Chicago the week of January
seventh.*

*I want very much to have him meet you and hope that this
will find you in town.*

Affectionately,
Louise Hill

At the same time a second and private letter of information
goes by mail.

My dear Ruth,

I have sent you a letter introducing George Perrin. He is young, about thirty-five or so, good-looking, very good company, and an altogether likable person.

Alas, he does not play cards, which is not important; but knowing how much you play, I thought it only fair to warn you so that you might invite him to something other than a card party.

I know you will like him; and I hope you will be able to get together.

Affectionately,
Louise Hill

Procedure on arrival:

A letter of introduction is always handed to you unsealed. (It is correct for you to seal it at once in the presence of its author.) You thank your friend for having written it and go on your trip.

If you are a man and your introduction is to a lady, you go to her house soon after you arrive in her city, leave the letter with your card, if you have one, at her door, without asking to see her. If she herself opens the door, you introduce yourself and give her your letter of introduction. She should—unless prevented by illness—at once invite you to cocktails, lunch, or dinner, or at least name an hour when she would like you to come to see her.

If your letter is to a man, you mail it to his house, unless the letter is a business one. In the latter case, you go to his office and send in your business card and the letter. Meanwhile, you wait in the reception room until he has read the letter and calls you into his office.

If you are a woman, you mail your letter of social introduction and do nothing further until you receive an acknowledgment from the recipient. But the obligation of a written introduction demands that only illness or mourning can excuse her not asking you to her house—either formally or informally.

When a man receives a letter introducing another man, he calls the person introduced on the telephone and asks how he may be of service to him. If he does not invite the newcomer to his house, he may arrange a hotel reservation or ask him to lunch or dinner at a restaurant, as the circumstances seem to warrant. But it is absolutely necessary that he show this stranger what courtesy he can.

The indirect letter of introduction:

When the Newcomers go to live in Strangetown, an indirect letter of introduction is better than a direct one. By indirect is meant a letter written by Mrs. Neighbor at home to a friend of hers in Strangetown. Mrs. Neighbor merely writes to Mrs. Oldhouse, "My friends, the Newcomers, are going to live in your neighborhood"; this leaves the former free to make advances only insofar as she feels inclined.

Because, as has already been explained, a letter of introduction makes it obligatory for the recipient to do something for the Newcomers, no matter how inconvenient it may be, it can be a very real burden. If you are ill or in mourning—the only excuses possible—you must send a note explaining your lack of hospitality, and if possible, a deputy—your husband, your sister, or even your nearest friend—to explain and insofar as possible to take your place. But with the indirect letter, you and the Newcomers have the same opportunity to know each other well, if you like each other, and are bound only by inclination.

THE LETTER OF CONDOLENCE

Intimate letters of condolence to those close to you are too personal to follow a set form. One rule, and one only, should guide you in writing such letters. Sit down at your desk; let your thoughts be with the person you are writing, and say what you truly feel and nothing else.

Don't dwell on the details of illness or the manner of death; don't quote endlessly from the poets and Scripture. Write as simply as possible and let your heart speak truly but briefly. Forget that you are using written words. Think merely how you feel—then put your feelings on paper. Grace of expression is important, but sincerity counts most of all.

Suppose it is the death of a man who has left a place in the community that will be difficult to fill. You think of all he stood for that was fine and helpful to others and how much he will be missed. So you say just that: "Dear Steve—what a prince he was! I don't think anything will ever be the same again without him." Ask if there is anything you can do at any time to be of service to his people. Nothing more need be said. A line expressing a little of the genuine feeling that you had for Steve is worth pages of eloquence.

Sometimes a letter from one who has suffered an equal loss, who in sincerity writes words of encouragement and assurance that in time the pain will grow less instead of greater, is of genuine help. But such a letter must never be written by anyone whose own suffering has not been equally devastating. A glib list of qualities that did not exist is meaningless. A letter of condolence must, above everything, express a genuine sentiment. The following are merely guides for those at a loss to construct a short, appropriate message.

My dear Mrs. Neighbor,
    We are so shocked to hear of the sorrow that has come to you. If there is anything that either my husband or I can do, I earnestly hope that you will ask someone to call upon us.
                        Alice Rivington Blake

My dear Mrs. Neighbor,
    I know how little words written on a page can possibly mean to you at such a time. But I must at least tell you that you are in our thoughts and in our hearts, and if there is anything at all that we can do for you, please send us a message.
                    With deepest sympathy,
                            Mary Newling

Where death comes after a long illness, and you want to express sympathy but cannot feel sad that one who has long suffered has found release, you might write: "Your sorrow during all these years—and now—is in my heart, and all my thoughts and sympathy are with you."
(For letters of invitation and acceptance, see Chapter 44, Informal Invitations, and Chapter 46, Acceptances and Regrets.)

7

Greeting cards

Birthday, anniversary cards and other messages of friendship are charming evidences of good wishes from family and friends. But such cards are pleasant only if you take the trouble to add a little note in your own handwriting expressing something of your own feelings about the occasion. *(See also Chapter 32, "Funerals," for the use of "Thank you for your sympathy" cards.)*

Christmas cards:

There is virtually no limit to the list of those to whom one may send Christmas cards, beginning with dearest friends and ending with the slightest acquaintances. However, the custom in many communities of sending a card to everyone with whom you have a nodding acquaintance is ridiculous and contrary to the spirit of Christmas.

Christmas cards should be sent to those whom you really wish to greet, but who are not quite close enough to you to exchange gifts, to those good friends you may not have seen for some time, and most of all to those who do not live near you and with whom your Christmas card may be your only communication.

A Christmas card to someone in mourning:

A card to someone who is in mourning can be kind if it illustrates the promise of peace or if its message is a loving friendly thought. But please do not send a picture of a grave or gravestones, nor a gay card shouting "Merry Christmas and Happy New Year." Whether or not those who are in mourning

51

send cards depends entirely upon their own feelings. Naturally they would not send cards to mere acquaintances, but there is no impropriety in wishing their friends happiness.

Cards to business acquaintances:

When it is company policy to send a Christmas card to a client, it is preferable to send it, addressed to the man at his business address in the name of the company—"The Hollister Hardware Company wishes you a Merry Christmas and a Happy New Year"—rather than to his home in the name of the president or other officer. But if the client is known to the executive socially as well as through business, it may be addressed to husband and wife, even though she is not known to him personally. It should be signed, however, by the executive —not by him and his wife. This also applies to people working with you, or for you, in your own company.

Engraved cards:

Few people send engraved cards today unless they are prominent in public life or hold an official position. These cards are very simple—they may contain the message and a little decoration: a straight gold border or a simple design of holly leaves around the edge. The title is included in the signature and the message usually reads, "Mr. and Mrs. Christopher Holly send you their best wishes for a Merry Christmas and a Happy New Year," or "Governor and Mrs. Herbert Black wish you a Merry Christmas and a Joyous New Year." Engraving of names on Christmas cards (as opposed to printing) follows the rules for the engraving of names on visiting cards. For example, a woman's name should never be engraved without the title of Mrs. or Miss, although a man's card may be left without a title.

Is husband's or wife's name written first?

When the cards are sent by husband and wife, the one who writes the names courteously writes his or her own name last. To very close friends, the last name need not be written. When cards are printed, there is no rule about whether the husband's or the wife's name shall be first, but the last name is always used. However, when children's names are included, the father's name comes first—always. For example: "John and Mary and John, Jr." A baby's arrival at any time during the year is announced by adding his name on the Christmas cards—"John and Mary and their new son Timothy." Cards sent to intimate friends, by a family having several children, might be "From The John Smiths—All Five," or "From The Smiths—John, Mary, Johnny, Marie and Tim."

On printed cards sent by a widow and her grown son together, or a widower and his grown daughter, the name of the parent is on one line and that of the son or daughter on the line below. Or if written by hand, the parent's name comes first: "Henry Brown and Mary," or to those who call the parent by the first name, "Henry and Mary," each signing his or her name.

Engaged people often send cards together to their intimate friends with their first names either written by hand or printed to match the rest of the printing on an informal card.

When a card is intended for the whole family, the envelope is addressed to Mr. and Mrs. Brightmeadow; on the card itself and below the wording of the message write in ink "Love to the children, too" or "We all in our house send best Christmas wishes to all of you in your house," or whatever message is suitable.

PART THREE

AS OTHERS SEE YOU

8

The general rules

"Do not attract attention to yourself in public" is one of the cardinal principles of etiquette. Naturally, then, one should shun conspicuous manners and conspicuous clothes. Avoid staring at people or pointing at them. Noise is unattractive, so don't talk in strident tones, and avoid loudly pronouncing people's names or making personal remarks that may either attract attention or proclaim a person's identity. Do not expose your private affairs, feelings or innermost thoughts in public—you are knocking down the walls of your house when you do.

WALKING ON THE STREET

Older convention ruled that a gentleman, whether walking with two ladies or with one, took the curb side of the pavement to protect his fair companion from runaway horses. Today it seems senseless for him to keep circling behind the lady every time they cross a street. Modern rules of behavior approve of his walking either on the curb side of the pavement or on the lady's left, as he chooses.

A gentleman never sandwiches himself between two ladies when walking or sitting with them. From one side, he can look in the direction of both while talking with either one, whereas when he is between them, he must turn away from one when he talks to the other. In addition, the women may have a tendency to talk "across" him, forcing him to turn back and forth as if he were at a tennis match.

The problem or packages:

Today, the etiquette of toting is determined by practicality. A lady carries such feminine articles as her purse, gloves, umbrella and hatbox, and any lightweight packages. A gentleman carries the heavy items for her—suitcases, golf bags or groceries—for a reasonable distance and asks if he can assist her when she has many small packages.

Though a man willingly carries a woman's field glasses, camera, polo coat or anything that might seemingly be his own, he should not be asked to carry a slender, colored umbrella with a long, delicate handle or a conspicuously feminine coat. A woman makes sure that any packages she asks a man to carry for her are wrapped neatly and securely or she is likely to find herself wondering why John Newbeau never calls her any more.

THE PROFFERED ARM OR THE HELPING HAND

A gentleman offers his arm to an elderly lady, to an invalid or to any lady when he thinks she may need his support. In the daytime, she need not take it unless she wishes. At night, however, when walking for some distance or going down the steps of a house, she courteously accepts his offer. When he offers his arm, he says, "Will you take my arm?" or perhaps "Wouldn't it be easier if you took my arm here?"

The only other occasions on which a gentleman offers his arms to a lady are when he takes her in at a formal dinner or when he is an usher at a wedding. In crossing a ballroom, couples walk side by side rather than hand on arm.

A gentleman does not grab a lady by the arm or the elbow and shove her along. Only when he is helping her into a car, a taxi, or a bus does he put his hand under her elbow. When he helps her out of such a vehicle, he alights first and offers her his hand.

GENTLEMEN BEFORE LADIES

In all ordinary circumstances, indoors or out, the gentleman precedes only if the way is dangerous or uncertain. Over dangerous footing, he goes first and offers his hand, which the woman takes to steady herself. He gets out of a car or bus or train first and holds the door for her, as well as stepping ahead of her to open the door for her when she enters it. He also precedes her down a very steep or slippery stairway: "Let me go first; the steps are bad." He also steps into a boat first and offers her his hand.

A LADY NOT ON THE LEFT

In former days a lady was never seated on a gentleman's left, because according to the etiquette of the day a lady "on the left" was *not* a "lady." Today in America all that remains of this rule is that, when equally practical, it is always more polite that a gentleman seat a lady on his right. (The few surviving rules about sitting on the right include the seating of a guest of honor on the right of the host or hostess or chairman, and the military rule by which the senior officer walks as well as sits on his junior's right.)

In her own car a lady sits, if practical, on the right-hand side of the rear seat if she is being driven by a chauffeur. This can be awkward, however, because in getting into the car on the left side of a one-way street, the hostess would have to precede her guest to avoid climbing over her. Therefore, it is really more practical for the lady who enters first to sit in the farthest corner, whether right or left.

THE QUESTION OF PAYING

It is becoming less customary today for a gentleman to offer to pay a lady's way, especially if they meet by chance. For example, if a young woman and a man happen to find themselves taking the same train and she stops at the newsstand to buy magazines, the man instinctively starts to pay for them. If she knows him very well and the total is small, she perhaps lets him pay. But if he is someone she knows slightly or if the magazines she has bought are higher-priced ones, she answers, "Don't bother; I have it!" and puts the money on the counter, to which he makes no protest. She also buys her ticket and tips the porter for carrying her bag. On the other hand, if she has gone on his invitation to spend the day in the country, or to lunch or dinner, or to a theater, he of course pays for everything.

A group of people going on an excursion or dining together

in a restaurant should agree beforehand on the handling of the finances. Going "Dutch" (each individual or couple paying his own way) is more often done than not. To avoid the confusion of several people trying to divide and pay the bill, it is better for one man (or woman, but only if it is a women's group) to pay the entire bill, and the others to pay him their share later.

LIFE IN CROWDED CITIES

In today's congested cities, behavior that was once strictly private can all too easily become public. In city apartments sound seems sometimes to be intensified by distance. In the same room with the children, their play does not seem overloud, nor does the radio or television set when we are engrossed in the program. But to the family living on the floor below, the patter of little feet sounds like a stable full of horses and the toys they drop seem made of iron! Certain noises can't be helped; babies must sometimes cry, children scream, dogs bark, or someone gets a hacking cough. Considerate people try to soften such sounds by shutting a window temporarily and by trying to train both children and dogs.

In nearly all communal buildings there are always those few who show little feeling for others because their own sensitivity is, as it were, on another wave length. Sounds that greatly annoy some of us—the unceasing sound of a television set, for example, or a record player—do not disturb others at all, whereas some things which we don't mind can be unbearable to our neighbors. If we make every effort to remember this we will not be classed with the insensitive few.

Public cleanliness:

We are all aware of the increasing messiness—sometimes filthiness—of the lounges and dressing rooms of hotels, theaters and movie houses to say nothing of the waiting rooms at railroad terminals, and rest rooms of overcrowded department stores or sports stadiums. Food-eaters, gum-chewers and newspaper-discarders are conspicuous offenders, and wall-scribblers often do permanent damage. The present scarcity of employees responsible for keeping order makes the orderliness of these places the responsibility of the public—and more especially you and me.

I particularly appeal to people who throw ashes no matter where, set wet tumblers down on no matter what, drop wet raincoats on the nearest upholstered chair, burn table edges with forgotten cigarettes. Some women leave indelible lipstick on napkins and towels, shake face powder on whatever is near them and leave hairs in the sink when they arrange their hair-do. Their behavior suggests that in their own homes their beds are seldom made! They live in disorder and are unaware of the disorder they make others endure.

If everyone would act as a deputy warden, the situation would improve. Instead of courteously refraining from criticizing others, we must not only become conscious of our own behavior but do what we have been trained NOT to do— frankly correct others. If a woman tosses a used paper towel at a receptacle and leaves it lying on the floor when it misses its mark, why not pick it up and put it in the receptacle? We might even add, "Did you notice you missed the basket?"

Most troublesome to all who have the care of public places is the discarding of chewing gum. I was told by a railroad official that chewing gum ground into the marble floor of a crowded terminal meant patient hand-scraping at great cost to the building maintenance department. Washrooms in railroad stations and department stores and other public places are put completely out of order by people who carelessly throw all manner of waste into toilets. In washrooms without attendants, conditions sometimes become so bad that a locked door is the only answer. The owner of a big department store wrote me he had been forced to hang a large sign on the door leading from the customer's rest room into the washroom reading: "This washroom can remain open for your convenience only so long as you cooperate in helping to keep it in order."

Every city has the same problem in keeping its streets clean. All the campaigns, the "Keep our city clean" weeks, the signs, the trash receptacles and the fines imposed for littering fail to solve the problem. It is the duty of each one of us to take pride in keeping our cities and towns places of cleanliness and beauty and to impress others with the importance of the problem.

I was myself a witness to the following example of the length of carelessness to which a nice person can go: Just ahead of me on the street, a prominent citizen bought a Sunday paper, walked along the street ruffling through its pages hunting for a particular article. Finding it, he stopped, tore it out, then dropped the entire paper on the sidewalk at his feet, stepped over it, and walked on.

CONSIDERATION FOR THOSE WHO SERVE YOU

To show lack of consideration for those who serve us in any capacity— whether in restaurants, hotels, stores or in public places—is always a mark of ill breeding as well as inexcusable selfishness. The person who is afraid to show courtesy and consideration save to one whom he thinks it would be to his advantage to please has an exceedingly insecure dignity and questionable values.

9

In restaurants

ON ARRIVING
Checking hats and coats:

On entering a restaurant, a man leaves his hat and coat in the checkroom near the entrance. A woman may either check her coat or wear it into the dining room. If she keeps it with her, she wears it until she is seated, then drops the shoulders of the wrap over the back of her chair with her escort's help. In the daytime, if she wears a hat, she keeps it on—though today's trend is toward hatlessness, a hat is always correct with a street dress. At night, she wears a hat with daytime clothes, perhaps an evening hat or small veil with a cocktail or dinner dress and no hat, ever, with a formal evening dress.

Being seated:

After the coats have been checked, the couple or the group wait just inside the entrance until the headwaiter comes forward to ask about the number in the group and preference as to the location of the table. If there is no host (or hostess), some one member of the group assumes for all the duties that are ordinarily assigned to the host. If many people are involved, an informal kind of appointment may be made beforehand: "John, won't you please handle things this noon?" This avoids the confusion of several people addressing the waiter at once. Naturally this temporary host assumes no financial burdens not properly his.

After the table is reached, the waiter pulls out the choice seat first (meaning the seat that faces the room or perhaps a lake view). If you are a woman with a man, you naturally take it, unless you prefer another. If so, you stand beside the other chair saying, "I think I'd like to sit here." A lady who has another lady as her guest offers her the best seat, but when the hostess is a much older person, the young guest naturally refuses, saying, "Oh no, Mrs. Friendly, won't you sit on the banquette?"

When no waiter is at hand to seat them, the man seats his guests. If he is with two women, he helps first one and then at least makes the gesture of helping the second. He always helps a guest before his wife, who by that time has probably seated herself.

The women generally follow the headwaiter and the gentlemen follow them. But if a man is giving a dinner for six or more, it causes less confusion if he goes in ahead of his guests so he may indicate where they are to sit. When a husband and wife are hosts, the wife seats the guests, usually going ahead with the most important lady.

If they are only four and none is married, the ladies seat themselves facing each other. When one married couple invites another to dinner, the host and his wife sit opposite each other exactly as they do at a table for six or ten. If, however, neither couple is giving the party, they may sit in any fashion they prefer. At a table of eight or other multiples of four, the most important gentleman sits opposite the host with the hostess on his left.

If there is dancing and an older or more important woman is a guest, the host invites her for the first dance; then he dances with the other ladies and finally with his wife. The other men invite the women on either side of them to dance before asking others from seats farther away. A woman should never be left alone at a table.

At a restaurant with continuous sofa-seats or banquettes along its walls, two people dining together are seated side by side against the wall and the table is pushed in front of them. If there are four, the ladies are seated on the banquette and chairs are placed for the gentlemen facing them across the table.

In a restaurant with booths, the women go in first and sit against the far wall, facing each other across the table. The men then sit next to them, also facing each other. If a woman and two men are lunching or dining, the woman takes her place first against the wall. If one of the men is related to her, he sits across from her and the one not related sits beside her. If this grouping is reversed, the two ladies sit next to the wall and the man who is the husband of one sits beside the other.

COCKTAILS AND WINE

When the group is seated, the waiter may ask if anyone would like a cocktail. The host asks the others what, if anything, they would like and then gives the order to the waiter. No one should be urged to drink cocktails once he has refused. If there are some who say "no" to liquor, the host asks if they would like ginger ale or tomato juice perhaps, while the others are having their cocktails. To prolong the cocktails beyond one or two when others are left with nothing in front of them is impolite.

If wine is to be served, it is ordered after the food has been chosen from the wine steward if there is one, otherwise from the waiter. The host, or the best qualified man, chooses a wine that goes well with the greatest number of choices of food. For instance, if more people have ordered chicken or fish, choose a white wine; but if more are having a steak dinner, pick a red. A vin rosé, or pink wine, is often a happy compromise, as it goes well with almost any menu. However, if you have a definite preference for red or white wine, either is perfectly correct with any food.

You may choose expensive imported wines if you wish, but some of the domestic wines at lower prices are delicious, too, and one should not feel it necessary to spend a great deal to enjoy a fine wine with dinner. If you do not recognize the names on the wine list, ask your headwaiter's advice, explaining the type you prefer, dry or sweet, domestic or imported.

ORDERING THE MEAL

When a man takes a woman to dinner, he orders the meal after asking her what she would like. When he knows the restaurant well or when foreign food is served with which she is not acquainted, he suggests some choices to her. If they are both unfamiliar with the type of food served, he asks the waiter to recommend one of the specialties of the restaurant.

Unless she knows that her host is well off, she should show some consideration for his pocketbook and either ask for a *table d'hôte* dinner, if one is offered, or choose only a soup or appetizer, a main course and a dessert. The man may add more, with her permission, but she should give him the opportunity of economizing.

Four people, or even six, may order in the same way, telling their choices to the host, who then gives them to the waiter. If the group is larger, however, it is easier for the waiter to go around the table, taking a complete order from each guest in turn.

Table d'hôte and à la carte:

Table d'hôte means a set price for a complete meal, irrespective of how many courses are ordered. "Club" breakfasts and lunches, "blue plate" dinners or any meals at fixed prices are *table d'hôte*. *A la carte* means that you order from a list of dishes and you pay for each dish ordered, often including the bread and butter.

Usually, the price follows each item on an *à la carte* menu, whereas no prices are listed on a *table d'hôte* bill of fare except at the top where the price for the complete dinner is generally printed. Often a separate card or a box inset on the *à la carte* menu reads, "Special dinner $3.00" or whatever the price may be; you order whatever you choose on this special list for three dollars, but any item taken from the regular bill of fare is charged for as an extra.

On another popular type of menu a price follows each entrée

and it says below that this price includes the choice of an
hors d'oeuvre or a soup, a salad and a dessert, choice of coffee,
tea or milk. Any additional items are charged for.

Special types of meals:

The *smorgasbord,* a delightful importation from Sweden, is
a very special buffet, extremely popular in the United States.
When a man invites a woman to dine in this fashion, he may
leave her sitting at the table and go to the buffet alone and fill
a plate for her, but this eliminates much of the fun of dining
in such a restaurant. Few women would want to miss seeing
the delectable displays of food and choosing a little of each
appealing food that is offered.

Japanese and Chinese restaurants often offer interesting
variations in service and food. Some of the former have a
section where the guests may, if they wish, remove their shoes
and sit on cushions on the floor at low tables in Japanese
style. In Chinese restaurants you may try eating with chop-
sticks. Some restaurants suggest that each person at the table
order a different dish; these are placed in the center of the
table so that the diners may serve themselves from any or all
of them, a delightful way to experiment with various dishes
and helpful in ordering the next time you go to a similar restaurant.

PAYING THE CHECK

When everyone has finished his meal, the host catches the
eye of the waiter or headwaiter and says, "The check, please."
The check is brought face down on a small plate and presented
to the man who ordered the dinner. He checks it quickly for
mistakes, and returns it to the plate with the necessary money.
If he finds an error, he beckons the waiter and points
it out quietly; the waiter makes the adjustment, either himself
or with the help of the headwaiter or cashier. Never make a
"scene." If the management is unpleasant about making a
correction, simply pay the check, leave as quickly as possible
and do not return to that restaurant.

When it says at the bottom of your check "Please pay
cashier," leave the tip on the table, collect your coats or belongings, and leave, with the host following the group, who

wait in the entry while he pays the bill. (If he needs change in order to have the right amount for a tip, he pays the check and quickly returns to the table so that the waiter knows he has not been forgotten.)

Credit cards:

Numerous credit-card companies exist, a great convenience for those who dine out or entertain frequently. A credit card, sent to you on request with your name, address and a number, may be used as identification at any restaurant or establishment that is a member of the credit organization. The customer signs the checks and gives it and the card to the waiter for processing. The card is returned to its owner, and the restaurant sends the check in to the credit-card company, which in turn bills the customer at the end of the month. The tip may be added to the check, but remember that if you do this, the percentage charged by the credit-card company may be deducted from the amount your waiter receives. You should therefore adjust your tip accordingly.

TIPPING

It is impossible to give definite rules for tipping, because it depends upon where you go, what you order, and the service that is given you—or that you exact. If you patronize luxurious restaurants and wear expensive clothes or if you are critical and difficult to please, greater "compensation" is expected.

Waiter and headwaiter:

Fifteen percent for the waiter is standard in any restaurant, twenty percent in a night club or if you've been very exacting or the service has been excellent; ten percent is too little almost anywhere, except perhaps at a lunch counter and never less than ten cents there. Tipping waitresses less than waiters is not only unfair but incorrect—because the service rendered is the same.

If you are having a party of ten, twelve, or more, fifteen percent is quite adequate for the waiters who serve you and perhaps five dollars for the headwaiter if he has given you particularly good service. If he does nothing beyond seating you and handing you a menu, you give him nothing.

Wine steward and bartender:

If the wine steward serves you, he receives twelve to fifteen percent of the wine bill. The bartender receives 10 percent if you have drinks at the bar.

Checkroom and dressing room:

The fee to the checkroom boy or girl who takes care of a man's hat and coat in most restaurants is twenty-five cents, in a very expensive one, fifty cents. Fees to the maid in the dressing room of any restaurant or hotel are the same.

In the ladies room there is usually a small plate with a few coins on it in a conspicuous place. If the attendant hands you a towel or performs some other service, you are expected to leave a coin of the same denomination as those on the plate— usually a quarter.

A HOST'S RESPONSIBILITIES

The host considers the choice of restaurant: do his guests like exotic food or good plain cooking? If they are from out of town, do they have the proper clothes with them for an elaborate restaurant? Do they wish to see a place with a world-wide reputation? Or if a man is taking a girl to dinner, would she like a small, intimate spot or would she prefer to dance to a good orchestra? If he picks a well-known restaurant, he reserves a table ahead of time, and on a weekend evening, it is always safer to make a reservation. If he has ordered the dinner in advance, he observes the dishes as they are served to make sure that everything is as he requested; if there are any omissions he quietly calls them to the attention of the waiter and tactfully makes sure that they are supplied. If dinner has not been ordered beforehand, the host takes his guests' orders and gives them to the waiter or, if the party is too large, makes sure that the waiter gets the order correctly from each person.

When paying the check, the host does not display the total, but puts the money (or the signed check if he pays by credit card) quietly on the plate and nods to the waiter to remove it. If he has not had the exact amount, including the tip, the waiter brings his change, but if the sum includes both bill and tip, the host thanks the waiter and indicates that he is ready to leave by rising or remarking, "Perhaps we should be moving along if we don't want to miss the overture."

If the headwaiter has been especially helpful, given him the best table or taken special care in serving the meal, the host unobtrusively slips a bill (from one dollar to five dollars, depending on the size of the group) into his hand and thanks him as he leaves the restaurant.

WOMEN DINING OUT

When a woman invites a man:

When a woman invites a man to dine with her for personal rather than business reasons and it is understood that she is paying the bill, embarrassment is avoided if she has a credit card or possibly a charge account at the restaurant. The act of signing a slip of paper simplifies the whole affair. Many women without charge privileges prefer to give their guest a sum of cash large enough to cover the bill before they enter the restaurant. This is also an excellent solution if the husband finds he has insufficient money with him (his wife saves him embarrassment by passing him the necessary sum without calling attention to his situation).

If a woman is entertaining a customer for her business company, the company usually has accounts in nearby restaurants, and she signs the check as their representative. If no such arrangements have been made, she pays cash. If her guest protests, she explains that he is her company's guest and the amount of this check is going on her expense account. Or, if she has a credit card, she may use it and present the bill to her employer.

When women dine together:

When several women are dining out together, the problem of the check is one that can cause confusion among the waiters, the nearby diners and the women themselves. One way to avoid such confusion is to get separate checks. Or one woman may pay the entire check and the settling up can be done later.

Women and makeup at table:

A well-bred woman always avoids making up in public; cosmetics and food do not go together. At the end of a meal, she may quickly powder her nose and put on a little lipstick, but that is all. One never-to-be-broken rule is: don't ever use a comb anywhere outside a dressing room. Don't even slightly rearrange or put your fingers on your hair in any place where food is served.

RESTAURANT COURTESY

When a group about to dine together enters and sees people whom some know and others do not, the members generally continue on directly to their table, nodding "hello" as they pass. However, there are occasions when introductions are suitably performed. The men at the table rise when a woman is being introduced, as they do whenever a woman stops to talk. But when a woman stopping at a table is introduced to other women seated there, the latter never rise—not even if they are young and the visitor quite old.

Men at the table do not rise when another man stops on his way by. When someone comes across the room to speak to one of the diners, that man only stands to shake hands. The visitor then asks him please to be seated while he finishes what he has come to say. But if he intends to say more than a few words of greeting, he asks a waiter for a chair or quickly makes a later appointment with the one he wishes to talk to.

Then there is the unobserving woman who, on entering a restaurant, passes a table where her friends the Evanses are dining; she stops for a greeting that lengthens into a prolonged dialogue, while the polite husband stands and watches the food on his plate grow cold. From time to time the visitor earnestly urges, "Oh, *do* sit down!"—which Mr. Evans may quite properly do. Usually, however, the poor husband feels too conspicuous to sit down while the woman remains standing.

One husband solved the problem this way: Gustav Gourmet, just about to eat a perfect soufflé in a noted restaurant, was forced to stand for a friend of his wife's who stopped at their table. "Oh, *please* sit down! You must not let your soufflé fall!" said she and, having given this permission, went on talking. Thereupon he solved the problem by lifting the plate and eating—standing.

10

The opera, the theater and other indoor entertainments

THE OPERA
Seating in a box at the opera:

When people dine with their hostess before the opera, they usually arrive together. The gentlemen help the ladies to take off their coats. If there is an anteroom, one of the gentlemen draws back the curtain between the anteroom and the box. The ladies enter, followed by the gentlemen, the last of whom closes the curtain again. If there are two ladies besides the hostess, the latter places her more distinguished or older guest in the corner of the front row nearest the stage. The seat farthest from the center is always her own. The older guest takes her seat first, then the hostess takes her place, whereupon the third lady goes forward in the center to the front of the box and stands while one of the gentlemen places a chair for her between the other two. If there are eight, one of the ladies sits in the second row with two gentlemen beside her and the other two in the back row.

A common practice today is for three or four couples to subscribe to a box at the opera together, sharing the cost. So that each member of the group may enjoy the better seats and no two men be always relegated to the back row, these friends may agree to switch their seating arrangements around, even though it violates the old rule of "no gentlemen in the front row."

Between the acts:

Both ladies and gentlemen may visit friends in other boxes between the acts, but the lady always has an escort. They may go out to enjoy the refreshments provided by the opera houses or simply to mingle with the other patrons at the opera. No lady is ever left alone in the box, however, and all who have been out of the box during the intermission return promptly when the signal is given for the raising of the curtain, a courtesy to the performers as well as to the audience. Their is never any conversation during the overture or the performance. An enthusiastic audience may applaud at the end of an aria and, of course, after each curtain.

Dressing for the occasion:

In the boxes, many of the men wear white tie and tails, and their companions wear long evening dresses and their most brilliant jewelry—this is particularly true on Monday evenings in New York and other large opera houses. Other men prefer a dinner jacket, and the ladies choose an evening, dinner or cocktail dress. In the orchestra or grand tiers, either a dinner jacket or a business suit is correct, and you will feel comfortable in whichever you choose. A lady may wear a long or short dinner dress or, if her escort is in a business suit, a silk dress or a cocktail suit.

In the balconies, daytime clothes are more commonly worn by both men and women.

THE THEATER

Dinner and a play:

When an unattached man invites friends to go to the theater, he may take them to dinner in a restaurant beforehand; but if a host and hostess have a house or apartment not too far distant from the theater, they are likely to have their dinner party at home. Young people especially like to dine out together, and the evening is usually Dutch treat. Or one member of the group may ask the others to meet at his (or her) home for cocktails and a chat, but the cost of dinner and the tickets is divided among them. However, many friends prefer to meet at the theater and, perhaps, have refreshments afterward at some convenient restaurant.

It is absolutely essential that a host arrange for theater tickets well in advance. In New York, for instance, if you buy your tickets at the box office, you must plan weeks ahead in order to get the desired seats for popular plays. You may also buy tickets from a ticket agency which charges a certain amount more than the box-office price.

Arriving at the theater:

On arriving at the theater, the host (or hostess) holds the tickets so that the ticket-taker may see them, but he allows his guests to pass in ahead of him. At the head of the aisle, if the usher is there, he gives her the stubs and steps back, and the ladies precede him down the aisle. If, however, the usher is already partway down the aisle, the host may lead the way until he reaches her. For a large party, the hostess may tell her guests in what order they are going to sit, so that they may arrive at their row in more or less that order.

The only fixed rule about seating in the theater is that a man sits on the aisle. In a group of four, it is more pleasant if one man goes in first, followed by the two women, and finally the other man. A woman would probably sit next to the man who was not her husband. When the party is larger, a woman usually leads the way into the row, and the others alternate, men and women, leaving the host, or one of the men if there is no host, on the aisle. In the case of a man and a woman alone, she, of course, goes in first and he follows, sitting on or nearest to the aisle. There are exceptions to this rule: Arthur Norman, for example, is stone-deaf in his right ear and his wife always sits on his left no matter where that position happens to place her. Others for comparable reasons do the same.

When the play is over:

The man on the aisle, or nearest the aisle, stands in the aisle for a moment so that the lady who follows can walk with him or precede him. Only when the crowd is really dense does a man go first to make a wedge for her. In a theater party of six, the first man lets the woman who sat next to him go ahead of him, then joins her.

Dressing for the theater:

Today Mrs. Franklin who decides to combine her trip to the theater with an afternoon's shopping, may quite properly appear at the theater in a wool dress or even a suit, although it should not be a sports suit. Many women carry an extra piece or two of jewelry in their purses with which to dress up their "basic" black dresses for the evening.

When a hostess plans a theater party, perhaps to celebrate an anniversary, she may wish to make the evening more gala by requesting that the men wear "black tie." The only other time more formal dress is required is the opening night when one sits "down front." Then ladies wear cocktail or dinner dresses, and gentlemen tuxedos.

Courtesy at the theater:

Don't be late! If your taxi breaks down or something else causes unavoidable delay, you should wait at the back of the theater until the first scene is over. Then the usher can show you quickly to your seat.

Hats off! Every woman should be agreeable about removing her hat if asked to do so. Even better, courteous women take them off without having to be asked. A high hairdo can also block the view of the one behind it. In such cases one can only wish the wearer had been more considerate.

"Excuse me, please" is the natural expression of courtesy when having to disturb anyone in order to get to or leave your seat. If someone is obliged to get up to let you pass, say, "Thank you," or "I'm sorry"; if you have to pass someone a second time, say, "I'm sorry to disturb you again," and "Thank you," as they let you go by.

In passing strangers, both men and women face the stage and press closely to the backs of the seats of the row in front of them and are careful not to drag a bag or a coat across the heads of those sitting in that row. When you are seated and others must pass you, you may either turn your knees sideways, if there is space enough so passersby do not have to step over your knees; otherwise you must of course stand, but sit down again—quickly! Every second you stand, you are cutting off the view of all who are seated behind you.

Occasionally older men as well as women practically refuse to allow anyone to pass because of their reluctance to gather up opera glasses, program and bag and stand to let each person on a long aisle leave and come back. But if you haven't sufficient self-control to be amiable why not avoid all annoyances and stay at home?

Quiet, please! Finish that one important story or joke or find that misplaced glove at intermission time. If you want to discuss the plot or the performance, wait until the act is over.

Smoking between the acts:

A woman usually goes out to the lobby with a man who wishes to smoke between the acts. If she does not smoke, it is quite proper to leave her briefly during one intermission, but he should not leave her at each curtain-fall to sit alone until the house is darkened for the curtain's rise.

THE MOVIES

Except for a premiere or an elaborate benefit performance, casual clothes are proper—although "casual" must be determined by the location of the theater and the other activities of the evening. For example, slacks might be quite proper in the country, with a stop at your favorite ice-cream stand to follow, but quite out of place in the city, especially should your escort suggest, say, dancing afterward.

Talking, coughing, jingling bangles—not to speak of rattling cellophane when opening candy boxes—are annoying and disturbing to everyone in the audience. If those behind you insist on talking, it is bad manners and does no good to turn around and glare. The only thing you can do is to say amiably, "I'm sorry, but I can't hear anything while you talk." If they still persist, you can ask an usher to call the manager. Those who discuss private affairs might do well to remember that every word said above a whisper is easily heard by those sitting directly in front.

11

Conducting meetings

Almost all of us are involved in several kinds of meetings each year and most of us find ourselves from time to time in the position of having to take charge. Therefore, some generalized suggestions may be useful.

MEETINGS OF LARGE ORGANIZATIONS

The president of chairman of any large organization runs its meetings in strict accordance with the rules of parliamentary procedure found in the standard reference book, *Robert's Rules of Order,* available in any library or bookstore. In addition he controls the meeting politely but firmly, preventing unpleasant wrangling and keeping the discussion from wandering from the business of the day. His appearance is one of good grooming, appropriate for the time of day and the type of meeting.

Board meetings:

The chairman of the board of any organization holds meetings, probably once a month and possibly oftener. Meetings of a large organization (a hospital or a community fund drive, for example) are run with some degree of formality. Preparatory work includes providing adequate seating, pads, pencils and, if possible, copies of the minutes of the last meeting and the agenda for that day.

You open the meeting (no more than ten minutes need be allowed for latecomers) with "Will the meeting please come to order?" and a word of welcome. The secretary reads the minutes of the last meeting. Whereupon, you ask, "Are there any additions or corrections?" If there are none, you state, 'The minutes stand approved as read." If there are corrections, the secretary makes them and you say, "The minutes stand approved as corrected." If the minutes have been distributed to each board member in advance, the reading of them may be dispensed with, provided you first ask for a motion and a second from the floor to that effect which may then be put to a vote. Next you call for the treasurer's report, then the reports of the committee chairmen. Those who have no report simply say, "I have no report to make this month." If there are no questions about the reports, you bring up the business to be discussed, following your prepared agenda.

As chairman you recognize those who wish to speak, one at a time, and see that no one speaks for too long, intervening if an argument gets too heated by saying, for instance, "I'm sorry, Mrs. Harris, but you have spoken for more than your allotted time, so I will have to ask you to sit down"; or you may rap for attention, saying, "The meeting will please come to order. Mr. Robertson, kindly confine your remarks to the subject and do not go into personalities." If he persists in going on, you can simply ask him to sit down, as he is out of order. By directing the discussion firmly along appropriate lines, limiting speeches, and staying in charge, a good chairman hastens immeasurably the successful conclusion of the business meeting.

MEETINGS HELD IN THE HOME

When a group is formed to raise funds for a charity, to back a political candidate or put on a play, meetings may be held in the home of the chairmen or of any member of the group who volunteers. Coffee is usually served before or after a morning meeting, tea or coffee in the afternoon. The member at whose home the meeting is held may provide the refreshments or others may volunteer to contribute.

No matter how informal these gatherings, a chairman, appointed or elected to plan and direct the meeting, and a secretary to take notes or minutes, are essential for the orderly continuity of the work. If funds are involved, a treasurer is needed to handle them and keep an exact account of receipts and expenditures.

The group need not follow any particular rules but may run

its meetings as it wishes—semi-formally with minutes being read and the roll being called. Or it may be a social meeting with open discussion over a cup of coffee and a piece of cake—provided the chairman directs the discussion into the proper channels. Otherwise, friends tend to become involved in a discussion of babies or neighborhood politics and forget the purpose of the meeting. Each member should express views about the current topic and be willing to discuss and act on suggestions, so that the chairman is not left with all the responsibilities.

As to clothing, ordinary standards of neatness are observed; of course, this excludes mud-encrusted shoes or hair curlers. A skirt and sweater, or slacks if you live in the country, are perfectly acceptable. If the group is made up of young mothers, babies and children are usually brought along to play together in some safe spot other than the conference room!

PART FOUR

ADVICE FOR TRAVELERS

12

Planning the trip

Planning a trip is "half the fun." But to the joys of poring over maps and collecting suggestions from friends, add certain practical preparations without which travel can be a nightmare instead of an adventure. Touring castles in Spain will be far more enjoyable if you fortify yourself with a good meal and a comfortable night's sleep.

RESERVATIONS

Advantages of a travel bureau:

The easiest way to plan your trip is to go to a travel bureau, preferably one recommended by a well-traveled friend. Tell the bureau where you want to go, when and how, and let them work out the best possible plan for you. They can do it not only better but much more economically than you can and at no extra cost to you, as they get their commission from the transportation company, the resort or the hotel.

An important point for the inexperienced traveler to realize is this: while a competent travel bureau will engage, if you wish, the best rooms in deluxe hotels, secure automobiles by the week or month, either with or without chauffeurs, and arrange any other elaborate accommodations, they will, with equal

interest, provide the same quality service for those traveling on
a limited budget.

Making your own reservations:

If you do not wish to use a travel agency, make your
reservations well in advance. Arrangements for an extensive
trip to a popular area may reasonably be made six months or
more ahead of time. Reconfirm the reservations a week or two
before your departure. Request a receipt or acknowledgment
(and carry it with you) to be shown on your arrival to the
innkeeper or hotel manager as proof of your reservations.

Make your travel reservations at the same time that you
make hotel reservations, and secure your home-bound tickets
then too. Many people have found themselves in Europe at the
end of the tourist season with days of waiting for a plane seat
still ahead of them.

A tip to parents: When your son or daughter sets off for a
summer of traveling, possibly with knapsack on his back and
no planned stopping places other than a list of youth hostels
(inexpensive lodgings for bicyclists and motorcyclists found
in every European country), be sure that he or she has a return reservation, either with him or held at the airline or
steamship office for him. It is all too easy for a youngster to
cable home, "Unable to get reservations until September 15"
—three weeks longer than you had expected to finance him!

Using a guidebook:

If you are able to travel during the "off" season you may not
need reservations. To be able to drive at random, following
whatever highway or byway catches your fancy, stopping for
the night wherever you happen to be, staying as long as you
wish in some charming city, is the ideal way to travel. There
is but one requirement—a good guidebook. Places recommended by all reputable guidebooks are visited regularly by
their staffs and their information is as accurate and current as
it is possible to make it. Thus you may avoid poor or dirty
accommodations and dishonest proprietors.

(For additional suggestions about hotel and transportation
see also Chapters 13 and 14.)

Protection of your house:

When you leave an empty house or apartment, take these steps:

Cancel milk delivery and newspaper delivery. Ask the post office to either hold or forward your mail—mail and newspapers piling up at your door only advertise your absence to unwelcome intruders. Have all laundry and cleaning delivered before you leave.

In a house leave a light or two burning, or install an automatic light that goes on at dusk. Check all locks on windows and doors and be sure that you take a key with you! Leave a spare key with a friendly neighbor and ask him to check the house occasionally. Notify the police of your absence and ask them to keep watch over your house. Give them the name of anyone who might be coming into the house legitimately.

Never give your travel plans or dates to your local newspaper in advance. There are people who watch the papers every day in order to take advantage of just such information.

TRAVEL DOCUMENTS

Several weeks before your departure, apply for your passport, visas if they are required, and health certificates which must be attended to in person. After you have filled out the forms and paid the fee at the passport office, your passport may be sent to you by mail. You must also go in person to the consulate of the country from which you wish to get a visitor's permit or visa.

It is advisable to get some foreign money in small bills and change (check the amount you are permitted to take in or out of some countries). Be sure to take the bulk of your money in American Express or other traveler's checks which can be replaced if lost and are accepted everywhere as readily as cash. A letter of credit is a good idea if you want to have something to depend on for extra and unexpected expenses.

(See also Chapter 15.)

13

Motels and hotels

MOTELS:

All over America, and recently in foreign countries, motels are becoming more and more luxurious. The larger ones, particularly those belonging to national chains, are equipped with every facility including swimming pools, shuffleboard courts, sunbathing areas, television sets and individual coffee-makers in each room. At one motel I know, a drive-in movie is directly behind the motel, so that you can sit comfortably in bed and see a movie before going to sleep with the sound piped into each unit through a private speaker!

Those motels connected with a chain generally have a restaurant on the premises, but if you are staying at a smaller motel, you may have to go a little distance to find a good eating place. Ask the clerk at the desk to recommend one or two. If you are looking for entertainment—dancing, movies and so on—you may be better off in a hotel in the heart of the city.

The advantages of motels:

Because the majority of motels are on the outskirts of towns you need not drive into heavy urban traffic to reach them. Your car is parked directly in front of your room or unit and you unload only what you need for the night. One may travel in shorts, slacks—whatever is most comfortable for driving. One simply goes to the office of the motel, registers, pays for the room (if you are staying for one night only), receives the key and drives to the allotted unit. No tips are necessary. In the morning you depart when you wish, without any further formality.

Because of the immense popularity of motels as stopping places, it is wise, especially for a woman alone, to make reservations in advance. If you stay in a chain motel, they will be delighted to call ahead to the member motel in or nearest to your next destination and reserve a room for the following night.

HOTELS
Accommodations:

If possible, write or telegraph in advance for accommodations. At the time of a convention or a big football game, or any other occasion of crowded hotels, you should write months in advance. Have your letter or telegram state clearly the hour of your arrival, number of persons, the accommodations you wish, the approximate length of your stay, and ask for a confirmation.

A typical telegram and letter follow:

KINDLY RESERVE DOUBLE ROOM WITH BATH FOR WIFE AND SELF AFTERNOON DECEMBER THIRD TO FIFTH. PLEASE CONFIRM.

JOHN G. HAWKINS

Manager of the Lake Hotel
Chicago, Illinois

Dear Sir:

Please reserve two single rooms with baths or with a bath between for my daughter and me. We are due to arrive in Chicago at five o'clock on the afternoon of December sixth and shall stay a week.

I prefer moderate-priced rooms not higher than the fourth floor.

Very truly yours,
Mrs. George K. Smith

Kindly confirm reservation to
Brightmeadows, Ill.

(This is one of the few occasions when "Mrs." belongs with a woman's signature.)

The arrival at a hotel:

At a first-class hotel, a doorman opens the door of your car or taxi and deposits your luggage on the sidewalk. A bellboy carries your bags into the lobby and deposits them near the registration desk, usually a long counter manned by one or more men.

You go to the desk, and, if you have written ahead, you say to the room clerk, "I am Mrs. George K. Smith. I telegraphed you Tuesday and received your confirmation on Thursday." The clerk asks you to write your name:

A gentleman writes: "John Smith, New York." If alone he does not use "Mr.," but if his wife is with him, the title to their joint names is correct: "Mr. and Mrs. John Smith, New York." Or he writes his name, John Smith, and his wife's, Mrs. Smith, below. He does not add his street and house number in a registration book. A registration card or form, however, usually includes space for the house address. His signature is exactly the same whether written in a book or on a card. Neither "John Smith and Wife" nor "John Smith and Family" is good form. The whole family should be registered.

John T. Smith	New York
Mrs. Smith	"
Miss Margaret Smith	"
John T. Smith, Jr.	"
Baby and nurse	"

Or, if the children are very young, he writes:

Mr. and Mrs. John T. Smith, New York, 3 children and nurse [if there is one]

"Miss precedes the names of girls over five; boys are registered with no title—just "John" or "Henry.""

One exceptional occasion when a lady signs her name "Miss" or "Mrs." is in a hotel register. "Miss Jean McLean" is correct or "Mrs. George K. Smith"—never "Sarah Smith."

If Mrs. Smith arrives first, she fills in the blank for both herself and her husband. Then on his arrival, he says to the room clerk, "Mrs. Smith has already arrived and registered. What is the number of our room, please?"

After you have registered, the clerk hands the room key to the bellboy who gathers up your bags and starts for the stairs or the elevator. You follow. In your room, he turns on the lights and opens the window or tests the air-conditioning unit. His tip is usually twenty-five cents for each large bag and extra for several small parcels.

Service in a hotel:

The telephone is your base of operations. You tell the operator the hour you wish to be called, ask for the desk, inquire about mail or messages, call the porter's desk about luggage or trains or reservations, or the newsstand for magazines, newspapers or theater tickets, room service when you want food or drinks sent up to you, and valet or maid service if you need a dress or a suit cleaned or pressed. If there is no regular valet service, you ask a chambermaid, "Where can I have my dress [or suit] pressed?" She answers, "I will do it for you," or tells you who will.

In the morning, for instance, if you want breakfast in your room (there is an additional charge for this), you say, "Room service, please," then give your order, chosen perhaps from breakfast menus in your room. Presently the waiter brings in a tray with your order, puts it on a table, or in a large hotel he wheels in a long narrow table completely set: cloth, china, glass, silverware, etc. You may pay him in cash, or sign the check and have it put on your hotel bill.

You may receive the waiter when you are sitting up in bed or clad in a robe. Waiters are used to carrying trays into the presence of wearers of all varieties of pajamas and negligées. He returns later for the table, or, if you do not wish to be disturbed, you may put it outside your door. His tip is the usual fifteen percent of the check.

Pilferage:

An inexplicable urge to pilfer small or large objects seems to come over many otherwise decent, honest citizens when they are guests in a hotel. Bath towels, mats, ashtrays, dining-room silver and even blankets and bed linen disappear in such quantities as to be a major expense in every large hotel. These pilferers, normally law-abiding persons, when accused of stealing, say, "Not at all—the management expects these things to disappear!" I suggest that any time you are tempted to take home such a souvenir, you say to yourself, "That ashtray [or bath towel] is the property of the hotel, and if I take it home with me, I am no better than a common thief."

Hotel manners:

If you have a private sitting room, you can have everyone you please take a meal in it with you, or visit with you, as long as you observe the ordinary conventions of behavior. But it is against the rules of any reputable hotel for a guest to receive a visitor of the opposite sex in a bedroom without first speaking to the desk clerk. Noisy parties and men or women visitors at unconventionally late hours are not permitted in any high-class hotel.

The woman staying alone in a hotel—and it is quite correct for even a very young girl to do so—and having no sitting room of her own receives her men visitors in any one of the public rooms of the hotel and entertains in the restaurant or dining room. It is not so much a question of suitable age as of suitable behavior. A woman or girl who is dignified and whose friends are the sort that pass that sharpest of character readers, the house detective, will never have an uncomfortable moment. But the woman who thinks a hotel is a brier-patch where she can hide away all the things she oughtn't to do will find that she might as well have chosen to hide in a show window.

A hotel guest—whether a woman or a man—going down to the dining room alone may wish to take a book or newspaper, because nothing is duller than to sit staring into space while waiting for one's order.

A woman may wear a hat in a hotel restaurant or dining room if she wishes. Of course, if she is dressed in evening clothes, she does not wear a hat.

When you call on friends at a hotel, you either inquire for them at the desk and the clerk telephones their rooms or you go to the house telephone and ask the number of their room, call them, and then go up in the elevator. Or your friends may wish to join you in the lobby or the lounge.

When you leave the hotel:

When you are ready to leave, go to the cashier—or telephone from your room—asking that your bill be made out.

Then you telephone for a bellboy to carry down the luggage. Downstairs you tip him, pay the bill at the desk, leave the key and a forwarding address for mail to be sent after you.

TIPS

The following schedule of tips applies to transient visitors staying in the hotel (or the motel with services) for not more than a week. Permanent or long-term residents tip on a monthly or even twice-yearly basis. The amount varies according to the quality of the service, and the quantity requested. Hotel residents must arrive at their own conclusions, possibly with the help of other permanent guests and even the hotel management.

To a dining-room waiter in a first-class restaurant: between fifteen and twenty percent of the bill, but never less than twenty-five cents in a restaurant with a tablecloth on the table. In an American-plan hotel, you give the waiter or waitress at the end of each week about ten percent of the week's board per person, but less if the family is large. When going to the dining room for the first time, you give from two to five dollars to the headwaiter if you would like a table in a particular location. When you leave, you tip him proportionately to the service rendered: one or two dollars a week, if he has done little, and five dollars for a family. For a one-night stay, no tip is necessary.

Other tips:

Chambermaid: one dollar a week a room, or fifty cents a week in a small inexpensive hotel. If you stay one night only, fifty cents for each person in a room in a large hotel, or twenty-five cents in a small one. If you cannot find her leave it in an envelope addressed "Chambermaid" on the bureau.

Doorman: nothing for putting a bag on the sidewalk; twenty-five cents if he helps take luggage into the hotel or calls a taxi

Bellboy: twenty-five cents for each large bag; twenty-five cents for paging

Porter: fifty cents for bringing a trunk to the room fifty cents or one dollar if there is much baggage twenty-five cents for ice, drink setups, newspapers, packages, telegrams, etc.

Checking a man's coat and hat: twenty-five cents

Attendant in the woman's dressing room of a hotel or restaurant: twenty-five cents

Attendant at the coat rack at the entrance to the dining room: twenty-five cents

Valet: tip only if he brings a large amount of clothing back to your room when you are there; his charge for cleaning or pressing is included in the hotel bill

Barbers, manicurists and beauty-parlor specialists: fifteen percent of the bill, but not less than twenty-five cents

Bootblacks: twenty-five cents

People who frequent expensive hotels and take first-class accommodations on trains, ships or planes are expected to give larger tips than people traveling economically.

One piece of advice: Whether or not you approve of the system of tipping, you will not get good service unless you tip generously but not lavishly. If you do not care to order elaborate meals, do not go to an expensive hotel and expect your waiter to be contented with a tip of ten cents for your dollar snack!

EUROPEAN HOTELS

Large, first-class hotels in Europe are essentially the same as our best hotels in the United States. When you leave the beaten track, however, for those less well-traveled be prepared for certain differences in facilities and service.

All services other than actual accommodations and meals are provided by a concierge; he and his staff handle luggage and mail, make reservations, rent cars, shop for you, deliver packages, arrange tours, and are altogether indispensable.

Instead of a telephone in each room, many foreign hotels have a pushbutton device with little pictures of waiters, maids or valets beside each button to indicate which to push. This system helps to overcome the language barrier.

Small hotels seldom have bathrooms with every room. Many rooms do have washbasins; in small towns there may just be a pitcher of water and a bowl. In these hotels, you use the public bathrooms on each floor used by all guests; these are usually marked "W.C."—a universally known abbreviation for "water closet." Washcloths and toilet soap may or may not be provided, so carry your own!

The hotels in small towns may not be luxurious, but the friendliness more than makes up for the lack of comfort: the chef who proudly invites you to see his spotless ktichen, the chambermaid who smilingly brings you a cup of coffee when she awakens you in the morning, and the concierge who is eager to show you the beauty of *his* town, leave you feeling that the physical comforts are not so important as you thought.

14

On plane, train or ship

PLANE TRAVEL

Large, scheduled airlines offer two main classes of air travel: first class and economy. Both classes fly on the same plane. The economy class, occupying two-thirds or more of the space toward the rear of the plane, is divided from first class by a partition. Seats are generally three on each side of the aisle. Meals and snacks are included in the fare, but you must pay for alcoholic drinks. On long flights, most airlines show movies in both economy and first class. The difference in cost between economy and first class on a long flight is quite astronomical. For this difference, in the first-class section the widely spaced seats are two on each side of the aisle with plenty of room to stretch one's legs; tables may be put between the seats so that passengers may play cards or spread out their business papers. Cocktails are free, meals more elaborate.

Luggage:

The ideal luggage is a lightweight, firm metal, such as aluminum, or a composition. (Soft bags can be damaged or pierced if handled roughly.)

Each piece of luggage is weighed when you check in for an overseas flight, including those you carry with you onto the plane. The exceptions are handbags, cameras, binoculars, brief-cases, knitting bags, a book or two, etc. In general, overseas economy-class passengers are allowed approximately forty-four pounds, and first class, sixty-six. You may carry more, but you pay for the excess at a specified rate per pound. Any bag or package carried onto the plane must be capable of being stowed under your seat. No hard or heavy article is allowed on the shelf above the seats. On domestic flights each passenger is allowed two pieces of luggage free, regardless of weight. If you carry more than two, you will be charged at the usual rate for excess.

On arrival at the airport or terminal, a porter takes your luggage to be weighed in. If it is overweight on overseas flights, you pay the extra charge at this time. Tip the porter twenty-five cents for each suitcase. When your ticket is validated, the bags are tagged and the stubs given to you at the same time. You do not see the luggage again until it is brought into the "baggage claim" section at your destination.

Arriving at the airport:

On overseas flights, you are asked to arrive at the airport one hour ahead of departure time, half an hour for domestic flights. Seats are usually assigned as the passengers arrive, although some airlines allow you to choose from a chart displayed at the counter. Your boarding pass with the seat number on it is shown at the departure gate and again to the stewardess when you board the plane.

While in the air:

During the trip, the stewardesses, whom you signal by a light above your head, serve meals, bring magazines, hand out newspapers, bring extra blankets, even help care for babies by heating bottles, etc. Never tip a steward or stewardess or any other member of the crew.

Be sure to wear loose, comfortable, wrinkleproof clothing. On overnight flights some women like to change into slacks and bedroom slippers. Men may remove jackets, loosen ties, change into a sport shirt. A loose sweater and wool socks or slippers are a wise protection against low temperatures in the plane.

Obey "Fasten Seat Belts" and "No Smoking" signs promptly. (Only cigarette smoking is allowed.)

No animals are allowed in the cabin of a plane except a Seeing Eye dog. A pet must be in a carrier (his weight is counted as part of the amount of luggage you are permitted). He rides with the luggage or in a special pressurized compartment.

In the washrooms or lavatories on a plane, wipe out the basin thoroughly with your used towel before you throw it into the towel basket. Before combing your hair, lay a fresh towel over the washbasin or counter. When you have finished, throw the towel into the towel receptacle. All this is only good manners.

Friendliness among the passengers is characteristic of air travel. People talk freely to each other. But anyone can avoid conversation by simply saying, "I'd rather not talk if you don't mind, I'm very tired."

TRAIN TRAVEL

The official rate for a porter to take luggage from the entrance of a railroad station to a train is twenty-five cents for each piece unless otherwise posted; an additional tip is optional but expected. When traveling to an unknown destination, where there may be no porters, send larger bags and trunks ahead by railway express.

If you are spending the night in a single berth, upper or lower, carry a small overnight case with you, as the remainder of your luggage will be stowed at the end of the car. Even in a compartment or drawing room, avoid having to open large bulky suitcases.

On a day-long journey, speak or not, as you please, to your table companions in the diner. On a longer journey, if you happen to sit near the same person for a number of meals, it is good manners to enter into friendly conversation.

During the day in a Pullman section, the seat facing forward belongs to the occupant of the lower berth; the occupant of the upper berth rides backward. If your seat faces forward, courtesy demands that you ask the occupant of the other seat whether he or she minds riding backward—and if he does, to make a place at your side. The window seat naturally belongs to you—unless you prefer the other.

In a bedroom, compartment or drawing room, the porter should be called to make up the beds by ten o'clock or ten thirty at the latest. If you wish to have another drink or continue your talk, you may go to the club car or bar car. When you are in a berth in the open section of the car, divided only by curtains from the other passengers, all conversation ceases as soon as neighbors are in bed; if you are not sleepy, resort to a good book in your berth. Occupants of a section, even though strangers, consult each other on the time they like their berths made up for the night.

Going to bed in a Pullman:

The porter, on your ring, will make up your berth when you are ready to go to bed. If you have a roomette, drawing room, compartment or bedroom, you simply shut your door when he is finished, and go to bed. Since all bathroom facilities are included in your space, you do not go to the public dressing room at all. If, however, your berth is in the open car, you wash and prepare for the night in the dressing room while the porter makes up your bed. If you have an upper berth the porter brings a stepladder for you to get up and down to your berth. You may remove your clothes in the dressing room, put on a bathrobe and return to your berth. But most people, after washing, return to their berths, close the curtains and go through the gymnastics of undressing in an impossibly small space! In the morning you ring for the stepladder and dress, again as much as you can in your berth, because there is no privacy—and less space—in the dressing room.

Tips:

Tip dining-car waiters as you would in any restaurant: fifteen percent of the bill, never less than a quarter; waiters or stewards in the bar car or club car, fifteen percent of the bill, and a quarter if they bring "setups" (ice, glasses, water and soda) to you in the Pullman car; the Pullman porter receives fifty cents to one dollar for each person on an overnight trip—more if he has given additional service other than making up the berths.

TRAVEL ON A SHIP
Luggage:

On your arrival at a pier, a porter puts your luggage on the escalator or elevator to the upper level. His tip is twenty five cents or more a bag. You go to the receiving end of the escalator where your porter puts the luggage on trucks for delivery on board the ship. (If another crew takes over upstairs, tips are also given to these porters.) You then show your passport and ticket at the proper desk and board the ship.

Be sure to arrive at the ship in plenty of time to be certain your luggage is on board. Your receipt stubs for trunks sent to the pier by express are turned in to the baggage master at his desk on the pier; the luggage will be stored in the hold or sent to your stateroom, as requested. If you are sharing a cabin with strangers, unpack all but one or two pieces and send the rest to the hold.

Reserving dining-room table and deck chair:

Immediately after being shown to your cabin, it is well to go to the dining room and reserve a table at the sitting you wish for the voyage. Next, go to the main deck and see the head deck steward about a steamer chair and tell him your preference for its location.

Social life on board:

When friends come to the ship to wish you "Bon Voyage!" you may want to give a party. If you have a large, comfortable stateroom, your steward will bring soda and soft drinks, hors d'oeuvres, ice and glasses to your cabin. If you are in a small room, possibly shared with strangers, you may have your party in one of the bars or lounges. In either case, board the vessel early and make the arrangements with your cabin steward or the head waiter. During the rest of the trip you may entertain your new shipboard acquaintances in the same way. Tip the stewards who serve such a party fifteen percent of the bill at the time, rather than adding it to your regular tip at the end of the trip.

In first class, on a luxury liner, some people dress in evening clothes—tuxedos for the men and dinner dresses for the women—every night except the first on board. This is not necessary, however, except on the night of the Captain's party (usually the next-to-last night out), and cocktail dresses and business suits are acceptable on other evenings.

No formal introductions are necessary on board in any case—you introduce yourself to your neighbors and, with luck, you quickly find congenial people with whom you will become friends for the length of the voyage: in deck chairs, around the swimming pool, in the lounges or in the game rooms. Only remember that some people honestly wish to be left alone.

A cruise ship is like a large house party where the guests speak to each other as a matter of course. A "cruise director" (on small ships this is the purser) acts as host or hostess, arranges for deck or bridge games and introduces dancing partners. Any young girl or man on board who is without friends is expected to go to the director and ask to be introduced to congenial people.

On any ship, the Captain usually entertains at cocktails, once for first-class and once for tourist-class passengers. He may also give smaller parties for prominent persons, personal friends or those sitting at his table. These invitations should always be accepted, if possible, and a written refusal sent if you cannot attend. The Captain is always "Captain Sawyer" and the other officers "Mr." At mealtime, those seated at the Captain's table or that of any senior officer must treat him as they would a host in a private home. These passengers arrive at the same time as the officer. If he is delayed, they wait for him before starting, unless he sends word to go on without him. At other tables it is not necessary to arrive all together as long as each person or group sits down well within the limits of that sitting.

Tips:

There are definite minimum amounts that passengers are expected to give. In first class, your cabin steward receives ten dollars, the dining-room steward ten dollars and the headwaiter five dollars. One or two dollars to the busboy, if there is one, would make him very happy. Lounge and bar stewards receive fifteen percent at the time they render their services, the chief deck steward five dollars and his assistant, if he has one, three dollars. Fifteen percent of the amount of the wine bill goes to the dining-table wine steward.

All these suggestions for tipping are per person, on a transatlantic trip.

Tips in the cabin and tourist classes are lower, in proportion to the difference in the passage fare. A good general rule for shipboard travelers is to allow approximately ten percent of the fare for tips. Divide about half of this allowance between the cabin and dining-room stewards, and distribute the rest to others who have served you. Obviously, passengers occupying suites are expected to tip more generously than those in modest accommodations.

To anyone on the ship who has taken pains to please you, show by your manner in thanking him that you appreciate his efforts, as well as by giving him a somewhat more generous tip when you leave the ship.

On no account attempt to tip a ship's officer! Thank the purser as you would any other acquaintance for courtesy. If you go to see the doctor, or if he is brought to see you, he will probably send you a bill for his services. If he does not and you have had a real illness, it is proper to send him, in an envelope when you leave the ship, the amount that probably would have been charged by your own doctor. If you are ill enough to be hospitalized, an extra charge will be added to your fare.

15

Currency and language

MONEY MATTERS

The rates of exchanging dollars for each country's currency vary from time to time, but revised and inexpensive wallet-sized guides may be bought at stationery stores or gift shops and are distributed by many travel bureaus, ticket agencies, etc. It is wise to learn by heart the corresponding sum for such standard amounts as a quarter, a dollar and five dollars. The rough equivalent of a quarter is still a standard tip for small services all over the world and if you know the amount equal to one dollar, it is easy to arrive at that corresponding to ten dollars.

And a word about bargaining. In large city stores all over the world the prices are just as firm as they are at Macy's in New York City. In small towns or rural marketplaces, however, especially in Latin countries, bargaining is often part of the fun of making a sale. Not only is the tourist considered simple-minded if he pays the "asking price," but he has ruined the day for the vendor.

In most restaurants in Europe, there is a charge on the bill for service. When this is fifteen percent or more, you need not tip an additional fifteen percent, but you should leave something. If there is no service charge, or a very small one, you tip the usual fifteen percent.

THE LANGUAGE BARRIER

Although people will tell you time and again that it is not necessary to speak a foreign language because "everyone in Europe speaks English," it simply is not so. Outside the cities and areas frequented by tourists, there are literally millions of foreigners who neither speak nor understand one word of English. I cannot stress enough the importance, first, of knowing a few words of the language of whatever countries you are planning to visit and, second, of carrying a small pocket dictionary with you.

You will find invaluable a few such words and phrases as: "yes" and "no," "please" and "thank you," "hello" and "good-bye," "how much?" "where is . . . ?" and "how do you get to . . . ?" and "ladies' room" and "men's room."

"Beautiful," "wonderful," "nice," "kind," etc.—these single words, said admiringly and sincerely about the place or people you are visiting, will warm the heart of any native. Nothing pleases a native of any country, including our own, more than realizing that a visitor has taken the time and made the effort to learn a little of his country's language. Anyone who has walked through a little alley in a tiny town on a Greek island and seen the beaming smiles and eager response of the old ladies who sit there in the sun and hear "Ka-lee-*meh*-ra" instead of "Hello" or "Good morning" will know that this is true.

16

Representing America abroad

As a result of travel by jet airplane, people at the farthest reaches of the earth have become our neighbors. Every traveler will increase his enjoyment of his trip if he attempts to make friends and exchange ideas with the people of the country he is visiting. When traveling we should know something of the customs that determine the different points of view. The best way to learn is to read books about the people and places you intend to visit.

OUR ATTITUDE

At first thought, it would seem that there could be no difficulties of understanding between us and those whose language is the same as ours—especially the British, the Australians and New Zealanders. But slight frictions develop even when there is no language problem. Sensitive perception of the feelings of others is something few possess instinctively. Therefore, we must train ourselves to see the point of view of the people of each country we visit, adapt ourselves to their ways and not expect them to adapt to ours.

Our travel attitude also determines the amount of enjoyment we get from our trip. Which one enjoys his travels more —the man who goes with an open mind, eager to see the best in each country and forget the inconveniences, or the man who finds it too hot in Spain, broods all day because he had no hot water for shaving, or can't find a hamburger stand to buy his favorite lunch? Do not voice your disappointments in public; rather attempt to find and dwell on the parts of your stay that you *do* enjoy. Don't hesitate to show your appreciation and enthusiasm for the country you are in.

Don't compare everything you see with the United States. Every country has something to offer that we do not. The people there do not necessarily envy us our material wealth—they may prefer their simpler, less complicated existence.

Adaptability is a happy, rewarding trait. Latins live in warmer parts of the world. The combination of temperament and the necessity of adapting themselves to hot weather has resulted in a relaxed, unhurried attitude in all things, and *"mañana"* is the order of the day. This is one of the most difficult adjustments for Americans to make. To arrive in a country where no one cares whether everything is ready, where one arrives for appointments hours late, and meals are served hours later than one is used to, is often quite a shock. Soon, however, if he is perceptive, the traveler finds that the Latin countries have something unique to offer, and it becomes as difficult to return to a clock-watching society as it was to leave it behind in the first place.

Our greatest fault, it is said, is that we think the best of everything should be eagerly handed to us because we can pay for it! Could anything be more ill-bred? We must learn how to pay for it graciously if we are going to be given more than just what dollars can buy! Dollars, pounds, francs, pesos, lire don't buy a single gesture of welcome, of admiration, of sympathy. But a little thought, a little preparation, a wish to learn and to understand, these will reap the beautiful reward—the foreigner's friendship.

OUR CONDUCT

Appearance:

Clothing should be appropriate: thin clothes for warm climates, dark clothes for large cities, a "dressy" suit or dress for dining out, and the proper clothes for any sports you intend to take part in. Do not wear shorts or slacks except at resorts, or for golf, tennis, boating, etc. Such attire only proclaims the ignorance of the tourist who so offends local custom. In fact, clothing is usually more formal in large cities abroad than in our cities. Men are seldom seen in anything but dark business suits, and well-dressed women wear dark suits or dresses. The tropics are different. There women wear sleeveless cottons; men wear a loose cotton or linen shirt-jacket, worn outside the trousers and sometimes beautifully pleated or embroidered. Women should always carry some sort of head-covering, if only a scarf, for some churches refuse them admittance without it.

Avoid talking in a loud voice or gesturing wildly even in your effort to speak a strange language. When you see a friend from home across the square or in a crowded restaurant, don't shout and wave violently to attract his attention; approach him quietly as you would ordinarily do at home. Europeans are usually most polite about waiting their turns. We could learn a lesson from them.

Don't stare or criticize customs different from those at home. When you see a Greek gentleman toy with his "worry beads" or a peasant family, the mother burdened with a heavy load while the father rides the donkey, accept what you see as an interesting facet of life abroad.

Taking pictures:

If you wish to include a native of the country in your pictures, first ask his permission. He may quite naturally resent it otherwise. In countries where the natives wear a national costume, people are accustomed to being photographed by tourists, but it is still polite to ask their permission unless you are just taking a picture of a large crowd. Children's fears may be overcome by the offer of a small tip or candy. Where they are used to many tourists, they will often crowd around you, offering their services as models.

Latin customs:

In Latin countries a man must not expect to meet a well-brought-up girl one night and take her out the next. He must be presented to her family, gain their approval, and then arrange, at least on the first few dates, to include mutual friends. A woman seldom goes out alone after dark; any Latin man would consider himself un-masculine if he did not attempt to approach her for a flirtation. Young girls should stay in groups of three or four, and older women should be accompanied by at least one friend.

The manners of Europeans and South Americans are more "flowery" than those of Americans. Women always shake hands when introduced, and hand-kissing is still practiced. European gentlemen remove their hats to ladies and bow with a flourish. Ladies are always seated on the gentleman's right, except in a theater when this would place her on the aisle.

Europeans, and especially Latins, have a great love of giving presents: foods and flowers—especially those baked in their own ovens or grown in their gardens—or any trifling or more expensive gift.

In accepting these, we show our pleasure warmly—and as soon as possible thereafter we respond to this gesture with a simple, appropriate gift. Flowers are always sent to the hostess when you are invited to dinner. They are also sent as a "thank you" and to greet visitors.

17

An audience with the Pope

Although there are often hundreds of people in a day who wish an audience with the Pope, no one is denied. The great majority of audiences are group or collective. Relatively few can be granted one of the three types of audience that are considered to be personal.

Requests by Americans for these group audiences as well as for the personal ones should be cleared by the North American College, and then sent to the Office of the Master of the Chamber known as *Ufficio del Maestro di Camera di Sua Santità* which is in the Vatican. They are presented in person, or sent on arrival in Rome, to the Monsignor in charge whose name and address can be obtained from the concierge of your hotel. One must fill out a form requesting the kind of audience desired and show his credentials, which for a Roman Catholic may be simply a letter of introduction from his parish priest or a prominent layman. The length of one's stay in Rome, his address and telephone number, are also included on the form so that he can be notified of the day and hour of his audience. Non-Catholics as well as Catholics are granted audiences, and their requests for audiences must be arranged through prominent Catholic laymen or members of the Catholic clergy.

The reply, and the invitation if the answer is favorable, is sent within a few days. You may receive a general admission ticket, meaning no reserved seat, or, if you are considered sufficiently important, a reserved seat in a special section.

THE GENERAL AUDIENCE

General audiences are usually held at noon. It is not necessary to have tickets, and anyone may attend. Those without reserved places should arrive very early if they wish an advantageous location—people often start arriving as early as 10 A.M.

At noon, the audience rises as the Pope appears, seated on a portable throne called the Sedia Gestatoris, carried by eight Swiss Guards. At the end of the aisle, he usually leaves the portable throne for a fixed one. He delivers a short address; then the audience may kneel as he gives his benediction to all those present, as well as to all articles they have brought with them to be blessed. The group rises and if the Pope has time, he greets each person in the special area. He mounts his portable throne and is carried out, and the audience is over.

For general audiences women must have their hair covered, wear black or dark dresses with necklines that are not too low and skirts that are not too short; their forearms must be covered. Men wear jackets and long trousers.

OTHER AUDIENCES

The "private" audience is reserved for cardinals, heads of state, ambassadors or others of first importance. The second type of audience is the "special," which is almost as important as the "private," and is granted only to people of high rank or to those who have an important subject to present to the Pope. The third type of audience is the *"baciomano,"* which is also considered personal, as each visitor comes into the personal presence of the Pope, kisses his ring, and exchanges a few words with him, addressing him as "Your Holiness."

In this third type of audience, visitors stand in a single file around the room and when the Pope enters they kneel and do not stand again until the Pope leaves the audience chamber or makes a sign for them to rise. He passes from one visitor to another, extending his hand to each so that all may kiss his ring. He also may ask a question and exchange a few words with each. It is customary, as it is in the general audience, for visitors to take with them one or more rosaries or other small religious objects, which, after the visitor has received the Papal blessing, are also considered to have been blessed.

The rules of dress for visitors to the Pope are not so strict as they once were. But even now for a private or special audience, men traditionally wear evening dress with tails or sack coat and women long-sleeved black dresses and veils over their hair. No one may wear any but the most functional jewelry.

NON-CATHOLICS

At a general audience, every person present must kneel, rise and sit at the prescribed time. Non-Catholics, if they do not ordinarily do so, need not make the sign of the cross.

In private audiences, those being received will be told when they arrive the proper manner of kneeling and kissing the Pope's ring. If they object to these requirements on the grounds of their religion, there may be some slight modification. But the procedures are strictly followed, and rather than make an issue, those who feel they do not wish to follow them would be wiser to forego the private audience.

PART FIVE

FORMAL ENTERTAINING

18

Formal dinners in private homes

The requisites for a perfect formal dinner, whether a great one for two hundred people or a little one for eight, are as follows:

Guests who are congenial to one another (the most important requirement).

Good *food,* a suitable menu perfectly prepared and served, *table furnishings* in perfect condition, suitable to the occasion and the surroundings, freshly laundered linen, brilliantly polished silver, shining glassware, *service* competent and expertly suited to *your* requirements.

A *cordial, hospitable host* and a *charming hostess* whose tact, sympathy, poise and perfect manners are in evidence at all times.

For all dinners, these requisites are much the same, but the necessity for perfection increases in proportion to the formality and the importance of the occasion. A perfect dinner is not necessarily a *formal dinner,* which cannot be given without the help of servants. However, if the guests must help themselves from a buffet, or if the hostess has to rise to clear the table, the dinner immediately becomes informal.

EXPERT SERVICE

The lack of butlers, footmen or kitchen maids need not keep you from entertaining formally. The hostess who wishes her dinner to be formal can either hire temporary help or resort to a catering service that provides not only servants but excellent meals, either prepared by a cook sent to your home or partially cooked in their kitchens and finished in yours.

A small (for no more than twelve) formal dinner may be beautifully handled by a cook, a butler and a footman or a maid (at a truly formal dinner, those who serve the meal should be men). More than twelve necessitates a second footman and a cook's assistant. Either the host's chauffeur or a man hired for the occasion assists the ladies from the cars or taxis, directs the parking and, later, brings the cars to the door when the party is over. (In the country his job is that of a chauffeur—in the city he acts as a doorman.) If there is a permanent cook in the house, she prepares the meal and only the butler and footman are hired for the evening. They serve and also assist her with the cleaning up.

The hostess sets the table, arranges flowers and does all else that will relieve her help of responsibilities other than the preparation and serving of the meal.

The cook arrives early in the day, the butler and footman and doorman come a little later and take care of any last-minute polishing or arranging. If cocktails are served, the butler mixes them in advance and has them ready to serve as each guest arrives. Before the guests arrive, the footman takes his place in the hall to direct the guests or help with their wraps; the butler stands near the hostess to announce guests, pass cocktails or assist her in any way. It is up to him to see that all runs smoothly so that the hostess may devote her attention to her guests.

The butler, footman and waitress leave after all the guests have gone, the glassware is washed and the ashtrays emptied. The cook may leave after the cooking utensils and dinner service have been washed and the kitchen made immaculate. If the help has been hired from an employment agency, you may be billed later, but you tip those who have served you when they are ready to go. If hired by you personally, you simply pay them before they leave at the rate you have agreed upon. Be sure that you establish the method and amount of payment at the time the servants are hired; this avoids any unpleasantness at the end of the evening.

SELECTING YOUR GUESTS

The proper selection of guests is the first essential in all entertaining. It is a mistake to invite too many great talkers to the same gathering. Brilliant men and women who love to talk want listeners, not rivals. Very silent people should be sandwiched between good conversationalists or at least voluble talkers. Never seat the silly or dull near the learned and clever, unless the dull one is a pretty woman with a talent for listening and the clever one is a man with an admiration for beauty and a love of talking.

Making a dinner list is a little like making a Christmas list. You put down what *they* will like (you hope), not what you like. Those who are placed between congenial neighbors remember your dinner as delightful, but ask people out of their own groups and seat them next to their pet aversions, and wild horses will not drag them your way again.

THE IMPORTANCE OF DINNER INVITATIONS

Invitations to formal dinners may be engraved or written by hand. Occasionally they are even issued by telephone. *(See Chapter 43.)* They must be answered immediately by return mail, or those which were telephoned, by telephone. Only illness or an unavoidable accident excuses the breaking of a dinner engagement. To break one engagement in order to accept a more desirable one is inexcusable. The rule is: Don't accept an invitation you don't care about.

If a guest is forced to drop out at the last moment, the hostess tries to fill in by inviting an intimate friend by telephone. Good manners require the friend to accept if possible.

SEATING YOUR GUESTS

Who is the guest of honor?:

The guest of honor is the oldest lady present, or a stranger whom you wish for some reason to honor. The guest of honor is *always* taken in to dinner by the host and placed on his right. The lady of next greatest importance sits on the host's left and is taken in to dinner by the gentleman on whose right she sits. The hostess is always the last to go into the dining room at a formal dinner unless the President of the United States or the governor (but only in his own state) is present. Then the hostess goes in to dinner with the guest of honor, who leads the way, and the wife of the President or governor follows immediately with the host.

In Washington, even though the dinner be given for a guest of medium rank, the ladies of highest rank have the honor-places on either side of the host. The lady for whom the dinner is actually given is merely "among those present," unless those of higher rank agree to waive precedence, which Mrs. Frances Perkins did when she was Secretary of Labor, saying always to seat her where no one else wanted to sit.

The order of table precedence:

The lady of highest rank is on the host's right. The lady of next highest rank is on his left. The third lady sits on the right of the man of highest rank, the fourth lady on the left of the man of second rank, and so on. The lowest in rank is nearest the center. If the dinner is not official and there is no particular distinction in rank or age, the hostess may seat her guests in whatever order she thinks will achieve the most congenial and pleasant conversation. The lady she places on her husband's right is automatically the guest of honor. The "lady of honor" is "taken in" by the host and seated at his right. At ordinary dinners, therefore, the hostess goes in to dinner with the man of the second highest rank. But if the man of honor is of such importance that she must go in with him as well as place him at her right, the lady who sits on the right of the gentleman of honor and the gentleman who sits on the hostess's left go in to dinner together and then separate. He sees her to her place, then goes around the table until he finds his card. The diagram (with arrow lines indicating ladies and gentlemen who go in together) makes this seemingly complicated situation clear:

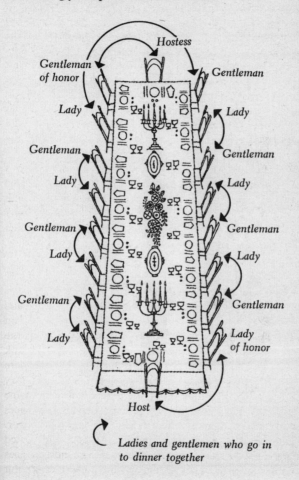

Ladies and gentlemen who go in
to dinner together

Seating a party of eight, twelve or sixteen:

At dinners of eight, twelve or sixteen, where either two ladies or two men must sit at the head and foot of the table, the hostess usually relinquishes her place and the host keeps his. The hostess moves one place to her left rather than to her right, and the male guest of honor is seated at one end of the table on her right. An example of this, with the lines showing service:

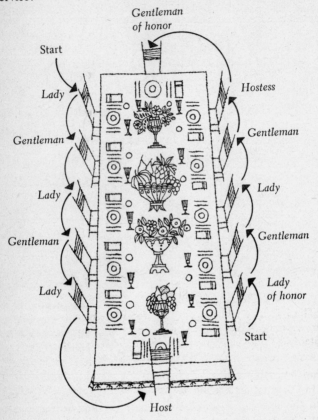

This diagram shows the correct seating arrangement for a group that has a hostess but no host:

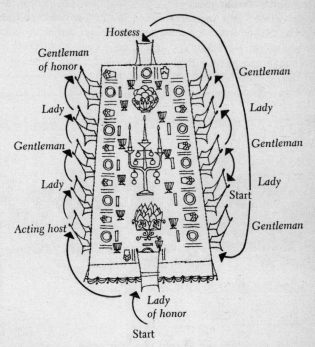

The order of table precedence for such special situations, for example when there is no host, can be worked out suitably by applying common sense to the standard forms.

The envelopes for the gentlemen:

In the entrance hall on his arrival, or just before he goes into the drawing room, each gentleman is offered a silver tray on which are small fold-over cards arranged in two or three neat rows. His name is on the front of one and his partner's name inside. Or, her name may be written on a small one- by two-inch card put into a matching envelope on which his name appears.

If there are many separate tables, the tables are numbered with standing placards (as at a public dinner) and the table number written on each lady's name card. (Do not call it an "escort card.")

The place cards:

The place cards are plain, about an inch and a half high by two inches long. The courtesy title and surname—"Dr. Gooding" or "Mr. Ashley"—are used except when there is more than one guest with the same surname; then it becomes Mr. Russell Albright and Mr. Lee Albright.

SETTING YOUR TABLE

One unbreakable rule is that everything must be geometrically spaced: the centerpiece in the actual center, the places at equal distances from each other, and all utensils balanced.

A tablecloth of white damask, best for a formal dinner, requires a pad under it. (Lacking a felt pad cut to the dimensions of your table, a folded, white blanket serves very well.) Naturally, the cloth must be smooth and perfectly laundered. Lace tablecloths are excellent on a refectory-style table. Handkerchief-linen tablecloths, embroidered or lace-inserted, are suited to all low-ceilinged, old-fashioned rooms. With either lace or linen, no felt or other padding is used.

The centerpiece may be an arrangement of flowers in either a bowl or a vase—low enough for guests to see over—or a distinctive ornament in silver, glass or china.

The individual places:

The distance between places at the table must allow guests elbowroom and room for the servants to pass the dishes properly. About two feet from plate center to plate center is ideal, though a small round table may require less room even if the seats touch at the front corners.

Plates are put around the table at equal distances. For the position of the silver, see diagrams A and B.

A

The silver is arranged so that one uses the utensils farthest from the plate first, taking the next in order for each succeeding course. Fork prongs are always up and the cutting edge of the knives toward the plate. Butter knives and plates are never used on a formal dinner table.

A dinner napkin folded square and flat is laid on each place plate. If the napkin is very large, the sides are folded in so as to make a flattened roll a third the width of its height. If the napkin has a corner monogram, it may also be folded diagonally in half and the two long ends folded under.

B

Napkins are put at the side only when food is put on the table before seating the guests. Bread should not be put in the napkin. The place cards are put on top of and in the center of the napkin or, if unsteady on a folded napkin, on the tablecloth above the napkin at the center of the place setting.

Finishing the table:

Two pairs of candlesticks are placed at the four corners about halfway between the center and the edge of the table, or two candelabra at either end halfway between the places of the host and hostess and the centerpiece. The candelabra are high enough and the candles as long as the proportion can stand, so that the light does not shine into the eyes of those at the table.

Dishes or compotes, holding candy, fruit, fancy cakes or other edible trimmings, go at the corners, between the candlesticks or candelabra and the centerpiece. Nuts may be put on the dinner table either in two big silver dishes or in small individual ones at each of the places, but they are removed with the salt cellars and pepper pots after the salad course. Pepper pots and saltcellars are put at every other place.

Olives and celery are passed during the soup course. When fish or meat or salad has its own accompanying condiment, sauce or relish, it is also passed. Pickles are incorrect on a dinner-party menu.

Cigarettes and ashtrays:

A small ashtray may be put at each place and cigarettes in a tiny holder in front of each diner or in larger holders spaced evenly about the table. The smoker does not light his cigarette until he has finished his main or salad course. Some hostesses even today prefer that their guests do not smoke until coffee is served, and no ashtrays or cigarettes are placed on the table. Others have them passed at the end of the salad course.

FOOD AND DRINK

Cocktails:

If cocktails are served, two or three varieties are prepared in the pantry or kitchen and passed (on a tray) to each

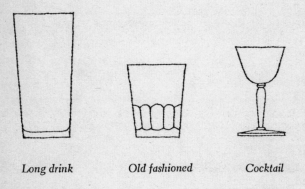

Long drink   *Old fashioned*   *Cocktail*

guest as he arrives, the butler indicating what they are: "Would you care for an Old Fashioned or a martini?" Glasses of tomato juice or some other nonalcoholic beverage are always on the tray for those who do not care for liquor. Only one cocktail need be served. Formal dinners should start as nearly as possible at the hour stated on the invitation.

The menu:

The menu for a modern dinner, no matter how formal, consists of no more than six courses:

1. soup, fresh fruit cup, melon or shellfish (clams, oysters, shrimp)
2. fish course

3. the entrée, or main course (usually roast meat or fowl)
4. salad
5. dessert
6. coffee

Balance an especially rich dish by a simple one: for example, fish timbale with a thick creamed sauce followed by spring lamb or a filet mignon; broiled fish by an elaborate meat dish. Highly flavored Spanish or Indian dishes are not appropriate for a formal dinner. Avoid the monotony of too many creamed dishes: cream soup with creamed chicken; or too many sweet dishes: fish with apricot sauce and duck basted with currant jelly.

Vary the textures: for example a poor menu is clear soup, smelts, broiled squab, miniature potato croquettes and string beans, lettuce salad with cheese straws, ice cream. There is no substance here. Substitute roast squab instead of broiled and a thick cream soup or a fish such as salmon. Too many women order trimmings rather than food and men go away hungry.

Wines with dinner:

Sherry (in a small V-shaped glass) customarily is served with the soup; it is put into a decanter and served at room temperature.

White wine: any dry white wine is served with fish or with an entree.

Burgundy, stronger than claret, is especially suitable with red meats, duck and all game. Claret and burgundy should both be at room temperature. The decanting of vintage wines is a delicate, important operation. Clarets and white wines, if not decanted, are lifted as gently as possible, without changing the side on which the bottles are lying, into straw baskets such as those used in restaurants.

The white wines are carried carefully to a refrigerator; red wines, to the dining room or pantry whose temperature approximates sixty-eight degrees. All these wines are left in their baskets until just before they are to be served and then, as gently as possible, they are decanted. Be careful not to let any sediment, which has settled at the bottom of the wine, get into the decanter.

Champagne is served with the meat course; when it is the only wine, it is served as soon as the first course has begun. Its

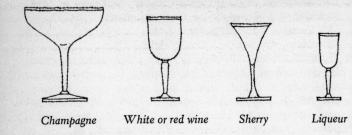

| Champagne | White or red wine | Sherry | Liqueur |

proper temperature depends upon its quality. Only very thin glasses are used.

An excellent vintage champagne is packed in ice without salt. Champagne of not especially fine vintage is put in the refrigerator for a day and then chilled further by putting it into a cooler with a very little salt as well as ice and, occasionally, holding the bottle by the neck, turning it back and forth a few times. In doing this, take care not to leave the bottle in the salt and ice too long or the champagne may become sherbet! When opening, wrap the bottle in a towel or napkin as a protection in case it explodes.

THE GUESTS ARRIVE

The hostess receives:

The hostess stands near the door of her drawing room and as guests enter or are announced, she greets them with a welcoming smile, a handshake and says something pleasant to each: "I am very glad to see you," or "I am so glad you could come!" Elaborate phrases should be avoided. She takes your hand with a firm pressure and gives you—if only for the moment—her complete attention so that you go into her drawing room with a feeling that you are under the roof of a friend.

Although engrossed in the person she is talking to, she must be able to notice anything amiss elsewhere. No matter what goes wrong, she must notice it as best she can and at the same time cover the fact that she is noticing it. If a dish appears that is unpresentable, as quietly as possible she orders the next one to be brought in. If a guest knocks over a glass, her only concern seemingly is that her guest has been made uncomfortable. She says, "I am sorry! But the glass doesn't matter!"

And she has a fresh glass brought (even though it doesn't match) and dismisses all thought of the matter.

If the conversation lags, both the host and hostess must keep it going. At the small dinner the skillful hostess displays what Thackeray calls the "showman" quality. She brings each guest forward in turn to the center of the stage. To a clever but shy man, she says, "Harold, what was that story you told me—" then repeats briefly an introduction to a topic in which Harold particularly shines. Or she begins a narrative and breaks off suddenly, turning to someone else—"*You* tell them!"

The duties of the host:

Mr. Oldname, who stands near his wife as the guests arrive, comes forward and, grasping your hand, adds his own greeting to his wife's gracious welcome. You join a friend standing near or he presents you, if you are a man, to a lady; or if you are a lady, he presents a man to you. At formal dinners introductions are never general and people do not as a rule speak to strangers except those next to them at the table or in the drawing room after dinner. The host therefore makes a few introductions if necessary.

A hostess who is either a widow or unmarried asks the man she knows best to act as host. He gives his arm to the guest of honor and leads the way to the dining table, where he sits opposite the hostess. After dinner he leads the men to the smoking room and later to the drawing room to "join the ladies."

WHEN DINNER IS ANNOUNCED

It is the duty of the butler to "count heads" so that he may know when the company has arrived. As soon as he has announced the last person, he notifies the cook. Then he approaches the hostess, bows and says quietly, "Dinner is served."

Seating your guests:

The host offers his right arm to the lady of honor and leads the way to the dining room. All the other gentlemen offer their arms to the ladies appointed to them and follow the host, in an orderly procession, two and two; the only order of precedence is that the host and his partner lead, while the hostess and her partner come last. If by any chance a gentleman does not know the lady whose name is on the card in his envelope, he must find out who she is and be presented to her before he takes her in to dinner.

At a dinner of less than ten, the ladies are not escorted in to dinner but walk in with whomever they please, in groups of two or three to avoid crowding at the door.

The guests look for their place cards, assisted by the hostess, who may carry her seating plan with her. The gentlemen help the ladies on their right into their seats, with the exception of the male guest of honor, who seats the hostess, leaving the man on her left to walk around and seat the lady on the right of the guest of honor.

The late guest:

Fifteen minutes is the established length of time that a hostess may wait for a belated guest. When the late guest finally enters the dining room, she goes up to the hostess and apologizes for being late. The hostess remains seated, the guest shakes hands quickly so that all the men at table need not rise. The hostess simply says something conciliatory, such as, "I was sure you did not want us to wait dinner." The guest begins her dinner at the course presently being served.

CORRECT SERVICE

At a formal dinner in a house with a large staff, the butler always stands behind the hostess's chair except when giving one of the men under him a direction or when pouring wine. In a smaller house, where he has no assistant, he does everything himself or, if he has a second man or a waitress, he passes the principal dishes and the assistant follows with the accompanying dishes or vegetables.

No serving dishes are ever put on the table except ornamental dishes of fruit and sweetmeats. The meat is carved in the kitchen or pantry; vegetables, bread and condiments are passed and returned to the side table.

From the setting of the table until it is cleared for dessert, a plate remains at every place. If oysters or clams are served as a first course, the plate holding them is put on top of the place plate; so is a plate holding fruit or cold seafood in a stemmed glass. Only the used plate is removed and the soup plate is put in its place. But when the soup plate is removed, the underneath plate is removed with it; at the same time the plate for the next course is put down in their place. A first-course cold dish offered on a platter instead of being served on individual plates would have been eaten on the place plate, then a clean plate would have been exchanged for the used one, and the soup plate then put on top of that. *A plate with food on it must never be exchanged for one that has held food.* A clean one must come between. Dessert plates are put down on the tablecloth.

Dishes are presented at the left of the person being served, and plates are removed at the right unless, because of space, that is very inconvenient. Glasses are poured and additional knives placed at the right—forks are put on as needed at the left. Individual plates are not removed until the slowest eaters have finished.

Dishes are passed to the right or passed alternately right and left so that the same gentleman shall not always get the last piece on a dish.

The hostess is never served first:

To have oneself served first is the height of discourtesy to one's guests. In all first-class restaurants, each dish is presented to the host for his approval before it is passed or served to his guests but he does not help himself. Nor should a hostess in her own house. The person seated on the host's right is always served first.

Filling glasses:

As soon as the guests are seated and the first course is put in front of them, the butler goes from guest to guest, on the right-hand side of each, and fills the water goblet. He then serves the wine, asking each guest, "Sherry, sir?" (or "madam?"). All wines are poured at the right of each person and without lifting the glass from the table. Sherry is served with the soup (or Chablis with oysters) and then champagne is served straight through to the end from its own bottle with a napkin around it (put on like a shawl) and wrapped tight.

Serving bread:

As soon as soup is served, dinner rolls, crackers and toast are passed in a flat dish or a basket. A guest helps himself with his fingers and lays the roll or bread on the tablecloth—there are no bread plates at a formal dinner because no butter is served. Whenever no bread is left at anyone's place at table, more should be passed.

Presenting dishes:

Dishes are presented held flat on the palm of the servant's left hand; every hot one has a napkin placed as a pad under it. A heavy meat platter is steadied by holding the edge of the platter with the right hand protected by a second folded napkin. Each dish is usually supplied with a serving spoon and a large fork. Peas, mashed potatoes, rice, etc., may be offered with a spoon only.

The serving table:

The serving table is in a corner near the door to the pantry or kitchen and hidden by a screen from the guests at table. It holds stacks of cold plates, extra forks and knives, the finger-bowls and dessert plates. At informal dinners all dishes of food are left on the serving table on a warming tray but at formal dinners, dishes are never passed twice and are therefore taken directly to the pantry after being passed. When clearing the table for dessert, the plates of whatever course precedes dessert are removed, leaving the table plateless. Saltcellars, pepper pots, unused flat silver and nut dishes are taken off on the serving tray and the crumbs brushed off each place at the table with a tightly folded napkin onto a tray held under the table edge.

Dessert service:

There are two methods of serving dessert. The first is to put the fork and spoon on a china dessert plate. After the dessert the fingerbowl is brought in on a separate plate. In the second method, the fingerbowl as well as the fork and spoon are brought in on the dessert plate. The diner puts the fingerbowl above his plate, and the fork and spoon each to its proper side. The fingerbowl is less than half filled with cold water; a few violets or a gardenia may be floated in it, but never a slice of lemon.

Fruit, when served, is passed immediately after the dessert or ice cream; then decorative sweets are passed: chocolates, caramels, peppermints, candied orange. Coffee is usually served elsewhere later.

AFTER THE MEAL

At the end of the dinner, the hostess looks across the table and, catching the eye of one of the ladies, slowly stands up. In a moment everyone is standing. The gentlemen offer their arms

to their partners and conduct them back to the living room or
the library or wherever they are to sit during the rest of the
evening. Each gentleman then leaves his partner and, with the
other men, follows the host to the room where after-dinner
coffee, liqueurs and cigars and cigarettes are passed. At the end
of twenty minutes or so, the host, at the first lull in the conversation, suggests that they "join the ladies" in the living room.

In a house where there is no extra room to smoke in, the
gentlemen remain at the table for their coffee, etc., while the
ladies go to the drawing room, where coffee, cigarettes and
liqueurs are passed to them.

Afterdinner coffee is served in one of three ways: (1) The
footman proffers a tray of cups, saucers and sugar; the butler
follows with the coffeepot alone and pours into the cup held in
the guest's hand. (2) A tray with filled cups is proffered by the
butler to the guests who help themselves. (3) The tray of cups
and sugar is held on the servant's left hand. The guest puts
sugar into one of the cups and the servant pours coffee with
the right hand. Liqueurs are offered exactly as coffee in the
second or third manner. The guests pour their own, or, saying
"Cognac" or "Mint, please," their choice is poured for them.
Cigarettes are arranged on a tray with matches or a lighter.

TAKING LEAVE

Today, although it is the obligation of the guest who sat on
the host's right to make the move to go, it is not considered ill-
mannered, if the hour is growing late, for another lady to rise
first, go to her hostess and say, "Good night. Thank you so
much." The hostess answers, "I am so glad you could come!"

In the dressing room or in the hall, the maid helps the ladies
with their wraps. The butler at the door goes out on the front
steps and says, "Mr. Sewell's car." The host's chauffeur (or a
man hired for the evening) signals to Mr. Sewell's chauffeur;
on the arrival of the car he reports to the butler who says to
Mr. Sewell, "Your car is at the door, sir." Or, if Mr. Sewell is
driving his own car, the chauffeur brings the car round and
holds the door for him.

Bridge players leave as they finish their games, sometimes a
table at a time or, most likely, two together. (Husbands and
wives are never, if it can be avoided, put at the same table.)
They stop to say good night to their hostess and thank her.
She expresses her pleasure that they could come.

SOME ADVICE FOR THE GUESTS

Refusing wine or food:

If you do not wish wine, it is best to allow a little to be poured into your glass. A guest should, however, feel free to say "No, thank you," to anything offered him, if he wishes.

Gloves and napkins:

Ladies always wear gloves to formal dinners and take them off at the table—entirely off! It is hideous to leave them on the arm, merely turning back the hands. Both gloves and bag are supposed to be laid across the lap and the napkin, folded once in half across the lap, on top of the gloves and bag. However, both gloves and bag more often than not land on the floor. There is one way to keep these three articles from disintegrating—cover the gloves and bag with the napkin put cornerwise across your knees and tuck the two side corners under you like a lap robe with the gloves and bag tied in place, as it were. It is either that or have the gentleman next to you groping unhappily under the table at the end of the meal.

Conversation:

Guests, of course, are expected to converse with their neighbors on both sides of them. Not to do so is rude not only to one's neighbors but to the hostess as well.

19

Luncheons

The formal luncheon differs from the formal dinner only in minor details. I shall confine this chapter to the differences. *(For all other matters, see Chapter 18.)*

THE INVITATIONS

The word "lunch" is used much more often than "luncheon" —"luncheon" is rarely spoken but it is written in books like this one and sometimes in third-person invitations.

Although invitations may be telephoned, formal invitations to lunch are nearly always written in the first person and rarely sent out more than a week in advance. For instance:

> *Dear Mrs. Kindhart* [or *Martha*]:
> *Will you lunch with me on Monday, the tenth, at half past one?*
> *Hoping so much for the pleasure of seeing you,*
> > *Sincerely* [or *Affectionately*],
> > *Jane Toplofty*

If Mrs. Toplofty's luncheon were given in honor of somebody, the phrase "to meet Mrs. Eminent" would be added immediately after the hour. At a very large luncheon for which the engraved card might be used, "To meet Mrs. Eminent" is written across the top. *(See also Chapter 43.)*

ARRIVAL OF THE GUESTS

The hostess sits in the living room in some place that has an unobstructed approach from the door. After leaving her wrap, each guest comes into the room preceded by the butler or the maid who quietly announces the new arrival's name. Or the guests may greet the hostess unannounced. The hostess takes a step forward, shakes hands and says, "I am delighted to see you." If the guest does not speak to anyone, she makes the necessary introductions.

When all the guests have arrived, or have had time to enjoy a cocktail if it is offered, the butler or maid notifies the kitchen, approaches the hostess and bows slightly. If necessary to attract the hostess's attention, he or she says quietly, "Luncheon is served."

If there is a guest of honor, the hostess leads the way to the dining room, walking beside her. The gentlemen stroll in with those they happen to be talking to or, if alone, fill in the rear, but never offer their arms to ladies in going in to a luncheon.

COCKTAILS

Cocktails may or may not be served before lunch. The preference leans toward sherry, Dubonnet or a cocktail made with fruit juice, such as a daiquiri. As always, tomato juice or plain fruit juice should be available for those who wish it.

THE TABLE

Although colored damask is acceptable, traditionally the the lunch table is set with place mats of linen, needlework or lace. A runner, matching the mats but two or three times as long, may be used in the center of the table and on it are arranged flowers or an ornament and two or four dishes of fruit or candy. No candles are used at a luncheon. On a large table, four slim vases with small sprigs of flowers or any other glass or silver ornaments may be added.

The places are set as for dinner with a place plate, a fork, a knife or a spoon for each course. The lunch napkin, matching the table linen, is smaller than the dinner napkin and is folded like a handkerchief in a square of four thicknesses and laid on the plate diagonally, with the monogrammed (or embroidered) corner pointing down toward the edge of the table. The upper corner is then turned sharply under in a flat crease a quarter of its diagonal length, the two sides rolled loosely under (see diagram). At a large luncheon, place cards are used as they are at dinner.

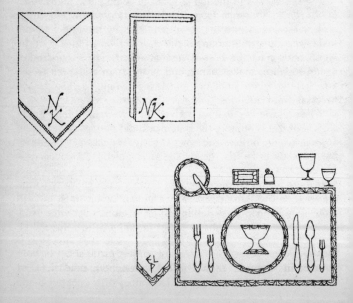

The bread-and-butter plate:

The bread-and-butter plate, part of the luncheon (and breakfast or supper) service goes at the left side of each place just above the forks with the butter knife on the plate placed diagonally from upper left to lower right, with knife edge toward the table edge.

Hot breads are an important feature of every luncheon—hot crescents, baking-powder biscuits, bread biscuits, dinner rolls or corn bread—and are passed as necessary. Butter in balls or curls rather than in squares is put on the plate beforehand and passed throughout the meal until the table is cleared for dessert. Bread-and-butter plates are removed at the same time as the large plate.

SERVING LUNCH

A formal luncheon may be served by one or two waitresses instead of by men alone. The service is identical with that of dinner. Carving is done in the kitchen and no food is set on the table. The places are never left plateless, except after the salad course when the table is cleared and crumbed for dessert. The dessert plates and fingerbowls are arranged as for dinner.

THE MENU

Five courses at most (not counting the ornamental sweets or coffee as a course)—and more usually four—are sufficient for the longest and the most elaborate luncheon possible. For example: (1) fruit or soup in cups; (2) eggs or shellfish; (3) fowl or meat (not a roast); (4) salad; (5) dessert. The menu in a private house is seldom more than four courses and eliminates either 1, 2 or 5.

A popular first course is melon, grapefruit or any sort of fruit cut into very small pieces and served in special bowl-shaped glasses set into long-stemmed larger ones, with a space for crushed ice between the two, or in champagne glasses, which are kept in the refrigerator until sent to the table.

Soup at a luncheon (or at a wedding breakfast or a ball supper) is never served in soup plates but in two-handled cups. It is eaten with a teaspoon or a bouillon spoon or is drunk from the cup which is lifted to the mouth with both hands. It is usually a clear soup: in winter, a bouillon, turtle soup or consommé; in summer, chilled jellied consommé, madrilene or vichyssoise.

Lunch-party egg dishes are innumerable (see any cookbook); substantial dishes such as eggs Benedict or eggs stuffed with pâté de foie gras and a mushroom sauce should be balanced by a simple meat course, such as broiled chicken served with a salad. With a light egg course, eggs in aspic for example, serve meat and vegetables. If you serve fruit *and* soup, omit the eggs.

For an informal luncheon, if you do not wish to leave out a course, choose the simplest dishes: a bouillon or broth, shirred eggs or an omelette, then chicken or a chop with vegetables, a salad of plain greens with crackers and cheese, and a pudding, ice cream, mousse or any other light dessert. There should always be at least one course of hot food. If you offer hot soup (or at supper, tea or chocolate), the rest of the meal may be cold.

The menus suggested above are for lunch parties. For women you know are dieting, the menu would be greatly modified. In other words, when lunching with intimate friends, you have the kind of food you know they like.

BEVERAGES

In the winter, one light wine such as a dry Rhine wine or a claret may be served with lunch. Sherry may also be served with soup. White wine might be served in the summer, but iced tea or iced coffee are the usual choices. Iced tea at lunch is prepared with lemon, sugar, and orange juice if you wish, and poured into ice-filled glasses (often decorated with sprigs of fresh mint) already at each place. But coffee is passed around in a glass pitcher on a tray that also holds a bowl of powdered sugar, a pitcher of cold milk and another of cream as thick as possible. The guests pour their coffee to suit themselves into tall glasses half full of broken ice and furnished with long-handled spoons.

After lunch, the men remain with the ladies and have coffee in the living room.

20

Teas and receptions

Afternoon parties range from the very dignified reception, through the more or less formal tea dance or tea, to the casual cocktail party. The reception today is primarily a public or semipublic gathering in honor of a prominent personage or an important event. Receptions usually take place on the diplomatic or civic levels and are handled by a competent staff. The major difference between a reception and a tea is one of atmosphere. A reception always takes itself seriously. A tea, no matter how formal, is friendly and inviting.

THE INVITATIONS

Afternoon teas are given in honor of visiting celebrities, new neighbors, or a new daughter-in-law, to "warm" a new house, for a house guest from another city, or just because the hostess feels hospitably inclined.

The invitation is a visiting card of the hostess with "Jan. 10, Tea at 4 o'clock" in the lower corner, opposite the address, and, if appropriate, "To meet Mrs. Harvey Montgomery" across the top of it. Or it may be telephoned. *(See also Chapter 43.)*

THE TEA TABLE

The tea and the coffee or hot chocolate may be passed on trays, but more often the hostess prefers to have them poured at a table. Many choose their dining-room table from which to serve; however, the tea table may be set up in any room with adequate space and easy access and exit so that the guests can circulate freely.

Except on a metal and glass table a cloth must be used. It may barely cover the table or hang half a yard over the edges. A tea cloth may be colored, but the conventional one is of white linen with needlework or lace, or both, or appliquéd designs.

A large tray is set at either end of the table, one for the tea and one for the chocolate or coffee. On one tray is the kettle, in which the water was boiling before being brought in. A flame under the kettle keeps the water hot. There are also an empty teapot, a caddy of tea, a tea strainer and slop bowl, cream pitcher and sugar bowl, and, on a glass dish, thin slices of lemon. On the coffee tray is a large coffee-filled urn or pot, also with a flame under it. A pitcher of cream and a bowl of sugar complete the tray. If chocolate is served instead of coffee, all that is needed is the pot of steaming chocolate.

If the trays are carried in by the maid, the flames under the pots are lighted as soon as the trays are set down but never before, to avoid any possibility of a spark catching fire to her apron.

The table:

The cups and saucers are placed within easy reach of the ladies who are pouring, usually at the left of the tray, because they are held in the left hand while the tea (or coffee) is poured with the right. On either side of the table are stacks of little tea plates, with small napkins matching the tea cloth folded on each one. Arranged behind these, or in any way that is pretty and uncluttered, are the plates of food and whatever silver is necessary. If the table is not large enough to hold all the plates and food, some may be placed on a sideboard or on a small table in a convenient location.

SERVANTS NOT NECESSARY

Because nothing needs to be passed to the guests, it is perfectly possible for a hostess to give a formal tea without the help of servants. The hostess would then set out the tray with everything except the boiling water before her guests arrive. After she greets the guests, she fills the tea-tray kettle from the kitchen kettle and carries it in to the tea table.

MAKING GOOD TEA

The most important part of the tea service is boiling water and plenty of it. Nothing is easier than tea-making; nothing is rarer than the hostess who knows how! To make good tea, first rinse the teapot with a little boiling water to heat it, and pour out. Then put in a rounded teaspoonful of tea leaves or one teabag for each person, or half this amount if the tea is superquality. Pour on enough *actually boiling* water to cover the tea leaves about half an inch. Then let it steep at least five minutes (for those who like it very strong, ten) before additional boiling water is poured on. Now pour half tea, half boiling water for those who like it "weak"; pour it straight for those who like it strong. The cup of *good* tea should be too strong without the addition of a little lively boiling water which gives it freshness.

When tea has to stand a long time and for many guests, the ideal way to make it is in a big kettle on the kitchen stove, very strong, and let the tea actually boil three to four minutes on the range; then pour it through a sieve or filter into your hot teapot. The tea will not become bitter. Moreover, you do not need a strainer at the table. It does not matter if it gets quite cold. The boiling water added to the strong infusion will make the tea hotter than most of us can drink immediately.

DRINKS SERVED AT TEA

At a tea or reception to which men have been invited, the hostess (or maid or butler) often asks a guest who has refused a cup of tea if he or she would like anything else, a whiskey and soda or a cocktail. If there is a servant, he will serve the drink after it has been made in the pantry. If the hostess has no help, she may ask the guest to mix his own drink from a bar that has been set up in an inconspicuous place separate from the tea table.

THE LADIES WHO POUR

The pouring is usually done by two intimate friends of the hostess especially invited beforehand. Sometimes after an hour, the first two are relieved by two other close friends of the hostess.

A guest says to the deputy hostesses pouring, "May I have a cup of tea?" (or coffee or chocolate). The one pouring smiles and answers, "Certainly! How do you like it? Strong or weak?"

If the visitor says, "Weak," *boiling* water is added and, according to the guest's wishes, sugar, cream or lemon. (Good tea calls for milk, though it seems always to be called cream.) If either hostess is surrounded with people, she smiles as she hands her the cup, and that is all. If the hostess is free, the guest makes a few pleasant remarks, such as an observation or two about the beauty of the table or how delicious the little cakes look. The guest then moves away with her tea or chocolate and joins a group of friends.

21

Balls, dances and debuts

FORMAL BALLS AND DANCES

There are two fundamental differences between balls and dances. First, only those of approximately one age are asked to a dance; ball invitations are sent to personal friends of the hostess, regardless of their ages. Second, because fewer people are asked to a dance, the decorations and refreshments may be but do not have to be simpler.

Great private balls have become almost unheard of in recent years. Two types of balls have replaced private ones all over the country—the charity ball and the debutante ball. Though you may never give a private ball, your daughter may be among the group of girls to be presented or you may be asked to serve on a charity committee.

How and where to start:

A public ball is run by a committee, whose chairman is comparable to the hostess, but without the full burden of responsibility. Special duties are allotted to each member of the committee: one takes charge of invitations, one of decorations; others are responsible for the orchestra, the food, the ticket money, etc. In the following paragraphs, however, wherever the word "hostess" is used, you may substitute "committee member" if the ball is other than a private one.

The hostess preparing to give a ball may enlist the aid of many people. The club or hotel where it is to be held provides the servants, the food and the drinks; or, if the ball is in her home, a caterer provides the same services. A good florist sees to the decorations, and there are social secretaries available to help the hostess with the lists and invitations. Nevertheless she must make the final decisions on all the details important to the success of the party.

The first thing the hostess does is to find out which evening the facilities of the club or hotel she prefers are free. She then telephones and engages the best orchestra she can for that evening. If possible, there are two orchestras, so that the moment one finishes playing, the other begins. Good music is of more importance than the choice of place. Also try to select an evening not already taken by another hostess or organization in order to avoid conflict either on lists or, in a small town, on the services of caterers, florists, etc. Next the hostess makes out her list and orders and sends out the invitations.

Asking for an invitation:

Invitations to balls, private or public, are always formal. There are, however, many variations in good taste. (*For these forms, and also for less formal invitations appropriate to the smaller dance, see Chapter 43.*)

It is always permissible to ask a hostess if you may bring a man who is a stranger to her; men who dance are always in demand, and the more the better. But it is rather difficult to ask for an invitation for an extra girl, no matter how pretty, unless she is to be looked after by the person asking for the invitation. In that case, the hostess is delighted to invite her. Invitations are never asked for persons whom the hostess already knows. This definitely established rule of etiquette assumes that she would have sent them an invitation had she cared to. However, an intimate friend may quite properly remind her of someone who, in receiving no invitation, has probably been overlooked.

The one who has arranged for the invitation for the stranger should, if possible, accompany him to the ball and introduce him to his hostess. "Mrs. Norman, I would like to introduce John Franklin, my roommate, whom you were kind enough to say I might bring." If the stranger arrives alone he introduces himself and identifies the guest who arranged for his invitation. "Mrs. Norman, I am John Franklin, Bob Whiting's roommate. He was kind enough to ask you if I might come, and he is joining me here later."

A ball in a private house:

A ball always has an awning and a red carpet down the front steps or walk of the house. A chauffeur at the curb opens the car doors. Appurtenances such as the awning, red carpet, coat racks and ballroom chairs, as well as crockery, glass, napkins, waiters and food, can be supplied by hotels or caterers.

The room selected for dancing should be emptied of furniture. If there are adjoining rooms such as a large hall or a library for those not dancing, the floor space of the dancing room is increased considerably by having no chairs at all in it— a far better arrangement than the stiff alignment of straight chairs around the dance floor. The floor itself must be smooth and waxed.

Decorations:

Decorations may be as simple or as elaborate as the pocketbook and the taste of the hostess or committee dictate. At Christmas there might be a beautifully decorated tree in one corner; at another time, Japanese lanterns and Oriental flower arrangements. Whether at home or in a public ballroom, some greens behind the orchestra, some flowers on the tables and wherever else they are most effective are all that are necessary for even the most elaborate ball.

The guests arrive:

The hostess is ready to receive on the stroke of the hour specified in her invitations. If the ballroom opens on a foyer or entrance hall, she usually receives there. Otherwise she receives in the ballroom near the entrance. Guests are announced as they arrive, and after shaking hands with the hostess, pass into the ballroom.

The perfect host and hostess:

The duty of seeing that guests are looked after, that shy youths are presented to partners, that shyer girls are not left at the wallflower outposts, that the dowagers are taken in to supper and that elderly gentlemen are provided with good cigars, falls to the perfect host. But both host and hostess try to see that their guests are having a pleasant time.

The perfect guest:

Guests have responsibilities too. Every young man must dance at least once with the hostess, the girl or girls the dance is given for, the hostess of the dinner he went to before the dance and both girls he sat beside at dinner. At a dance to which he has brought a girl, he dances the first dance with her. He also makes sure that she is not stuck too long with any one partner and he takes her home after the dance.

The helpful ushers:

The hostess chooses from among the young men she knows best a number who are tactful and self-possessed to act as ushers. The appointment cannot be refused. Ushers are identified as deputy hosts by white or other distinguishing boutonnieres. They see that the wallflowers remain chair-bound as little as possible and relieve any young man who has too long been planted beside the same "rosebud." An usher may introduce any man to any girl without knowing either one of them personally and without asking permission. He may also ask a girl (if he has a moment to himself) to dance with him, whether he has ever met her or not. The usher in turn must release every stag he calls upon by substituting another, and the second by a third, and so on. In order to make a ball "go," meaning to keep everyone dancing, the ushers have on occasion spent the entire evening in relief work.

The manners of the guests:

When a man is introduced to a girl, he says, "Would you care to dance?" She may reply, "Certainly" or "Yes, I'd like to very much," or she simply smiles, gets up and dances. At the end of the dance, whether it has lasted one minute or sixty, the man says, "Thank you" and perhaps he adds, "That was wonderful!" to which she replies, "Thank you, it was great fun."

If a girl is sitting in another room or on the stairs with a lone man, a second man should not interrupt or ask her to dance. But if she is sitting in a group, he can go up and ask, "Would you like to dance?" She smiles and either says, "Yes" or "Not just now—I'm very tired."

To refuse to dance with one man and then immediately dance with another is an open affront to the first one. A girl who is dancing may not refuse to change partners when another cuts in, even if she and her partner have taken only a dozen steps together.

When a stag sees a girl whom he wants to dance with, he steps forward and places his hand on the shoulder of her partner, who relinquishes his place to the newcomer, who then dances with the girl until a third in turn does the same to him.

When cutting, the following rules must be observed: (1) The partner who was first dancing with a girl never cuts back on the man who took her from him. He can cut in on her next partner if he wants to, especially if he is giving her a rush. (2) He must not continue to cut in on the same man when the latter dances with other partners.

Supper is served:

A sit-down supper may be served by the caterer at an elaborate ball, but a buffet supper that begins at one o'clock and continues for an hour or more, to which people may go when they feel like it, is pleasanter and easier to manage. Small tables are set up at which guests may sit down to eat after they have served themselves at the buffet. They sit where they please, either a group making up a table or a man and his partner taking any two vacant chairs. A girl is always taken in to supper by the young man who is her escort. If there are unescorted girls at the party, the ushers (or the host, if there are no ushers) see that some of the stags take them to supper or that they are included in a group.

Hot dishes are still served at some balls, but many times the supper consists of a variety of sandwiches, platters of cold meats and accompanying dishes. There may be coffee, chocolate or bouillon or bowls of iced fruit punch. Champagne may be served if it is in accordance with the customs of your community and your own taste, and if guests are of legal drinking age.

SMALLER DANCES

Less formal dances may be given for any number of reasons, perhaps to introduce a new neighbor, or simply because your friends like to dance.

Evening dances:

Invitations are either telephoned or written on a visiting or an informal card. For a dance for young people, invitations are sent out on printed "party" invitations, which have attractive drawings on the outside and spaces for writing time, address and type of party on the inside. Include at the bottom an R.S.V.P. with a telephone number beside it and a hint about clothes. At young peoples' informal parties, even dances, clothing may be anything from suits for the boys and "party" dresses for the girls to Bermuda shorts for both. *(For additional details, see Chapter 44.)*

When the dance is held in your own home rather than a public room, the most important thing is a large enough clear space and a floor properly prepared for dancing. If possible, remove all the furniture from the room; if not, take out whatever you can and move the rest close to the wall, roll and put away the rugs and wax the floor. For decorations, a few flowers—on a mantle, for instance—are sufficient.

Tea dances:

An afternoon tea dance often takes the place of the old-fashioned debutante ball. It may also be given to introduce a new daughter-in-law or someone you feel responsible for who has moved to your community.

Invitations are written on the visiting card of the hostess with "To meet Mrs. Grantham Jones, Jr." across the top. It is equally correct to use the inside of a fold-over card or an informal, or they may be telephoned.

Nowadays houses large enough for dancing are comparatively few. As a result, the tea dance is usually given at a club or in a small ballroom of a hotel. Do not choose too large a room. An undecorated public room needs more people than a room in a private home to make it look filled and give the effect of success. A screen of greens back of the musicians, a few green vines here and there and flowers on the tables form the typical decorations.

Whether in a hotel, club ballroom or a private drawing

room, the curtains are drawn and the lights lighted as though
for a dance in the evening.

Usually only tea, chocolate (or sometimes coffee), breads,
sandwiches and cakes are served. At the end of the table or on
a separate table nearby are bowls or pitchers of orangeade or
lemonade or punch for the dancers. Guests go to the table and
ask whoever is serving for chocolate, coffee or tea and help
themselves to the sandwiches or cakes, which they eat standing
at the table.

Outdoor dances:

If you have a smooth terrace, a stone patio, perhaps beside a
swimming pool, or even a built-in dance floor on the lawn, an
outdoor dance on a summer evening is a romantic and gay way
of entertaining. Small tables are set up near the dance floor,
with enough chairs for all who are not dancing. The bar, if you
serve liquor, and the table with refreshments are nearby.

Have plenty of light for the orchestra (if you have one) to
see their music and also for the bartender and waiters. When
your guests are ready to sit down, uneven ground or steps may
be a hazard if not well lighted. For an outdoor dance, insure
the guests' comfort in case of rain: either have a tent or marquee large enough to cover chairs, tables and dance floor, or be
prepared to move the entire party into your house.

The importance of good music:

Good music is essential to the success of every dance. Therefore spend as much as your pocketbook can afford on it. Hire
the best orchestra obtainable even though you have only three
pieces. If you plan to use a phonograph, choose records specifically intended for dancing and ones that will appeal to your
guests. If you borrow records from your friends—and many
people do in such a situation—be sure the owner's name is
clearly printed on the label in indelible ink or put on with
marking tape.

Dance manners:

Good manners at a dance are the same for young and old
alike. Whatever the local customs about cutting in, a man must
dance with his hostess and he must dance the first and last
dances with the lady he brought to the party, be it friend or
wife. Where the guests are married couples and there are few

extra men, the only time to change partners may be during the intermission or when the music starts again. At this type of party, there are almost always tables to which the couples return between dances, and the men must ask their wives, as well as the women next to them and their hostess, to dance. If the hostess is at another table, a man does not ask her to dance until all the women at his table have partners or there are several men and women remaining at the table, so no one woman is left alone. Under no circumstances should the men hold a "stag party" in the bar, leaving the women at the table without partners.

When the dance is over, every guest finds his host and hostess, thanks them and says "good night."

DEBUTS

"Presenting a debutante to society" may seem to echo social customs long past. Yet, when her daughter is eighteen, a mother may want to present the young lady to the adult world with a certain degree of formality. For this "coming-out," she has a choice of several forms:

(1) The most elaborate is a private ball; (2) less elaborate and more common is a small dance that presents the debutante to her own and her parents' friends; (3) a tea dance (see Chapter 20) and, (4) the most popular today, the big dance for all or several of the debutantes in the area. In a large city, a group of parents may get together and share the expense of a single coming-out party for their daughters. Or it may be given by an organization that invites a group of girls to participate. Many balls or cotillions of this kind are benefit affairs, handled by a committee of the sponsoring charity; the parents of the girls invited to participate are expected to give a substantial donation to the charity involved as a fee for their daughter's participation. (For invitations and their answers see Chapters 43 and 46.)

Debutante balls:

The debutante "receives" standing beside her mother, or whoever else may be hostess, and farthest from the entrance, whether that happens to be on the latter's right or left. As they enter, the guests approach the hostess first, who, as she shakes hands with each, turns to the debutante and, repeating the name that has been announced to her, says, "My daughter" or

"You remember Cynthia, don't you?" or merely "Cynthia." Then each guest shakes hands with the debutante. If there is a queue of people coming at the same time, the guest need only say, "How do you do?" and pass on. If there are no others entering at the moment, each one makes a few pleasant remarks —for instance, "How beautiful your bouquets are!" A friend of her mother probably says, "Cynthia dear, how lovely you are tonight!" A young man exclaims, "My, you look wonderful tonight!" The girls assure her, "Your dress is simply divine!"

At a ball when the guests begin coming at eleven o'clock, the debutante receives until about twelve o'clock—or later if guests continue to arrive. Then she is free to join the dancing. She usually dances the first dance with her father and the next two with the young men she has asked to be her escorts for the evening.

It is still customary to send a debutante flowers at her coming-out party: bouquets or baskets or other decorative flowers. They are sent by relatives, friends of the family, and her father's business associates. Her escorts send corsages. The flowers are banked as a background for her when she stands to receive. The debutante always holds one of the bouquets while receiving, sometimes the same one, sometimes several in succession so as not to show partiality to any special giver.

The debutante goes to supper with her escorts. If she does not wish to center her attention on one man, an easy way out is to ask a brother or other relative. She makes up her own table which includes her most intimate friends. Her table is usually in the center of the dining room, is somewhat larger than the tables surrounding it and has a card on it saying "Reserved."

Debut dances:

Since many young people are at home only during school vacations, evenings available for parties are limited in number. In many communities, two girls whose guest lists overlap arrange for one of them to be presented at a dinner dance and the other at a late dance on the same evening, a convenient arrangement for both families. The one who serves the dinner provides drinks and refreshments for a limited time after dinner. The other girl only needs to worry about a light supper served around one o'clock, and the champagne, punch or whatever she chooses to serve for the rest of the night.

The two debutantes attend each others' parties. The one giving the second party leaves the first with her escorts immediately after dinner to help her mother with last-minute arrangements. The dinner dance usually starts at seven thirty or eight o'clock; the debutante and her hostess receive until dinner is served at eight thirty or nine. The late dance begins at approximately eleven o'clock.

Tea dances:

Tea dances are described earlier in this chapter. The only addition necessary to make it a "debutante tea dance" is the presence of the hostess and the debutante at the entrance as a receiving line.

Assemblies, cotillions and community dances:

Coming out as a member of a group, large or small, is becoming more and more common. These "mass debuts" are a great success because of the relatively small expense to each family involved. A girl's mother may give a small debut party or tea at home and still accept an invitation to participate in one of the assemblies or cotillions. Customs vary widely in different areas. Whatever local practices have become traditional and are accepted by the participants are, in that city or town, quite correct. Some committees invite both boys and girls (other than those "coming out") to the dance; others invite only the girls and request that they bring two escorts. When this is done, the girls send in the names of the escorts as soon as they have accepted and the committee then sends the boys a formal invitation. The girls pay for their escort's ticket if it is a charity-sponsored ball. At most multiple debuts, the committee itself does not invite guests, but each debutante's family is allowed a certain number of invitations and they pay for those they invite.

The party may be a dinner dance or, more often, a late ball. The members of the committee often have dinners beforehand for the debutantes and their escorts. This may also be done by the families of the girls themselves.

The father's part:

The role of the father at a private debut is that of the good host at any party. He does not stand in the receiving line but stays nearby, greets friends and acquaintances and sees that everything is running smoothly. He dances the first dance with his daughter, then he dances with his wife, with the grand-

mothers if they are present and wish to dance, and then with
the other guests, young and old alike.

At many cotillions and community debuts, the fathers participate in a parade and a simple cotillion dance with their
daughters. They cross the ballroom, one couple at a time, and
each father presents his debutante daughter to the hostess or to
the committee giving the dance. Although the young men
guests nowadays may wear tuxedos to debut parties, the escorts
of the debutantes who are coming out and the father must wear
white tie and tails.

The debutante's dress:

At a ball, the debutante wears the prettiest evening dress she
can buy, preferably white, suggesting something light, airy, gay,
and above all, young. A pastel color is acceptable, but not scar-
let or a bright blue, and never black. At a multiple debut, the
girls wear the same color, almost invariably white, but they
choose their own style. The mothers of the debutantes wear
evening dresses in any color except black.

At an afternoon tea the debutante wears a cocktail dress.
Her mother wears an afternoon dress. Both mother and daughter wear gloves, and neither wears a hat.

Some hints for the "belle of the ball":

Let us suppose that *you* are the debutante! Don't let your ex-
citement overwhelm your sense of courtesy. Listen to a name
that is said—look at the one to whom the name belongs, put
out your hand cordially. As friends who have sent you flowers
approach, thank them; also later write an additional note of
thanks to older people. To your relatives or your own intimate
friends, your oral thanks are sufficient.

PART SIX

INFORMAL ENTERTAINING

22

Cocktail parties

Cocktail parties are a popular form of entertainment. They require little preparation, are limited as to time, and you can entertain many more people at once in a small house.

"PAY-BACK" PARTIES

An unattractive custom nowadays is that of giving large "pay-back" cocktail parties. A hostess who has been invited to many parties invites on one evening all those to whom she is indebted and creates one large horror! The guests are not chosen for compatibility, there are not enough places to sit down, the noise level reaches an intolerable pitch. If you incur social obligations with any frequency, do make the effort to give small parties from time to time and avoid the necessity of a yearly "pay-back."

COCKTAILS BEFORE A DANCE

A pleasant form of entertaining is having a group of friends for cocktails before a dinner dance or some other function. Invitations are sent out on visiting cards, note paper or a printed cocktail-party invitation card. They state "Cocktails before the dance at the Happy Course Golf Club, 6:00 to 8:00," the place and date. Add "R.S.V.P." because the hostess usually makes the

139

reservations for those of her guests who wish to go on to the other event.

Invitations may be telephoned, a correct, practical method; the hostess knows immediately how many will be joining her at the club or dance and so can make the reservations sooner.

When you are the guest, you pay the cost of admission, dinner, drinks and anything else at the later party unless your hostess specifically says or writes that she expects you *as her guest*. If you are not a member of the club involved, find out in advance whether you may sign as a member of another club or pay in cash. If either is not permitted, ask your host if you may sign his name and add your initials so you may pay him for your share when he receives his bill.

COCKTAIL BUFFETS

Many hostesses choose the cocktail buffet for entertaining all except the smallest and most informal groups. Here the food offered is sufficiently substantial so that the guests need not have dinner afterward. Since they are expected to linger longer than at a regular cocktail party the invitation frequently states only the hour of arrival, perhaps six thirty or seven, and makes it clear that the gathering is a "cocktail buffet."

The menu may vary from simple to very elaborate. The least is a platter of sliced cold meat (ham, chicken or roast beef), slices of buttered breads, accompanying dishes such as carrot sticks, celery, olives, raw cauliflower, and possibly some sandwiches already made. This type of buffet may be eaten standing near the table without a plate. The meat is placed on a slice of bread and eaten like a sandwich and the raw vegetables picked up and dipped in a sauce. Often a smoked ham or turkey is placed whole on the table; when the platters of sliced meat are running low, the host, or any of the guests, carves additional slices as required.

The table is covered with a tablecloth and napkins are available. If there is room, a centerpiece of flowers or fruit is attractive, but it is better to leave it off and use a prettily decorated cake (or even one of the main dishes) in the center rather than crowd the table.

A more elaborate buffet includes one or more hot dishes, generally casseroles kept warm on an electric hot plate or served in a chafing dish over a flame. In this case, there are stacks of plates and rows of forks, or you may choose a hot dish such as bite-sized meat balls or frankfurters, tiny hot potatoes dipped in salt, and hot bread or rolls with a cheese fondue, all of which may be speared with a toothpick.

JUST COCKTAILS

If the number of guests is small, the invitation is almost always by telephone. For a larger party, they may be written on your own informal, on note paper or on a visiting card. *(See Chapter 44 for the correct forms.)* Or you may buy an attractively printed card made for the purpose.

The time is usually stated, "Cocktails *from* 5:00 to 7:00." Even though R.S.V.P. is omitted, thoughtful guests let the hostess know whether they are planning to attend the party. If there is an R.S.V.P., the telephone number is written beside it, as this type of invitation may always be answered by telephone. Every sort of hors d'oeuvre or appetizer is acceptable provided it can be eaten with the fingers: olives (chilled, or wrapped in bacon and broiled), tiny broiled sausages, thin bread rolled around cheese or bacon, skewered and toasted, crackers spread with sandwich paste, crabmeat or lobster in bite-size pieces, or shrimp on little wooden picks so that they can be dipped in mayonnaise or colorful sauces. Don't forget a pile of cocktail napkins—cloth or paper—on the tray.

WHAT DRINKS TO SERVE

As a general rule, a host should count on each guest having two or three drinks. In the winter, martinis, whiskey "on the rocks" and whiskey in a tall glass with water or soda are popular; in warm weather a cocktail mixed with fruit juice and gin or rum or tall drinks made from these same ingredients are excellent. Always have nonalcoholic drinks available: tomato juice, other fruit juices, Coca Cola, ginger ale. Never urge a guest to have a drink—or *another* drink—if he has once refused.

BARTENDERS AND WAITERS

For a cocktail party of more than twelve and if you have no maid in your home, it is wise to hire a bartender for the evening. The bartender attends to the drinks. He may stand behind

a large table loaded with every sort of cocktail glass, ice, and
bottles of each kind of liquor and soft drink to be served. The
guests go to the bar themselves and request the kind of cocktail they wish. A gentleman usually asks the lady accompanying him her preference and she waits at a little distance from
the bar while he gives the order to the bartender and brings her
the cocktail. If a group of women are talking together, it is perfectly correct for one of them who wishes another drink to go
to the bar herself.

You may prefer to have the bartender pass a tray of drinks,
already mixed, to each guest as he arrives. After the first serving, he watches for empty glasses and, when he sees one, approaches the guest and says, "May I bring you another drink?"
The guest replies, "Thank you, I am drinking bourbon and
soda," and hands him the glass to be refilled.

One important note: Be sure that you instruct the bartender
in advance exactly how you like your cocktails mixed and insist
he use a measure. If you let him measure "by eye" your liquor
supply may run out long before you had planned. Or you may
have some unexpectedly boisterous guests on your hands!

HINTS FOR HOSTS AND GUESTS

At a small party, the hostess introduces a newcomer to all
the guests, but at a large one, after introducing him to two or
three people, she leaves him on his own, her roof serving as an
introduction. There is no need to shake hands. A girl has trouble enough managing pocketbook, hors d'oeuvres, cigarette
and cocktail.

Self-help:

When there is no extra help for the evening, the host is the
bartender and the hostess the waitress. She passes the trays of
hors d'oeuvres once or twice, often with a friend helping her,
and then leaves the food in a conspicuous spot (on a hot plate
or in a chafing dish if the hors d'oeuvres are hot) and the guests
help themselves. She carefully removes trays or dishes even before they are completely empty. One cold limp shrimp in a dish,
or a mayonnaise-smeared platter left on a table is most unap-
petizing.

If the choice is limited, the host-bartender may say, "Will
you have a martini or bourbon?" Also, he may ask the men to

refill their own glasses, as well as those of any ladies who wish another.

If there are only a few guests, the host hangs their coats in a hall closet. If there are more wraps than a closet can conveniently hold, the men and women put them in separate bedrooms, laid neatly on the beds. Or a rack may be placed near the door.

Overstaying your welcome:

Although the hosts must be ready on time, the guests may arrive as much as an hour or so after the start of the party. A late arrival, however, should not mean a late departure. After a half hour or so beyond the indicated departure time, the hostess may take steps to hurry the last survivors out. The most practical way is simply to remove the liquor and close the bar, after which the party will soon be over.

23

Informal dinners

Every dinner party that varies even slightly from the rules laid down for "formal dinners" is informal. There are all degrees of informality. If a hostess who has several servants (or hires several for an evening) serves only three courses, or her husband carves the roast, or if she uses linen mats rather than a damask tablecloth, it becomes an informal dinner. Many of the suggestions in Chapter 18, "Formal Dinners," will be useful, for the rules for the informal dinner are derived from the rules for the formal dinner.

SIT-DOWN OR BUFFET?

The first consideration is the size of your party. Eight is the maximum number that can be served comfortably at a sit-down dinner without help. If your table can seat more than eight, you may have a semi-buffet, with the guests serving themselves from a sideboard, but sitting together at the table. Otherwise, you must plan a buffet dinner. *(See Chapter 24.)*

PREPARATION AND PLANNING

Careful planning and preparation for a sit-down meal are of utmost importance. If you wish to enjoy the company of your guests, you choose dishes that can be prepared in advance and served with a minimum of last-minute fuss. Omit fancy hors d'oeuvres—salted nuts or "niblets" are preferable to elaborate spreads. Try to spread out your preparations over several days. Cigarette boxes may be filled, flowers arranged (choose those that will last several days), silver polished, and even your table set ahead of time. If you have a freezer, prepare in advance whatever dishes can be frozen.

THE INVITATIONS

Invitations may be written on visiting cards or note paper, but they are usually telephoned. They are extended between ten days and two weeks ahead of time and the person invited must answer promptly, either by mail or by telephone. *(See also Chapter 44.)*

SEATING YOUR GUESTS

Give considerable thought to the seating of your guests, for you can make or break a party by the congeniality of dinner partners. In a group of six or ten, the host sits at one end of the table opposite the hostess. If there are eight or twelve at the table, she must move one seat to the left, putting the male guest of honor on her right opposite her husband. The lady guest of honor sits on the host's right. If there is no particular guest of honor, the hostess might choose the oldest lady present or one who has not visited her house for some time. She alternates the men and women, spacing them as evenly as possible, keeping her place at the end of the table unless this puts too many women in a row. She still seats the honored guests at her right and her husband's.

SOME MENU SUGGESTIONS

There are certain practical aspects to consider. Try to avoid dishes that require many extra condiments or sauces; restrict your courses to two or three. If you decide on only two, a main course and a dessert, you may serve more substantial hors d'oeuvres beforehand. Some hostesses serve soup or a fish course, such as cold salmon or shrimp, in the living room. If this is done, the host helps his wife by removing the empty plates and ashtrays while she is seating the guests in the dining room in order to have the living room neat when they return there for coffee. If there is a maid, she does this tidying up while the guests are eating their main course.

A roast is always delicious, and there is something mouth-watering about watching the meat being carved. Creamed or curried chicken within a ring of noodles or rice is pretty. Or try a special dinner—shrimp steamed in beer, lobsters flown from Maine, a Spanish paellan—in short any unusual treat.

A word of caution—don't experiment with a new dish at a party. Try it out at least once on the family. Because the appearance of a dish is almost as important as its flavor, choose a menu with variation in color and texture—never a white sauce on chicken served with rice and cauliflower.

CHOOSING AND SERVING WINE

Unless the meal is strictly formal, the host may choose any wine he thinks his guests would prefer. Whether that is the dry or the sweet variety is a matter of your own taste. The most important consideration is that the wine complement the food you are serving it with. *(For details about the traditional choice of wine, see Chapter 18.)*

SETTING YOUR TABLE

Set the table as for a formal dinner, with a damask or lace cloth; or it may be set with individual place mats as for a luncheon. Gay, colorful cloths add much to a table set on a terrace or in an informal room.

If a tablecloth is used, you do not need butter plates, but with place mats, they are necessary to avoid soiling the polished surface with the buttered or crumbly rolls. All flat silver necessary for the meal is put at each place, the silver to be used last nearest the plate, the one to be used first on the outside. The service

plate is not used. In many houses, the salad dressing ingredients are arranged in a set of bowls and bottles that, with the salad bowl, are put in front of the hostess who mixes the dressing herself.

If a course is to be served before the entrée, it may be on the table when the guests come in to dinner. Fish or shrimp in long-stemmed glass bowls are brought in on a plate, and both removed to make way for the hot plates of the main course. If your first course is soup, practical soup dishes are little pots with lids; they keep the contents hot while the guests are seating themselves.

The butter should already be on the butter plates, the water glasses filled and any wine should either be chilling in a coolor beside the host or in a decanter on the table. Salad is often served with the main course on a salad plate or a bowl set at the left of each place.

If the host is to carve a roast, or serve the meat and vegetables, the stack of warm plates is placed in front of him along with the foods to be served and the necessary implements. If there is a course already on the table, however, the hostess or maid brings the entrée in from the kitchen after the plates have been removed.

GREETING THE GUESTS

The host and hostess stay near the door, or if the living room is out of sight of the door, they go together to greet their guests when the doorbell rings.

Dinner should be planned for forty-five minutes to an hour later than the time on the invitation if cocktails are served, or twenty minutes later if not, to allow late arrivals a moment of relaxation.

INFORMAL SERVICE

With one maid:

Before dinner, the maid may be on hand to take coats from the guests and serve hors d'oeuvres if cocktails are offered. Then she goes to make the last-minute preparations, and announces dinner, or signals the hostess, who tells the guests that dinner is ready.

If a first course is served, the maid removes the plates when everyone is finished and either replaces each one with a hot plate or places a stack of hot plates in front of the host, depending on how she is to serve the main course. She may do this in one of two ways.

First, if all the food is ready in the kitchen, she passes it to the guests, the meat first and then the vegetables. When the maid serves in this way she starts on the host's right with the lady who is guest of honor and continues around the table counterclockwise, serving the host last. Some hostesses insist that they be skipped and the maid return to serve them next to last, but this is awkward.

All dishes are served from the left and, if convenient, removed from the right. The condiments, breads, sauces and salad are usually passed around the table by the guests themselves; if the group is not large, the maid may pass one or more of them when she has finished with the main dishes. A competent maid may pass two vegetable dishes at the same time, holding one in each hand.

When the hostess sees that all her guests are finished, she rings and the maid clears the table. Everything is removed except the glasses and the silver for dessert. The maid then crumbs the table, using a clean folded napkin to sweep the crumbs onto a small plate held just below the edge of the table.

Dessert may be brought in from the kitchen already on the plates and placed before the guests in the same order as was the main course. Or the plates may be set before the guests and the dessert passed to each one in turn. If she prefers, the hostess may serve it herself at the table.

The less formal way, often used for family dinners when guests are not present, is to have all the dishes to be served arranged about the host; as he fills each plate, the maid lifts it and passes it to each person, from the left, starting as before, with the lady on the host's right. When everyone is served, she removes the serving dishes to be kept warm in the kitchen and passes them herself for a second helping when the hostess signals. Or if they have covers, they may be left where they are. When the host wishes to offer his guests another portion, he rings for the maid and says, "Mary, would you please bring me Mrs. Harris's plate"; she holds it for him to fill and returns it to Mrs. Harris. If dessert is served by the hostess, the maid passes the plates around in exactly the same manner as she passed the first course.

THE HOSTESS ALONE

When you are giving a dinner party with no help, begin the meal with the main course and provide the equivalent of a first course by serving plenty of substantial canapés with your cocktails or before you enter the dining room.

You receive your guests and stay with them until all have arrived. Then you leave them with your husband and go into the kitchen, take the roast or other meat out of the oven, put it at your husband's place, set the vegetable dishes beside it, and invite everyone to "Come in to dinner."

Your husband carves the roast or serves the casserole. He may serve the vegetables, you may serve them, or the vegetable dishes may be passed around. When the salad is mixed, pass the bowl, each guest in turn holding it for the one on his right. Dessert may be put on each plate in advance, or you may serve it at the table as your husband did the roast.

In most cases, when the guests see you start to rise to clear the table, they will stand up, saying "May I help you?" Firmly refuse, telling them, "No, really, it is easier to do it myself." The only exception is when you have a daughter, sister or very close friend at the table and have asked her in advance if she would mind helping.

You remove the dishes two at a time, not stacking them, and either put them on a side table or take them to the kitchen. Bread-and-butter plates, salts and peppers and condiment dishes are also taken off, but you need not crumb the table. Each time that you take something out to the kitchen, you may bring back dessert plates, salad and salad plates, or whatever is needed for the next course. If you wish, you may put a dessert plate at each place you have cleared as you return to take the next plate. Or as soon as you have removed your husband's plate, you may put a stack of dessert plates and the dessert in front of him so that he can serve it while you are finishing the table-clearing. Any system that speeds the changing of courses is acceptable, so that your guests do not feel that you are going to too much trouble.

You need not clear the dessert dishes; when everyone is finished, you say "Shall we have our coffee in the living room?" Don't accept a guest's offer to help do the dishes. The thoughtful guest does not insist.

AFTER-DINNER COFFEE

When the guests are seated in the living room, take the cream out of the refrigerator and pour the coffee into whatever pot you are going to serve it from—glass, silver, or, best of all, one that has a flame under it to keep the coffee hot. It may be made and served in an electric coffeemaker, which can be plugged in again in the living room. Arrange the coffee and cream on a big tray, set with sugar, spoons, cups and saucers. It is a nice gesture to offer either a large cup or a demitasse, so many hostesses put some of each size on the tray. When it is all ready, you or your husband carry it in and set it on a coffee table or on any table that has a chair nearby. You serve the coffee, asking each guest, "How many lumps of sugar?" and "Cream?" Either you or your husband may pass the cups around, or the guests may step up and you hand it to them directly. It is thoughtful to offer caffeine-free coffee as an alternate to regular after-dinner coffee.

HINTS FOR GUESTS

A guests should arrive within fifteen minutes of the time for which he is invited. When dinner is announced, you respond promptly, rise and encourage your companions to go with you

—"Shall we go in to dinner? I think Nancy would like us to."
Unless she says, "Please bring your drink with you," don't.

When you are told which is your place, wait for the hostess to
seat herself before you sit down, unless she says, "Please sit
down, I must bring in another dish." Men, as at any meal, help
the women on their right to be seated. At a large party, you
need not wait until all the guests are served to start. Your hostess should say, as the plates are passed, "Please start. I don't
want your dinner to get cold," but if she neglects to do so, pick
up your fork after four or five have been served. The others
will follow suit.

When your hostess rises to clear the table, don't jump up to
help unless she has asked you to beforehand. However, you
may offer to pass the cups around when she serves coffee after
dinner.

Most important—remember to talk to the guests on either
side of you or to enter with enthusiasm into a general conversation if the table is small.

If games are suggested after dinner, no matter how you feel
about them, look as though you think it's a fine idea. Often,
especially if the guests do not have much in common, entertainment that you would ordinarily avoid can be the means of
pulling a party together and making it a success.

24

Buffet dinners

Three great advantages of a buffet dinner are: you can
accommodate many more guests than your dining-room table
will seat, lack of service is no handicap, and it has enjoyable
informality. If people are not sitting beside those they find

particularly congenial, women as well as men are free to move elsewhere.

WITH OR WITHOUT HELP

Just before the hostess announces dinner, she attends to lighting the candles, putting out iced water, and arranging the platters, casseroles or serving dishes on the table. But the food can be all ready—in double boilers or chafing dishes or, if cold, in the refrigerator. After eating, the guests take their empty plates back to the dining room themselves, putting them on a side table—not on the buffet—and serving their own dessert. Their hostess and her husband may remove the dessert plates or the guests may do it themselves. If the dining room has a door, it can be closed, or a screen can be pulled across the entrance, once all the plates have been taken there. If, however, the dining area is a part of the living room, the hostess removes the soiled plates to the kitchen while the guests are drinking their coffee.

If she has a maid or a hired waitress, she advises the waitress when to put the food on the buffet table, watching to see that her guests are ready. The maid takes out empty plates as they set them down. She may, if the hostess wishes, pass the dishes around for second helpings. Because everyone will not finish simultaneously, she has adequate time to remove the food from the buffet table and replace it with dessert plates and dessert or salad and cheese or whatever is chosen to finish the meal.

After the waitress has removed the last of the plates, she brings in the coffee tray and the hostess pours; the maid is then free to clean up the kitchen and dining room.

THE INVITATIONS

The invitation is usually written on an informal, on your note paper or across the top of the face of your visiting card. *(See Chapter 44.)*

The invitation must be answered promptly either by telephone or sent on a visiting card, merely saying "Sat. Oct. 2 with pleasure." *(See also Chapter 46.)*

SEATING ARRANGEMENTS

There are two ways of seating guests at a buffet dinner. First, they may simply return to the living room, hold their plates on their laps and set their glasses on the nearest table. Your guests will be more comfortable if you set a small folding table by each chair.

The second way of seating guests is to set out small tables —sturdy card tables, perhaps—in your living room, dining room or library. If you have the space, most men and women prefer to be seated in this way. The tables are covered with bridge-table size cloths. Places are set exactly as for an informal dinner with silver, napkins, glasses. The guests serve themselves, going for second helpings and removing their used plates. If the living room is used, the hostess takes the tables out after the meal to make room for after-dinner activities.

SEMI-BUFFET

A pleasant way of serving a small group of friends or a family party is to arrange the food on the sideboard or a side table and set the dining-room table as for a sit-down dinner. Two variations are possible. First, after the guests are seated, the host serves each plate from the buffet, asking the guests, "Do you like your meat rare or well done?" or "Do you take cranberry sauce and stuffing?" The hostess passes the plate, seating herself with her own plate next to last, the host helping himself last. She may say as she hands the plates around, "Please start, so that your dinner won't get cold." In the other variation, the guests may serve themselves as at a regular buffet and carry their plates to the table. The hostess serves herself after the guests, and the host is the last.

THE INVALUABLE ELECTRIC HOT PLATE

I recommend an electric hot plate or tray, because on them, plates can be heated and your meal kept warm for an almost indefinite period of time. Furthermore, with an electric appliance on the buffet table, there is no need to take the dishes to the kitchen to be kept warm for second helpings. And, finally, it is unnecessary to watch and replace fuel for flame-heated chafing dishes.

SETTING THE BUFFET TABLE

Unless there is ample space, ornamental objects are omitted. Flowers are lovely, but if it is a question of choosing between decorative flowers and edible fruit, a centerpiece of dessert fruit is preferable. If the table is crowded and candles are not needed to see by, they are better left off. Candelabra are more compact than candlesticks and give better light.

If the party is large, leave the table in the center of the room, so that two lines of guests may serve themselves at once. The most important dish is divided into two parts and one plate or casserole placed at each end of the table. The plates are in two stacks beside them, and the napkins and silver neatly arranged next to the plates. Dishes of vegetables, salads, bread and butter, and sauces and condiments are on each side of the table and the guests need to pass down only one side. If the table is set against the wall, arrange the utensils and food in a way that makes for the best flow of traffic, so that the guests need not double back.

If you use a white damask cloth, silver candelabra and an elaborate centerpiece, your buffet will appear quite formal. But you may just as properly use pottery dishes with a hot-plate pad under them and a bowl of fruit in the center of the table. It is not the elegance of the utensils and decorations you use that

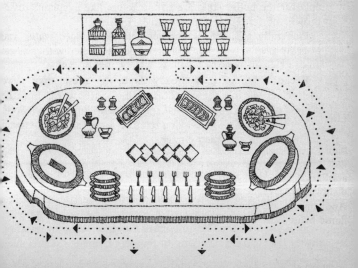

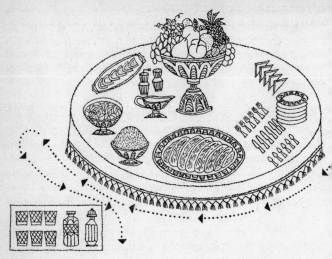

makes your table attractive, but the combination of dishes, linen, and silver and the way in which they are arranged on the table.

Color plays an enormous part in the beauty of a buffet table. If you have copper bowls, keep all the autumn tints in mind: green, red, russet, and yellow on a bare table. Especially suitable for the buffet table are strong colors like eggplant, russet brown, lobster red, leaf green and dark blue.

Generally a punch or another cold drink, iced water and possibly beer left in its cans or bottles, together with glasses, are on the sideboard as well as a large urn of coffee.

Because the coffee is already there, the guests may serve themselves during the meal as well as afterward, but the hostess may take an additional tray, set with cups, a coffeepot, cream and sugar into the living room to serve those guests who did not want it with their dinner.

THE MENU

Whatever kinds of food you choose, be sure they are good of their kind and easy to eat with a fork alone (this is not important if you are seating your guests at tables). Otherwise, merely use a reasonable amount of common sense in selecting dishes that will be satisfying to the people invited. Don't feed hungry men bouillon, dabs of hors d'oeuvres, fruit salad and meringues; rather provide three or four substantial dishes—at least one of these should be hot. Substantial dishes include most meats, fish in a sauce such as Newburg, potatoes and the heavier desserts. Nearly everything made in a baking dish or casserole is ideal for a buffet meal as it is hearty and easily kept hot.

If you have many guests, you may serve two main dishes, possibly a lobster Newburg at one end of the table and beef Stroganoff at the other, but choose two dishes that will be complemented by the same vegetables and condiments.

Here are some menu suggestions, ranging from an elaborate buffet to a simple family-type meal. Use any combination that appeals to you, omitting or adding to each menu as you wish.

Veal Scaloppine or Roast Turkey
Mashed Potatoes
String Beans with Mushrooms
Cranberry Sauce, Stuffing, Gravy
Buttered Rolls
Fresh Fruit Compote
Cookies
Coffee

Italian Spaghetti and Meatballs or Lasagna
Mixed Green Salad
Choice of Roquefort, French, Italian Dressing
French or Italian Bread, Butter
Lemon Ice
Coffee

Hungarian Goulash or Beef and Kidney Pie
Noodles
Glazed Carrots
Green Salad with Mandarin Oranges
Buttered Rolls
Coffee

Curried Lamb or Chicken
Rice Ring
Chutney, Raisins, Ground Nuts
French Bread, Butter
Raw Spinach Salad
Ice Cream and Cake or Cookies
Coffee

For a summer evening:
Three or four varieties of cold sliced meats such as
Ham, Turkey, Roast Beef, Lamb, or Cold Cuts
Scalloped Potatoes
Vegetable Salad
Buttered Rolls
Vanilla Ice Cream with Green Mint Sauce
Cookies
Coffee

THE PARTY ITSELF

When the guests have arrived and the cocktails, if served, are finished, the door into the dining room is opened and people in more or less of a queue file around the dining table. The women as well as the men help themselves, although, quite correctly, a man may ask a woman what she would like, fill a plate and take it to her.

If people continue to sit and wait to be served, the hostess directs them, "Please go into the dining room and help yourself to what you like." If they stand blockading the table, carrying on a long conversation, she says, "Won't you please take your plate and go into the other room again and sit down?"

The only serving detail is the clearing away of used dishes. In a house with servants, every plate is removed as soon as it is put down, and filled ashtrays are constantly replaced; the glasses of those seated are refilled from time to time, and the main dishes passed for second helpings. But the servantless hostess asks one or two members of her family—or an intimate friend—to help her put used dishes in several spaces provided, from which she can stack them and take them away as unobtrusively as possible.

nformal luncheons

f you are one of those who have a very small dining room, r no dining room at all, but have a living room or a patio arge enough to permit two or three small tables to be set up, a uncheon of eight or twelve, perhaps followed by bridge, is elightful. Each card table is set with a cloth, white or colored, yard and a half square; any style will do, but they should, f possible, be exactly alike. Simple matched cloths are better han assorted, elaborate ones. A small flower arrangement nakes a pretty centerpiece.

ERVING THE LUNCHEON

he hostess alone:

If you are serving without a maid, a buffet luncheon is the visest. The food is set out as for a buffet dinner. For a ladies' uncheon, the fare is simpler than for a dinner. A delicious but ight meal is more appreciated than one dressed with rich auces and ending with "gooey" sweets.

After you announce that luncheon is served, your guests file ast the table and help themselves, taking their plates to the ard tables and seating themselves with whomever they wish. f you are having a course before the entrée, it is put on the ables before your guests arrive; they sit down and finish it efore going to the table for the main course. If there is no naid, the guests take their empty plates and leave them on a ide table as they go to get their next course. While they are nelping themselves, you remove the soiled dishes to the kitchen.

157

The same procedure is followed for the salad or dessert. You
then ask them to leave the tables and sit on more comfortable
chairs to have their coffee; you clear the tables and, if bridge
is to follow, set out the cards, two decks, two score pads and
pencils on each table. (*For further details about card parties
see Chapter 27.*)

With the help of a maid:

When you have a maid, she can serve eight or twelve guests
quite easily if the first course is already on the table. She clears
the plates by standing at the table corner, taking two at a time,
one in each hand. A menu limited to a single dish and salad is
best, as she must pass the food from each person's left. The
salad may be all ready in small bowls or plates, which she
brings in two at a time to place on the guests' left. Rolls, butter,
iced water and any other beverage are put on the table beforehand.

When dessert is finished, the waitress carries the coffee tray
to another room and readies the tables for bridge, while the
hostess pours the coffee.

ON FOOD AND DRINK

If you wish to serve cocktails before lunch, the drinks should
be of a milder type than those served before dinner. Sherry,
Dubonnet, vermouth, either "on the rocks" or in a wine glass,
are ideal, but if you know your friends prefer them, serve
martinis, daiquiris, or Bloody Marys.

Two or three courses are sufficient at any informal luncheon.
Four of the following menus have been planned with the idea
that you can have all the preparation finished in advance. But
the sole and the soufflé dishes must be cooked and served at
the exact moment.

Fresh Fruit Cup
Filet of Sole Amandine
Spinach Salad with Chopped, Hard-Boiled Egg, Tart Dressing
Buttered Rolls
Orange Chiffon Cake
Coffee

Clam or Oyster Chowder with Oyster Crackers
Fruit Salad and Cottage Cheese
Melba Toast
Chocolate Mousse
Coffee

Cold Salmon with Green Mayonnaise Sauce
Sliced Cucumber and Tomato
Protein and White Toast
Lemon Chiffon Pie
Coffee

Curried Chicken with Rice Ring
Mixed Green Salad
Baking Powder Biscuits
Jell-O made with Fresh Fruit
Coffee

Little Neck Clams or Oysters
Cold Sliced Roast Beef, Horseradish Sauce
Potatoes au Gratin
Watercress and Tomato Salad
Fresh Strawberries and Sour Cream
Coffee

Cheese Soufflé
(if your guests can be trusted to arrive on time)
Asparagus Vinaigrette
Croissants
Fresh Fruit and Cookies
Coffee

Beverages:

In summer iced tea and coffee are delicious, or give your
guests a choice by passing a tray with a pitcher of each, or
have both available close to the buffet table. A bowl of fruit
punch prepared with floating slices of orange and lemon and
surrounded by glasses or cups adorned with fresh sprigs of
mint looks refreshing. A pitcher of ice water, from which the
guests may help themselves, should be in evidence.

26

Barbecues

If you have a built-in grill in your yard or patio, you are fortunate, but a portable grill serves just as well. A table near the fire holds the food and the plates, cooking utensils, etc. There must be seating facilities for every guest. A garden wall or steps leading to the patio may be used as seats, if cushions are provided. Small chairs can be rented for very little from a caterer.

You may give your flair for color and decoration a free rein: checked or striped tablecloths, ones with splashy designs of fruits or flowers are gay. They may be of cotton or linen, but plastic ones are more practical. If your cloth is patterned, solid-colored paper napkins and plates are best.

Disposable plastic or plastic-coated paper plates and cups are excellent if they are of a sturdy material—avoid the flimsy cardboard-paper type. For a hot drink, the cups must have handles (the package should be labeled "for hot drinks" or they will leak).

Some hostesses prefer the new hard plastic sets of "china" in lovely patterns; although unbreakable, they feel much like real china. Drink containers, too, come in a variety of unbreakable materials. The barbecue cook will like colorful enameled flameproof pots and pans.

For decorations, string lanterns above the table and make a centerpiece of gay paper parasols for a Chinese dinner. A fishnet tablecloth with colorful felt cutouts of fish sewed on is decorative for a lobster dinner. Fresh flowers arranged in a container that fits into the barbecue theme are always attractive —yellow daisies, for instance, arranged in a copper kettle.

At most barbecues, the host is the cook, but the hostess may also act as chef.

MENU SUGGESTIONS

I am going to give you some sample menus, intended only as a guide. In each, the main dish—meat, fish or fowl—is prepared on the grill, and unless specified, the others are prepared in advance and kept on the stove indoors or brought out to sit on a corner of the grill where the temperature must be neither too hot nor too cold.

The least expensive, but always popular, especially with young people:

Hamburgers and/or Hot Dogs
Buttered Rolls
Casserole of Baked Beans
Potato Chips
Celery and Carrot Sticks
Watermelon Slices

In the following menu, pieces of meat or shrimp, mushrooms, tomatoes, onions and bacon are marinated and threaded alternately beforehand on long skewers, ready to be laid on the grill:

Beef, Lamb or Shrimp "Kabobs"
Rice
Watercress and Tomato Salad
Hot Rolls
Chocolate Éclairs

Especially good for the seashore:

Grilled Swordfish
Casserole of Scalloped Potatoes
Spinach Salad
Croissants
Fresh Fruit Compote and Cookies or Cake

Messy to eat, but delicious:

Spareribs with Barbecue Sauce
Baked Potatoes
Coleslaw
Hard Rolls
Apple Pie with Vanilla Ice Cream

The classic barbecue menu:

Sirloin Steak
Potato Chips
French Fried Onions
Mixed Green Salad
French or Garlic Bread
Assorted Pastries

Beer, any soft drink and pitchers of milk go well with the informality of a barbecue, and, in very hot weather, iced tea and iced coffee. Pots of coffee kept hot on the grill are served either during or after the meal. If cocktails are served, instead of elaborate hors d'oeuvres, dishes of nuts or potato chips scattered about are sufficient.

A side table loaded with a variety of condiments is a nice touch. As each guest fills his plate (the host cuts and serves the meat), he passes by this table and helps himself to catsup, mustard, relish or sauce.

SOME GENERAL HINTS

Have plenty of light so the chef can tell whether the meat is done. Floodlights directed up into the trees give a beautiful effect. Japanese lanterns can be purchased strung on electric wires like Christmas-tree bulbs. Candles in hurricane lamps give a soft light. Some candles with insect repellent are excellent in summer.

A lunch-time barbecue may be followed by a swim if you have a pool or are near the beach, or you may organize a game of softball or badminton. Many adults enjoy a game of catch or touch football on a brisk day. Organized games and races for the children are almost a necessity.

In the evening, a phonograph may be plugged in for dancing if the patio or terrace has a suitable surface, or, with a stone fireplace, the fire may be built up to a blaze and the guests gather round it to sing or chat. If you notice your guests putting on sweaters or coats, be prepared to move the party into the house.

27

Other informal gatherings

Other ways of entertaining informally have special descriptive names but do not otherwise differ much from the informal gatherings discussed in earlier chapters. A housewarming, for example, may be a cocktail buffet with a tour of the new house added, or a surprise party might be an informal dance given in someone else's home. Therefore, a hostess may want to combine the suggestions made here with those from another appropriate chapter.

HOURS FOR PARTY-GIVING

The hour chosen for a meal or a party or a game or a visit should always be that of neighborhood custom. If weddings in the evening are customary in your neighborhood, then have your wedding in the evening too. If, on the other hand, a nine o'clock dinner hour and a noon wedding are customary, then even though you forage in the refrigerator an hour or more before dinner, at nine you dine and at noon you marry.

If neighbors pay visits in the evening—or if morning is the hour preferred—you take your protesting husband with you in the evening—or go by yourself in the morning—no matter how inconvenient either hour may be to you. If you cannot manage to have a party at the time decreed by custom, find another way to entertain your friends.

HOUSEWARMINGS

You may invite your friends to a housewarming whenever you see them or by telephone. Invitations on visiting cards are quite suitable too. A housewarming is generally a cocktail party or a cocktail buffet. It may be as simple or as elaborate as you wish, but it is fun to keep the style of your house in mind when you plan your decorations. For instance, if it is an Early American type, a brown tablecloth set with copper or pewter may be more appealing than lace with crystal or silver. *(For additional suggestions, see Chapter 22.)*

The guest generally takes a small gift to a housewarming, something of permanent use, rather than flowers: a few pretty dish towels or place mats or a brush for the fireplace.

OPEN HOUSE

The door is open to all those invited at any time between the hours stated on the invitation. Most open houses nowadays are held to celebrate a holiday—New Year's Day, Christmas Eve or Fourth of July, and are decorated accordingly. They also may take the place of a housewarming.

Invitations are generally sent out on informals or commercial cards bought for the occasion. Because an answer is never expected, refreshments are simple and expandable. Dips, bowls of nuts, or other "nibbles," and a punch rather than individual drinks are good choices. People drop in to greet their hosts and generally stay no more than a half hour to an hour.

Food and beverages are set out on the dining-room table or, if your refreshments are restricted to one or two plates of food and a punch bowl, on a table in the hall or living room. You may surround a bowl of eggnog with holly twigs or a fruit punch with flowers, but otherwise, only the attractive arrangement of glasses, little napkins (cloth or paper) and food is necessary to assure the charm of your refreshment table.

BRUNCHES

Brunch is a combination of breakfast and lunch that relies heavily on breakfast for its menus but is taken closer to the usual hour for lunch. Brunches are often given on the day after a large party, but no such excuse is necessary if you find the late morning hours convenient for you and your friends.

Informality is the rule. In the country, slacks or simple dresses are worn by the women, or if the party is beside a swimming pool, people may come in shorts and bring their bathing suits. In the city, any daytime dress or a suit is correct for a woman; a man usually wears a sports jacket rather than a business suit.

Invitations may be telephoned ahead of time, but with this kind of gathering the host may simply say to his friends as they are leaving someone else's party, "Would you come over around eleven thirty tomorrow for a late breakfast?" or "Would you all come for a late breakfast after church tomorrow?"

The food is attractively and conveniently laid out on a buffet table. Breakfast and lunch dishes are combined: a platter of scrambled eggs surrounded with bacon or little sausages, accompanied by hot rolls or toast, and sautéed potatoes and broiled tomatoes; or platters of waffles to be covered with maple syrup or with creamed chicken. Pitchers of fruit juice and pots of coffee are on a table beside the buffet.

CARD PARTIES

On planning your tables:

The first thing to do is to make a list of those to be invited. Then divide those who accept into groups of four and try to seat at each table only those who like to play together. The tables may all be different—one with good players, another with beginners, one where the stakes are high, another where they play for nothing—but do your best to put those who play approximately the same kind of game at the same table. Don't put people who take their game seriously with others who unceasingly chatter and keep asking, "What's trump?" Above all, don't seat players by drawing names out of a hat.

On each table you leave a slip of paper on which you have written the names of the four players who are to play there together. They cut for their seats and partners. See that each table is comfortably lighted, taking care that no light reflects the shiny surface of the cards. If you have any doubt about light, sit in each place, hold the cards in your hands, lay a few on the table and see.

Refreshments:

The kind of refreshments you offer at a card party depends, of course, on the time of day and the guests. Small sandwiches and tiny cakes, accompanied by tea or coffee, are suitable at four o'clock for a group of women. For the men at an evening gathering, a selection of cold meats and cheeses and a variety of breads for do-it-yourself sandwiches are served with coffee and beer. The food may be arranged on the dining-room table, and, having served themselves, the guests may return to the cleared card tables, or take their plates to comfortable chairs in the living room.

A note of warning: If you have invited avid card players, don't interrupt their game to serve some lavish concoction of whipped cream, etc. Give another kind of party if you wish to indulge yourself in the kitchen!

Prizes:

If it is customary in your community to play for prizes, select first prizes for the highest scores made by a woman and a man; at a party to which no men are invited, a second prize is usually given. All prizes are attractively wrapped before being presented. Those who receive the prizes open the packages at once and show appreciation when thanking the hostess.

DESSERT CARD PARTY

A dessert card party is a happy compromise for the hostess who wishes to do more than simply invite her guests to play cards. Dessert for four or eight may be served in the following way: The dining table is set for the dessert course only, with individual place mats, a china dessert plate, a lunch napkin on the plate, a fork at the left and a spoon at the right, and a glass of water. The table is set with a coffee tray in front of the hostess. While her friends are having their dessert, the hostess pours the coffee, and it is handed around the table. After coffee, they begin playing on tables already set up in the living room.

If there are more than eight, the dining table is set up as a buffet, using a pretty tablecloth or place mats or round lace doilies (paper ones will do) under the stack of plates and the dishes on which the dessert is served. The guests serve themselves and take their plates to the living room to eat, but unless the hostess asks them to, they do not sit at the card tables which have already been set up and readied for bridge.

They help themselves to coffee; if they wish to start playing immediately, they may take their cups with them to the bridge tables.

STAG DINNERS

A man's dinner is called a stag or bachelor dinner. It is given by a man for men only. It usually celebrates some special event or person, as a welcome or farewell, or, most frequently, as the groom's last party with his good friends before his wedding. A man's dinner is usually given at the host's club or in a private room in a hotel or restaurant. If he gives a stag dinner in his own house, his wife (or mother or sister) should *not* appear. For ·his wife to come downstairs and receive the guests with him is definitely out of place. He discusses his plans and the menu with his wife, who will prepare it ahead of time and set out the dishes on a buffet table. After the men have eaten, she removes the plates and cleans up if they have gone to a room separated from the dining room; if not, she leaves the cleaning up until the next day.

THE SURPRISE PARTY

The preparation for a surprise party may be done in different ways. For an evening party, you might make your plans for a date on which you know John and Mary White are having dinner alone at home. The company who are to surprise them meet nearby, then troop in a procession to storm the house. Or you may arrange to have the Greens invite John and Mary for dinner. While dinner is progressing, the others who are giving the surprise party take possession of John's and Mary's house. On some pretext, the Whites and Greens return to the White's house where the party is in full swing. Refreshments are always brought by the unexpected guests, and they never leave a mess for Mary to clean up when they have left.

Such parties usually take place on John's or Mary's birthday or some other anniversary, particularly wedding anniversaries celebrated in paper, wood, tin or crystal. A word of warning: to celebrate a golden wedding anniversary with a surprise party may cause too great a disturbance to older people.

SEWING GROUPS

The hostess at whose house a sewing group meets provides a supply of different-sized thimbles, extra needles, and several pairs of scissors and spools of thread. The purpose of the group may be to make garments for a nursery, hospital or other organization; or the members sew for themselves, do needlepoint or knit. Sometimes a sewing circle is also a lunch club that meets weekly or fortnightly at the houses of the various members. They sew from eleven until about one and then have a sit-down or buffet luncheon. More often coffee and light refreshments, such as coffee cake, cookies or doughnuts, are served approximately halfway through a session that may run from ten to twelve or from two to half past four.

28

Showers

Showers are friendly gatherings held in honor of a bride-to-be or in welcome of a new clergyman or in expectation of the arrival of the stork—for almost anything, in fact, that imagination can invent. The setting can be almost anything—a luncheon, a dinner, an afternoon tea, an evening party, or even a morning coffee. The only distinguishing characteristic of the shower is the giving of presents to the guest of honor.

Bridal showers are never given by members of the bride's immediate family, because a gift is obligatory. It is correct to give a shower for someone who is being married for the second time, whether she be widow or divorcée. But the hostess keeps in mind the elaborateness of the wedding plans and takes hers accordingly. The bride-to-be who is having a quiet, simple wedding might easily be embarrassed by an extremely elaborate shower.

THE INVITATIONS

Invitations to showers are often telephoned: "I'm having a kitchen shower for Betsy Jones on Tuesday at three o'clock." Or they may be written on a visiting card—"Larder shower for Dr. Smythe" or "Stork shower for Helen"—with the day and the hour. Or a shower card from a stationer's shop is entirely appropriate. Make it perfectly clear to the guests the kind of shower it is to be, including all details you have that may be helpful. For example, if you know that Betsy Jones's kitchen is to have red trim, let the guests know, too, so they can choose appropriately colored items.

THE HOUR

A shower for a bride may be given at any hour of the day or evening. Evening is chosen when men as well as women are invited. Originally shower presents were most often things to wear, and therefore showers were for girls only.

The shower for a clergyman is usually given in the early evening. A stork shower is always given in the early afternoon and only intimate girl or women friends are invited. Sometimes a combination of stork shower and surprise party is given at the house of the mother when the baby is five or six weeks old. Although a surprise party, it would be excusable for someone to give her a hint half an hour in advance, so that she and the baby will be found ready for company. The guests usually bring light refreshments with them, certainly in the case of a surprise shower for an unmarried clergyman.

THE GIFTS

The type of shower allows wide leeway in the choice of presents. At a stork shower, they include anything for a new baby. A larder shower, often given for a new clergyman, includes everything eatable. The shower for a bride is sometimes specified as a linen or a kitchen shower or a general shower.

At a "round-the-clock" shower, each guest is given an hour of the day on her invitation and brings a present appropriate

for the hour. For example, at a bridal shower, if her hour
10 A.M., she might take a dustpan and brush; if it is 6 P.M
she might take a set of four or six glasses.

PRESENTING THE GIFTS

When everyone—or almost everyone—expected has arrive
Betsy Jones opens the packages one by one and thanks ea
giver. "Thank you, Susie—how lovely!" The cards of dono
should be enclosed.

If the party is at tea time, the guests are then offered lig
refreshments of tea or coffee and cakes. If it is in the evenin
coffee or punch and sandwiches are suitable, as are cider a
doughtnuts, or liqueurs or highballs, especially if men a
included.

Unlike wedding presents which are sent from the shop whe
they are bought, gifts for a shower are brought by hand a
given personally. Sometimes the packages are taken at t
door and put unopened with the others on a table in anoth
room. In some localities all the presents are sent to the hoste
several days beforehand. She leaves the packages as they ar
but puts each in a uniform outer gift wrapping. When all a
wrapped, the presents are piled on a table or behind a scre
or perhaps in full view against one wall of the living room.

9

House parties and overnight guests

THE INVITATIONS

Invitations for house parties and overnight guests are generally telephoned, or, if your guests live in another town, written on your note paper.

June 15th

Dear Ellie,

John and I are hoping that you and Bob and the children can spend the weekend of the fourth with us in Edgartown. There is a 4:00 P.M. ferry that would get you here in time for dinner, and there are ferries leaving at 5:00 and at 8:00 on Sunday. The fishing should be great, and our children are counting on Sally and Jimmy for the annual picnic. Please come—we have wanted to show you our island for so long.

Affectionately,

Ann

With the rising popularity of winter sports, more and more people are acquiring lodges in the mountains, and ski weekends are becoming almost an institution in all sections of the country with nearby slopes.

January 4

Dear Joan,

The forecast is for snow and more snow, and Dick and I are hoping that you and Bill will spend the weekend after

*next skiing with us at Stowe. Come as early as you can
Friday the 8th, and stay until Sunday night, so as not to m*
a minute of it. The Hortons are coming, too, and perha
you could drive up together. To find us, you turn off Ro
7 on Skyline Drive, exactly three-tenths of a mile beyond
traffic light in Hampton; we are the second house on
right.

No formal clothes, only your ski outfits and slacks or
skirt for the evening. Plenty of woolies and flannels—
cold.

We're counting on you, so do say "yes."

> *Love to you both,*
> *Barbara*

In your letter or on the telephone, always give the details
transportation or, if your guests are coming by car, the rou
If they will be arriving by public transportation, tell them to
sure to let you know at what hour they will arrive, so that y
can meet them at the station or airport. It is also wise
indicate what the main activities will be. "We're planning
deep-sea fishing expedition on Saturday," "The Joneses ha
asked us to a beach picnic on Sunday," or "There is to be
dance at the club on Saturday night."

ROOM FOR YOUR GUESTS

Temporary arrangements:

Few families today have a room in their house intend
solely for the use of guests. When friends spend a night or
weekend (or more), the children are moved around to vaca
a room, or the library or den is put in readiness. Toys a
hidden from sight, clothes are removed from the closet (whi
should have an adequate supply of hangers), sufficient draw
space is cleared so that the guest may unpack his suitcase, a
the room is made sparkling clean. If he is to share a bath wi
other members of the household, his towels are hung on
rack in his bedroom, so that children do not inadvertently u
them. A vase of flowers on the bureau or table will make t
room inviting.

ANNING THE MEALS FOR YOUR GUESTS

When you must entertain without help, the more planning
 preparation that can be done ahead, the more effortless
 pleasant the result. House parties generally last for no
re than two days and nights or possibly three. With the help
 freezer, or even the freezing compartment of your refrig-
tor, meals can largely be prepared in advance. A casserole,
ming in the oven, can be ready at whatever hour your guests
ve, early or late. A steak cooked on the beach in summer
over the coals of the fireplace in winter, served with potato
ps and salad, takes little effort. You may wish to treat your
sts to a dinner in a local restaurant that specializes, perhaps,
foods native to the region. At most summer resorts, yacht
os or nightclubs provide dinner and dancing on Saturday
ht.

or lunches, you may prepare the ingredients for a chef's
d, lobster rolls, chowder and sandwiches in advance, ready
e mixed or spread at the last moment.

The one meal that the hostess cannot organize in advance is
akfast. Because one of the joys of a weekend away from
ne is being able to sleep as late as they want, guests should
 be awakened unless there is an activity planned in which
 truly wish to participate. The hostess precedes all her
sts to the kitchen, makes coffee, prepares fruit or juice, and
ks sausage or bacon enough for all, keeping them warm on
ot plate or in a low oven. She puts butter, eggs and frying
—or pancake batter and griddle—by the stove, bread by
 toaster, and an assortment of cereals and milk and cream
the table, which she sets with places for everyone. She may
 for her guests, or she may eat her own breakfast and be
dy to help the latecomers as they arrive. If some of the
up want to make an early start, to the beach or to ski, for
ance, make plans the day before. The host and hostess may
ompany the ones who are leaving, as long as everything is
 in readiness for those who wish to sleep or relax and
angements have been made for their joining the group later
 if they wish.

A friendly custom is gaining popularity in many localities—
en two or three couples go to visit good friends, they offer
oring a roast or a casserole to provide one evening's meal.
re is no reason why the hostess should not accept such an

offer. On this type of intimate party friends feel more comfo
able if they can contribute.

THE PERFECT HOSTESS

The perfect hostess chooses guests who have the sa
interests and will enjoy each other's company. There is lit
pleasure in having one couple who enjoys staying up all nig
to play bridge, while the others wish to go to bed early in or
to be up at sunrise to go on a fishing expedition.

Arrangements for activities you know your visitors will enj
are made ahead of time. If they like tennis, sign up or reser
a court at a convenient hour, or if they would love to go
the dance at your club, make a reservation for a table. Lea
time for your guests to relax and visit with you and the otl
guests; they may want to see a special landmark or shop
stores carrying merchandise made in the area.

Certain rules are easy to observe once they are brought
one's attention. A host or hostess never speaks of annoyan
of any kind—no matter what happens. Unless actually una
to stand up, they should not mention physical ills any mo
than mental ones. If anything goes wrong with the househo
they must work a miracle and keep it from their guests. Shou
a guest be taken ill, the hostess assures him he is not givi
the slightest trouble, at the same time doing all that can
done for his comfort.

And above all, they must not be "overanxious." The ove
anxious host or hostess is one who fusses and plans continual
who thinks the guests are not having a good time unless th
are being rushed, tourist fashion, from this engagement to th
and crowded with activity and diversion every moment of th
stay.

DO'S AND DON'TS FOR HOUSE GUESTS

Having accepted an invitation, guests may, in an emergenc
shorten their visit, but they must not stay beyond the time th
were asked for unless very especially urged to do so. Ev
then they would be much wiser to go early and be missed rath
than to run the risk of outstaying their welcome.

You as a guest must conform to the habits of the fam
with whom you are staying, take your meals at their hour,
what is put before you and get up and go out and come in a

) to bed according to the schedule arranged by your hostess.
nd no matter how much the hours or the food or the
rangements may upset you, you must appear blissfully con-
nt. When the visit is over, you need never accept an invitation
● that particular house again; but while you are there, you
ust at least act as if you were enjoying it.

The ideal guest not only tries to wear becoming clothes
ut tries to get into an equally becoming frame of mind, never
entioning the misfortunes and ailments he has experienced or
itnessed.

The perfect visitor never keeps people waiting. You are
ways ready for anything—or nothing. If a plan is made to
cnic, you like picnics above everything and prove it by
thusiastically making the sandwiches or the salad dressing or
hatever you think you make best. If, on the other hand, no
ae seems to want to do anything, the perfect guest always has
book to be absorbed in, or a piece of sewing or knitting, or
se beyond everything would love to sit in an easy chair and
) nothing.

It is not necessary, but it is courteous to take your hostess
gift—or better, if she has children, to take presents to them.
●me people prefer to send a present after their visit, having
ade note of something that their hostess would find useful or
at would go perfectly in one of the rooms. As to the children,
they are young, a collection of small amusing articles from
e ten-cent store often gives them more pleasure than a single
-esent of value.

Condense your luggage in both quantity and size, especially
you are being taken in someone else's car or going by train
● a place where there are no porters.

Beside the necessary sport clothes, a dinner coat (inquire of
our host if one is necessary) and one or at most two sports
ckets with the necessary shorts, shoes, ties, etc., will suffice.

If you are to swim, ride or play games, take your own bath-
g suit (preferably two in case of damp weather), riding habit,
nnis racket or golf clubs.

The guest no one invites a second time is the one who dog-
rs books, burns cigarette trenches on table edges, uses towels
r cleaning shoes, stands wet glasses on polished wood, tracks
to the house in muddy shoes. Other unwelcome guests are
ose who are late for every meal, help themselves to a car and
) off and fail to come back for meals on time.

Aside from the more or less general rules of behavior, the are some specific rules worthy of mention: A guest in som one's home never suggests taking his hosts to a meal in a r taurant. If, however, your host suggests dining at a restaura you might well say, "That sounds wonderful, and we wou love to be *your* hosts for dinner—you are giving us such wonderful time!" Otherwise, you show your gratitude by i viting them to a restaurant when they are in town or by sendi a suitable present.

If you have friends in the neighborhood and they invite y and your hosts over for a swim or to play tennis, never acce the invitation and then relay it to your hostess. Instead, make noncommittal reply such as, "May I call you back, as I'm n sure about Joan's plans?"

If you are not needed to make up a foursome at bridge a you are tired and want to go to bed before your hosts and t other guests do, it is perfectly all right to say to your hoste that you've had a "rugged" week at the office and would li to go to bed.

When you are visiting a house run with one maid or non avoid making your visit a burden through the extra picking your carelessness may entail. If the housemaid offers to pre a dress that has become mussed in packing, you accept h offer and later give her a larger gratuity—but do not ask f this service unless it is an emergency. A maid is always tipp by overnight guests. The amount for a weekend may ran from two to five dollars, depending on the type of work s does. If the hostess does her own housework, you make yo bed, tidy up your room and offer to help in clearing the tab and cleaning up in the kitchen.

When you are one who wakes with the dawn and the hous hold you are visiting sleeps on a Sunday morning, the lo wait for your coffee can be most unpleasant. The farsight guest with the early habit can prevent discomfort by carryi in a small case his own little electric water-heating outfit a a package of instant coffee or tea, sugar, powdered milk cream, and a few crackers. He can then start his day all himself without disturbing anyone. In an informal househol he may slip quietly into the kitchen and make himself a cup coffee and a piece of toast to sustain him until the others a ready for a full breakfast.

Perhaps the entire guest situation may be put in one se

tence. If you are an inflexible person, very set in your ways, don't visit! If you have confidence in your adaptability, go and enjoy yourself!

THE GUEST ON A YACHT

The main difference between being a guest at a country house and a guest on a yacht is that you live in very close quarters with your host and hostess and your fellow guests and must therefore be particularly on guard against being selfish or out of humor. If you are not a good sailor, do not accept a yachting invitation.

If you are involved in a racing cruise of any sort, you will almost certainly be expected to assist or act as crew, and presumably your host knows the extent of your sailing ability. You must be prepared to accept orders quickly, adjust yourself to his routine, respect his regulations, and forgive and forget any impatience or ill temper that he may show in moments of stress.

THE OVERNIGHT GUEST IN A CITY APARTMENT

Today an increasing number of people live in apartments where a guest room is a rarity. Sometimes a couch in the living room is converted into a comfortable bed at night for an overnight guest, or if a child is away at camp or boarding school, his room may be available. No matter how hospitable your host or hostess may be, a guest should remember that an extra person in small quarters is, inevitably, something of an imposition—no matter how charming the guest may be. Household regulations should be meticulously observed, and the visitor stays no longer than necessary, takes up as little room with his possessions as possible, and keeps his belongings neat. Above all, he should be prepared to fit in with the household schedule and not inconvenience his host or hostess.

PART SEVEN

SPECIAL OCCASIONS

30

The new baby

ANNOUNCEMENTS

Sometime before the birth of a baby, or immediately thereafter, the prospective parents select an announcement card at
a stationer's to be sent to their own friends and those friends
of the grandparents who are close to the family. After the
birth and as soon as the name is determined, the father notifies
the stationer and in a few days the cards are ready.

The nicest type of birth announcement, one that happily is
coming back into general use, consists simply of a very small
card with the baby's name and birth date on it, tied with a
white or pastel ribbon to the upper margin of the "Mr. and
Mrs." card of the parents.

A large variety of commercially designed announcement
cards, with space for the baby's name, date of birth and parents' names to be written in by hand, are much less expensive
and very popular. The least desirable include data on the baby's
weight and length and a picture of a baby saying coyly: "My
mommy and daddy want me to tell you I landed."

Robert Meadows, Jr.

July tenth

Mr. and Mrs. Robert Meadows

47 Pace Place

Announcement of adoption:

It is a nice gesture to send a card announcing this happy event to your friends and relatives. A card such as this will also bring assurance to the child later on of her place in the hearts of those who chose her to be their own.

Mr. and Mrs. Nuhome
have the happiness to announce
the adoption of
Mary
aged thirteen months

Newspaper announcement of birth:

In the week following the birth, the father may send a release to the local newspapers: "Mr. and Mrs. Robert Meadows of 202 Park Avenue, New York, announce the birth of a son, Robert, Jr., on July 10, 1967, at Doctors Hospital. They have one daughter, Jane, 4. Mrs. Meadows is the former Miss Mary Gilding." Or, "A daughter, Mary Jane, was born to Mr. and Mrs. Robert Meadows," etc. The same announcement may be sent to the editor of the church newsletter or bulletin.

CHOOSING A NAME

Avoid giving the baby a name that is too long or difficult to pronounce clearly or that forms an unpleasant combination with the last name. Choose instead a simple or biblical name or one with some significance, perhaps because it is the name of some member of the family or a beloved friend. When a son is given the same name as his father, he may be given a middle name different from that of the parent; in adult life he may prefer to be known as "R. William Meadows," instead of "Robert Meadows, Jr." Roman Catholic baptismal certificates must record a saint's name as the baby's first or middle name. Most Jewish babies are traditionally named for a deceased relative.

PRESENTS FOR BABY AND MOTHER

Everyone who receives a birth-announcement card writes a note of congratulations to the new parents. Or a note may be enclosed if a gift is sent. It is not necessary to send a present, however, even if you receive an announcement.

Gifts for the baby are addressed to the parents at home or you may bring your present with you when you visit the hospital. It is thoughtful to bring something for the new mother too, handkerchiefs or a plant or flower arrangement.

CHRISTENINGS AND OTHER RELIGIOUS CEREMONIES
Time of christening:

In the Catholic church, the baptism takes place when the baby is very young—usually not over a month old—and always in the church or baptistry (unless its baptism is *in extremis*). In Latin countries, babies are often baptized in the hospital within a day or two of their birth. In Protestant churches, the average age for christening is from two to six months, although in some denominations or under special conditions, children may not be christened until they are several years old. In all churches, the mother is present if she is able.

The godparents:

If your faith requires godparents, before setting the day of the christening, the godparents are asked and their consent obtained. They may be asked to serve when the baby's arrival is announced to them and occasionally before; or perhaps when they visit the hospital. In Protestant practice, there are usually two godfathers and one godmother for a boy, two godmothers and one godfather for a girl. A Catholic baby has one godparent of each sex, who must be Catholics, too. (Catholics are not allowed to serve as godparents for children of other faiths.)

If the godparent lives at a distance, a note is sent to him or he may be asked by telegraph: "It's a boy. Will you be godfather?"

If a godparent is unable to be present, a proxy acts for him or her at the ceremony, the consent of the real godparent having first been given. It is considerate for the real godparent to send a note to the clergyman authorizing the proxy.

Only a most intimate friend should be asked to be a godmother or godfather, for it is a responsibility not lightly to be undertaken and also one difficult to refuse. Godparents are usually chosen from among friends rather than relatives, because one advantage of godparents is that they add to the child's stock of relatives. Should the child be left alone in the world, its godparents become its protectors.

The obligation of being a godparent is essentially a spiritual one; therefore, the godparent should be of the same faith as the parents. The godparent is supposed to see that the child is given religious training and is confirmed at the proper time. Beyond these obligations, he is expected to take a special interest in the child, much as a very near relative would do.

At the christening, he gives the baby as nice a present as he can afford. The typical gift is a silver mug or porringer, inscribed: *"Robert Meadows, Jr./December 5th, 1965/From his godfather/John Strong."* Other typical presents are a silver fork and spoon, a silver comb and brush set, a government bond, or a trust fund to which the donor may add each year until the child is grown.

Christening invitations:

Usually, christening invitations are given over the telephone or in a personal note to "Dear Linda and Jeff" or "Dear Mr. and Mrs. Kindhart," and signed "Mary" or "Mary Meadows."

Dear Jane,

We are having Karen christened on Sunday at 3:00 in Christ's Church. Would you and Bob come to the ceremony at the church, and join us afterward at our house?

Affectionately,
Sally

Or a message is written on the "Mr. and Mrs." card of the parents, saying: *"Baby's christening, St. Mary's Church, Jan. 10, 3 o'clock. Reception at our house afterward."* All invitations to a christening should be friendly and informal.

Clothes for the christening:

The baby's christening dress may be one worn by the baby's mother, father or even a grand- or great-grandparent. Custom requires that everything the baby wears on this occasion be white. The traditional christening dress is long, made of sheer, soft material with lace and hand-embroidery trim, and worn with delicate, long petticoats. If there is no family heirloom, any long, or even short, plain white dress will do. Some very pretty and quite inexpensive christening dresses are available in the new miracle fabrics.

In Protestant churches, when the children are no longer babies, little girls wear white dresses. Little boys, however, wear an Eton jacket, dark blue with matching shorts; older boys wear a dark blue or dark gray suit.

Guests at a christening wear what they would wear to church. The mother wears a light-colored dress, never black, and a hat or veil.

The church ceremony:

The ceremony may take place at the close of the regular Sunday service, the guests remaining after the rest of the congregation leaves. Roman Catholic parishes generally schedule baptisms for a specified time on Sunday afternoons, and the parents make an appointment at the rectory in advance. At all christenings, guests seat themselves in the pews nearest the front.

After the clergyman enters, the baby's coat and cap are taken off and the godmother, holding the baby in her arms, stands directly in front of the clergyman. The other godparents stand beside her and relatives and friends nearby.

The godmother holding the baby pronounces its given name or names distinctly; if the name is long or unusual, print it on a slip of paper and give it to the clergyman beforehand, because whatever name the clergyman pronounces is fixed for life. More than one baby has been given a name not intended for him. The godmother does not state the surname.

In the Presbyterian church and others that do not require godparents, the father holds the baby and gives its name. There is no separate service—it is done during or immediately after the regular Sunday service.

As soon as the ceremony is over, the baby and all the relatives and friends go to the house of the parents or grandparents for a reception.

Baptism is a sacrament of the church, for which no fee is required. A donation, however, is presented in an envelope to the clergyman after the ceremony, commensurate with the elaborateness of the christening.

A house christening:

If permitted by the church to which the baby's parents belong, the house christening is a pretty ceremony. The only necessary decoration is the font. This is always a bowl—usually of silver—put on a small, high table covered preferably by a dark rather than a white fabric: old brocade or velvet. Flowers may be arranged around the bowl in a flat circle, the blossoms outside, the stems covered by the base of the bowl.

At the hour set for the ceremony, the clergyman enters the room and takes his place at the font. The guests make way, forming an open aisle. The godmother, or the father if there are no godparents, carries the baby and follows the clergyman; the other participants walk behind and all stand near the font. At the proper moment, the clergyman takes the baby, baptizes it and hands it back to the godmother or father, who holds it until the ceremony is over.

After performing the ceremony, the clergyman, if he wears vestments, goes to another room, changes into his street clothes, then returns to the living room as one of the guests.

The christening party:

The only difference between an ordinary informal reception and a christening party is that the latter features christening cake and caudle. The christening cake is generally a white "lady" cake elaborately iced. A real caudle is a hot eggnog, drunk out of little punch cups. Today punch is often substituted for the caudle. Guests eat the cake as a sign that they partake of the baby's hospitality and are therefore his friends, and they drink the punch to his health and prosperity. But by this time the young host or hostess is peacefully asleep in his crib.

Jewish ceremonies for the newborn:

On the eighth day after birth, in the ceremony known as *Brith Milah,* a boy is initiated into the Jewish covenant between man and God. The circumcision is accompanied by a religious ceremony during which the boy is named. After the ceremony, there is a light collation, usually at home since today the mother rarely stays in the hospital more than a week. The guests drink to the baby's future and toast the parents, grandparents and godparents (there is always a godfather and usually a godmother). Relatives and close friends are invited to the *Brith* by telephone or informal note. They dress as they would for any service in a synagogue and both men and women customarily wear hats.

Girls are named in the synagogue on the first Sabbath after birth when the father is called up to the Torah. Sometimes the naming is postponed until the mother is able to be present. In some Reform congregations, boys are also named in the synagogue (in addition to being named at the *Brith*) when both parents are present and a special blessing is pronounced by the rabbi. The mother may be hostess at the collation following the service. Friends and relatives are invited to attend the religious service during which the baby is named.

The ceremony of redemption of the first-born (if it is a son), the *Pidyon Ha-Ben,* is performed when the baby is thirty-one days old. According to ancient custom described in the Bible, the first-born son was dedicated to the service of God. It became customary for a *Cohen* (a descendant of the priestly tribe) to redeem the child from his obligation, entrusting him to the care of his father for bringing up in the Jewish faith. The *Pidyon Ha-Ben,* consisting of a brief ceremony and a celebration, is held in the home, informal notes of invitation being sent about ten days previously to close friends and relatives.

31

Graduation

Graduation or commencement programs at the high school level are much the same as at the college, but on a modified scale. "Commencement week" festivities for the students start in advance of graduation day, but the events to which families and dates are invited take place only on the last day or two before commencement. The events usually consist of any or all of the following: a senior class ball, attended at some colleges by dates only, and at others by parents and brothers and sisters of the graduates as well; a senior class play, attended by everyone; fraternity parties, tea dances, to which all the graduates' dates are invited; a varsity baseball game. Winding up all commencement week festivities, and attended by every guest, are the baccalaureate service on a Sunday morning and the commencement exercises themselves that afternoon or the following morning.

INVITATIONS AND RESERVATIONS

Colleges and universities provide each graduating student with the number of invitations he is allowed to send. The list of announcements should be limited to those really interested, because the recipients usually feel that they must send a gift.

It is essential for the families of the graduates to make reservations well in advance of graduation day, even as early as some time during the fall term, especially if the college is in a small town that does not have too many accommodations. If the graduate is engaged or has a serious boy or girl friend, the family makes a reservation for him or her too.

REQUIREMENTS FOR THE SENIOR'S DATE

The senior's date, whether or not he or she is engaged to the graduate, stays with the family of the student and goes with them to parties or games to which all guests are invited. She takes care not to monopolize the attention of the graduate. If a young man's family cannot attend the commencement, he or his date finds another graduate's family willing to adopt her for the occasion. If this proves impossible, the young man may ask one of his favorite professors if it would be possible for her to stay in his house. Under no circumstances may she stay alone in a motel or an inn.

CLOTHING

Clothing is much the same as for similar social events elsewhere. The senior dance is always formal, requiring an evening dress or a tuxedo. Girls generally wear shorts or simple cotton dresses for daytime sporting events or picnics and the boys wear shorts or slacks and a sport shirt. For the baccalaureate and commencement services, mothers and girl friends wear cool, short-sleeved dresses, in a print or a pastel color (never black). Hats or veils are worn at a chapel service, but are not necessary if the commencement ceremony is held out-of-doors. Men and boys wear lightweight suits of any color for the formal services.

PRESENTS

Parents may give the graduate a fine watch, a set of evening jewelry, an automobile, or even a trip to Europe. If these gifts are beyond their means, anything lasting and of the best quality is always appreciated: a nicely bound book on a favorite subject or a set of cuff links or other simple jewelry. A fiancé or a "steady" boy friend might choose a charm or a locket and a girl friend might consider a handsome wallet or a gold or silver tie clip.

The gifts from other relatives and friends may depend on the future plans of the graduate. If he or she is taking a trip, a passport case or a suitcase would be a good choice; if marriage is contemplated, something for the new home—a silver tray with the graduation date on it. A check is always welcome.

A note of thanks, written by hand and on note paper, goes promptly to everyone who has sent a present whenever the giver has not been at the commencement to be thanked in person.

Dear Aunt Mary,

I can't thank you enough for the check you sent me which will be such a help toward my summer in Europe. I'm looking forward to seeing you in the fall to tell you all about the trip.

With much love,
Jane

Or:

Dear Uncle Jim,

Thank you so very much for the cuff links you sent me. How did you know I very much needed them? I was disappointed that you couldn't make the graduation, but I'll drive down to see you and thank you in person as soon as possible.

Thanks again,
Bill

32

Funerals

When a person makes a will, he may want to put into it his wishes as to how and where he would like to be buried. These wishes are not irrevocable, but the family will naturally give them every consideration. If he does not include them in his will, he should discuss the question with those closest to him so they may be able to carry out his wishes.

He should know whether there is space for him (and his wife, if she wishes) in the family plot at a cemetery, or think about purchasing a plot for himself and his own family. If he wishes to be cremated, the law requires that his nearest relatives give permission. Therefore, he makes his desires very clear to his wife (or husband, if we are speaking of a woman), his children, and his brothers or sisters.

The head of the family should have a space set aside for a copy of his will and the name of the attorney who drew it up, a deed to a burial plot if he has one, a list of the location of safe deposit boxes, mortgages, bank accounts, etc., and any personal instructions he may wish to leave in case of his death. The other members of the family should know the location of these papers and something about their contents. The small amount of effort necessary to put such a sensible precaution into effect is nothing compared with the help it can be to a stunned and confused family at the time of death.

IMMEDIATE STEPS

When you hear of the death of a close friend, you go at once to the house, and offer to help out in any way you can. For a less intimate friend, you write a letter to the family at once. Telephoning is not improper, but it may cause inconvenience by tying up the line needed for notifying members of the family.

You may help by preparing food for the family or for the children, sending telegrams and answering the door. *(See also Chapter 51.)*

A very good friend or a relative who is not of the immediate family can help immeasurably by taking charge of the funeral arrangements, thus relieving those closest to the deceased of making difficult decisions when they are prostrate emotionally.

Notifying family and close friends:

If members of the immediate family are not already present, the first act of someone at the bedside of the deceased is to notify them. In the case of a long illness, where the family has become attached to the trained nurse, she may be the best fitted to do this and to look after many details. Members of the family and very close friends should be called on the telephone. If expense is a factor, friends and more distant relatives may be notified by telegram.

The death certificate:

The death certificate is filled out and signed by the physician in attendance at the time of death. If the death was sudden or caused by an accident, or if there was no doctor in attendance, the county medical examiner or coroner must be called in immediately to sign the certificate since no other steps can be taken until the death certificate is properly signed.

Notifying an attorney:

The next step is to notify an attorney, preferably the one who has drawn up the will of the deceased. If he, or his firm, is unavailable, then any other reputable attorney, perhaps one who has been retained by another member of the family or one who is a personal friend, may be called.

The funeral director and the clergyman:

The next most immediate matter is that of selecting a funeral home. If the family belongs to a church or synagogue, they may call the church office which will give them all the information about the funeral directors in the area and probably recommend one who will suit their needs. The family doctor can also provide this information.

The funeral director comes to the home as soon as possible after he is called and removes the body to the funeral home. All arrangements are discussed with him at that time—how elaborate a funeral the relatives wish, if the service is to be held at the funeral home, in the home of the deceased, or in a church, and the day and hour. The clergyman must also be consulted as to the time. If the family is not affiliated with a church, the funeral director or a friend can recommend a clergyman of any faith the family chooses.

Newspaper notices:

Notices of the death go to morning and evening papers in a large city and to the local paper (daily or weekly) in towns or suburbs. These contain the date of death, names of immediate family, place and time of funeral, and, frequently, a request that a contribution be sent to a charity instead of flowers to the deceased. The notice may be telephoned by the person making the funeral arrangements, but often the funeral director handles it as part of his services. When the notice reads "Please omit flowers," this wish should be strictly followed.

CONSTANTINE—Mary Phillips, on March 19th, 1967. Beloved wife of Henry S. Constantine, devoted mother of Henry S. Constantine, Jr., and Barbara Constantine Franklin, sister of Dorothy P. Hill. Reposing at the Frederick Carter Funeral Home, Farmingdale, Mass., Monday and Tuesday, 2:00 P.M.–9:00 P.M. Funeral Wednesday, 11:00 A.M., at Christ Church, Farmingdale. In lieu of flowers, please send donations to the New York Cancer Fund.

HASKELL—John Woods, suddenly, on February 12th, 1967. Beloved brother of Robert C. Haskell, George F. Haskell and Sally Haskell Simpson. Funeral service Friday, February 14th at 11:30 A.M. at the Riverside Funeral Home, 10 Lawton Street, Clinton, Mass.

When the notice reads "Funeral private" and neither time nor place is given, only very intimate friends are given this information, either by telephone or on the personal card of the relative or friend in charge: "Mr. Brown's funeral will be at Christ Church, Monday at eleven o'clock." Others are not expected to attend.

If the person who has died was prominent, probably the newspapers have a file on him and, in the case of an older person, an obituary already written. They should be notified immediately, and their information checked so that errors will not appear in the published articles. The paid notice of death is inserted as with less well-known people, when the details of resting place, funeral, flowers, etc., have been decided.

The clothing for burial:

The person in charge of arrangements, with the help of someone close to the deceased who would know of special preference, delivers the clothes to the funeral director. Members of some faiths, the Orthodox Jewish among them, still prefer to bury their dead in shrouds, but most religions have no restrictions on clothing for burial. Dresses in solid, subdued colors are of a style worn to church. Young girls are usually buried in white and children in their Sunday school clothes.

Men are also dressed as for church. Wedding rings are left on, but other jewelry is removed.

Emblem of mourning on the door:

The funeral director may hang streamers on the front door if the family so desires: white ones for a child, black and white for a young person, or black for an older person. Flowers are usually ordered by the family directly from their own florist, though the funeral director may order them. White flowers are used for a young person, purple for one who was older. Emblems are removed by a member of the funeral establishment before the family returns from the services.

HONORARY PALLBEARERS

The member of the family who is in charge asks (either when they come to the house or by telephone) six or eight men who were close friends of the deceased to be the pallbearers. For a man prominent in public life, there may be eight or ten of his political or business associates as well as his six or eight lifelong friends. Members of the immediate family are never chosen as their place is with the women of the family.

One never refuses an invitation to be a pallbearer except because of illness or necessary absence from the city. The pallbearers meet in the vestibule of the church a few minutes before the time set for the service.

Honorary pallbearers serve only at church funerals. They do not carry the coffin. (This service is performed by the assistants of the funeral director, who are expertly trained.) They sit in the first pews on the left and, after the service, leave the church two by two, walking immediately in front of the coffin, or, if there is no procession, ahead of the congregation.

SENDING AND RECEIVING FLOWERS

If there is a notice in the papers requesting that no flowers be sent, you send none. Otherwise, they are addressed "To the funeral of [name of the deceased]," either at the funeral home or the church. When you did not know the deceased, but only his close relatives, flowers may be sent to them at their home, with a card addressed to one of the family on which you might write "With sympathy," "With deepest sympathy," or, if appropriate, "With love and sympathy." A few flowers sent to any bereaved person from time to time—possibly long afterward—are very comforting in their assurance of continued sympathy.

The one in charge of arrangements for the family appoints one person to take charge of flowers; he or she carefully collects all the accompanying cards and on the outside of each envelope writes a description of the flowers that came with the card. Sometimes this is done by the florist and the cards are delivered to the bereaved family after the funeral. For example:

Large spray Easter lilies tied with white ribbon
Laurel wreath with gardenias
Long sheaf of white roses—broad silver ribbon

These descriptions are necessary when one comes to writing notes of thanks.

If friends have sent potted plants or cut flowers to the house, their cards are removed and noted for later acknowledgment.

If the family is Protestant, an hour before the time set for the service one or two women friends go to the church to help the staff arrange the bouquets or sprays, so that those sent by relatives are given a prominent position. But they leave the actual moving of heavy arrangements to the trained florist.

The sexton or one of his assistants will have collected the cards, noting the variety of flowers as above. He gives them to these friends who in turn deliver them to the one who is responsible for all the cards.

Friends of any faith may send a "spiritual bouquet" (a mass said for the deceased) to a Catholic family. Any priest will make arrangements for the mass and accept the donation. A card is sent to the family, stating the time and place of the mass and the name of the donor.

CALLING AT THE FUNERAL HOME

Usually the body of the deceased remains at the funeral home until the day of the funeral. Often the family receives close friends there, rather than at home. The hours when they will be there to accept expressions of sympathy are usually included in the death notice in the newspaper. People who wish to pay their respects but are not close to the bereaved may

stop in and sign the register that is always provided by the
funeral parlor. Their signatures are formal, including their
titles—"Dr. and Mrs. Harvey Cross" or "Miss Deborah Page,"
not "Bill and Joan Cross" or "Debbie Page." This simplifies
the task for those helping the family acknowledge these visits.
The family need not thank every caller by letter, but if someone has made a special effort or if no one of the family was
there to speak to him, they may wish to do so.

WHO ATTENDS THE FUNERAL

All members of the family find out when the funeral is to
take place and go to it without waiting to be notified. But if
the notice reads, "Funeral private," a friend does not go unless he has received a message from the family that they wish
him to come. The hour and location of the service in the paper
is considered an invitation to attend. It is delinquent not to go
to the public funeral of one with whom you have been closely
associated in business or other interests, or to whose house you
have been often invited, or when you are an intimate friend
of the immediate members of the family.

Wearing black is not necessary unless you have been asked
to be one of the honorary pallbearers, but dark, inconspicuous
clothes are advisable.

Enter the church as quietly as possible and seat yourself
where you think you belong. Only a very intimate friend takes
a position far up on the center aisle. If you are merely an
acquaintance, you sit toward the rear of the church.

FUNERAL SERVICES
At the church:

As the time appointed for the funeral draws near, the congregation gradually fills the church. The first few pews on one
side of the center aisle are always left empty for the family and
those on the other for the pallbearers.

The trend today is to have the casket closed. Protestants
may follow their own wishes. At a Catholic or Jewish service
it is obligatory that the casket be closed.

At most funerals, the processional is omitted. The coffin
may have one or several floral pieces on it, or in some churches
be covered with a pall of needlework—for a member of the
armed forces or a veteran, it may be draped with the flag. It is

placed on a stand at the foot of the chancel a half hour before the service. The family usually enters through the door nearest the front pews.

Should the family prefer a processional, it forms in the vestibule. If there is to be a choral service, the minister and choir enter the church from the rear and precede the funeral cortege. Directly after the choir and clergy come the honorary pallbearers, two by two; then the coffin covered with flowers, then the family—the chief mourner being first, walking with whoever is most sympathetic to him or her.

Usually each woman takes the arm of a man. But two women or two men may walk together. For example, if the deceased is one of four sons and there is no daughter, the mother and father walk together immediately after the coffin and they are followed by the two elder sons and then the younger, and then the nearest woman relative.

At the chancel, the choir takes its accustomed place, the clergyman stands at the foot of the chancel steps, the honorary pallbearers take their places in the front pews on the left and the casket is set upon a stand previously placed there for the purpose. The actual bearers of the casket, always professionals furnished by the funeral director, walk quietly to inconspicuous stations on the side aisles. The family occupies the front pews on the right side, the honorary pallbearers on the left; the rest of the procession fills vacant places on either side. The service is then read. Upon its conclusion, the procession moves out in the same order as it came in, except that the choir remains in its place.

If the family so wishes, one of the male relatives may stop at the back of the church to thank those who have attended the services. He need say nothing more than "Thank you" with perhaps a special word for close friends.

Outside the church, the casket is put into the hearse, the family enters automobiles waiting immediately behind the hearse; the flowers are put into a covered vehicle (open landaulets with floral offerings are in poor taste) to be taken in the procession to the cemetery. Or they are taken in the closed car by a different route and placed beside the grave before the hearse and those attending the burial service arrive.

At the house:

Many prefer a house funeral. It is simpler and more private and it obviates the necessity for those in sorrow to face people. The nearest relatives may stay in an adjoining room where they can hear the service, yet remain in seclusion. If the women of the family come into the living room, they wear hats, as in a church. All other women keep their wraps on. The men, if they are wearing overcoats, keep them on or carry them on their arms and hold their hats in their hands.

The coffin is usually placed in front of the mantel in the living room, or between two windows, but always at a distance from the door. It is set on stands brought by the funeral director, who also supplies enough folding chairs to fill the room without crowding. Phonographic recordings of organ and choir music are excellent and readily available.

It is unusual for any but a small group of relatives and intimate friends to go to the cemetery from the house.

At the funeral home or chapel:

The establishments of funeral directors generally have a nonsectarian chapel in the building. There are also reception rooms where the families may receive the condolences of their friends. Services are conducted in the chapel quite as they would be in a church. Sometimes there is a private alcove to one side, so that the family need not sit in the front pews.

The burial:

If the burial in the churchyard is within walking distance, the congregation naturally follows the family to the graveside. Otherwise, those attending the funeral, wherever the services are held, do not expect or wish to go to the interment. Except at a funeral of public importance, the burial is witnessed only by the immediate family and the most intimate friends.

Cremation:

Many people prefer the idea of cremation to burial. The service is exactly the same as that preceding a burial. The family may or may not accompany the body to the crematorium, as they wish. If they do, a very short service is held there also. The ashes may later be delivered to the family, to be disposed of in any way that the deceased would wish (as long

as it is not contrary to any law). Often, however, the urn is
deposited in a building or section set aside in the cemetery
or churchyard and sometimes it is buried in the family plot.

A memorial service:

In some circumstances a memorial service is held instead of
a funeral. Notice of this service is put into the obituary column
of the paper, or, in a small town, people are telephoned and
each given a short list of his own nearest neighbors whom he
is asked to notify.

These services are very brief. In general outline, two verses
of a hymn are sung, then follow short prayers and a very brief
address about the work and personality of the one for whom
the service is held. It is closed with a prayer and two verses
of another hymn.

Usually no flowers are sent except a few for the altar. On
those occasions when flowers are sent, they are arranged in
holders (not as sheaves) so that they may be put into the
wards of a hospital without having to be taken apart and rearranged.

Since this is more like a church service than a funeral, some
of the men in the family may, before joining the women, escort
guests to their seats as at a Sunday service.

CHURCH FEES

No fee is ever asked by the clergyman, but the family is expected to make a contribution in appreciation of his services;
the fee may be anything from ten dollars for a very small funeral service to one hundred dollars for a very elaborate one.

A bill rendered by the church office includes all necessary
charges for the church.

ACKNOWLEDGMENT OF SYMPATHY

When messages of condolence mount into the hundreds (for
example, when a public figure or a prominent business executive is involved) engraved or well-printed cards may be sent
to strangers:

The Governor and Mrs. State
wish gratefully to acknowledge
your kind expression of sympathy

The family of
Harrison L. Winthrop
wish to thank you for
your kind expression of sympathy

If such cards are used, a handwritten word or two and a signature *must* be added below the printed message when there is any personal acquaintance with the sender. Such cards are never sent to those who have sent flowers or to intimate friends who have written personal letters.

A most unfortunate custom has recently sprung up. The funeral director supplies printed cards and the recipient merely signs his or her name to it, a poor return for the thought behind a beautiful spray of flowers or even a bouquet of garden flowers.

A personal message on a fold-over card is preferable to any printed card; it can simply say, "Thank you for your beautiful flowers," or "Thank you for your kind sympathy," or "I cannot half tell you how much your loving kindness has meant to me."

If the list is very long, or if the person who has received the flowers and messages is unable to perform the task of writing, some member of the family or a near friend may write for her or him: "Mother [or whoever it is] asks me to thank you for your beautiful flowers and kind message of sympathy." The message should be written by hand.

(For suggestions on writing letters of condolence, see Chapter 6.)

MOURNING CLOTHES
For women:

An ever-greater number of persons today do not believe in going into mourning at all. However, a widow of mature years may still, if she chooses (and in some Latin countries they do), wear mourning for life. On the other hand, deep mourning for a year is now considered extreme and more than six months is very rare. The young widow, if she wishes to wear mourning, wears all-black for six months except in the country, where sports clothes of an inconspicuous nature are worn. She *never* remains in mourning for her first husband after she has decided to be married again.

A mother who has lost a grown son or daughter may wear

all-black for six months or a year, depending on her inclination. A daughter or sister, if she wishes, wears mourning for one season. When going into mourning in the spring or summer, for example, wear deep mourning until winter clothes are appropriate, then go back to regular clothes.

Mourning that attracts attention is unsuitable in an office. Inconspicuous mourning, on the other hand, is entirely proper. The fact that a woman invariably wears a black dress or a gray mixture suit attracts no attention if she has a little white at the throat. But if a woman does not wish to go into mourning at all and arrives at her office a day or so after the death of a close relative in the clothes she ordinarily wears, no one looks in the least askance.

For men:

A man may go into mourning for a few months by the simple expedient of putting a black band on his hat and on the left sleeve of his clothes. Also, he wears black shoes, gloves, socks and ties, and white instead of colored linen. In the country a young man continues to wear his ordinary sport clothes and shoes and sweater without any sleeve band.

The sleeve band is from 3½ to 4½ inches in width, of dull cloth on overcoats or winter clothing and of serge on summer clothes. A sleeve band on business clothes implies a bid for sympathy, which most men want to avoid. Many men, therefore, go to the office with no evidence of mourning other than a black tie and black socks.

THE BEHAVIOR OF THE FAMILY AFTER THE FUNERAL

As soon as possible after the funeral, the life of the family should return to its normal routine. There are many things that must be attended to at once, and while these may seem like insurmountable chores to a grieving husband or wife, the necessity of having to perform them and, above all, in so doing, to think of others rather than oneself is in reality a great help in returning to an active life.

Letters of thanks must be written to the clergyman, the pall-bearers and others who have performed some service for the family. The gifts of flowers must be acknowledged and each letter of condolence answered.

The return of the close relatives of the deceased to an active social life is, nowadays, up to the individual. If he or she is not wearing mourning, he may start, as soon as he feels up to it, to go to a friend's house, to a movie, play or sports event. A man or woman may start to have dates when he or she feels like it, but for a few months they should be restricted to evenings at the home of a friend, a movie, or some other inconspicuous activity.

Those who are wearing mourning do not go to dances or formal parties, nor do they take a leading part in purely social functions. But anyone who is in public life or business or who has a professional career must, of course, continue to fulfill his duties. In sum, each year the number increases of those who show the mourning in their hearts only by the quiet dignity of their lives.

Children:

A child should never be put into black at any time. They wear their best church clothes to a funeral, and afterward, whatever they ordinarily wear. Many people are uncertain about whether children who have lost a parent should participate in their usual school activities and after-school entertainments. The answer is "yes." The normal routine of a small child should not be upset—more than ever they need to romp and play. Older children take part in sports and school concerts or plays. However, they may not wish to go to a purely social party within two or three weeks, or even longer, after the death of a parent.

33

Engagements

PRE-ENGAGEMENT

It is important during the pre-engagement time that young people do not avoid the company of others and that they get to know each other's friends. A marriage in which either partner is incompatible with those who have always been part of the other's life has one strike against it to begin with. This is true also of the couple's families. Each should be entertained in the home of the other so that they can see the surroundings and the family to which they will be expected to adjust. The family that is to entertain the young people should be advised of the situation beforehand by their son or daughter, in order to avoid embarrassing the guest.

"Mother, may I bring Sally Foster up for the night next Saturday? We have been seeing a lot of each other, and I'm eager to have her see Waterbury and to introduce her to you."

Love,
Jim

or:

Dear Mom,
I recently met a most attractive man, Jerry Boy, from Syracuse, and I'm eager for you to meet each other. I wondered if it would be convenient for us to spend next weekend with you and Dad.
Please let me know as soon as you can.

Love to you both,
Sue

The parents receiving such a note or a telephone call realize that, unless they are told otherwise when the couple arrives, the engagement is still in the future.

THE FUTURE GROOM AND HIS FIANCÉE'S FATHER

After he proposes and she says "Yes" the prospective groom asks her father or whoever is head of her family for his consent. If her father refuses, the girl must either change her "Yes" to "No" or marry in opposition to her parents. The honorable young woman who has made up her mind to marry in spite of her parents' disapproval tells them that on such and such a day her wedding will take place and refuses to give her word that she will not marry. It is highly dishonorable for her to give her word when she intends to break it.

THE ENGAGEMENT RING

It is doubtful that the man who produced a ring from his pocket upon the instant that she said "Yes" often existed outside romantic novels. In real life, the fiancé first goes alone to the jeweler, explains how much he can afford and has a selection of rings set aside. He then brings his fiancée into the store and lets her choose from among them the ones she likes best, perhaps one of platinum and diamond design or a lovely ring in her own birthstone. Any good jeweler has a correct list of birthstones and can make suggestions as to the cut and color.

One popular trend today is that of using semiprecious stones, beside which the tiny diamond has lost its appeal: an aquamarine, amethyst, a topaz or transparent tourmaline is perfect for an engagement ring.

The engagement ring is worn for the first time in public on the day of the announcement. But *the engagement ring is not essential to the validity of the betrothal*. The wedding ring is a requirement of the marriage service. The engagement ring on the other hand is simply evidence that he has proposed marriage and that she has answered "Yes!" Countless wives have never had an engagement ring at all, many receive these rings long after marriage. Some brides prefer to forego an engagement ring and put the money it would have cost toward furnishing their future home.

IF SHE GIVES HIM AN ENGAGEMENT PRESENT

The girl may give the man an engagement present or not as she chooses: a set of studs and a matching pair of cuff links, or a watch. But she does not give him an engagement ring.

HIS PARENTS' CALL ON HERS

Following the acceptance of the engagement, the parents of the man go to call on the parents of the girl or telephone to arrange a meeting. If they do not live in the same city, letters of welcome are written to the girl and to her parents expressing pleasure at the match. The telephone can help two families who live at a distance to know each other. When they live some distance apart, it may be more practical for the bride's parents to visit those of the groom first, and this is perfectly correct.

ANNOUNCING THE ENGAGEMENT

Personal announcement:

A few days—perhaps a week—before the formal announcement the girl and man each write to or call aunts, uncles and cousins and their most intimate friends telling of their engagement. This is done so those closest to them will not read of it first in the newspapers. These relatives telephone or write the bride-to-be as soon as they receive the news, and call, when it is convenient. She answers the letters as soon as possible.

His people may ask her with her fiancé to lunch or to dinner and, after the engagement is publicly announced, give a more general party in her honor. If, on the other hand, they seldom entertain, they merely call or write to show their welcome.

In case of a recent death in either immediate family, the engagement is announced quietly by telling families and intimate friends.

The formal announcement:

The formal or public announcement is made by the parents of the bride-to-be either by notes or at the engagement party and after that publicly through the newspapers. Engraved announcements are not correct.

A week or more before you wish it to appear, the announcement goes with all the necessary information (including perhaps a picture of the bride) to the society editor of all the papers in which it is to be printed. If you live in the suburbs of a large city or in a small town, a copy is sent to the local paper (which may be a weekly). The date should be stated clearly, so that the announcement comes out simultaneously in all the papers.

The usual form is as follows:

Mr. and Mrs. Herbert Coles Johnson of Lake Forest, Illinois, announce the engagement of their daughter, Miss Susan Bailey Johnson, to Dr. William Arthur Currier, son of Mr. and Mrs. Arthur Jamison Currier of Atlanta, Georgia. A June wedding is planned.

Miss Johnson was graduated from Bentley Junior College. She made her debut in 1965 at the Mistletoe Ball in Chicago, and in May will complete her nurse's training at Atlanta General Hospital. Dr. Currier was graduated from the Hill School, Yale University, and the Yale Medical School. He completed his residency at the Atlanta General Hospital and is now in practice in that city.

When one parent is deceased: The announcement is worded the same way whether made by the mother or father of the bride.

Mrs. Herbert Coles Johnson announces the engagement of her daughter, Miss Susan Bailey Johnson, to Dr. William Arthur Currier . . . etc. Miss Johnson is also the daughter of the late Herbert Coles Johnson. . . .

If her parent has remarried:

Mr. and Mrs. John Franklin announce the engagement of Mr. Franklin's daughter, Miss Helen Susan Franklin, to . . . etc. Miss Franklin is also the daughter of the late Mrs. Sarah Ellis Franklin. . . .

If a parent of the groom is deceased:

Mr. and Mrs. Harry Brown announce the engagement of their daughter, Miss Mary Frances Brown, to Mr. Robert

Lewis, son of Mrs. Allen Carter Lewis, and the late Mr.
Lewis. . . .

When the bride is an orphan: The engagement is announced
by the girl's nearest relative, a godparent or a very dear friend.
If she has no one close to her, she sends the announcement herself:

The engagement of Miss Jessica Towne, daughter of the
late Mr. and Mrs. Samuel Towne, is announced, to Mr.
Richard Frost. . . .

This form may also be used if the parents live far away or if
she has, for some reason, separated herself completely from her
family.

If the parents are divorced: The mother of the bride usually
makes the announcement, but, as in the case of a deceased parent, the name of the other parent must be included.

Mrs. Jones Farnham announces the engagement of her
daughter, Miss Cynthia Farnham . . . Miss Farnham is also
the daughter of Mr. Henry Farnham of Worcester, Massachusetts. . . .

If divorced parents are friendly: When divorced parents remain good friends and their daughter's time is divided equally
between them, they may both wish to announce the engagement.

Mr. Gordon Smythe of Philadelphia, and Mrs. Howard
Zabriskie of 12 East 72nd Street, New York, New York, an-
nounce the engagement of their daughter, Miss Carla Farr
Smythe. . . .

If the bride is adopted: If the bride has been with the family
since babyhood and has the same name as her foster parents,
there is no reason to mention the fact that she is adopted. If she
joined the family later in life, however, and has retained her
own name, it is proper to say:

Mr. and Mrs. Warren La Tour announce the engagement
of their adopted daughter, Miss Claudia Romney, daughter
of the late Mr. and Mrs. Carlton Romney. . . .

Older women, widows and divorcées: A woman of forty or more, even though her parents are living, generally does not announce her engagement in the newspaper, but instead calls or writes her relatives and friends shortly before the wedding. A widow or divorcée announces her second engagement in the same way.

THE ENGAGEMENT PARTY

Invitations to engagement parties are written on informals or visiting cards and do not necessarily mention the reason for the party. They are generally sent in the name of the bride's parents or of the relative who is announcing the engagement. Occasionally the parents wish to include their daughter's name with theirs, and add "To meet Mr. John Watkins." Or, they may prefer, "In honor of Sally Jones and Robert Coolidge," clearly indicating the nature of the occasion. The invitations also may be issued by telephone.

Presents are never taken to an engagement party because only intimate friends or relatives give gifts and it might embarrass other guests.

The engagement party may be of any type that the mother of the bride prefers. Generally it is a cocktail party or a dinner. The guests are relatives and close friends of the bride and groom and probably a few close friends of the parents. The news may be told by the girl herself, or by her mother, as the

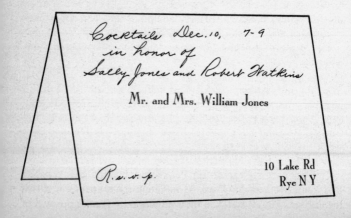

Cocktails Dec. 10,   7-9
in honor of
Sally Jones and Robert Watkins

Mr. and Mrs. William Jones

R.s.v.p.   10 Lake Rd
Rye N Y

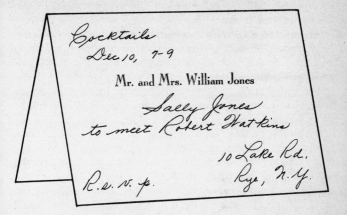

Cocktails
Dec 10, 7–9

Mr. and Mrs. William Jones

Sally Jones
to meet Robert Watkins

10 Lake Rd.
Rye, N.Y.

R.s.v.p.

guests arrive and find the fiancé standing with their hostess. Or, if the party is a dinner, it is announced by the father who proposes a toast to the couple.

As to a novel way of announcing an engagement, there is really no logical objection to whatever may be pleasing to you: you may float balloons with your names printed on them, distribute bouquets tagged with both names, or put it in telegrams used as place cards.

The toast:

When all glasses at the table are filled, the host rises, lifts his own glass, and says: "A standing toast: To my Mary and to her —Jim!"

Or: "I want you to drink to the happiness of a young pair who are close to the hearts of all of us: Mary [holding up his glass and looking at her] and Jim [looking at him]!"

Everyone except Mary and Jim rises and drinks a little of whatever the beverage may be. They then congratulate the young couple and Jim is called upon for a speech.

BEHAVIOR OF THE ENGAGED COUPLE

It is not necessary to demonstrate one's feelings with caresses and kisses in front of others. How much more attractive it is if the engaged couple indicate their affection by frank approval of whatever the other may do or say and by their radiant look. That is love as it should be.

An engaged man shows no marked interest in other women. If he is away at work or lives in another city, his fiancée may of course go out with friends, but both of the engaged pair avoid going out with any one man or woman alone.

The question of a chaperon differs with locality. There are few places left today where an engaged pair may not spend as many hours alone together as they wish, as long as it is not overnight. They may travel overnight by a public conveyance, provided their accommodations are not adjoining. They should never take an automobile trip that requires them to pass the night en route in a hotel or motel. Unmarried friends are not suitable chaperons, but married couples, even though of the same age, are. Otherwise, for any overnight stay, the engaged pair must be in the company of an older man, woman, or couple, either relatives or friends.

Presents that may and may not be accepted by the bride-to-be:

The fiancée of a young man who is saving in order to marry shows good taste by not allowing him to send her extravagant presents. If the bridegroom-elect has ample means, she may accept anything he chooses to select except wearing apparel or anything that can be classified as maintenance. He may give her all the jewels he can afford. He may give her a fur scarf, but not a fur coat; the scarf is an ornament, the coat wearing apparel. Her wedding dress and the clothes she wears away on her wedding day must not be supplied by the groom or, in most circumstances, by his family. Of course, if his mother has long known the girl, she may give her anything she chooses.

The engaged pair may properly open a joint bank account shortly before the wedding in order to deposit the checks they receive as gifts and draw on this account to help in furnishing their future home. She may select furniture for their home which he may rent, buy or have built. But she must not live in the house or use its furniture until she is given his name.

THE LENGTH OF THE ENGAGEMENT

The ideal duration is from three to five months. This allows time for the wedding arrangements to be made and for the couple to come to know each other well. If one or both are finishing school, but want to be engaged during the last year, or if a man is serving his military term and his fiancée wishes everyone to know that she will not be going out with other men, then it is proper to announce the engagement long before the wedding.

THE BROKEN ENGAGEMENT

If the engagement is broken, the ring and all other gifts of value must be returned to the former fiancé. Gifts received from relatives or friends are returned with a short note of explanation:

> *Dear Sue,*
> *I am sorry to have to tell you that Jack and I have broken our engagement. Therefore I am returning the towels that you were so sweet to send to me.*
>
> *Love,*
> *Sara*

A notice reading "The engagement of Miss Sara Black and Mr. John Doe has been broken by mutual consent" is sent to the newspapers that announced the engagement.

If the man dies before the wedding, his fiancée may keep her engagement ring. If it is an old family heirloom and she knows that his parents would like to have it remain in the family, she considerately offers to return it. She may keep any gifts that were given her by friends.

BUYING THE WEDDING RING OR RINGS

Shortly before the wedding, it is important that the bride go with the groom when he buys the wedding ring. Since she may not intend to take it off—ever—she should be allowed to choose the style she prefers. No ring is in better taste than the plain band of yellow or white gold or platinum. A diamond band is more suitable as a guard than as a wedding ring, since it will have to be taken off to be properly cleaned.

The wedding ring may be engraved with whatever sentiment the bridegroom chooses; today, this is usually only the initials and date.

If the bridegroom wishes to have a ring, the bride usually buys a plain gold band to match hers but a little wider. It may also be marked with initials or a sentiment. It is worn, like the bride's, on the fourth finger of his left hand.

ENGAGEMENT PRESENTS

A bride-to-be often receives a few engagement presents sent either by her relatives, her very intimate friends and her godparents or by members of her fiancé's family as special messages of welcome to her. Engagement gifts are usually table linen, towels, bed linen, such as a set of embroidered sheets, or possibly an inexpensive novelty gift. It is helpful if, shortly after the engagement is announced, the bride goes to the local stores and indicates her preferences in colors and styles so that engagement presents will fit in with her choice of trousseau.

Marking linen:

A monogram or initials on linen is most decorative. One initial with additional embellishment is more effective than two initials—and usually the cost is less.

The monogram should be in proportion to the size of the piece, neither too small nor too large. When articles are monogrammed, it is practical to mark everything with the bride's future initials.

Long tablecloths are marked on either side of the center, midway between the table center and the edge of the table. Small yard-and-a-half square tablecloths are marked at one corner midway between the table center and the edge. Square monograms look well set in line with the table edge; triangular or diamond-shaped ones look best at the corner.

Large damask napkins are marked in the center of one side, smaller ones in the corner—cross-cornered usually, but sometimes straight. To decide about the place for marking the napkins, fold the napkin exactly as it is to be folded for use, then make a light pencil outline in the center of the folded napkin.

Towels are marked so that when they are folded and hung on the rack the marking is centered.

Sheets are marked with base of the letters toward the hem—when on the bed, the monogram is right-side up and can be read by a person standing at the foot of the bed—and it is put at half the depth at which the sheet is turned back. Pillowcases are marked halfway between the edge of the case and the beginning of the pillow. On square French pillowcases the monogram is put cross-cornered with the top of initials at the corner.

PART EIGHT

ENGAGEMENTS AND WEDDINGS

34

Planning the wedding

A wedding, be it large and elaborate or small and simple, is always an important occasion—beautiful, impressive and the bride's day of days. But the groom is equally important and his wishes should be consulted from first to last. Because of the many details involved in even the simplest wedding, careful preparation is necessary if everyone is to enjoy the day itself. Without adequate preparation, father may be irritated, mother jittery, the bride in tears, the groom cross. This chapter and those that follow are dedicated to avoiding such miseries.

THE RESPONSIBILITIES, FINANCIAL AND OTHERWISE

All the expenses of the wedding itself belong to the bride's parents. A big fashionable wedding can total several thousand dollars; even a simple one may entail considerable outlay. Whatever size or style of wedding you choose, it is the careful, thoughtful planning—not the cost—that makes it beautiful. The simplest wedding is often the most tasteful. Whether a wedding is to be large or tiny, the reception is either at the house of the bride's parents or other relatives or close friends, or in rooms rented by her family. If, however, the bride were without family, she might perfectly well be married in the

church or the rectory and go afterward to the house of the
bridegroom's parents for the reception.

The bride's family's expenses:

1) The engraved invitations to ceremony and reception, and
the announcements (true engraving is required for an extremely formal wedding, but today's simulated engraving is entirely suitable when cost must be counted).

2) The service, if needed, of a professional secretary who
compiles a single guest list from the various ones provided her;
addresses the envelopes, both inner and outer; encloses the
proper number of cards; seals, stamps and mails all the invitations or announcements. She may also handle such details as
making arrangements with florists, orchestra, etc.

3) The trousseau of the bride, consisting not only of her
clothing but of her household linen as well.

4) Floral decorations for church and reception, bouquets
for the bride and bridesmaids, corsages for the bride's mother
and grandmother, and a boutonniere for the father of the bride.
In some communities, the groom provides the bouquets carried
by the bride and her bridesmaids, and the bride sends boutonnieres to the ushers.

5) Choir, soloists and organist at the church, and the fee to
the sexton.

6) Orchestra at the reception. This may mean twenty pieces
or one violinist or a phonograph.

7) Automobiles to take the bridal party from the house to
the church and to the reception.

8) The refreshments, including the wedding cake and the
beverages, for the reception.

9) The bride's presents to her bridesmaids.

10) Hotel accommodations for bride's attendants if they
cannot stay with friends and neighbors.

11) A wedding present to the bride in addition to her trousseau.

12) Photographs taken of the bride in her wedding dress
and candid pictures taken on the day of the wedding.

13) Rental of awnings, tent for outdoor reception and carpet
for church aisle if desired.

14) A wedding present or a wedding ring, or both, to the
groom, if the bride wishes to give them.

The bridegroom's expenses:

1) The engagement and wedding rings.

2) A wedding present to the bride, jewels or something for her of permanent value.

3) A personal gift to his best man and ushers, and their hotel expenses.

4) Wedding ties, gloves, boutonnieres for the ushers plus his own and his father's boutonnieres.

5) The bride's bouquet, where local custom requires it, and a corsage for her to wear when they go away.

6) His bachelor dinner (if he gives one).

7) The marriage license.

8) The clergyman's fee or a suitable donation to him.

9) Transportation for himself and his best man to the ceremony.

10) Expenses of the wedding trip.

WHEN, WHERE AND HOW BIG?

Before deciding the date of the wedding, the bride: (1) establishes the day her church or synagogue and the clergyman who will perform the ceremony are available and coordinates their time with that of the caterer, hotel or club; (2) decides the time of day for the ceremony, taking into account religion, climate, local custom, transportation schedules and the bride's and groom's own plans for their wedding trip; due consideration is next given to what is convenient for the relatives and friends who will be coming; (3) determines the number of guests based on the size of her house or the club and the amount she can spend. (Remember, a reception at a customary meal hour adds the expense of a substantial wedding breakfast or collation.)

THE INVITATIONS

When to order:

Two months before the wedding, the bride-elect and her mother go to the stationer's to select the size and texture of paper and the style of engraving for the estimated number of invitations or announcements that will be needed. Once the plates are engraved, the order may easily be increased if necessary. *(For details of forms, see Chapters 40 and 42.)*

Invitations are sent out three weeks before a formal wedding and two weeks or ten days before a small, informal wedding.

THE WEDDING LIST

Four separate lists of wedding invitations are made out: (1) the bride's, (2) the groom's, (3) the bride's family's (made out by her mother or other near relative), (4) the groom's family's (made out by his mother or a relative). If the families have long been friends and live in the same community, the invitations are divided more or less equally between them. If one hundred are to be included at the reception, some seventy names would probably be the same; each then could add fifteen of their own to the seventy already on their shared list. Otherwise each would limit her list to fifty. But if the groom's people live in another place so that not more than twenty will be coming, the bride's mother may invite up to eighty who will probably accept. Always allow for the few who accept but are unable to come.

Faraway friends are sent announcements or invitations to the church alone; these carry no obligation for a gift.

Invitations to a big church wedding are sent to all friends and relatives of both families, regardless of whether they can be present or not. Only a small church would limit the number of guests invited to the ceremony. For a house wedding or reception where the guest list is limited, the bride's family may tell the groom's family how many guests they may invite.

Lodging for out-of-town guests:

If the groom comes from another town, friends and neighbors of the bride, when possible, offer accommodations for his ushers and his immediate family. Otherwise they and his other relatives and friends stay at nearby hotels or motels for which the bride's mother reserves the necessary number of rooms, or she sends brochures and they make their own reservations. The rooms are paid for by those who stay in them.

CHOOSING THE BRIDE'S ATTENDANTS

The bride's closest sister is always maid or matron of honor. If she has no sister of suitable age, she chooses her most intimate friend. She may also have bridesmaids, flower girls, pages and a ring bearer. The last is a small brother or nephew who, all dressed in white, walks ahead of her and carries the ring, lightly attached by a thread to a small firm white cushion. The bride may ask one or two young girls, usually between seven and twelve, to be junior bridesmaids.

The bridegroom asks his brother, brother-in-law, best friend or father to serve as his best man. He then asks as many ushers as he will need to seat the guests in the church—at least one usher for every fifty guests. A married man may act as usher or a married woman as matron of honor. The husband or wife not officiating is, of course, invited to the wedding, and is asked to sit at the bridal table.

The bride and groom usually ask their attendants to serve in their wedding at the time the engagement is announced or shortly thereafter. Bridesmaids pay for everything they wear except their floral bouquets which are presented to them by the bride. Ushers provide their own attire too.

PLANNING THE CHURCH SERVICE

Some time before the wedding day, the bride and groom together visit the clergyman who will perform the ceremony, discuss the service they would like to have, whether they wish the choir or a vocalist to sing, possible pieces of music and any customs or rules peculiar to that church. If the marriage is to be performed by a minister or rabbi from another parish, the couple visit both him and the clergyman of the church or synagogue where the wedding is to take place.

THE FLOWERS

After the date and general plans for the wedding are decided upon, the bride and her mother get an estimate from the florist for church and reception decorations and for the bridesmaids' bouquets, and, if it is in accordance with the custom of the community, the bride's bouquet.

The bridegroom sends the bride a corsage to wear when she leaves the reception with him. He also buys the boutonnieres for his ushers, his best man and himself.

The church chancel is decorated as lavishly or simply as desired. There may be masses of flowers arranged as standards or a simple arrangement or two on the altar. Sprays of flowers may be tied to the pew ends. The colors, rather than being all white, may blend with those of the bridesmaids' costumes. At the reception the bridal couple often receives against a floral background, and a flower centerpiece may be used on the bridal table.

OTHER DECORATIONS AND ACCESSORIES

Other decorations may include a canopy at the church entrance and a carpet laid down the aisle of the church after the bride's mother is seated, to protect the bride's train. If the reception is held under a tent or a marquee, it is provided by the caterer for a home garden reception or by the club where the reception is to be held, and it is usually put up a day or two in advance.

MUSIC FOR CHURCH AND RECEPTION

At many weddings, the march from Wagner's *Lohengrin* is the choice for the wedding procession. The recessional is usually Mendelssohn's. But the bride and groom may select any music they are particularly fond of, providing, of course, that it is appropriate for a church ceremony. A singer, possibly a member of the bride's or bridegroom's family, may be asked to sing during the wedding ceremonies. All this is discussed with the organist.

The music at the reception may range from a full orchestra to a trio or even a phonograph to provide dance music. If there is to be no dancing, a wandering violinist or accordionist, playing the music chosen by the couple, acts as a happy background for toasts and conversation.

PLANNING THE "WEDDING BREAKFAST"

The "wedding breakfast" is the meal served at the reception, whether it be morning, noon or night. It may be an elaborate sit-down meal, a buffet, or simply sandwiches and hors d'oeuvres passed on trays. If the reception is held at a club or hotel, the bride and her mother discuss the menu and all other arrangements with the manager as soon as the wedding date is set.

The sit-down breakfast:

The sit-down breakfast is the most elaborate wedding reception possible. If not held at a club or hotel, it is supplied by a caterer, who brings all the food, tables, chairs, linen, china and glass as well as the necessary waiters. In the country a canopied platform is erected on the lawn. In the center a large table is reserved for the bridal party and another one for the parents of the bride and groom and specially invited friends. Place cards are provided for these two tables. Small tables are provided for the other guests who distribute themselves at them as they wish.

The menu may include: bouillon or vichyssoise, lobster Newburg or some other seafood; a main dish of beef Stroganoff with wild rice, or chicken in patty shells; any variety of aspic or salad; individual ices and little cakes. Small menu cards, perhaps with the initials of the surnames of bride and groom stamped on them, may be put on all the tables.

The stand-up breakfast or supper:

A single long table, set in the dining room of the home or club, is covered with a plain white damask cloth and adorned by a center piece of white flowers. On this table are piles of plates (white or white and gold), stacks of napkins and rows of spoons and forks at intervals. In evenly spaced places are cold dishes; chicken and celery salad or ham mousse with chopped hearts of lettuce and hot dishes such as creamed crabmeat, chicken à la king or chicken croquettes; besides these are finger rolls and sandwiches; for dessert, ice cream, fancy cakes and candies. On a side table are after-dinner coffee, champagne or punch.

The wedding cake, flanked by floral pieces, is placed either on the bridal table, if there is one, or in the center of the buffet table.

The simplest reception requirements:

An afternoon reception can be very simple: champagne or a fruit punch, in which to drink the bride's and groom's health, and the wedding cake are all that need be served. A slightly more elaborate reception would include either tea or coffee and thin sandwiches. The table decorations and wedding cake are white. The collation is set out on the dining table and the guests eat standing.

If there is to be no reception:

When the marriage takes place in a church and there is to be no reception, the bride and groom sometimes wait after the recessional in the vestibule of the church (with their parents and the bridal party) to receive the good wishes of their guests as they leave.

THE WEDDING CAKE

The wedding cake, usually ordered from a caterer, has several tiers and is topped by small figures of bride and groom, flowers made of frosting or real flowers. Members of the wedding party, the families, and as many guests as possible, are offered a piece. At some weddings, fruitcake is put into individual white boxes and tied with white satin ribbon. These boxes are stacked on a table close beside the front door and each departing guest takes one. To lower the cost, the individual pieces of cake, instead of being boxed, may be wrapped in white paper and tied with white or silver ribbon, possibly with a little flower or greenery put through the knot.

THE WEDDING PICTURES

Before the wedding, perhaps after the final fitting of the bridal gown, the photographer takes the formal wedding pictures of the bride. These are mailed to the newspapers two to three weeks before the wedding day.

Candid shots on the wedding day may be taken by a professional photographer or by a friend of the bride or groom who is an accomplished amateur. He may cover the entire day: the bride leaving the house before the wedding, the bridal party's arrival at the church, the bridal couple coming down the aisle after the ceremony, their departure from the church, the receiving line at the reception, shots of the bride and groom dancing, the guests, the toasts, the cutting of the cake, and, finally, the departure of the happy pair on their honeymoon.

WEDDING PRESENTS AND OTHER GIFTS

The presents are entered in a gift book as they arrive, listing the article, the name and address of the donor and where it was bought. Later when the thank-you note is written, that date is entered in the gift book. A letter of thanks on the day the present arrives keeps the job from getting out of hand later. These notes are always handwritten on personal stationery.

(For the wording of the bride's notes, see Chapter 6.)

When the presents are shown:

It is entirely correct to show the presents at the wedding reception. In a room other than that where the reception is being held, tables covered with plain white damask tablecloths or sheets are put like counters around the sides of the room and decorated perhaps with white ribbon and the sides with tulle net or pleated cheesecloth. The presents are arrayed in such a way as to make the prettiest display. The cards accompanying the gifts may be left or removed, as the bride wishes.

When checks are received, they must, of course, be displayed with the other gifts. This is done by overlapping them so that the signatures show but the amount is covered. A clear piece of glass is laid on top.

It is a time-honored custom to permit a bride to exchange duplicate gifts, except those chosen by her own or the groom's family. To keep sixteen saltcellars and have no coffee spoons would be putting sentiment above common sense.

Gifts for the bride's attendants:

The bride gives her presents to the bridesmaids at the rehearsal dinner, or when they arrive to help dress her for the wedding. (Or, if the bridesmaids give the bride a party before the wedding, she may give them her presents then.) Her present is usually something to wear: a bracelet, earrings, a pin, a clip or some other memento. The gift to her maid or matron of honor may match those given the bridesmaids or be quite different and more elaborate.

Gifts for the ushers:

The bridegroom's gifts to his ushers are usually put at their places at the bachelor dinner—if one is held. If not, they may be presented at the rehearsal dinner or just before leaving for the church. Cuff links, gold pencils and billfolds are popular gifts. The present to the best man is approximately the same as the gifts to the ushers.

The bride and groom exchange presents:

The bridegroom's gift to the bride may be a brooch, pendant, bracelet or perhaps a charm. The bride's gift to the groom is something permanent, ranging from cuff links to a watch or ring.

"DOLLARS AND SENSE" PLANNING

An overall budget will avoid the nightmare of unsolved financial problems and unnecessary debts. The Wedding Expense Chart below gives a realistic picture of the actual expenses of four different weddings. However, these figures are offered only as examples.

A GUIDE TO WEDDING COSTS

	Total Wedding Budget			
	$500	$1,000	$2,000	$4,000
Type of Wedding	Informal or formal	Formal	Formal	Formal
Number of Attendants	1 or 2	2 - 4	2 - 4	6 - 8
Number at Reception	50	100	100 - 200	100 - 300
Place of Reception	Home or in church facilities	Home, club or restaurant	Club or hotel	Club or hotel
Type of Reception	Stand-up reception	Buffet or home or club, sit-down in restaurant	Buffet or sit-down	Buffet or sit-down depending on number
Refreshments	Sandwiches and snacks	Sandwiches and hors d'oeuvres	Sandwiches and hors d'oeuvres	Hot meal
Items to Budget:				
Wedding Clothes	$125	$200	$400	$ 680
Invitations, Announcements, etc.	25	40	80	200
Flowers, Attendants at Church and Reception	50	80	160	400
Music (Church and Reception)	35	40	160	400
Transportation for Bridal Party to Church and Reception	none	40	100	160
Photographs—Formal and Candids	50	100	200	240
Bridesmaids' Gifts	25	40	80	120
Reception (Food, Beverages, Wedding Cake, Catering Service)	185	430	760	1,600
Contingency Fund (Any additional expenses not planned in budget)	5	30	60	200

35

Clothes for the wedding party

THE BRIDE'S WEDDING CLOTHES

A bride who has not been married before traditionally wears a white dress and a bridal veil. A bride over forty will probably feel more comfortable in a pretty cocktail dress in an off-white or pastel shade. Satin is suitable anytime, but is uncomfortably heavy for hot weather. Faille, velvet and moiré are excellent for autumn and midwinter. In the spring, lace and taffeta are lovely; in midsummer, chiffon, organdy, mousseline de soie, cottons, piqués and linens are cool and flattering. Lace adds dignity and is most becoming to a mature bride. The length of the train of the bride's dress depends somewhat upon the length of the church aisle and the bride's height. (A moderately short train extends one yard on the ground.)

For a civil ceremony before a justice of the peace, or a second marriage, the bride chooses the prettiest dress she has or can buy that will be appropriate to whatever the couple plan after the wedding ceremony—perhaps an afternoon or cocktail dress or suit. If they are leaving on a wedding trip immediately, she may be married in the suit or traveling dress she will wear away.

If the bride chooses to wear a veil over her face up the aisle and during the ceremony, the front veil is a short, separate piece about a yard square, gathered on an invisible band of some kind. It is taken off or thrown back by the maid of honor when she gives the bride's bouquet back to the bride at the conclusion of the ceremony.

The bride's slippers are of white satin or moiré and *com-*

fortable since she has to stand at the reception. If short gloves are the fashion, she merely pulls one glove off at the altar so that her ring can be put on. If elbow-length or longer evening gloves are worn, the underseam of the wedding finger of the glove is ripped for about two inches so that she may pull the tip off to have the ring put on. Or she may wear no gloves at all. A simple pearl necklace or possibly a pin of pearls or diamonds is the usual jewelry, but if the groom's present to the bride is jewelry, she always wears that on her wedding day.

THE BRIDEGROOM'S WEDDING CLOTHES

The groom plans his outfit according to the formality of the wedding. (The ushers' suits are the same style as the groom's.) The following are correct for every occasion:

1) *Formal wedding daytime:* Cutaway coat, or slightly less formal, black sack coat, waistcoat to match or gray (or white or fawn in summer); gray-striped trousers or black with white pinstripes; wing or fold-down collar for cutaway; stiff fold-down collar for sack coat; black and white tie or gray or white ascot; plain black shoes and socks (soles of the shoes should be blackened with waterproof shoe dye so that when he kneels at the altar, the soles look dark); white boutonniere; preferably white buckskin gloves or light gray; silk hat with cutaway; black homburg with sack coat—more often, no hat.

2) *Most formal wedding, evening:* Tailcoat, stiff white shirt, wing collar, white lawn tie, white waistcoat; white evening gloves; white boutonniere; patent leather pumps or oxford ties, black socks; silk hat or no hat.

3) *Informal wedding, daytime:* (when the bride wears a suit or daytime dress): Dark blue, black or very dark suit; white shirt; starched turn-down or soft-fold collar, bow or four-in-hand tie in conservative stripe or dark solid color; black socks and calfskin oxford shoes; white boutonniere; no gloves; gray or black fedora.

4) *Informal evening wedding:* (the bride wearing wedding gown or cocktail dress—if she is in a daytime dress, the groom wears outfit 3): Dinner coat (tuxedo) and black waistcoat or cummerbund; white shirt with piqué or pleated bosom; black silk bow tie; white boutonniere; no gloves; patent leather oxford shoes.

5) *Summer daytime wedding in the country:* Either dark

blue or gray flannel coat; white or gray flannel or white linen trousers; with blue coat, blue and white tie; with gray coat, black and white tie or plain gray; white buckskin shoes and white wool or lisle socks, or plain dark blue or gray socks (matching coat); no hat or gloves.

6) *Informal daytime wedding in torrid weather:* All-white Palm Beach suit; plain dark-blue tie, bow or four-in-hand; white socks; white buckskin shoes; white handkerchief.

7) *Evening wedding in a hot climate:* White dinner coat, double-breasted so as to avoid waistcoat; black tie, and other details same as (4).

(See Chapter 61 for correct accessories for evening and daytime formal wear.)

THE BRIDESMAIDS' COSTUMES

The costumes of the bridesmaids—slippers, dresses, bouquets, gloves and hats—are selected by the bride. The dresses may be long or short, straight or full, light or dark. Bridesmaids customarily wear and pay for what the bride chooses. They are always dressed exactly alike as to texture of materials and style, but their dresses may differ in color. The two who follow the ushers might wear green, the next two chartreuse, and the next two lemon yellow, and the maid of honor pale yellow. All carry the same kind of flowers.

The dress of the maid or matron of honor never precisely matches that of the bridesmaids; though it is usually similar in style, it is different or reversed in color. For an autumn wedding, the bridesmaids might wear deep yellow and carry rust and orange chrysanthemums and the maid of honor might wear rust and carry yellow chrysanthemums.

The bridesmaids almost always carry flowers. If sheaves, those walking on the right hold them on the right arm with the stems pointing downward to the left; those on the left hold their flowers on the left arm, with stems toward the right. Bouquets or baskets are held in front.

CHILDREN ATTENDING THE BRIDE

The clothes of junior bridesmaids are modified copies of those worn by the bridesmaids. Flowers girls and pages may be dressed in quaint old-fashioned dresses and white suits of whatever period the bride fancies. Or they can be dressed in their ordinary white clothes, with wreaths and bouquets for the girls and white boutonnieres for the boys.

Tiny boys and girls wear kid slippers with a strap and white socks. Their slippers may match their clothes or contrast in color.

WHAT THE BEST MAN AND USHERS WEAR

At the formal daytime wedding, the best man wears precisely what the bridegroom wears. To make sure that his ushers will be alike, a bridegroom may send each one instructions after he finds out their sizes in gloves and collars. For example: "Please wear for the wedding black calfskin shoes; plain black socks; gray striped trousers—the darkest available; morning coat [cutaway] and single-breasted black waistcoat; white dress shirt; cuffs to show three-quarters of an inch below coat sleeves. Stand-up wing collar; bow tie and gloves are enclosed; boutonniere will be at the church." Or, having received their measurements, he may rent all the suits at a local agency.

The clothes of the bride's father need not match those of the ushers, nor should the clothes of the bridegroom, best man and ushers match too precisely. Their ties, boutonnieres and gloves are exactly alike, being gifts from the bridegroom and not bought individually. But there may be slight differences in the stripes of the trousers, the shape of the waistcoats and the materials and measures of the coats. Since few young men nowadays possess cutaways or tails, such suits are usually rented.

CLOTHES OF THE PARENTS

At a wedding held at any hour between 8 A.M. and 6 P.M., the mother of the bride wears a light-colored dress, varying in degree of elaborateness according to the other wedding preparations. At a formal wedding her dress should be formal— even, if she wishes, to a long skirt. She always wears a hat and gloves and usually flowers. A mantilla veil, or flowers may take the place of a hat. In the evening, dinner dresses are in best taste, though not cut too low. If the church is likely to be cool, she carries or wears a furpiece. Or a light wrap is put in the pew for her just before she herself comes up the aisle, so that nothing spoils the effect of her dress.

The bride's father wears whatever is becoming to him or whatever the bridegroom is going to wear.

Since the two mothers stand together to receive at the reception, the bridegroom's mother chooses a dress similar in type to that chosen by the bride's mother. At a formal wedding, the bridegroom's father may wear the same type of clothes as those worn by the bride's father: cutaway in the daytime, tailcoat in the evening.

(For clothes worn by wedding guests, see Chapter 39.)

36

Parties, dinners and the rehearsal

PARTIES BEFORE THE WEDDING
Bridesmaids' luncheon and the bachelor dinner:

In many American communities, the bridesmaids give the bride a farewell luncheon (or a tea) in addition to the regular showers. The only difference from other lunch parties is that the table is decorated with the bride's chosen colors for the wedding. *(For a full description of bridal showers, see Chapter 28.)*

Bachelor dinners are generally in the private dining room of a restaurant or in a club. Toward the end of the dinner, the bridegroom rises and proposes a toast. Every man rises, and drinks the toast standing.

The rehearsal dinner:

Following the rehearsal on the afternoon before the wedding, a dinner is generally given for the bridal party and the immediate families of the bride and groom. It is a gala affair—telegrams and messages are read, and toasts are drunk to the couple and their families. Customarily, the parents of the groom give this party. If they come from another city, they may ask the mother of the bride to reserve a room in a club or restaurant for the dinner. If the groom's family cannot give the rehearsal dinner, a member of the bride's family or a close friend arranges it. The bride and groom and her parents usually leave shortly after dinner, but the rest of the group may stay on, especially if there is music and dancing. This, in many cases, is a reunion for the ushers and takes the place of a bachelor dinner.

THE REHEARSAL

A wedding rehearsal proceeds as follows:

First, as the wedding march is played, the ushers line up at the door, walk forward two and two. The bride and members of the families decide which pace looks well. It should be neither too fast nor too slow. The organist then marks the tempo on his music. The entire procession, including the bridesmaids and the bride on her father's arm, goes out into the vestibule and makes its entry. The procession is arranged according to height, the two shortest ushers leading. Junior bridesmaids, if any, follow the ushers. The bridesmaids come next, two and two, also according to height, the shorter in the lead. After the bridesmaids, the maid or matron of honor walks alone; then come flower girls, ring bearer, and last of all, the bride on the arm of her father, with small boy pages, if she has any, holding up her train. Each pair in the procession follows the two directly in front by four paces or beats of time. The bride counts eight beats before she and her father put their feet forward.

At the chancel:

At the foot of the chancel, the ushers divide. In a small church, the first two go up the chancel steps and stand at the top, one on the right, the other on the left. The second two go a step or two below the first. If there are more, they stand below again. In a big church they go up farther, some of them lining the steps or all of them in front of the choir stalls with the line sloping outward so that the congregation may see them individually. The bridesmaids also divide, half on either side, and stand in front of the ushers. The maid of honor stands on the left at the foot of the steps opposite the best man. Flower girls stand above or below the bridesmaids, wherever they look the best.

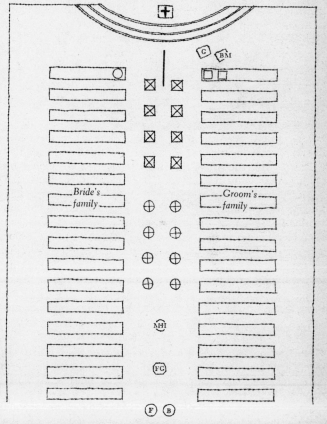

B, bride; F, father; FG, flower girl; MH, maid of honor; ⊕, bridesmaid; ⊠, usher; G, groom; BM, best man; ✠, clergyman

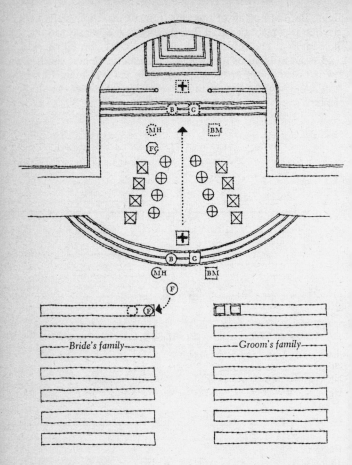

In Roman Catholic and Jewish ceremonies, the father of the bride joins her mother as soon as the groom joins the bride. He does not give his daughter away. The Protestant father remains at his daughter's left until he gives her away. Then he joins his wife.

In a church with two main aisles, the guests are seated according to aisles and not according to the church as a whole. All the seats on the right aisle belong to the bride's family and guests. The left aisle belongs to the bridegroom.

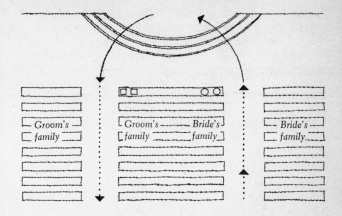

The bride's mother is seated in the front pew at the left of the bride's aisle—exactly as she would be in a center-aisle church. On the other side of the church the bridegroom's mother occupies the front pew on the right of the groom's aisle.

For the processional, the bride's (right) aisle is chosen. After the ceremony, the bride and groom come down the groom's (left) aisle. If the church is very large and the wedding small, so that only the right aisle is used, then the bride's family sits on the left of this aisle and the groom's family on the right, while the marriage takes place at the head of this aisle.

Entrance of the bridegroom:

The clergyman who is to perform the marriage comes into the chancel from the vestry or waiting room. The groom follows at a few paces behind him; he is followed by the best man. The groom stops at the foot of the chancel steps and takes his place at the right, as indicated in the diagram, and his best man stands behind him. The ushers and bridesmaids always pass in front of him and take their place as noted above. When the bride approaches, the groom takes a step to meet her.

Rehearsing the marriage service:

At the rehearsal, the bride takes her left hand from her father's arm, shifts her (makebelieve) bouquet from her right hand to her left, and gives her right hand to the bridegroom; he takes it in his own right hand and draws it through his left arm, at the same time turning toward the chancel. (If the marriage ceremony is to be read at the foot of the chancel, he merely takes her hand in his left one and they stand as they are.)

No words of the service are rehearsed, although the minister explains the order of the service and the responses.

The bride takes the bridegroom's left arm and goes slowly up the steps to the altar. The best man follows behind and to the right of the groom, and the maid of honor moves forward at the left of the bride. In pantomine, the bride gives her bouquet to the maid of honor and the best man hands the ring to the groom, thus insuring that they are at a convenient distance from each other for the actual ceremony.

The recessional:

The recessional is played, and the procession goes out in one of two ways. In reversed order, the bride and groom go first,

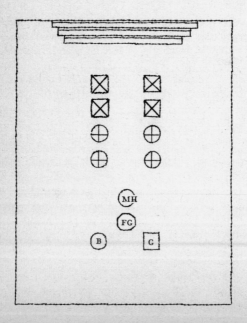

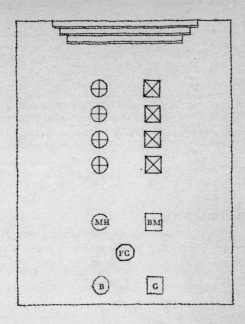

she on his right arm, then the maid or matron of honor, then bridesmaids, then ushers, all keeping step with the leaders. In this form of recessional, the best man goes out through the vestry, picks up the groom's coat, if he has one, and rejoins him at the front door.

In the other form of recessional, the maid or matron of honor and the best man walk out together behind the bride and groom. Then the bridesmaids and ushers pair off and follow two by two. In this case the groom's coat is put in the vestibule before the ceremony so that he need not go back to the vestry for it.

37

The wedding day

BEST MAN'S DUTIES

His first duty is to see that everything the groom needs for the honeymoon is packed and to take a bag to wherever the bridegroom is to change from wedding clothes into traveling ones. He should also check the travel reservations and hotel accommodations.

Next he sees that the groom is dressed in plenty of time for the ceremony and that the marriage license is safely stowed in the groom's wallet or pocket. He takes charge of the wedding ring and the clergyman's fee himself.

After the ceremony he sees the bride and groom into their car which is waiting at the entrance to the church. Then he returns to the vestry to give the fee to the clergyman before going to the reception.

At the reception he gives the first toast to the bride and groom. When the couple leave to change out of their wedding clothes, he helps the groom dress, sees that he has with him everything necessary for the wedding trip—money and plane, train or boat tickets. When the bride and groom are ready, he leads the couple through the waiting guests to the door and puts them into the going-away car. Earlier in the day he has loaded most of their luggage into the car, which was kept hidden— safe from practical jokers.

There is another way the best man can be useful. If the first stage of the wedding journey is to be to a hotel in town, after the bride and groom have changed, he takes their luggage to the hotel where accommodations have been engaged, has their bags placed in their room and registers for the newlyweds. He secures the hotel key, then returns to the groom and gives him the key. This maneuver allows the young couple to slip quietly into their room without attracting notice.

BEFORE THE CEREMONY

The bridesmaids meet at the house of the bride, where they receive their bouquets. When everyone is ready, the bride's mother drives away in the first car, with perhaps others of her children or one of the bridesmaids with her. Maid of honor, bridesmaids and flower girls follow. Last of all come the bride and her father. This car remains in front of the church entrance.

Meanwhile, about an hour before the ceremony, the ushers arrive at the church. Their boutonnieres, sent by the groom, are waiting in the vestibule. The ushers most likely to recognize the friends and members of each family are detailed to the center aisle. Those who will escort the mothers of the bride and groom are designated.

A few pews on either side of the center aisle are reserved for the immediate families of the couple. The left is the "bride's side" and the right the groom's. Guests may be sent pew cards (*see Chapter 40*) to show the ushers. If not, the ushers may be given a list of guests to be seated in the first few pews, generally marked by a bouquet or white bow on the end.

An usher offers his right arm to each lady as she arrives. If the vestibule is crowded and several ladies are together, he asks them to wait until he can come back or another usher is available. The usher, of course, does not offer his arm to a man.

If the guest has no pew card, the usher asks whether he prefers to sit on the bride's side or the groom's and seats him accordingly. Or, he may consult his guest list and if the guest's name is on it, seat him in a pew "in front of the ribbon."

SEATING DIVORCED PARENTS

If there is a friendly relationship between them, not only Mary's parents but both of her stepparents are present at the wedding. Her mother and stepfather sit in the front pew, her mother's immediate family behind them. Her father (after giving her away in a Protestant ceremony) sits with her stepmother and their family in the next pew.

According to the exactions of convention, the wedding of their daughter must be given by her mother. This creates a hardship if there is bitterness between divorced parents. The bride still drives with her father to the church, walks with him up the aisle and has him share in the marriage ceremony. After giving his daughter away, he sits in the pew behind the immediate family of her mother. His second wife may sit with him if the bride wishes, or she may not attend at all. The father does not go to the reception given by his ex-wife unless urged to do so.

If the wedding is given by the bride's father and stepmother while her own mother is also living, it means that the daughter has made her home with her father instead of her mother. The bride's own mother sits in the front pew with members of her family, but her second husband usually sits farther back. (Whether or not she attends the reception depends on the bride's wishes.) The father gives the bride away and then takes his place in the second pew with his present wife and their family.

The groom's mother and whomever she would like to have with her are given the first pew on the bridegroom's side of the church and his father and others of his family are seated in the third pew behind. At a large reception their presence need not be conspicuous nor make anyone uncomfortable.

THE LAST FEW MINUTES

Fifteen minutes before the wedding hour, the groom and his best man arrive at the church and enter the side door. They sit in the vestry or in the clergyman's study until the sexton or an usher comes to say that the bride has arrived. They then wait for and follow the clergyman to their places. *(See diagrams for procession provided in Chapter 36.)*

The groom's mother and father wait in the vestibule. As the bride's mother drives up, an usher notifies the groom of her arrival. The bride and her father arrive last. When the entire wedding party is in the church, the doors between the vestibule and the church are closed. No one is seated after this except the parents of the young couple. Latecomers stand in the vestibule or go into the gallery.

The groom's mother goes up the aisle on the arm of the chosen usher to the first pew on the right; the groom's father follows alone and takes his place beside her. The same usher or a brother or cousin of the bride, escorts the bride's mother to the first pew on the left. (When the bride has a stepfather he may follow her mother and the usher, in the same manner as the groom's father.)

If a carpet is to be laid, two ushers now pull it quickly down the aisle and drape white ribbon over the ends of the pews from the back of the church to the nearest reserved pew on each side of the center aisle. Then they take their places in the procession. The beginning of the wedding march should sound just as they return to the foot of the aisle.

THE WEDDING CEREMONY

The sound of the music is the cue for the clergyman to enter the chancel, followed by the groom and the best man. The groom stands on the right-hand side at the head of the aisle; but if the door opens onto the chancel, he sometimes stands at the top of the steps. To make it easier for him to put the ring on his bride's finger he does not wear gloves. The best man stands directly back and to the right of the groom; he keeps his gloves on.

The processional advances and performs exactly as it did at the rehearsal. *(See Chapter 36.)*

As the bride and groom stand at the foot of the chancel in front of the clergyman, he reads the betrothal. In a Protestant ceremony when the clergyman says, "Who giveth this woman to be married?" the father goes forward and the bride gives him her right hand. The father puts her hand into the hand of the clergyman and says "I do," (or if he prefers, "Her mother and I do"). He then takes his place next to his wife at the end of the first pew on the left. The clergyman, holding the bride's hand in his own right, takes the bridegroom's hand in his left and places the bride's hand in that of the bridegroom.

If the bride has neither father nor any near male relative or guardian, she may walk up the aisle alone. At the point in the ceremony where the clergyman says, "Who giveth this woman to be married?" her mother remains standing in her place at the end of the first pew on the left and bows her head to indicate "I do."

As the organist plays or the choir softly sings, the clergyman moves to the altar before which the marriage is performed. The bride and groom follow, her right hand on his left arm. The attendants take the positions they did at the rehearsal. *(See Chapter 36.)*

The bride and groom plight their troth.

When it is time for the ring, the best man produces it from his pocket, the minister blesses it, and the groom slips it on his bride's finger. (Since the wedding ring must not be put above the engagement ring, on her wedding day a bride either leaves her engagement ring at home or wears it on her right hand. Afterward she wears it above her wedding ring. At a double-ring ceremony, the maid of honor hands the groom's ring to the bride at the moment that the best man gives her ring to the groom, and the bride puts it on his finger immediately after she has received her ring from him. The ceremony then proceeds.)

AFTER THE CEREMONY

At the conclusion of the ceremony, the minister congratulates the new couple and the couple kiss. The organ begins the recessional. The bride takes her bouquet from her maid of honor, who then lifts the face veil, if one is worn. The bride turns toward her husband—her bouquet in her right hand—and puts her left hand through his right arm and they descend the steps.

The maid of honor hands her own bouquet to a second bridesmaid while she arranges and straightens out the train and veil. Bride and groom go down the aisle, followed by their attendants, in the way that has been rehearsed. *(See Chapter 36.)*

The conveyances are drawn up in the reverse order from that in which they arrived. The bride's car leaves first; next come those of the bridesmaids; then that of the bride's mother and father; next that of the groom's mother and father. The nearest members of both families follow.

As soon as the recessional is over, the ushers hurry back and escort to the door all the ladies who were in the first pews, according to the order of precedence; the bride's mother first, then the groom's mother, then the other occupants of the first pew on either side, then the second and third pews, until all members of the immediate families have left the church. Meanwhile other guests stay in their places. When the occupants of the first pews have left, the ribbons along the ends of the pews are removed and the other guests go out by themselves.

The clergyman's fee:

The fee of the clergyman may range from ten dollars to one hundred or two hundred dollars, depending on the means of the groom and the importance of the wedding. When the clergyman comes from a distance, his traveling expenses and hotel accommodations are paid by the groom or his family.

ORTHODOX AND REFORM JEWISH WEDDINGS

The Orthodox wedding ceremony differs from the Reform Jewish ceremony. In the Orthodox ceremony, the bride is veiled and is escorted by her father and mother under a cloth canopy supported by four poles, usually held by hand. Or the posts may rest upon a stationary platform, and the bride's parents simply escort her up the aisle. Sometimes the canopy is of flowers instead of cloth. The groom is escorted by his parents. The principals stand under the canopy or "chupah" before the Ark of the Covenant. Hats are worn by all men attending the ceremony.

The service is read in Hebrew. The groom places a ring upon the finger of the bride, repeating the following formula: "Thou are consecrated unto me with this ring, according to the law of Moses and Israel." The officiating rabbi then makes the benediction over the wine, giving the groom and bride the goblet, from which they drink. A document is read in Aramaic, giving in detail the pledge of fidelity and protection on the part of the groom toward the bride and indicating the bride's contribution to the new household. At the conclusion of the ceremony, a glass is broken, symbolizing the fact that one must never overlook the possibility of misfortune.

In the Reform service, English (or the native language) is used in addition to Hebrew, and the canopy may be dispensed with. The young couple may decide to include many elements traditionally associated with the Christian wedding ceremony; they should consult with their rabbi about this a few weeks beforehand. The groom is usually ushered in by his best man, and the bride is escorted on the arm of her father although he does not give her away. The attendants function as in a Christian ceremony. The groom repeats either the Hebrew formula or its English equivalent. The bride and groom also drink wine out of the same cup, symbolizing the cup of joy. The clergyman delivers a brief address on the significance of marriage.

ROMAN CATHOLIC WEDDINGS

The wedding of the Roman Catholic Church is customarily centered around the Nuptial Mass celebrated between eight A.M. and noon. It is wise for the engaged couple to make arrangements at the rectory several months in advance. Marriage banns are usually proclaimed from the pulpit three times or are published in the church calendar prior to the wedding. Often, though it is not obligatory, the Catholic members of the bridal party receive Holy Communion at the Nuptial Mass.

Whether the bride and groom and best man and maid of honor, or the whole bridal party, are permitted within the altar rail is determined by individual church practice. The bride's father does not give her away, so after escorting her down the aisle, he steps into the front pew to join his wife.

Although afternoon weddings usually take place between four and five o'clock, they may be held at any time from one to six. A Catholic wedding may take place any time during the year, but during the closed seasons of Lent and Advent, the Nuptial Blessing is not given, unless, under extraordinary circumstances, permission is granted by the bishop.

THE RECEPTION

On arriving at the house where the reception is to be held, the bridal party may pose for pictures before the other guests arrive. This finished, they form the receiving line.

The receiving line:

The actual receiving line is made up of the mothers, the bride and groom and the bride's attendants. The ushers and best man have no place in it.

The bride's mother greets the guests at the beginning of the line nearest the entrance to the room. The bridegroom's mother stands next to her. The two fathers may join the line if they wish, standing on their wives' left, but it is not necessary, and they are generally more useful and happier circulating and greeting their friends.

At an elaborate reception there may be an announcer who asks each guest's name, then repeats it aloud. The guests shake hands with the hostess, make some polite remark about the "beautiful wedding" or "lovely bride," continue in line to the bridal pair. If there is no one announcing, guests unknown to the hostess announce their own names.

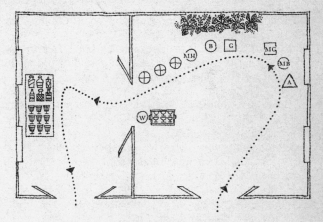

A, *announcer*; MB, *mother of bride*; MG, *mother of groom*; G, *groom*; B, *bride*; MH, *maid of honor*; W, *waiter*

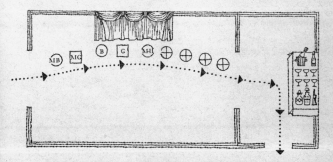

The bride stands on the bridegroom's right, the maid of honor next in line. The bridesmaids stand beyond the maid of honor, according to height.

Receiving their guests:

To a relative or friend of the bride, but a stranger to the groom, the bride always introduces her husband, saying, "Mrs. Neighbor, this is Jim," or, formally, "Mrs. Faraway, may I present my husband?" The groom says to an old friend of his, "Mary, this is Steve Michigan." And Mary says, "How do you do? Jim often speaks of you!" To all expressions of best wishes and congratulations, the bride and groom need only answer, "Thank you."

Refreshments are ready for guests as soon as they have passed down the receiving line.

When there is a bridal table, it may be at the side or end of a large room, decorated with white flowers. In front of the bride's place is its chief ornament, the wedding cake *(see Chapter 34)*. When the queue of arriving guests has melted away, the bride and groom go to their table or join their guests. Arm in arm they lead the way, followed by the ushers and bridesmaids.

The bride and groom always sit next to each other, she at his right, the maid or matron of honor at his left. The best man is at the right of the bride. Around the rest of the table are bridesmaids and ushers alternately. When there are no bridesmaids, the table is made up of intimate friends. The bridal table is always served by waiters even when the rest of the guests eat buffet style.

The table of the bride's parents:

When there is a table for the bride's parents, the groom's mother sits on the right of the bride's father, and opposite them the groom's father is on the right of the mother of the bride. The other places at the table are occupied by close relatives, very intimate friends of the parents or distinguished guests, who may include the clergyman who performed the ceremony.

The toast to the bride and groom:

At a sit-down bridal table, if champagne is served, it is poured as soon as the party is seated. The glass of the bride is filled first, then that of the bridegroom, and then on around the table, starting with the maid of honor at the groom's left and ending with the best man seated at the right of the bride. Then the best man proposes a toast to the bride and bridegroom. All (except the bride and groom) rise, raise their glasses and drink the toast. Then the groom rises and replies with thanks and a toast to his bride. At a small reception all the guests may join in drinking together to the couple's health and happiness.

Dancing at the reception:

If a regular two- or three-course meal, or wedding breakfast, is served, the first course is passed shortly after the bridal party sits down. The dancing starts after dessert has been eaten and the cake cut. But at a reception where sandwiches and snacks are passed or eaten from a buffet table, the bride and groom may start the dancing as soon as they wish. Guests watch and applaud while the bride and groom dance the first dance. Her father-in-law cuts in and then her father. The groom, meantime, dances with his mother-in-law and with his mother.

After this, the best man or a relative may cut in, the bride's father asks the groom's mother for the next dance and the groom's father asks the bride's mother. As the groom dances with each bridesmaid and the ushers with the bride, the guests may start cutting in, and dancing becomes general for the whole group.

Cutting the cake:

At a sit-down bridal table dinner, the cake is cut just before the dessert is served, and slices are passed with the ices or ice cream. If there is no bridal table, the cake may be cut later, often just shortly before the couple leave the reception.

The bride, with the help of the groom, cuts the first slice from the bottom tier (if it has more than one) with a silver cake knife. After this, a waiter cuts slices until the bottom tier has been cut away. The cake then is removed from the table, and the tiers are separated and cut into slices. The bride and groom may wish to save the figurines from the top.

THE DIVORCED FATHER SHARES IN THE WEDDING

When the divorced father of the bride wishes to have a share in his daughter's wedding, there is a practical solution. At the same time that the wedding invitations are sent out by her mother, the following invitations to a small second gathering are sent out by her father:

Mr. John Pater
requests the pleasure of your company
at the wedding supper of his daughter
Mary
and her bridegroom
James Martin
Saturday, the tenth of April
at seven o'clock
4 Monroe Place

If he has remarried, the invitation may read:

> Mr. and Mrs. John Pater
> request the pleasure of your company
> at the wedding supper of his daughter
> etc.

The mother chooses an earlier-than-usual hour for the reception. Then, instead of leaving the reception of the bride's mother in their traveling clothes, the bride and groom remain in their wedding clothes, and accompanied by her bridesmaids and his ushers, drive to the home of her father.

After the supper the bride and groom change into traveling clothes, which have been brought to her father's house earlier in the day, and depart.

THEY'RE OFF!

Unless the bride and groom have to catch a train, they usually stay until the crowd thins before going to dress for their journey. Then the bride signals to her bridesmaids and leaves the room. If the reception is in a house, they all gather at the foot of the stairs; about halfway up, she turns and throws her bouquet, and they try to catch it. If there are no stairs, she pauses at the entrance of the reception room to throw her bouquet. If the bride has no bridesmaids, she collects a group of other girls and throws her bouquet to them.

When the bridal pair appear in their going-away costumes, the guests all gather to bid them farewell, throwing confetti and rose petals after them as they run to the car.

38

Weddings in special situations

Not always do the bride-to-be and her fiancé choose to be married in church—and for a number of perfectly acceptable reasons. These occasions require our attention, for they should be as perfect of their kind as are the most elaborate of church ceremonies. Then, too, there are variations on the usual form, as when two sisters wish to be married at the same time or when the bride has been married before. Anniversaries, especially Golden Anniversaries, should be a re-echoing of the wedding day and so have been included here as special "situations."

THE HOUSE WEDDING

At a house wedding the procession advances through an aisle of white satin ribbons from the stairs or hallway to the improvised altar which may include a bench on which the bridal couple kneels. Chairs for the immediate families are placed within a marked-off enclosure, or if the room is small, all the guests stand.

The bride's mother stands at the door of the room in which the ceremony is to be and receives people as they arrive. The groom's mother takes her place near the altar with the rest of the immediate family. The ushers are purely ornamental, as no one is escorted to seats. The guests simply stand wherever they can find places behind the aisle ribbons. Just before the bride's entrance, her mother goes forward and stands in the reserved part of the room.

In a house, the procession starts from the top of the stairs. In an apartment, it starts in the foyer or bedroom hall. The wedding march begins, and the ushers come in two and two, followed by the bridesmaids, exactly as in a church, the bride coming last on her father's arm. The clergyman and the groom and best man have, if possible, reached the altar by another door. If the room has only one door, they go up the aisle a few moments before the bridal procession starts.

For a very small wedding, the clergyman enters, followed by the bridegroom; the bride then enters with her father, or alone; and the wedding service is read.

There is no recessional at a house wedding. The couple turn around as the clergyman leaves, and greet their guests where they are.

For music there may be beautiful phonograph recordings of organ and choir made for such weddings. The collation may consist of ginger ale or fruit juice, wedding cake, and varieties of sandwiches, with the refreshments placed on a small table covered with a tea cloth, or it may be much more elaborate.

At a simple stand-up breakfast, the food consists of one hot dish and one salad. Bouillon, ice cream and wedding cake are served as at a large wedding.

When only the immediate families and a few friends are present, they often all sit together at one lunch or dinner table.

A home wedding may be performed in the garden, with the wedding procession under the trees, and tables out on the lawn.

The bride's dress:

At a home wedding, the bride may have a formal wedding gown, long or short (without long train, however), or a daytime dress or suit worn with a hat or small veil.

THE EVENING WEDDING

All through the South and generally throughout the West, many weddings are celebrated at eight or nine o'clock in the evening. The details are precisely the same as those for the morning or afternoon. In large Southern cities, the bride and bridesmaids may wear dresses that are perhaps more elaborate and more "evening" in type, and the bridegroom and ushers wear full evening clothes. Guests, both men and women, dress as though going to a ball. For the church ceremony, the women wear light scarfs of some sort around their shoulders and over their hair.

At simpler ceremonies, especially in smaller communities, the guests wear what they would wear to evening service in church—a good dress and hat for a woman, and a dark daytime suit for a man.

THE EARLY MORNING WEDDING

Among Roman Catholics, an eight o'clock morning wedding is not unusual. The wedding may be carried out as follows:

The bride wears any simple dress. She would probably wear a veil, of tulle rather than lace, either falling to the hem of her dress or of finger length. She carries a bouquet of moderate size, unless she carries a prayer book, and she wears no gloves. Her attendants wear the simplest sort of morning dresses and hats; the groom and his best man, business suits or flannels. And the breakfast menu—really breakfast—might be fruit, coffee and hot biscuits.

MARRIAGE AT THE RECTORY

Marriages are often performed in the clergyman's study or in another room at the rectory or parish house.

When the bride and groom decide on a ceremony in the rectory, the clergyman is consulted ahead of time as to the date and hour. The bride and bridegroom go together and are met at the parsonage by the members of their families and the two or three friends invited. The bride and bridegroom stand before the clergyman, and the service is read. Afterward those present congratulate them, and that may be all. Or they may all go to the house of the bride or of a witness or to a restaurant and have lunch, tea or dinner together. At such a marriage, the bride rarely wears a white wedding dress and veil, but she may if she chooses—especially if there is to be a wedding dinner at someone's home afterward.

MARRIAGE BY A JUSTICE OF THE PEACE

The general procedure is the same as that for a marriage at the rectory. There are always two guests, preferably relatives but often friends, who act as witnesses as well. The bride wears a pretty daytime dress or suit.

THE RUNAWAY MARRIAGE

An elopement means that a young couple has run off and been married without the consent of the young girl's parents.

When the parents had approved before the marriage or when they have accepted it afterward, they send out the announcements in their name. Should the parents not send out the announcements, the married pair may, if they wish, send them out themselves. *(See Chapter 42.)*

If the bride's mother and father wish to give a belated reception after the marriage, the invitations are telephoned or sent on informals, and, if written, include the bride's married name—"in honor of Mr. and Mrs. Harvey Kirk, Jr."

THE DOUBLE WEDDING

At a double wedding, the two bridegrooms follow the clergyman and stand side by side, each with his best man behind him, the groom of the older sister nearer the aisle. The ushers —half of them friends of the first, and the others friends of the second bridegroom—go up the aisle together. Then come the bridesmaids of the older sister followed by her maid of honor who walks alone. The older sister follows, holding her father's arm. Then come the bridesmaids of the younger sister, her maid of honor, and last, the younger bride on the arm of a brother, uncle or the nearest male relative.

The first couple ascends the chancel steps and takes their place at the left side of the altar rail, leaving room at the right side for the younger bride and her bridegroom. The father stands just below his older daughter. The brother takes his place in the first pew.

The ceremony is a double one, read to both couples, with the particular responses made twice. The father gives both brides away—first his older daughter and then his younger. Then he takes the place saved for him beside his wife in the first pew.

At the end of the ceremony, the older sister and her husband turn and go down the aisle first. The younger couple follows. The bridesmaids of the older are followed by those of the younger and the ushers follow last, or bridesmaids and ushers pair off and go out together.

A bride at a double wedding may serve as maid of honor

for her sister. Each in turn holds the other's bouquet during her sister's ceremony. The parents of the two grooms must share the first pew, or draw lots for first and second.

REMARRIAGE

The groom's second marriage:

The fact that a bridegroom has been married previously has no bearing on the wedding preparations made by his maiden bride. She may wear a white gown and veil, and the wedding and reception may be as elaborate as she chooses.

The marriage of a widow:

The marriage of a widow differs from that of a maid in that she cannot wear a bridal veil or orange blossoms, emblems of virginity. Although a dress and hat of color are preferable, she may wear white. She does not have bridesmaids, though she may have a maid or matron of honor.

A widow either removes her first wedding and engagement rings or else transfers them to the fourth finger of her right hand as soon as she becomes engaged. When her second engagement ring is given her, she puts aside the first, and if her second marriage is to take place soon removes her wedding ring as well. She may keep the engagement ring for a daughter, have it reset, or, later she may again wear it on her right hand. This depends upon the feelings of her second husband.

Usually a widow writes personal notes of invitation to a quiet wedding, but this is no reason why she cannot have a lovely ceremony. Sometimes—especially if her family and the groom's are very large—she finds it necessary to send out engraved invitations. *(For the correct form, see Chapter 40.)*

The most tasteful wedding for a widow is held in a small church or chapel or in her home. A few flowers or some branched greens are placed in the chancel or at the altar rail. (Or flowers and greens decorate the improvised altar in her home.) There are a few ushers, possibly only honorary ones. There are no ribboned-off seats, as only very intimate friends are invited. Usually the bride wears an afternoon dress and hat or possibly a cocktail dress and tiny veil. There may be a fairly large reception afterward or the simplest afternoon tea. In any case, the breakfast, tea or dinner is, if possible, at the bride's house, and the bridal pair may stay where they are and have their guests take leave of them and then drive away afterward.

A divorcée remarries:

Whether or not a divorcée may be married in her church depends upon the circumstances of her divorce and the approval of her clergyman. Usually the remarriage takes place in her own house, performed either by a clergyman or a justice of the peace. A small reception follows. She wears a simple street-length gown with a hat, in any style she prefers, so long as it is not white; she does not wear a veil or orange blossoms. Engraved invitations are not in good taste. Handwritten notes or possibly messages on visiting cards are best.

Children of divorced parents are not required to attend the marriage ceremony unless they are fond of their future stepparent. They may, if they wish, attend the reception.

WEDDING ANNIVERSARIES

The eight universally recognized anniversaries are:

> 1 year, Paper
> 5 years, Wood
> 10 years, Tin
> 15 years, Crystal
> 20 years, China
> 25 years, Silver
> 50 years, Gold
> 60 years, Diamond

Because the first wedding anniversary is of great importance and the selection of paper gifts is comparatively limited, the trend is now toward making plastics also an accepted first-year gift.

Suitable parties to celebrate any of the earlier wedding anniversaries are a housewarming or a stork shower, a fancy-dress party, a barn dance, a treasure hunt. It can be a surprise party arranged for the bride and groom by their friends. The Silver Wedding is often celebrated by a big dinner or a dance to which everyone who was a guest at the wedding is invited, including the clergyman who performed the ceremony. The most important anniversary, the Golden Wedding, is usually celebrated by a somewhat formal afternoon or evening at home or by a family dinner either in the evening or at midday, after which other relatives, friends and neighbors come in to offer their congratulations. Some couples may wish to reaffirm their marriage vows on an anniversary such as the twenty-fifth or even the fiftieth.

Gifts not obligatory:

A gift is not obligatory, especially when the anniversary year is one that suggests an item of value. Sometimes the invitation carries a line reading "Please omit gifts." Intimate friends usually take or send something; flowers are always appropriate.

39

The wedding guest

The mere fact of receiving a wedding announcement or even an engraved invitation to the church obligates you to much or to nothing, according to your own personal situation or your impulse of the moment. In other words, an announcement informing you that a marriage has taken place between Mary Anthony and John Ballard may require no more attention than it takes to change the name of the bride in your address book. On the other hand, the wedding of a dear friend or a godchild necessarily entails certain responsibilities.

"THE HONOUR OF YOUR PRESENCE . . ."

When an invitation to the ceremony, the reception, or both includes R.S.V.P., you must reply at once, so that the family can make definite preparation. Failure to reply causes extra trouble and expense. *(For the correct form of acceptances and regrets, see Chapter 46.)*

An invitation reading "and Family" includes every member of the family living under the same roof from the child of walking-and-talking age up to great-grandparents. Married daughters or sons who live in their own houses are sent separate invitations. However, guests should not take small children unless they have been specifically invited.

THE WEDDING PRESENT

Wedding presents should, if at all possible, arrive before the ceremony. If you are not an intimate friend of the bride or groom or of their families and are invited to the church ceremony only, you are not expected to send a present. When you accept an invitation to a wedding reception, however, you should send a present. An invitation by written note indicates that you are considered an especially dear friend, and you will therefore want to send a gift.

An occasional few special friends and perhaps close relatives send presents to someone being married for a second time, particularly if one of the couple has never been married before.

An announcement of an elopement does not require a present, though affection for the bride or the groom or their families may prompt you to send one.

If, because of illness or absence, your present is not sent until after the wedding, a note accompanies it, giving the reason for the delay. Delayed presents are sent to Mr. and Mrs. Newlywed at their own new address or, if you do not know their address, in care of the bride's family.

What kind of gift:

Typical wedding presents include almost anything ornamental as well as useful for the furnishing of a house or the setting of a dining table, from a piece of silver, or an ashtray, to a lamp or an occasional table or chair. Objects of plain silver or untooled leather are enhanced by engraved or tooled initials; linen is more personal when it has an embroidered monogram or initials. But unless you know for certain that your gift will not be duplicated, it is safer to send presents unmarked.

Even if you have never met the bride, your present is sent to her. Often friends of the bridegroom pick out some things suitable for him, such as a masculine-looking desk set, which is sent to her, though obviously for his use.

Checks given as wedding presents are not necessarily drawn to the bride, but to the couple jointly. The check to be cashed after the wedding is drawn to John and Mary Smith.

A visiting card or a signed blank card is always enclosed with a wedding present with some such sentiment as "All best wishes for your happiness." If you know the bride well you sign it "John and Mary Friendly." If a friend of her parents or John's, you write "With best wishes from" and place it so that "Mr. and Mrs. Your Name" engraved on your card forms the signature. Unless you are certain that the bride knows it, be sure your address is included.

WHAT TO WEAR TO A WEDDING

Today few men wear anything more formal than plain business suits, whether dark blue or dark gray. During hot weather, especially at simple seashore and country weddings, light suits or white or light gray flannel trousers with plain flannel coats are suitable. The sport coat is out of place.

In the South and wherever evening weddings are customary, tailcoats are still seen. More frequently, the tuxedo coat is the one worn in the evening. In simpler communities, men wear plain navy blue suits on all dress occasions in the evening as well as during the day.

At a formal evening wedding the women wear low-necked, sleeveless evening dresses, with flowers or clips or hair ornaments or perhaps a lace scarf over their hair and shoulders in church. At a very simple wedding in the evening or during the day, they wear afternoon dresses, with small hats.

When not going to the reception, clothes worn habitually to church are correct.

Children wear their best party clothes.

AT THE CHURCH

If you have arrived early enough to be given an aisle seat, it is entirely proper for you to keep it, no matter who or how many enter the pew later. *(For additional details on seating arrangements, see Chapter 37.)*

When the service is over and the recessional has passed by, those in the pews farther back wait in their places until the immediate families in the front pews have left.

FROM CHURCH TO RECEPTION

When invited to the reception, you provide your own transportation from the church to wherever the reception is to be held.

AT THE RECEPTION

At the house, club or hotel, someone at the entrance tells you, "Ladies' dressing room to the right, men's through the hall on the left." A woman leaves her wrap but retains her hat and gloves. Men remove coats and hats. At the door of the room in which the reception is held, there may be an announcer who asks your name. You give it with title: "Miss Pauline Panic" or "Mrs. John Jones" or "Dr. Henry Roberts." He then repeats in a clear voice, "Miss Pauline Panic," and you start down the line. The bride's mother offers you her hand and greets you. You comment on the bride's beauty, the day, or the wedding in general. If the groom's mother is standing next to her, you shake hands with her too. Make your remarks brief in order not to keep those behind waiting. You congratulate the groom and wish the bride happiness; a thoughtful guest mentions his or her name if it is not known to either of them. You greet any of the bridesmaids with whom you are acquainted. Otherwise you walk by with a smile for each.

The bride's father sometimes stands beside his wife, but he usually circulates among his guests just as he would at a ball or any other party where he is host. Therefore, you speak to him either on your arrival or whenever you encounter him elsewhere.

It is courteous, especially if he is a stranger, to introduce yourself to the groom's father and tell him how much you like his son or his new daughter-in-law.

After greeting the bride and groom, you mingle with the guests and make your way slowly to wherever refreshments are being served. You either ask one of the waiters to serve you or help yourself to what you want, lingering as long as you wish.

If you are a stranger at a sit-down breakfast, you sit down at an unoccupied table and let others join you.

When you wish to leave, you do so without formal leave-taking of any kind.

PART NINE

ON THE SUBJECT OF INVITATIONS, INFORMALS, CARDS

40

Wedding invitations

The engraved forms of invitations and announcements are governed by fixed rules. All formal invitations are recognized as such because they are worded in the third person; their acceptances and regrets are answered in this same form and by hand.

Invitations to the largest and most elaborate of weddings consist of an invitation to the church ceremony, a card of admission or "pew card," and, for relatives and close friends, an invitation to the reception. But many variations are possible and perfectly correct, as we shall see.

When a guest is expected to attend the church service only, no invitation to the reception is enclosed. When the wedding is in a small church or chapel and the reception in a very big house, many receive invitations to the reception and few to the ceremony. If both the church and the reception are limited to the few who are sent handwritten invitations or are given oral invitations, then engraved announcements in place of invitations of any kind may be sent to the friends who could not be included as well as to acquaintances.

Invitations to a large wedding are sent three weeks beforehand; those to a simpler wedding may be mailed as late as ten days before the wedding day.

(For wedding announcements and reception invitations, see Chapters 41 and 43.)

CORRECT STYLE

Correct invitations to any wedding, whatever its size, are engraved on the first page of a double sheet of heavy paper, ivory or white, either plain or with a raised margin called a plate-mark or panel. Its size is governed by the current fashion, but usually it is about 5½ inches wide by 7⅜ inches deep and folds once for insertion into its envelope. Or it may be about 4⅜ by 5¾ inches and go into the envelope without folding. The engraving is in whichever lettering style the bride chooses at her stationer's.

If the family of the bride's father has a coat of arms, it, or a crest only, may be embossed without color at the top center of the sheet. When the invitations are sent out by the bride's mother (or any woman alone), a coat of arms is not used. With a crest, plain script is the best taste for the engraving.

Two envelopes:

Two envelopes are used: the inner one has no mucilage on the flap and is addressed to Mr. and Mrs. Brown with neither first name nor address. Then it is put into an outer "mailing envelope" that has mucilage on its flap; this envelope is then addressed by hand.

Addressing the envelopes:

In all formal correspondence never abbreviate the state name.

Mr. and Mrs. George Brown
26 Parkway
Hometown, Illinois

Never address an envelope:

Mr. and Mrs. James Greatlake
      and Family

Miss Mary Greatlake, or the Misses Greatlake, may be written beneath the names of their parents, but a separate in-

vitation should be sent to "The Messrs." All members of the
family not living at the family's home address are sent separate invitations.

The names of children under twelve or thirteen are written
on the inner envelope this way:

Priscilla, Penelope, Harold and Jim

and enclosed in an outer envelope addressed to "The Misses
and Messrs. Greatlake."

Folding and inserting:

When preparing to send out the invitations, all the envelopes
are addressed first. An envelope-size invitation is inserted in the
inner envelope, folded edge down, with the engraved side toward the flap. An invitation designed to fit an envelope half its
size will require a second fold, which should be made with the
engraving inside, and inserted, folded edge down, into the envelope. With the unsealed flap of this filled inner envelope away
from you, insert it in the mailing envelope. If the invitation is
folded, all insertions (such as the reception card or pew card)
are placed inside the second fold with the type facing the flap
of the envelope. If the invitation is not folded a second time,
they are inserted in front of it (nearest you), with the reception card next to the invitation and any smaller cards in front
of that.

Engravers generally use tissue sheets to protect the pages
from the fresh ink and recommend that they be kept to prevent the ink from smearing.

CORRECT WORDING

The wording of the wedding invitation never varies. For
example, the invitation to the ceremony itself always "requests
the *honour*"—spelled with a "u." The invitation to the reception "requests the *pleasure* of your company." But it is perfectly proper for communicants of the Roman Catholic Church
to use a form in which the phrase "at the marriage of" is replaced by *"at the marriage in Christ* of" and, where appropriate, add beneath the name of the groom the lines *"and your
participation in the offering of the Nuptial Mass."*

In the examples of correct wording, spacing and styles of

engraving that follow, note the omission of punctuation, ex
cept after abbreviations and initials and when phrases requirin
separation by punctuation occur in the same line.

Mr. and Mrs. Charles Robert Oldname

request the honour of your presence

at the marriage of their daughter

Pauline Marie

to

Mr. John Frederick Hamilton

Saturday, the twenty-ninth of April

at four o'clock

Church of the Heavenly Rest

New York

Doctor and Mrs. John Huntington Smith
request the honour of

Miss Pauline Town's

presence at the marriage of their daughter
Mary Katherine
to
Mr. James Smartlington
Tuesday, the first of November
at twelve o'clock
St. John's Church

General forms:

The wording of an invitation to a house wedding gives a
house address in place of the name of a church, and R.S.V.P.
is added at the bottom left.

Wedding and reception invitation in one:
  Occasionally, the invitation to the reception or to the breakfast is included in the invitation to the ceremony.

Mrs. Alexander Oldname

requests the honour of your presence

at the marriage of her daughter

Barbara

to

Mr. James Town, junior

Tuesday, the twenty-first of October

at three o'clock

Church of the Resurrection

Ridgemont, New York

and afterwards at the reception

Bright Meadows

R.s.v.p.

Invitation to a wedding in the house of a friend:
  Invitations are issued by the parents of the bride even though the wedding takes place at a house other than their own. The names of the parents at the head of the invitation means that *they* are giving the wedding, though not in their own house.

Mr. and Mrs. Richard Littlehouse

request the honour of your presence

at the marriage of their daughter

Betty

to

Doctor Frederic Robinson

Saturday, the fifth of November

at four o'clock

at the residence of Mr. and Mrs. James Sterlington

Tuxedo Park, New York

R.s.v.p.

When the reception follows a house wedding, it is not mentioned in the wedding invitation, as it is assumed that everyone invited will stay on.

When the bride has a stepfather:

When the bride's own father is not living and she has a stepparent, or her mother has divorced and remarried:

> Mr. and Mrs. John Huntington Smith
> request the honour of your presence
> at the marriage of her daughter
> Mary Alice Towne
> etc.

When the bride's mother is widowed or divorced:

If the bride's mother is giving the wedding alone:

> *Mrs. Bertram Jones*
> *requests the honour of your presence*
> *at the marriage of her daughter*
> *Helen Jeffrey Jones*
> etc.

When the bride is an orphan:

Though good taste does not permit "Miss" or "Mrs." as titles before the bride's name, the three cases that follow are exceptions.

If the bride has no relatives and the wedding is given by friends:

> *Mr. and Mrs. John Neighbor*
> *request the honour of your presence*
> *at the marriage of*
> *Miss Elizabeth Orphan*
> *to*
> *Mr. John Henry Bridegroom*
> etc.

If she has brothers, the oldest one customarily sends out her wedding invitations and announcements in his name. When another relative takes the place of a parent, his or her name is used. The bride whose several sisters or brothers are younger than she may prefer to send her invitations in her own name. The following form might be used:

> *The honour of your presence*
> *is requested*
> *at the marriage of*
> *Miss Elizabeth Orphan*
> *to*
> etc.

When the bride is a widow or divorcée:

Invitations to the marriage of a widow—if she is very young —are sent in the name of her parents exactly as were the invitations for her first wedding, except that her name, instead of being simply "Priscilla," is now written "Priscilla Banks Loring," thus:

Doctor and Mrs. Maynard Banks
request the honour of your presence
at the marriage of their daughter
Priscilla Banks Loring
to
etc.

Engraved invitations are never sent out for the remarriage of a divorcée. However, the fact that the groom has been divorced does not affect the invitation to, or announcement of, his new bride's marriage.

When the bride has a professional name:

When the bride has a career, uses a professional name and therefore has many professional friends to whom she would like to send invitations, but who are unlikely to recognize "Pauline Marie Oldname," the invitations may have her professional name engraved in very small letters and in parentheses under her Christian name:

Pauline Marie
(Pat Bond)

to

Mr. John Frederick Hamilton

This is most practically done by having the name (Pat Bond) added to the plate after the order for regular invitations has been completed. As many invitations as are to go to her professional friends are then struck off with this addition.

When principals are in the services:

On the wedding invitations, the name of a bridegroom whose rank is below Commander or Lt. Colonel is given:

John Strong
2nd Lieutenant, United States Army
or
Ensign, United States Navy

The title of higher ranking officers precedes their name, and the service may or may not be included on the line below.

Colonel John Spring
United States Air Force

The name of a noncommissioned or an enlisted man in the armed forces is engraved John Strong, and Signal Corps, U.S.N.R., or whatever designation is his, in smaller type directly beneath the name on the wedding invitations. Or if the bride chooses to include Pvt. 1st Class, U.S.A., or Apprentice Seaman, U.S.N.R., she may do so.

The name of the bride who is in the armed forces is engraved:

marriage of their daughter
Alice Mary
Lieutenant, Women's Army Corps

When the bride's father is in the armed forces and absent on duty, his name appears as follows:

Major (overseas) and Mrs. John Jones
request the honour of your presence, etc.

An officer in the Reserves does not use his title unless he is on active duty.

High-ranking officers continue to use their title and include their service on the line below with "retired" following the service.

General George Harmon
United States Army, retired

The double-wedding invitation:

Mr. and Mrs. Henry Smartlington

request the honour of your presence

at the marriage of their daughters

Marian Helen

to

Mr. Judson Jones

and

Amy Caroline

to

Mr. Herbert Scott Adams

Saturday, the tenth of November

at four o'clock

Trinity Church

The elder sister's name is given first.

When two brides who are friends wish to have a double wedding, the wording includes the surnames of both parents and brides:

Mr. and Mrs. Henry Smartlington
and
Mr. and Mrs. Arthur Lane
request the honour of your presence
at the marriage of their daughters
Marian Helen Smartlington
to
Mr. Judson Jones
and
Mary Alice Lane
to
Mr. John Gray
etc.

When the bridegroom's family gives the wedding:

When the young bride comes as a stranger from abroad, or from any distance, without her family, the groom's family may give the wedding and send the invitations in their name. This is the only other case where the title "Miss" is used.

Mr. and Mrs. John Henry Pater
request the honour of your presence
at the marriage of
Miss Marie Mersailles
to
their son
John Henry Pater, junior
etc.

Announcements, but not invitations, may be sent from abroad by her own family.

Personal invitations:

The most flattering wedding invitation is a note of invitation personally written by the bride:

Dear Mrs. Kindhart,
Dick and I are to be married at Christ Church Chantry at noon on Thursday the tenth. We both want you and Mr. Kindhart to come to the church and afterward to the reception at the home of my aunt, Mrs. Salde, at Two South Beach Street.
With much love from us both,

Affectionately,
Helen

CARDS FOR RESERVED PEWS

To the family and those intimate friends who are to be seated in specially designated pews, a card (approximately 2 by 3 inches) may be enclosed, with "Pew No.   " engraved and the number filled in by hand. The style matches that of the invitation.

A more usual and less expensive custom is for the mother of the bride and the mother of the bridegroom each to write on her personal visiting card the number of the pew that each intimate friend or member of the family is to occupy.

Pew No. 7

Mrs. John Huntington Smith

600 East Fifty-Seventh Street

A similar card for a reserved front pew and inscribed "Within the ribbon" may be enclosed with the invitations, or "Within the ribbon" may be written on a visiting card and included with the invitation.

Pew cards are often sent, or given in person, after acceptances have been received, when the families of the bride and groom know how many reserved seats will be needed.

ADMISSION CARDS

Except in the case of a wedding held in a cathedral or other church which attracts sightseers, admission cards are no longer used. If it is necessary, a card of approximately 2 by 3 inches is engraved in the same style as the invitations:

Please present this card

at

The Washington Cathedral

Saturday, the first of August

Only the holders of these cards will be admitted to the church at the time of the wedding.

AT-HOME CARDS

At-home cards (slightly smaller than the reception card) may be included with the invitation:

At home

after the fifteenth of November

3842 Olympia Drive

Houston 19, Texas

(For At-Home cards to accompany wedding announcements, see Chapter 4.)

41

Invitations to wedding receptions

INVITATIONS TO A RECEPTION FOLLOWING THE CEREMONY

The invitation to the breakfast or reception following the church ceremony is usually engraved on a card to match the paper and engraving of the church invitation. If the latter is folded for the envelope, the card is a little smaller than half the full size of the invitation. For the smaller invitation that does not fold, it is approximately 2½ to 3 inches high by 3½ to 4 inches wide:

Reception

immediately following the ceremony

Essex County Country Club

West Orange

The favour of a reply is requested
Llewellyn Park, West Orange

Although better suited to the unfolded church invitation because of its larger size, this longer form is also perfectly correct:

Mr. and Mrs. John Huntington Smith

request the pleasure of

Miss Pauline Town's

company at the reception
following the ceremony
43 Park Avenue

R.s.v.p.

R.s.v.p. and R.S.V.P. are both correct. In France and in diplomatic circles the capital letters are the correct form.

Reception at the club of a friend:

When the wedding reception is given at a club through the courtesy of a friend of the hostess, the following announcement is always engraved in the lower right corner: "Through the courtesy of Mrs. John Smith Jones." This is put in the right corner because the left corner is reserved for the R.S.V.P.

INVITATION TO THE RECEPTION ONLY

On occasion, the church ceremony is private and a big reception follows. In these circumstances, the invitations to the ceremony are given orally and general invitations to the reception sent out for a somewhat later hour. The size and style of these invitations are exactly the same as those to the wedding itself:

> *Mr. and Mrs. John Huntington Smith*
> *request the pleasure of*
> [name or names written in] *company*
> *at the wedding breakfast* [or reception]
> *of* [or for] *their daughter*
> *Millicent Jane*
> *and*
> *Mr. Sidney Strothers*
> *Tuesday, the first of November*
> *at half after twelve o'clock*
> *555 Park Avenue*
> *R.S.V.P.*

A RECEPTION FOLLOWING A HOUSE WEDDING

When the reception follows a house wedding, no separate invitation is needed, as it is assumed that those attending the wedding will stay on.

42

Wedding announcements

When the number of guests who can be accommodated at the marriage service or the reception is limited, announcements are sent to those friends of both families who would otherwise have been invited to be present. They require no gift or acknowledgment except what your own interest and impulse suggest. Announcements are never sent to anyone who has been invited to the wedding or the reception. And they should always be sent as soon after the wedding as possible.

CORRECT STYLE AND WORDING

The form (paper, engraving, envelopes) of the wedding announcement is the same as the wedding invitation in almost everything except wording. *(See Chapter 40.)*

Three forms of phrasing are equally correct: "have the honour to announce," "have the honour of announcing," or merely "announce." Although "Tuesday, April 24, 1967" is not incorrect, "Tuesday, the twenty-fourth of April" on one line and "One thousand nine hundred and sixty-seven" on the next is most formal.

𝔐𝔯. 𝔞𝔫𝔡 𝔐𝔯𝔰. 𝔍𝔬𝔥𝔫 𝔉𝔞𝔦𝔯𝔭𝔩𝔞𝔶

have the honour of

announcing the marriage of their daughter

𝔐𝔞𝔡𝔢𝔩𝔢𝔦𝔫𝔢 𝔄𝔫𝔫𝔢

to

𝔐𝔯. 𝔊𝔢𝔬𝔯𝔤𝔢 𝔉𝔬𝔩𝔩𝔬𝔴𝔢𝔰 𝔥𝔦𝔤𝔥𝔰𝔢𝔞𝔰

Ensign United States Navy

Tuesday, the twenty-seventh of March

One thousand nine hundred and sixty-five

Washington, D. C.

The variations in wording necessitated by special circumstances (when the bride has a stepfather, or professional name,
etc.) correspond to the variations in wedding invitations *(see
Chapter 40)* with the following exceptions.

Whenever possible, announcements go out in the name of
the bride's nearest kin, whether they have been present at the
wedding or not. For example, invitations to a wedding given by
the groom's parents carry their names, whereas announcements
of the same marriage carry the names of the bride's parents.

Announcements for a young widow's marriage are the same
as for a first wedding:

Mr. and Mrs. Maynard Banks
announce the marriage of their daughter
Priscilla Banks Loring
etc.

The announcement of the marriage of a widow of maturer
years reads differently:

Mrs. William Phillip Hoyt
and
Mr. Worthington Adams
announce their marriage
on Monday, the second of November
One thousand nine hundred and sixty-five
at Saratoga Springs
New York

The parents of a young divorcée may announce her second marriage in the same form as if she were a widow:

Mr. and Mrs. Harvey Strong
announce the marriage of their daughter
Mary Strong Brooks
etc.

Or a divorcée may, with her husband, announce her own marriage:

Mrs. Strong Brooks
and
Mr. Robert Hanson
announce their marriage
on Saturday, the tenth of May
etc.

The bride who is an orphan and the bridegroom may announce their own marriage this way:

Miss Elizabeth Orphan
and
Mr. John Henry Bridegroom
announce their marriage
etc.

Or, if the wedding was given by a relative or friend, the announcement may be made in this way:

Mr. and Mrs. John Neighbor
announce the marriage of
Miss Elizabeth Orphan
etc.

AT HOME CARDS

When announcements are sent, the At Home notice may be engraved in the lower left-hand corner:

After the first of December
25 Elm Street, Greattown

Or cards in the same form as those used with wedding invitations may be enclosed *(see Chapter 49)*. Either form is perfectly correct. There is a third possibility, also. Because the marriage has already taken place, the card may read:

Mr. and Mrs. John Newlywed
will be at home
after November twelfth
25 Elm Street
Greattown

43

Other formal invitations

All formal invitations are engraved on white cards, either plain or plate-marked like those for wedding receptions, or written by hand on personal note paper.

Formal third-person invitations are sometimes written on paper headed by a very small monogram, but are never engraved on paper headed by an address. If the family has a coat of arms, it or the crest may be embossed without color on engraved invitations.

The size of the card of invitation varies with personal preference. The most graceful proportion is three units in height to four in width, or four high by three wide. The lettering is a matter of personal choice; the plainer the design, the safer. Punctuation is used only when words requiring separation occur on the same line, and in certain abbreviations, such as R.S.V.P. The time is never given as "nine-thirty" but as "half past nine o'clock" or, the more conservative form, "half after nine o'clock."

If the dance or dinner or whatever the entertainment is to be is given at one address and the hostess lives at another, both addresses are given.

BALLS AND DANCES
To a private dance:
The form most often used by fashionable hostesses is this:

Mr. and Mrs. Harold Gilding

request the pleasure of

Miss Sally Waring's

company at a small dance

Monday, the first of January

at ten o'clock

400 Lake Shore Drive

R.s.v.p.

The expression "small dance" is often used no matter what the size of the ball, but it is not absolutely necessary.

Mr. and Mrs. Sidney Oldname

request the pleasure of your company

at a dance

Monday evening, January the third

at ten o'clock

The Fitz - Cherry

Kindly send response to
    Brookmeadows,
    Long Island

Even when the ball is given for a debutante daughter, her name does not necessarily appear, and the above forms may be used.

Other proper invitations in such cases are these:

Mr. and Mrs. Alexander de Puyster

request the pleasure of

Miss Rosalie Grey's

company at a dance in honour of their daughter

Miss Alice de Puyster

Monday, the tenth of January

at ten o'clock

One East Fiftieth Street

R.s.v.p.

Mr. and Mrs. James Town
Miss Pauline Town
request the pleasure of

Mr. and Mrs. Greatlake's

company on Monday, the third of January

at ten o'clock

400 Lake Shore Drive

Dancing
R. s. v. p.

The most formal invitation:

The most formal invitation to a private ball, no matter where it is given, announces merely that Mr. and Mrs. Somebody will be "At Home"—both words written with capital letters; the word "Dancing" is added in the lower left or right corner. It is engraved, usually in script, on a card of white bristol board about 5½ inches wide and 3¾ inches high. Like the wedding invitation, it is plain or it has an embossed crest without color. The precise form is this:

Mr. and Mrs. Davis Jefferson

At Home

Monday, the third of January

at ten o'clock

Town and Country Club

Kindly send reply to
Three Vernon Square

Dancing

(It may be engraved in whatever style of lettering the family prefers.)

The invitation to a public ball:

The word "ball" is rarely used except in an invitation to a public one, or at least a semipublic one, such as may be given by a committee for a charity or by a club or association of some sort. For example:

The Entertainment Committee of the Greenwood Club
requests the pleasure of your company
at a Ball
to be held at the club house
on the evening of Thursday, the seventh of November
at ten o'clock
for the benefit of
The Neighborhood Hospital
Tickets five dollars

Invitations to a debutante assembly:

An invitation to present the debutante at an assembly reads thus:

The Committee of the Westchester Cotillion

invites

Mr. and Mrs. David S. Williams

to present

Miss Penelope Williams

at the Cotillion

on Friday, the ninth of September

at ten o'clock

Shenorock Shore Club

Rye, New York

An invitation to debutantes not being presented at the ball
reads thus:

The Committee of the Mayfair Assembly

has the honor to extend to

Mrs. David S. Williams

an invitation for her daughter

Miss Penelope Williams

to attend

The Mayfair Assembly Dinner Dance

on

New Year's Eve

Saturday, December 31, 1964

Hotel Pierre Roof

nine o'clock

R.s.v.p.

An invitation to other guests invited to the ball:

The Governors of the Tuxedo Club
invite you to subscribe to
The Autumn Ball
to be held at
The Tuxedo Club
on Saturday, the twenty-second of October
Nineteen hundred and sixty-six
at eleven o'clock
Tuxedo Park, New York

R.S.V.P.

These invitations are accompanied by a card stating the
amount of the subscription, where it should be sent, etc. A list
of the debutantes being presented, the committee, and sometimes the patrons, is printed inside the invitation.

INVITATION TO BE A PATRON

When patrons are asked to serve by written invitation, the correct wording is as follows:

> *The Committee of the Midwinter Ball*
> *has the honour to invite*
>
> *to be a Patron of the Ball*
> *for the benefit of*
> *The Children's Hospital*
> *at the Hotel Grand*
> *Friday evening, the thirtieth of October*
> *at nine o'clock*

Usually a card with return envelope is enclosed with the invitation for the convenience of the patron's answer.

INVITATIONS TO RECEPTIONS AND TEAS

Invitations to receptions and teas are somewhat smaller than those to a ball. The words "At Home" with capital letters may be changed to "will be at home" with small letters or "at Home" with a small "a." The time states a beginning and a terminating hour. A man's name appears only on a very unusual occasion. If the tea is given for a debutante, her name is put under that of her mother, and sometimes under that of her sister or the bride of her brother.

To a tea dance:

> *Mrs. Grantham Jones*
> *Miss Muriel Jones*
> *at Home*
> *on Tuesday, the third of December*
> *from four until seven o'clock*
> *The Hilton Hotel*
> *3751 Wildwood Boulevard   Dancing*

Or to a tea for a debutante:

> *Mrs. James Town*
> *Mrs. James Town, junior*
> *Miss Pauline Town*
> *will be at home*
> *Tuesday, the eighth of December*
> *from five until seven o'clock*
> *850 Fifth Avenue*

When a man's name is included:

Mr. Town's name might appear with that of his wife if he were an artist and the reception were given in his studio to view his pictures; or if the reception were given to meet a distinguished guest, such as a bishop or governor, in which case "In honour of the Right Reverend William Ritual" or "To meet His Excellency the Governor of California" would be engraved at the top of the invitation.

Suitable wording for an evening reception:

> *To meet the Honorable George Stevens*
> *Mr. and Mrs. James Town*
> *at Home*
> *Tuesday, the eighth of December*
> *from nine until eleven o'clock*

Note the use of the small *a* and a capital *H*.

THE CARD OF GENERAL INVITATION

Invitations to important entertainments are nearly always especially engraved so that nothing is written except the name of the person invited. But for the hospitable hostess, a card engraved in blank, so that it may serve for dinner, luncheon, dance, reception or whatever she may care to give, is a great help.

Mr. and Mrs. Harold Foster Stevens

request the pleasure of

company at

on

at   o'clock

Two Knob Hill

Already-engraved cards similar to the example below may be purchased at any stationers.

Mr. and Mrs. Charles Watson James

request the pleasure of the company of

Mr. and Mrs. Maxwell

at *Cocktails*

on *Tuesday, December 4th*

at 6 o'clock

R. s. v. p.   *785 Meadow Rd.*

INVITATION BY MORE THAN ONE HOSTESS

The name of the hostess at whose house the party will be is usually put first. If one is a great deal older, her name may

head the list. The invitation should make very clear where the
event is to take place and where the acceptances and regrets
are to be sent. For example, for the luncheon at Mrs. White's
house:

Mrs. Walter David White
Mrs. Henry Edward Black
Mrs. Theodore Jamison Gray
request the pleasure of your company
at luncheon
Tuesday, the tenth of November
at half after one o'clock
123 Sutton Place

R.S.V.P.
Mrs. Walter David White

For the luncheon at a club or hotel:

Mrs. Walter David White
Mrs. Henry Edward Black
Mrs. Thedore Jamison Gray
request the pleasure of your company
at luncheon
Tuesday, the tenth of November
at half after one o'clock
Hotel Pierre

R.S.V.P.
Mrs. Walter David White
123 Sutton Place

INVITATION SENT BY AN ORGANIZATION

For example:

The Alpha Chapter
of
Beta Chi Delta
requests the pleasure of your company
on Monday, the twenty-third of February
at four o'clock
at a tea dance
at the Beta Chi Delta House
2 Campus Row

INVITATION TO COMMENCEMENT

Each school, college and university follows its own established customs for Commencement Week. *(See Chapter 31.)*

Of the varying forms of invitation to commencement exercises sent, the following is the most usual:

The President and Faculty
of Hotchkiss College
request the pleasure of your company
at the Commencement Exercises
on Wednesday morning
the twentieth of June
at eleven o'clock
in the Sterling Gymnasium

HANDWRITTEN INVITATIONS

When the formal invitation to dinner or luncheon is written instead of engraved, note paper stamped with a house address or personal device is used. The wording and spacing follow the engraved models.

Mr. and Mrs. John Lindhost
request the pleasure of
Mr. and Mrs. Robert Gilding Jr's
company at dinner
on Tuesday, the sixth of December,
at eight o'clock.

If the device stamped on the paper does not contain the address, it is written below the hour. A telephone number never appears on a formal invitation. Note: "Jr." is used when appropriate.

An invitation should never be written like this:

Mr. & Mrs. J. Kindhost request the pleasure of Mr. & Mrs. James Town's company at dinner on Tuesday etc

This incorrect example has three faults: (1) Invitations in the third person must follow the prescribed form, and this does not. (2) The writing is crowded against the margins of the note paper. (3) The full name "John" should be used instead of the initial "J."

THE FORMAL INVITATION BY TELEPHONE

It is proper to telephone formal invitations as well as informal ones. Such calls, if placed and received by members of the household staff, follow a prescribed form:

"Is this Lenox 2-0100? Will you please ask Mr. and Mrs. Smith if they will dine with Mrs. Grantham Jones next Tuesday, the tenth, at eight o'clock? Mrs. Jones's telephone number is Regent 4-0011."

The person receiving the call repeats the invitation and writes it down.

The answer:

"Mr. and Mrs. Huntington Smith regret very much that they will be unable to dine with Mrs. Jones on Tuesday, the tenth, as they are engaged for that evening. Please thank Mrs. Jones for asking them."

Or:

"Please tell Mrs. Jones that Mr. and Mrs. Smith will dine with her on Tuesday, the tenth, at eight o'clock, with pleasure."

44

Informal invitations

With the exception of invitations to house parties, those sent to out-of-town guests, and those requiring a certain amount of formality, the invitation by note is almost a thing of the past. On informal occasions, the telephone is used almost exclusively. Be perfectly clear, however, about dates and hour and leave your guests in no doubt about what is intended. If you feel that a written invitation is needed, you have a choice of several possibilities.

VISITING-CARD INVITATIONS

For an informal dance, for a tea to meet a guest, or for bridge, a lady may use her ordinary visiting card. *(See Chapter 47.)* Because the Post Office will not accept very small envelopes, a practical size should be ordered for mailing. Although larger, they match the card in color and texture.

The following examples are correct in every detail—including the abbreviations; they are written in black ink.

To meet
Miss Millicent Gordon

Mrs. John Kindhart

Tues. Jan. 7
Dancing at 9 o'ck.

1350 Madison Avenue

Wed. Jan. 8.
Bridge at 2. o'ck.

Mrs. John Kindhart

R. s. v. p.   1350 Madison Avenue

INFORMALS

The use of informals (small folding cards, described in Chapter 47) for invitations is correct and practical. When the card is engraved with your name:

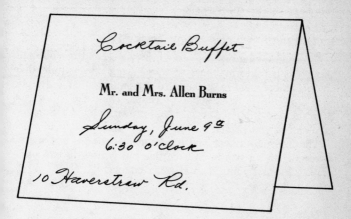

Cocktail Buffet

Mr. and Mrs. Allen Burns

Sunday, June 9th
6:30 o'clock

10 Haverstraw Rd.

If the card is monogrammed or unmarked, the informal invitation includes your name. If the card is going to a close friend, the signature need only be the first name, but to others you must include the last name.

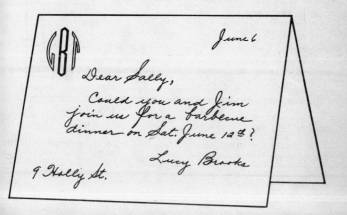

June 6

Dear Sally,
Could you and Jim
join us for a barbecue
dinner on Sat. June 12th?

Lucy Brooks

9 Holly St.

THE "SINGLE NOTE" CARD

A useful variation of the informal is an unfolded card, about 4½ by 3½ inches, with the address engraved in the upper right corner and the name slightly above the center, leaving room beneath for the message.

HANDWRITTEN NOTES AND ANSWERS

Informal invitations are written in the second person, and, though called informal because they have greater latitude than the prescribed pattern of the third-person invitation and reply, they too follow a fairly definite formula. The colon is not used after the salutation in a social note—either no punctuation or a comma, as you prefer.

The informal dinner and luncheon invitation is not spaced according to set words on each line but written in two paragraphs. From a younger to an older couple:

Jan. 2, 1964

Dear Mrs. Steele,
   Will you and Mr. Steele dine with us on Thursday, the seventh of January, at eight o'clock?
   Hoping so much to see you then, I am

Very sincerely,
Caroline Robinson Town

Or to a woman engaged to a man unknown to the writer of this invitation:

Jan. 2, 1964

Dear Phyllis,
   Will you and your fiancé lunch with us this coming Saturday, at one o'clock?
   Looking forward to meeting him,

Affectionately,
Caroline Town

Acceptance:

Dear Mrs. Town,
   We would be delighted to dine with you on Thursday the seventh at eight o'clock.
   Thanking you for your kind thought of us,

Sincerely yours,
Jane Steele

Regret:

Dear Mrs. Town,
    We are so sorry that we cannot accept your kind invitation for Saturday because of another engagement.
    With many thanks for thinking of us, and I will bring John over to meet you soon.

                                        Sincerely,
                                        Phyllis Steele

(For invitations to a house party, see Chapter 29; to an engagement party, see Chapter 32.)

A BACHELOR'S INVITATIONS

The bachelor's invitations are the same as those sent out by a hostess. In giving a party of any size he may write on his visiting card.

Saturday, April 7.
at 4. o'clk.

Mr. Anthony Dauber

To hear Tonini play.

Park Studio

45

Recalling and requesting invitations

WITHDRAWING AN INVITATION

If because of illness or for some other reason, invitations have to be recalled, the following forms are correct. They are always printed, because there is no time for engraving.

> *Owing to the sudden illness of their daughter*
> *Mr. and Mrs. John Huntington Smith*
> *are obliged to recall their invitations*
> *for Tuesday, the tenth of June*

When an engagement is broken off after the wedding invitations have been issued:

> *Mr. and Mrs. Benjamin Nottingham*
> *announce that the marriage of their daughter*
> *Mary Katherine*
> *to*
> *Mr. Jerrold Atherton*
> *will not take place*

REQUESTING AN INVITATION

Ordinarily one never asks for an invitation for oneself anywhere. But when regretting an invitation, it is quite proper to explain that you are expecting weekend guests. Ordinarily the hostess-to-be says, "I'm sorry!" But if she is having a big buffet lunch or a tea or cocktail party, she may say, "Do bring them. We will be delighted to have them!"

An invitation for any general entertainment may be requested for a stranger—especially for a house guest—still more especially for a man.

> Dear Mrs. Eminent,
>
> My nephew, David Park, is staying with us. May he come to your dance on Friday?
>
> > Very sincerely yours,
> >
> > Caroline Robinson Town

If the nephew had been a niece instead, Mrs. Town would have added, "If it will be inconvenient for you to include her, please do not hesitate to say so." This gives Mrs. Eminent a chance to answer that since her list of men was rather short she would be glad to have Mary come if Mrs. Town can find a man to escort her. A young girl may ask her hostess if she may bring a man to her dance.

46

Acceptances and regrets

The form of acceptance or regret depends upon the form of the invitation received, for the degree of formality or informality must be the same. The telephone presents no problems. For the handwritten answer, there are formulas that are invariably used.

THE FORMAL ACCEPTANCE OR REGRET

Whether the invitation is to a dance, a dinner, or whatever, the answer is identical save for the name of the occasion. (In the following form you may substitute "a dance," etc., for "dinner.")

> *Mr. and Mrs. Donald Lovejoy*
> *accept with pleasure*
> *the kind invitation of*
> *Mr. and Mrs. William Jones Johnson, Jr.*
> *for dinner*
> *on Monday, the tenth of December*
> *at eight o'clock*

The formula for regret:

> *Mrs. and Mrs. Timothy Kerry*
> *regret that they are unable to accept*
> *the kind invitation of*
> *Mr. and Mrs. Harvey Brent Smith*
> *for Monday, the tenth of December*

In accepting an invitation, the day and hour are always repeated. But in declining an invitation this is not necessary.

To more than one hostess:
If the names of two or more hostesses appear on an invitation, the envelope is addressed to the one at whose house the party is to take place; or if it is to be at a club or hotel, to the name and address indicated below the R.S.V.P. (Without such indication, you must address it to all of them at the hotel or club.)

But when you write your answer, you repeat the same order of names that appeared on the invitation, no matter how the envelope is to be addressed:

> *Mrs. Donald Lovejoy*
> *accepts with pleasure*
> *the kind invitation of*
> *Mrs. White and*
> *Mrs. Black and*
> *Mrs. Grey*
> *for Tuesday, the tenth of November*
> *at half after one o'clock*

TO A WEDDING

An invitation to only the church requires no answer (unless the invitation is a personally written note). An invitation to the reception or breakfast is answered on the first page of a sheet of full-sized letter paper or on fold-over note paper; although it is written by hand, the spacing of the words must be followed as though they were engraved.

Acceptance:

> *Mr. and Mrs. Robert Gilding, Jr.*
> *accept with pleasure*
> *Mr. and Mrs. Smith's*
> *kind invitation for*
> *Tuesday, the first of June*

Regret:

> *Mr. and Mrs. Richard Brown*
> *regret that they are unable to accept*
> *Mr. and Mrs. Smith's*
> *kind invitation for*
> *Tuesday, the first of June*

The alternate form, "The kind invitation of," is equally correct.

Combination acceptance and regret:

It is entirely proper for a wife or husband to take it for granted that either one alone will be welcome at a general wedding reception and to send an acceptance worded as follows:

> *Mrs. John Brown*
> *accepts with pleasure*
> *Mr. and Mrs. Smith's*
> *kind invitation for*
> *Saturday, the tenth of June*
> *but regrets that*
> *Mr. Brown*
> *will be absent at that time*
> or
> *will be unable to attend*

If the wife could not attend, the wording would merely transpose Mr. and Mrs.

FORMULAS FOR OTHER OCCASIONS
To an organization:

> *Miss Mary Jones*
> *accepts with pleasure*
> *the kind invitation of*
> *The Alpha Chapter*
> *of*
> *Beta Chi Delta*
> *for Monday afternoon, February 23rd*

To a committee:

If the name of the committee or its organization is long or complicated, you may write your reply in the following form:

> *Mr. and Mrs. Geoffrey Johnson*
> *accept with pleasure*
> *your kind invitation*
> *for a Ball*
> *on Saturday, the first of January*

To a multiple debut:

> *Doctor and Mrs. Ronald Graham*
> *Miss Joan Graham*
> *accept with pleasure*
> *your kind invitation*
> *for a dinner dance*
> *Saturday, February 10th*
> *at nine o'clock*

INFORMAL REPLIES

When an invitation is sent on a visiting card or an informal, the reply may be telephoned or written briefly on your own card.

Visiting-card replies:

> *Accepts with pleasure!*
> *Wednesday at 4.*
>
> Mrs. Robert Gilding, junior
>
> 14 Water Street

> *Sincere regrets*
> *Wed. Jan. 8*
>
> Mr. and Mrs. Henry Osborn

Informals:

In replying on an informal, use the same degree of formality as was used in the invitation.

EPL

June 4

Dear Sue

We'd love to come to dinner on June 10 at 8:00.

Thanks so much
Betsy

Brook Street   Holyoke   Mass.

So sorry we can't make it on the sixth. We'll be at the Cape.

Gloria

If your informal is engraved as a visiting card:

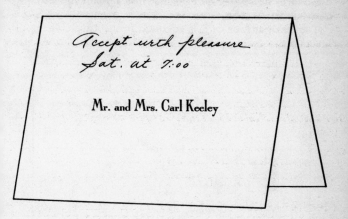

Accept with pleasure
Sat. at 7:00

Mr. and Mrs. Carl Keeley

On a plain informal:

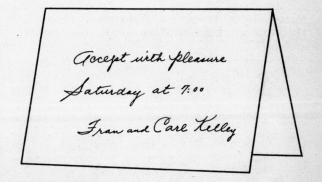

Accept with pleasure
Saturday at 7:00
Fran and Carl Kelley

ANSWER CARDS

Regrettably the custom of sending "answer cards" with invitations to debut parties and subscription dances is too widespread to be ignored. It arose out of sheer necessity because teen-agers appeared at parties without having answered the invitation sent to them. Today, when parties are served and food prepared by catering services, a hostess must be able to tell them the exact number of guests expected. Therefore, while we deplore the lack of good manners which makes sending these cards necessary, we recognize that it seems the only way to obtain the answers.

The small answer card is engraved in the same style as the invitation:

```
┌─────────────────────────────────────────────┐
│                                               │
│      Mr. Allen Fordyce                        │
│                                               │
│      ☐  accepts                               │
│                                               │
│      ☐  regrets                               │
│                                               │
│              Friday, January second           │
│              Columbus Country Club            │
│                                               │
└─────────────────────────────────────────────┘
```

Most invitations include a self-addressed return envelope.

Having returned the card, the receiver does not send a formal reply.

47

Visiting cards, informals and business cards

VISITING CARDS

Nowadays, the visiting card (in its matching envelope) has taken the place of the written note of invitation to informal parties of every description. A card with "With deepest sympathy" written at the top is enclosed with flowers sent to a funeral, or it may be left at the home of the deceased. They are also enclosed with presents. (Most shops provide small white cards and envelopes if you do not have your own with you.)

A married woman's card is usually 3 to 3½ inches wide and 2¼ to 2½ inches high. (Very young girls use a small card.) A man's card is narrower: from 3 to 3¼ inches long and 1¼ to 1⅝ inches high. The cards are white or cream-white glazed or unglazed bristol board of medium thickness, and they are not plate-marked. (Those made of thin parchment paper are convenient if a greater quantity must be carried.)

Either shaded Roman or script is good form. Matching envelopes, large enough to obey postal regulations, may be ordered at the same time.

People in cities often have the address in the lower right corner. People with both town and country houses occasionally have separate cards for each.

Initials are used only when names are awkwardly long. A man may have his cards engraved "Mr. John H. T. Smith" or "Mr. J. H. Titherington Smith." His wife's card uses the same form.

A married woman's card (approximately 3¼ inches by 2¼ inches):

Mrs. John Foster Hughes

"Mr. and Mrs." cards:

Mr. and Mrs. John Foster Hughes

14 Willow Road

A married man's card: A man's card is engraved with his title, Doctor or Mr., even though he has "junior" after his name. (Doctor is preferred to Dr.) The size is 3¼ inches by 1½ inches.

Mr. John Foster Hughes, Jr.

A widow's name: A widow always continues to use her husband's Christian names: Mrs. John Hunter Titherington Smith (or Mrs. J. H. Titherington Smith), but never Mrs. Sarah Smith. If a widow's son has the name of his father, the widow may add "Sr." to her name when her son marries, especially if they live in the same village where no street address is used.

John Smith, Jr., John Smith, 2nd, and their wives: The fact that a man's name has "Jr." added at the end in no way takes the place of "Mr." His card is engraved "Mr. John Hunter Smith, Jr." and his wife's "Mrs. John Hunter Smith, Jr." "Junior" may be engraved in full; when it is, it is not spelled with a capital *j*. John, second, or John, third, may have 2nd or 3rd after their names, but II or III in Roman numerals is preferable.

It is improper, unless he has a good reason, for a man to continue adding "Jr." to his name after the death of his father or grandfather. But he may wish to retain the *Jr.* if he lives in the same locality as his mother and his wife might be confused with the older Mrs. Smith, or if the widow, who is perhaps the young stepmother of the son, does not wish to be known as *Sr.* If a father has been so celebrated that the son cannot possibly take his place (and sometimes for other professional reasons), it may be practical for the son to keep his identity as junior.

The same considerations apply in continuing to call a boy "John Smith, 3rd" if John Smith, Jr. (or 2nd) has died. *Junior* always means the son—or possibly the grandson—of a man of the same name; *2nd* means the nephew or cousin of a man of the same name. The following diagram makes the order clear.

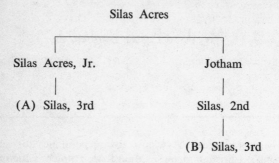

Because there is no way to distinguish between (A) and (B), the latter is usually given a different middle name and is christened Silas John Acres. Since this changes the name, he has no suffix, and his son could be called Silas John Acres, Jr.

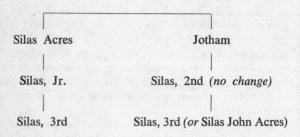

A divorcée's card: Some women, if they have no children and if their divorce has been a bitter one, prefer to give up their married name entirely and return to being "Miss Susan Coleman." This is permissible. The proper name for a divorcée, however, is her maiden name combined with her husband's surname. Miss Susan Coleman, who is divorced from Franklin Butler, becomes Mrs. Coleman Butler, and her cards are engraved in this form.

A professional woman's card: A woman who has earned a professional title uses her title or professional name in public, while in private life she uses the name of her husband. A spinster who is a practicing physician uses the title of Doctor socially as well as professionally. (If she is a doctor of philosophy, she calls herself "Doctor" only in a classroom or when she is introduced as a speaker.)

The solution for a woman who is a medical doctor is to have two cards—one for business, engraved "Helen Corbin, M.D." or "Doctor Helen Corbin," and one for social use, engraved "Mrs. Richard Ford Corbin." On a "Mr. and Mrs." card, she remains "Mrs." If her husband is also a doctor, the card reads "Dr. and Mrs. Richard Ford Corbin."

A boy's card: A boy never puts "Mr." on his cards until he leaves school or becomes eighteen: many use cards without "Mr." until they have finished college.

Cards of a young girl: A young girl's cards, after she is fourteen, have "Miss" before her name: "Miss Sarah Smith," not "Miss Sally Smith."

Titles on cards: A doctor, a clergyman, or a military officer in active service, and holders of title-bestowing offices all have their cards engraved with their titles: Doctor Henry Gordon (an M.D.); The Reverend William Goode; Colonel Thomas Doyle; Judge Horace Rush; Senator James Widelands. A person holding high degrees does not add their letters to his name, and his cards are not engraved "Professor." The double card reads Doctor and Mrs. Henry Gordon, Judge and Mrs. Horace Rush, etc. It is always best to engrave titles in full.

Card for a governor:
> *The Governor of Nevada*

on a card slightly larger or more nearly square than an ordinary man's card.

Card of a mayor:
> *The Mayor of Chicago*

or, if he prefers,

> *Mr. John Lake*
> *Mayor of Chicago*

A diplomat uses his title and United States of America rather than America or American. Titles of courtesy have no place either in a signature or on a visiting card: The American title of courtesy, "The Honorable," is never correct on a card.

The professional card of a doctor or surgeon is James Smith, M.D. His social card is Doctor or Dr. James Smith, as he prefers. (Dr. is not incorrect; but Doctor is somewhat better form.)

(For the use of visiting cards as invitations, see Chapter 44; as messages of condolence, see Chapter 33.)

INFORMALS

The small fold-over cards known as informals are convenient when you want, for example, to write a very brief note but one that requires more space than is afforded by a visiting card. If you wish, you may have them engraved. Or you may simply have your monogram in the upper left corner.

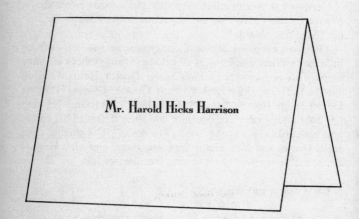

Mr. Harold Hicks Harrison

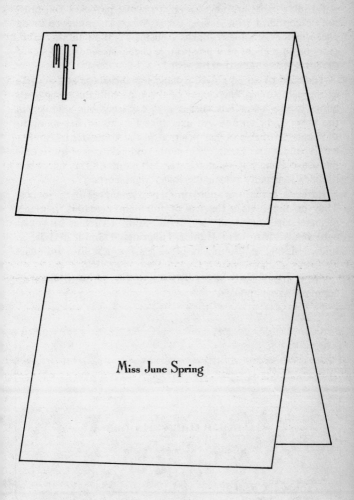

Informals are correct and practical for invitations *(see Chapter 44)*, but they cannot substitute for visiting cards when you make a formal call. They are enclosed with a gift only if you wish to write a personal message on the inner page.

BUSINESS AND PROFESSIONAL CARDS

Business cards are never used for social purposes and must not be confused with visiting cards. When an employee or an executive of a company makes a business call on another company or on a client or a prospective client, he sends in his card or leaves it as a record of his visit.

The card of an employee usually has the name and address of the company in the center of the card with the employee's name in the lower left corner and the telephone number in the lower right corner. An executive has his or her name in the center with his or her position in the company in smaller letters under the name. The name and address of the company are then put in the lower left corner. The telephone number is usually put in the lower right corner.

Business cards are approximately 3½ inches by 2 inches. They do not require the use of full names; that is, a man's business card may read "Mr. John Smith" (whereas his social card reads "Mr. John Hunter Titherington Smith") if he is known simply as "John Smith" in his business life and signs his letters in that form.

Professional cards differ from business cards in that no company name appears.

HAROLD HICKS HARRISON

500 WALL STREET
NEW YORK, N. Y.   MARket 6-7272

PART TEN

PROTOCOL IN OFFICIAL CIRCLES

48

An invitation to the White House

FORMAL

An invitation to lunch or dine at The White House is a command and automatically cancels any other engagement not of the utmost importance. The reply is written by hand. It is mailed the day the invitation is received or delivered by hand to The White House. The reason for refusing such an invitation must be stated in the note of regret—unavoidable absence from Washington, the recent death of a close relative or actual illness.

The correct forms for replies are:

Mr. and Mrs. Richard Worldly
have the honor to accept
the kind invitation of
The President and Mrs. Washington
for dinner on Thursday, the eighth of May
at eight o'clock

Mr. and Mrs. Robert Franklin
regret extremely
that owing to Mr. Franklin's illness
they will be unable to accept
the kind invitation of
The President and Mrs. Johnson
for dinner on Friday, the first of May

The note to a disappointed hostess:

Mr. and Mrs. Richard Worldly
regret extremely
that an invitation to The White House
prevents their keeping
their previous engagment for
Tuesday, the first of December

INFORMAL

Informal invitations to dinner or luncheon at The White House may be sent by letters, telegrams or telephone messages from the President's secretary or his wife's secretary. The replies are sent in the same form to whoever issued the invitations and written on personal stationery.

A typical invitation:

Dear Mrs. Heathcote,
Mrs. Harrison has asked me to invite you to have lunch with her at The White House on Thursday, the sixteenth of May. Luncheon will be at one o'clock.
                              Yours truly,
                              Eleanor Smithers
                              Secretary to Mrs. Harrison

The reply reads:

Dear Miss Smithers,
Will you please tell Mrs. Harrison that I shall be delighted to lunch with her at The White House on Thursday, the sixteenth of May. Thank you very much.
                              Sincerely,
                              Frances Heathcote

To the luncheon Mrs. Heathcote wears a dress that she might wear to any similar gathering; a hat and gloves are obligatory.

DINNER AT THE WHITE HOUSE

An engraved invitation to The White House means black tie unless white tie is specified on the invitation. For black tie the men wear stiff shirts and collars and a dinner jacket. Women wear evening clothes, and if it is a white-tie dinner, long gloves.

All the names of guests expected at The White House are posted with the guards at the gate. You announce your name and wait a few seconds until you are recognized.

After the guests arrive, the President and his wife enter and speak to each guest and shake hands. Guests, of course, remain standing.

At a formal dinner, the President goes into the dining room first with the highest ranking woman guest. His wife follows with the highest ranking man guest.

DETAILS OF WHITE HOUSE ETIQUETTE

The following details represent the conventional pattern followed and adapted by each administration.

When you are invited to The White House, you must arrive several minutes before the hour specified so that you may be standing in the drawing room when the President makes his entry. The President, followed by his wife, enters, makes a tour of the room, shaking hands with each guest. When your turn comes, you bow. If he talks to you, you address him as "Mr. President." In a long conversation you vary "Mr. President" with "Sir" occasionally. You call the wife of the President "Mrs. Washington" and treat her as you would any formal hostess. You do not sit down as long as either the President or his wife remains standing. No one leaves until after the President has withdrawn from the room. Then the guests bid each other good night and leave promptly.

Requests to see the President on a business matter are made through one of the Presidential aides—the one closest to the subject you wish to discuss—or through your congressman. For a business appointment with the President, you always arrive a few minutes ahead of the appointed time. If a buzzer rings when you are in a corridor, an attendant will ask you to step behind a closed door. The buzzer means that the

President or members of the family are leaving or entering. This precaution is for their safety and privacy.

Don't smoke unless you are invited to.

Do not take a present unless you have cleared it with an aide, otherwise the Secret Service men may become alarmed.

Nor should you *send* anything to The White House without receiving permission from his secretary or one of his aides.

49

The flag of the United States

GENERAL RULES

The following rules and customs are followed to show our respect for our flag.

Every day in the year between sunrise and sunset is a proper time to fly the flag; although customarily it is not flown in inclement weather unless a particular occasion requires its display. It may also be displayed at night as part of a patriotic display.

On Memorial (or Decoration) Day, May 30th, the flag is displayed at half-staff until noon and at full staff thereafter till sunset. Flag Day is June 14th.

The flag is never used as decoration on a portion of a costume or athletic uniform, as embroidery on cushions, scarves or handkerchiefs, or on paper napkins or boxes. It is never so used that objects may be placed on it or over it. When the flag is used in the unveiling of a statue or monument, it is never used as a covering of the object to be unveiled. It is unlawful to use the flag in a registered trademark which comprises "the flag, coat of arms, or other insignia of

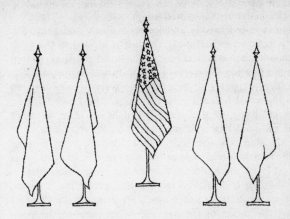

the United States or any simulation thereof." It is never displayed in connection with advertising of any kind. For festoons, rosettes or other draperies, bunting of blue (uppermost), white and red is used, but never the flag itself.

DISPLAYING THE FLAG

When displayed over the middle of a street, the flag is suspended vertically with the union (the blue field) to the north in an east-west street, or to the east in a north-south street.

When displayed with another flag from crossed staffs, the

flag of the United States is on the right (the flag's own right) and its staff in front of the staff of the other flag.

The flag is raised briskly and lowered slowly and solemnly.

When it is flown at half-mast, the flag is hoisted to the peak for a moment, then lowered to the half-mast position. Before lowering the flag for the day, it is again raised to the peak.

When flags of states or cities or pennants of societies are flown on the same halyard with the flag of the United States, the latter is always at the peak. When flown from adjacent staffs, the national flag is hoisted first and lowered last.

When the flag is suspended over a sidewalk from a rope, extending from house to pole at the edge of the sidewalk, it is hoisted out from the building, toward the pole, union first.

When the flag is displayed from a staff projecting horizontally or at an angle from a windowsill, balcony or the front of a building, the union of the flag should go clear to the peak of the staff (except when at halfmast).

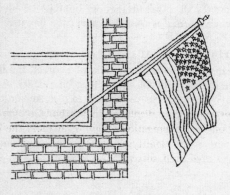

When the flag is used to cover a casket, it is so placed that the union is at the head and over the left shoulder. The flag is never lowered into the grave or allowed to touch the ground.

When the flag is displayed in a manner other than flown from a staff, it should be flat, not tucked or draped, whether indoors or out. When displayed vertically against a wall or in a window, the union is uppermost and to the observer's left.

When carried in a procession with another flag or flags, the American flag is either on the marching right or, when there is a line of other flags, in the center of that line.

When a number of flags of states or cities are grouped and displayed from staffs, our national flag is at the center or at the highest point of the group. If the flags of two or more nations are displayed, they are flown from separate staffs of the same height and the flags are of approximately equal size. International usage forbids the display of the flag of one nation above that of another nation in time of peace.

When the flag is used in a church, on the chancel or on a platform, it is placed on a staff on the clergyman's right, other flags on his left. When displayed in the body of the church, the flag is on the congregation's right as it faces the chancel.

When used as an identifying symbol on an automobile, it is flown on a small staff affixed on the end of the front bumper, on the right looking forward and within the line of the fender. When used this way, the staff should be tall enough so that the flag clears the car hood. Alternately, a small flag may be flown from the radiator cap. If the flag has become soiled or wind-torn, replace it promptly.

The flag is *never* hung upside down except as a signal of distress.

CARE OF THE FLAG

Every precaution should be taken to prevent the flag from becoming soiled or torn. Do not permit it to touch the ground or water or a floor, and in handling it do not let it brush against other objects. If it gets wet, hang it smoothly until dry; never roll or fold it while still damp.

Flags should be drycleaned, not washed.

PART ELEVEN

GOOD MANNERS FOR EVERY DAY

50

On the telephone

THE BUSINESS TELEPHONE

Answering the office phone:

When telephone calls go through a switchboard, the operator usually answers the ring by giving the name of the company, and sometimes adds some such greeting as "ABC Company, good morning." When the call is transferred or goes directly through, the person answering identifies himself and his department: "Mr. Hugo, accounting department." If answering for someone else, as a secretary does, she gives her employer's name as well as her own: "Mr. Carlson's office, Miss Norton speaking." If her employer is not in, or if she wishes to protect him from unnecessary calls, she offers to help the caller if she can or, if not, take a message: "He's not available at the moment. May I take a message?" or "He's attending a meeting this morning. Could I help you?" If he is in his office, she asks, "May I tell him who is calling?" With an evasive caller, she may have to ask for his name directly: "Who is calling, please?"

She should keep a pad and pencil next to the phone so that she can take a message.

Placing a call:

As soon as your call is answered, identify yourself, and unless the person you are calling knows you well, name your organization. "This is Robert Kramer, of the Hobbs Company. May I speak to Mr. Hughes?"

To a woman, a salesman announces himself correctly as "This is Mr. Sales of the Blank Company." But to a gentleman, he may omit the "Mr."

A young woman in business says, "This is Miss Caesar of the Wheel Tyre Co."

A most discourteous telephone habit is that of the business man who tells his secretary to call Mr. Jones and then is not waiting to take the call. The secretary, for example, dials the number; a voice announces, "A. B. Jones Company"; the secretary says, "Mr. Brown is calling Mr. Jones." Promptly Mr. Jones says, "Hello, Brown!" only to hear a secretary explain, "Mr. Brown is busy on another wire. He'll be with you in a moment." If you have placed a call, do not pick up another incoming call until you have finished your business with the person you called first.

THE TELEPHONE IN THE HOME

"Hello" correct at home:

The correct way to answer a house telephone is still "Hello." In all big cities, telephones are rung so persistently by every type of stranger who wants to sell something or to ask a favor that many prominent people keep their personal telephone numbers unlisted. The last thing that they want to do, therefore, is to announce, "Miss Star speaking." It is far more practical to say "Hello" and let the one calling ask for Miss Star. If she herself answers, a friend recognizing her voice says, "Hello, Mary. This is Kate."

Who is calling, please?:

When the telephone in the home is answered by someone other than the head of the household, the response to "May I speak to Mrs. Brown, please?" is usually, "Just a moment, please." If, however, Mrs. Brown has told the maid (or a child) that she can only take certain calls, the one answering says, "Mrs. Brown can't come to the phone just now: may I have your name and she will call you as soon as she can?"

If the caller refuses to leave a message or give his name, he need not expect Mrs. Brown to speak to him.

Giving one's name:

When talking with strangers, titles are always used, but in other situations the following rules hold good: An older person announcing herself or himself to one who is much younger says, "This is Mrs. Elder" or "Miss Spinster" or "Mr. Elder."

A young lady, whether married or single, says, "This is Marie Manners," or to one whom she knows socially, but who is not on a first-name-calling basis, "Hello, Mrs. Knox? This is Marie Manners." Mrs. Knox answers, "Good morning, Mrs. Manners!"

A gentleman calling a lady always says, "This is George Smartling"—never "Mr. Smartling".

If a young man calls a friend and the answering voice is that of a friend or a member of the friend's family, he says, "This is Jim Brown" or "This is Jim." If the voice is that of a maid he says, "This is Mr. James Brown. May I speak to Mr. Gray?"

Invitations by telephone:

When Mrs. Jones issues an invitation by telephone, she says simply: "Is that you, Mrs. Smith [or Sarah]? This is Alice Jones [or Alice, if the other is an intimate friend]. Will you and your husband [or John] dine with us next Tuesday?"

Mrs. Smith: "I'm so sorry, we can't. We are busy that night." Or "We'd love to" and repeats, "Next Tuesday at eight," to be sure there is no misunderstanding of date or time.

Invitations for a weekend visit are often telephoned: "Hello, Ethel. This is Alice. Will you and Arthur come for the weekend on the sixteenth?" "The sixteenth? That's two weeks from tomorrow. We'd love to!" (If Mrs. Jones is not telephoning herself and the message is given by or received by a butler or a maid, see the discussion of the formal invitation by telephone, Chapter 43.)

It is a bad habit to preface an invitation with "Hello, John. Are you going to be busy Monday afternoon?" This puts John in an awkward position. If he answers, "No," he may feel he has to accept the invitation that follows whether he wants to or not. If he answers, "I have an engagement," he may lose

out on an attractive invitation. A young woman who says sh
has an engagement and is then told, "Too bad you can't con
because John Brilliant was looking forward to meeting you
cannot change her mind without being rude to all concerne

Three important don'ts:

1) When the number you get is evidently wrong, don't as
"What number is this?" Ask instead, "Is this Main 2-3456?"

2) Don't answer and then say, "Wait a minute," becau:
the doorbell is ringing or the pot is boiling over; say instea
"I'll call you back in a few minutes!" And do so.

3) Don't let too young a child answer the telephone. Th
caller's message may be garbled beyond recognition.

LONG-DISTANCE CALLS

When making a long-distance call, do not shout—amplifie
on the circuits will step up your voice all the way. On ove
seas calls, wait for the other person to finish speaking befo
you start. It is a one-way-at-a-time circuit, and if both spea
at once, both are shut off until one or the other stops talkin

If you call long distance often, especially in these days ·
direct dialing, a telephone timer, a small second-countir
gadget that rings a bell before each three minutes, is a mu
for economy's sake. If you are making a personal call, yo
may ask the operator, when you put in your call, to interru
when the three minutes are up.

ON A PARTY LINE

When it is realized that the usual number of families sha
ing a party line is four (and the maximum ten) and that :
long as one person is talking, no outside call can reach ar
other person on that line, the consideration required of eac
sharer is obvious. For this reason the telephone company h
taken pains to make—and expects the subscribers to keep
the following rules on a party line: When you find the li
in use, hang up for three minutes before signaling again. I
an emergency, call out clearly "EMERGENCY!" and the
"Our barn is on fire," or "Johnny's had an accident," or wha
ever it is. But unless all on the line hang up, your telephone
cut off.

The operator is not permitted to cut in on a busy wire. B

a busy signal goes on and you must get through for some
reason—such as missing a train or plane—ask for the super-
visor of the station called and briefly explain. At her discre-
tion, she may then cut in, and ask those talking to hang up.

PAYING FOR YOUR CALLS

Many guests mistakenly hesitate to proffer payment for
their calls. The definite rule is this: Should one be obliged to
make a single local call, one would not ordinarily offer payment for it, but one must pay for every long-distance call. Request in advance that the operator let you know the time and
charges upon completion of your call. Then leave this amount
with a slip, giving the date and the number called. Or if one
has made many calls during a long stay, the complete list of
telephone calls and telegrams sent, with the amounts of each
and their total, may be handed to the hostess and paid for
when one says good-bye. No matter how rich the host may be,
it is correct to pay this debt.

If a guest does not offer to pay for his long distance calls,
it is quite correct—and fair to him and to you—to give him
an itemized bill for them.

THE TELEPHONE COURTESY TEST

The number of times you can answer "Yes" to the following questions will show you how good your telephone man-
ers are:

1. Do you make sure of the correct number so as not to
risk disturbing strangers by "calling from memory"?

2. Do you make conversations with busy people as brief as
possible?

3. When calling friends who do not recognize your voice,
do you resist playing a game of "Guess who?" and announce
yourself promptly?

4. Do you try to time your calls so as not to interfere with
the occupations of those you call most often?

5. Do you make business calls well before the close of
office hours, especially if calling a person you know is a com-
muter?

6. In a business office, do you explain to personal friends
inclined to talk at length that you will call them after hours?

7. Do you treat wrong-number calls as a mutual incon-

venience and answer, "Sorry, wrong number," in a tone o
polite sympathy instead of showing ill-tempered annoyance

8. On a dial telephone, do you always wait for the dial tone

9. When the number you are calling is not answere
quickly, do you wait long enough for someone to lay asid
what she may be doing before you hang up?

10. Do you, when making a number of calls on a part
line, space them so that others on the line may have a chanc
to use their telephones?

51

Calls and callers

The custom of making formal calls is pretty much a thin
of the past. But certain circumstances still require them. I
Washington, members of diplomatic or military circles ex
change calls. Members of the miltary or the diplomatic servic
arriving at a new post call on their superiors. Calls are ex
changed between officers on military posts.

In addition, there are certain visits that all of us must make
A visit of condolence is paid at once to a friend when a deat
occurs in the immediate family. You ask if Mrs. Jackson fee
like seeing you and, if you are admitted, you ask if there i
anything you can do. If you barely know the family you ma
simply leave your card with "With deepest sympathy" writte
at the top. A lady does not call on a man, but writes him
note of sympathy. *(See also Chapter 32.)*

When going to see, or inquire about, a friend who has bee
very ill, it is thoughtful to take a gift of a book or fruit c
flowers or perhaps, if you know of something she likes an
is allowed to eat, you may take something from your kitcher

Everyone invited to a wedding may call upon the bride o

er return from the honeymoon. When a man marries a girl
rom a distant place, his friends and neighbors should go to
ee her as soon as she is at home.

A visit of congratulation is paid a new mother, and, of
ourse, it is always very pleasing if you can take a present to
ne baby.

OW TO MAKE A FIRST VISIT

In large cities, neighbors seldom call on each other. But
vhen strangers move into a neighborhood in a small town or
n the country, nearby residents usually call on them. The
ewcomers wait for the old residents to call on them, but by
ppearing friendly and outgoing they may hasten this "break-
ng the ice."

When a stranger moves in near you, you call, and if the
ady herself opens the door—or you find her sitting on her
orch—you say, "How do you do—I'm Nancy Jones, I live in
ne brick house across the street." The new neighbor says,
How kind of you to come to see me!" and invites you into
er living room or asks you to join her on the porch. After
en to fifteen minutes, you usually leave, unless your hostess
ays, "Oh, do stay a little longer." When you are ready to go,
ay, "Do come and see me soon!" The new neighbor says,
I'll be glad to," and both of you make your farewells.

Returning a first visit:

First visits should be returned with considerable punctuality.
Vhen hospitality is shown you by two or more hostesses to-
ether, you are indebted to both or all equally, if you know
nem equally. If you know only one of the hostesses, you need
ot return the hospitality of the other (or others) unless the
pportunity arises. When returning the hospitality of these
everal hostesses, it is never necessary that you invite them
ogether.

ISITING THE SICK *(Also see Chapter 33.)*

There are a few do's and don'ts that may be helpful for
isitor and patient in a hospital or a home.

Don't bring as your gift foods such as chocolates or cakes
hat the patient may not be permitted to have.

Whenever possible, bring flowers with their own container.

Most florists will arrange flowers in inexpensive (even dis
posable) containers at no additional charge. Of course, heavily
scented flowers have no place in the sickroom. Potted plant
give the patient many moments of pleasure.

Don't worry a patient about anything that you feel migh
upset or disturb him. If you wish to speed his recovery, bring
him only cheerful, encouraging news. Don't talk to other
about his illness in front of him, or ask him to discuss it unles
he volunteers.

Make up your mind before you arrive that you will stay n
more than fifteen or twenty minutes, and stick to it, no matte
how much your friend may beg you to stay. If other visitor
arrive while you are there, leave sooner, so that they may hav
their share of the patient's time without overtiring him.

The vast majority of hospital patients nowadays find them
selves in semiprivate rooms or larger wards. Therefore voice
of visitors are naturally kept lower. Any smoking that is don
must have the permission of all the occupants of the room
When in doubt, don't smoke. If you are going to the snac
bar or restaurant to bring a dish of ice cream or a candy ba
to your friend, ask the other person in a semiprivate room i
you can bring him anything at the same time.

If another patient in a room wishes to rest, draw the cur
tains between the beds to give him as much privacy and quie
as possible. On the other hand, if he and your friend have be
come friendly, include him in the conversation and your visi
will be doubly appreciated.

It is perfectly proper for a woman to send flowers to an
man she knows when he is seriously ill or convalescing—cu
flowers, a plant, or a terrarium which requires very little care

52

Motoring

BAD DRIVING MANNERS CAUSE ACCIDENTS

The driver who shoves to get ahead, tries to beat the lights, crowds another off the road and never considers anybody's rights but his own can easily cause a fatal motor crash. Amazingly enough, these same people in other circumstances are perfectly well behaved.

Equally dangerous is the annoying snail who crawls along in the center of the road, or on the left, or in the passing lane of a superhighway. Behind him horns blow, but he does not budge an inch. Or if he does, he starts for his proper lane, then goes right back; the passing car is then forced to brake suddenly and risk being rammed by a third car. Timid Caspar Milquetoast also drives at ten miles below the speed limit on a narrow, twisting road through hilly country and accumulates a long line of impatient drivers behind him who end by taking desperate chances on passing too close to a curve or the top of a hill.

At night, apart from being legally required in most states, it is a courtesy to dim your headlights, so other drivers coming toward you are not blinded.

In order not to confuse the driver following you, don't put your arm outside the car to shake ashes off your cigarette or throw away your cigar. Don't put your hand out and point at the scenery, and don't let anyone else in your car wave his hand out of a window.

It is unnecessary to emphasize that alcohol and gasoline do not mix. The drunken driver and the exhilarated driver who have had one or two cocktails take chances that they would not think of taking when they have had nothing to drink.

CITY DRIVING MANNERS

Blowing a horn in a traffic line when it can do no good is merely annoying to others. Sounding a horn at a pedestrian caught midstreet by a changing light is dangerous—it may cause him to jump into the path of another car. A polite young man does not announce his arrival to a lady by standing at the curb outside her door and yoohooing; neither should he sit at the wheel and blast away at the horn. He alights and rings the door bell.

Don't rush traffic lights—that is, never start before the light is green. At a crossing where the lights have turned against you, stop far enough back so as not to block the path of pedestrians crossing the street. Slow down at a puddle so you don't splash pedestrians. On a green light, give pedestrians who are caught in the middle of the roadway a chance to get across. Don't start with a jerk to pass an elderly woman; fright is likely to root her to the spot. Slow down to a crawl when you see the sign "School Crossing."

Nerve-racking drivers:

We are all made nervous by the driver who keeps looking out all the time and admiring the view, turns around to talk to those in the back seat, or who lets go of the wheel while he lights a cigarette or tries to get a new station on the radio.

DRIVING SPORTSMANSHIP

It is just as unfair and unsporting to lag when the traffic light turns green (holding up the cars behind you) as to beat the light by starting while it is still red. The fair-minded driver, if driving slowly, keeps well over to the right so that another may pass him safely. When making turns, turn the steering wheel enough so you can stay on the right when you turn right and on the left when you turn left. Don't monopolize space for two parked cars nor park so close to others as to prevent them from pulling out. In marked parking places, stay within the marks. Slow up a little at a side road and let a car whose driver has been trying to enter your unbroken procession come into the line ahead of you.

MANNERS OF PEDESTRIANS

First rules for pedestrians include: Don't cross before the light turns green or the signal reads "Walk." Don't cross streets in the middle of a block. Don't dart forward after hiding behind a parked car. Don't, when the lights change while you are in the middle of the street, turn and run back to the side you started from. Keep on going exactly as you were. On a road that has no sidewalk, always walk facing the oncoming traffic.

SOME TIPS FOR MOTOR TRIPS

When starting out on a motor trip, make certain that your equipment is in the best possible condition. Check your tires, fuel, oil, brakes and automatic transmission before starting and during the trip. Replace windshield-wiper blades if rough or worn. Have headlights, turn indicators and brake lights checked.

Avoid fatigue. On long trips stop to stretch your legs, take some refreshment and allow your engine and tires to cool off. If you have a companion who is licensed to drive, stop and change drivers every two hours. Plan to arrive at your destination by four in the afternoon to allow time for a rest, a little sightseeing and a leisurely dinner.

Traveling with children:

Traveling with children who are old enough to read, write or play games need not be a problem. Take along a supply of papers, crayons or one of the excellent game books that are sold just for the purpose. Verbal games, such as "Twenty Questions," help to pass the hours. For little children, a mattress laid in the back of the station wagon or a little playpen with a well-padded mat on the back seat is a boon. The baby can move about safely and the older child will enjoy the luxury of being able to stretch out and sleep for a while.

For comfort and safety:

Fatalities are far less frequent among drivers and passengers wearing properly installed belts or shoulder harnesses. They should be snugly fastened, so that you are not thrown hard *against* the belt by a sudden stop. Keep a pair of sunglasses in the glove compartment of your car. Many people find that prolonged glare can cause severe headaches.

In an emergency:

If you have an emergency such as a flat tire or a broken fan belt, *pull off the road,* raise the hood and tie a white handkerchief or cloth to your door handle. This is the universal signal of distress on the road, and any policeman, and often a kindhearted motorist, will stop to offer assistance. On a superhighway, stay near your car, or in it. On a smaller road, if there is a house or shop nearby where you can go to call for help, walk well off the road and return to the car immediately after making your call.

CAR POOLS

The "car pool" is a practical, economical arrangement for people who go to work at the same hour. There are several basic rules of courtesy.

Be on time! Don't carry quantities of articles or let those you must carry obstruct the driver's view to the side or in the rear-view mirror. Open or close windows only after asking permission of the other passengers. Observe the same rule of courtesy about smoking. Don't bring an extra passenger without asking the driver if there is room. Shake a wet umbrella (and raincoat) before getting in the car. Let the driver know in advance when he is not to pick you up.

53

For those who smoke

TIMES WHEN NO ONE MAY SMOKE

One may not smoke in a church or during any religious service or ceremonial proceedings. One may not smoke in a sickroom unless the patient himself is smoking or gives permission. Good taste still forbids smoking by a woman on a city street. No one should smoke or carry a lighted cigarette when dancing.

Smoking is forbidden on local buses, in theaters, in most museums, and in many big city stores.

SMOKING DON'TS

Never light a cigarette, pipe or cigar when a "No Smoking" sign is displayed.

Never lay a cigarette (or cigar) on the edge of a table or other piece of furniture! Find an ashtray to put it in—or ask for one.

Striking a match directly toward someone is dangerous— the head may fly off and cause a painful burn. A lighted cigarette should not be thrown into a fireplace; it may start up an unwanted fire. Never toss a cigarette out the window—it may land on an awning or a pile of dried leaves. Don't throw filter-tipped cigarettes on a lawn or terrace where the fireproof, rainproof tip will remain until someone rakes or sweeps it away. Worst of all is the smoker who leaves his lighted cigarette in the ashtray to burn itself out, making others present ill from the smell.

A FEW HINTS ON SMOKING MANNERS

If each place at the dining-room table is set with cigarettes, a lighter and an ashtray, naturally people may smoke as soon as they choose. But in the houses of those who do not put them on the table or who have them passed only after dessert, it is bad manners to light one's own cigarette and smoke throughout the meal. And do be careful that the smoke from the cigarette you are holding is not blowing into the face of your neighbors.

Smokers should carry their own cigarettes. When a man is about to smoke, it is polite to offer a cigarette to those next to him, or in his immediate group. And a warning—the feminine cigarette "sponge" is no more popular than the male.

A man should light a woman's cigarette if he is close to her, but not if he is on the other side of a table. A woman smoker carries her own matches or lighter and *uses* them.

Pipe smokers need to exercise caution when emptying a pipe, using only a large sturdy ashtray lest they break a fragile one, or spray their ashes over the table tops.

A word to cigar smokers: Don't leave cigar butts in ashtrays —dead cigars have a strong odor that is unpleasant. Ask permission to smoke a cigar in mixed company.

54

In clubs

Membership in many athletic associations may be had by walking in and paying dues and many country golf clubs are as free to the public as country inns. But to join an exclusive club, a man must have among the members friends who like him enough to be willing to propose and second him and write letters for him; furthermore he must be disliked by no one— at least not so much that a member might raise a serious objection to his company.

You may join a club by invitation or by having application made for you. To join by invitation means that you are invited to be one of the founders or charter members, or you may at the invitation of the governors become an honorary member; or in a small or informal club you may become an ordinary member at the suggestion of the governors. A charter member pays dues, but not always an initiation fee. An honorary member pays neither dues nor initiation fee; he is really a guest of the club—a mayor, for example, may be an honorary member just for the duration of his term in office. A life member pays his dues for twenty years or so in a lump sum and is thereafter exempted from dues even though they may be increased in later years or he lives to be a hundred.

Different clubs offer different types of memberships: at a country club, a "golfing member" uses only the golfing facilities, a "house member," only the restaurant and facilities of the clubhouse. Regular members of a club may be resident (that is, they live within fifty miles of the club) or nonresident (they live beyond that distance and pay smaller dues but have the same privileges).

BECOMING A MEMBER
"Putting up" a name:

Since no sensible man would want to join a club in which the members are not his friends, he says to a member of his family or an intimate friend, "Do you mind putting me up for the Nearby Club? I think that Dick would second me." The friend answers, "Delighted to do it!" and Dick says the same. A man has no right to ask anyone who is not really one of his best friends to propose or second him.

More likely the suggestion to join comes from a friend, who remarks one day, "Why don't you join the Nearby Club? Let me put you up, and I'll ask Dick to second you." And he arranges with Dick to do so.

Let us suppose that Jim Struthers is to be proposed by Donald Cameron and seconded by Henry Bancroft. Jim's name is written in the book kept for the purpose and signed by both proposer and seconder:

Struthers, James
    Proposer: Donald Cameron
    Seconder: Henry Bancroft

Then the name is posted with other names on the bulletin board in the clubhouse. Sometimes a list of proposed names is also sent to each member. Cameron and Bancroft each write a letter of endorsement to the governors of the club to be read by that body when they hold the meeting at which Struther's name comes up for election.

Board of Governors,
The Nearby Club

Dear Sirs:
    It affords me much pleasure to propose for membership in the Nearby Club Mr. James Struthers. I have known Mr. Struthers for many years and consider him qualified in every way for membership.
    He is a graduate of Northsouthern University, class of 1941, and is a member of the Center Club. He is now with the firm of Jones, Fairbanks & Co.
                              Yours very truly,
                                  Donald Cameron

Because in most clubs, the number of members is limited by the bylaws, there may be a waiting list. Therefore before making a decision as to which clubs you wish to join, find out about the length of waiting time and discuss the possibilities with your sponsor.

Meeting the governors:
Cameron selects with Struthers six or more of his friends who are members of the club (but not governors) and asks them to write letters endorsing Struthers. Since the candidate cannot come up for election unless he knows several of the governors personally so that they can vouch for him at the meeting, Cameron and Bancroft must personally present Struthers to several governors. At many clubs the governors appoint an hour on several weekend afternoons before elections when they are in the visitors' rooms at the clubhouse in order to meet the candidates whom their proposers must present.

Importance of good letters of endorsement:

Jim Struthers, having well-known sponsors and also being well liked himself, is elected with no difficulty. But young Breezy was put up by two not very well-known members who wrote halfhearted endorsements themselves and did nothing about getting letters from others. Two men who disliked his "manner" wrote that they considered him "unsuitable." As he had no friends strong enough to stand up for him, he was turned down. If a candidate is likely to be blackballed, the governors do not vote on him but inform the proposer that the name of his candidate had better be withdrawn. Later on, if the objection to him is disproved or overcome, his name may again be put up.

Qualifications for election:

When the candidate is elected, a notice is mailed to him next morning, telling him that he has been elected and the amount of the initiation fee and the dues, which he sends at once. Only now is he officially a member and free to use the club. A new member is given a copy of the club book, which contains a list of the members, the constitution and the bylaws or "house rules" which he must study and follow carefully.

COUNTRY CLUBS

Country clubs vary greatly in both characteristics and expense. It is as difficult to be elected to some of them as to any of the exclusive clubs in the cities, inasmuch as they are open to the family and friends of every member, whereas a city club is used only by the member himself.

Furthermore, many country clubs have one open door unknown to city clubs. People taking houses in the neighborhood or vacation visitors in a resort are often granted "season privileges." On being proposed by a member and upon paying a season's subscription, new householders are accepted as transient guests. In some clubs, this subscription may be indefinitely renewed; in others, a man must come up for regular election at the end of three or six months' or a year's time.

Hundreds of country clubs have very simple requirements for membership: one or two members who will vouch for a candidate's integrity and good behavior are sufficient.

In almost all country clubs the atmosphere is informal:

members speak to each other without introductions, form
tennis games and golf foursomes with comparative strangers.

WOMEN'S CLUBS

There is no difference between women's and men's clubs. In
every state of the Union there are women's clubs of every
kind and grade: social, political, sports, professional. Some
are housed in enormous and elegant buildings designed especially for them and others in only a room or two, usually in
a hotel. No clubs are more nearly perfect in appointment or
more smoothly run than the best women's clubs.

IN THE CITY CLUB

There is no place where a person has greater need of
restraint and consideration for the reserves of others than in a
club. It is courteous of a governor or habitual member on
noticing a new member or a visitor to go up and speak to
him, but the latter should not be the one to speak first. In the
dining rooms of many clubs, there is a large table, sometimes
known as the social table, where members who are lunching
alone may sit and where the conversation is general, and all
are expected to talk whether they are friends or total strangers.

The fundamental rule for behavior in a club is the same as
in the living room of a private house. In other words, heels
have no place on furniture; ashes belong in ashtrays; books
should not be abused; and all evidence of exercising should
be confined to the courts or gymnasium, and the locker or
dressing room.

VISITORS IN A CLUB

All men's clubs have private dining rooms where members
can give dinners that include nonmembers, and many have a
special dining room for women guests.

When a woman gives a lunch or any party in a club, either
a women's club or in the "open" dining room of a men's club,
she waits for her guests in the lobby, entrance hall, or, if there
is one, the reception room. As her guests arrive, they join her
and stand or sit near her. If the room is filled with others,
she herds her own group, as it were, a little apart. When all
have arrived, they go to the dining room and sit at the table

prepared in advance for them. If they are more than four, the food is ordered in advance.

Almost always, a member is allowed to introduce a stranger —one who lives at least fifty miles away—for a varying length of time determined by the bylaws of the club. In many city clubs, the same guest cannot be introduced twice within the year. In country clubs, members usually may have an unlimited number of visitors. When these are golf or tennis players, the host is responsible for green's fees or court charges.

When a member introduces a stranger, he takes him to the club personally, writes his name in the visitors' book and introduces him to those who may be in the room at the time. If it is not possible for the stranger's host to take him to the club, he writes a formal letter to the secretary of the club for a card of introduction. This letter then goes in the club's files.

Secretary
The Town Club

Dear Sir [or *Dear Mr. Jones*]:
    Kindly send Mr. A. M. Strangleigh, of Wilkes Barre, Pa., a card extending the privileges of the Club for one week. Mr. Strangleigh is staying at the Carlton House.
                                        Yours very truly,
                                            Henry Bancroft

The secretary then sends a card to Mr. Strangleigh.

The Town Club
Extends its privileges to
Mr. Strangleigh
from Jan. 7 to Jan. 14
Through the courtesy of
Mr. Henry Bancroft

Mr. Strangleigh goes to the club by himself. A visitor who has been given a card to a club has, during the time of his visit, all the privileges of a member except that he is not allowed to introduce others to the club and he cannot give a dinner in a private dining room. The guest arranges at the club's office to have his charges rendered to himself, is scrupulous about asking for his bill upon leaving and pays it immediately. Otherwise his bill must be paid by the member who issued the invitation.

UNBREAKABLE RULES

Failure to pay one's debts or behavior unbefitting a gentleman is cause for expulsion from every club. If a man cannot afford to belong to a club, he must resign while he is still in good standing. If later on he is able to rejoin, his name is put at the head of the waiting list. If he was considered a desirable member, he is reelected at the next meeting of the governors. But a man who has been expelled—unless he can show that his expulsion was unjust—can never again belong to that club.

RESIGNING FROM A CLUB

To resign from a club, one writes a letter of resignation to the secretary well before the date on which the next yearly dues will be due. The letter would read something like this:

Mrs. James Town
Secretary, Colonial Club, New York

My dear Mrs. Town,
It is with great regret that I find it necessary to resign from the club and to ask you therefore to present my resignation at the next meeting of the governors.
Very sincerely,
Mary Smartlington

55

At the table

THE "WHYS" OF GOOD TABLE MANNERS

Most rules for the table were made to avoid ugliness. To let anyone see what you have in your mouth is offensive. To make a noise is to suggest one of the lower animals. To make a mess is disgusting. Chairs scraped on the floor and knives and forks rattled against the plate are unpleasant to those nearby. But if you consider what impression your actions will make on the others at the table, few problems will arise that cannot be solved by common sense alone.

ARRIVING AT THE TABLE AND GRACE BEFORE MEALS

At the informal gatherings and family meals that all of us have each day, a man holds the chair for the woman on his right. But if the men or boys do not arrive simultaneously with the women, the women (and girls) seat themselves without delay.

Giving a family blessing or thanks before meals is a gracious custom. Some families sit with bowed heads and touch nothing until the grace has been said, others remain standing— both forms are correct. The mother or the father may offer the prayer, but it is sweet to allow the younger members of the family to take turns in asking grace. The following three are typical examples.

Bless us, O Lord, and these Thy gifts, which we are about to receive from Thy bounty, Through Christ our Lord. Amen.

Lift up your hands toward the Sanctuary and bless the Lord.
Blessed art Thou, O Lord our God, King of the universe,
who bringest forth bread from the earth. Amen.

Bless, O Lord, this food to our use, and us to Thy service,
and make us ever mindful of the needs of others, in Jesus'
name. Amen.

POSTURE

Sit at a distance from the table that is comfortable, but not
so close that elbows are bent like a cricket's, nor so far back
that food may be dropped in transit from plate to mouth.

Elbows are *never* put on the table while one is actually eating. To sit with the left elbow propped on the table while
eating with the right hand or to prop the right elbow or fore-
arm on the table while lifting fork or glass to the mouth is
ugly and awkward.

Elbows are permitted when people are lunching or dining in
a restaurant and it is difficult to hear above music or conversation, without leaning far forward. And in leaning forward, a
woman's figure makes a more graceful outline supported on
her elbows than doubled forward over her hands in her lap
as though she were in pain! *At home* there is no reason for
elbows. *At a dinner of ceremony,* elbows on the table are
rarely seen, except perhaps at the ends of the table, where one
has to lean forward in order to talk to a companion across the
table corner. Even in these special situations, *never* when one
is eating.

Slouching or slumping at the table is most unattractive and
tipping one's chair is unforgivable. It not only looks dreadfully
sloppy, but it is fatal to the back legs of the chair. Ideal
posture at the table is to sit straight but not stiffly, leaning
slightly against the back of the chair; when you are not
actually eating, your hands should be in your lap; this will
automatically prevent you from fussing with implements, playing with bread crumbs, drawing on the tablecloth, and so forth.
Keep hands away from the face, from nervous scratching and
from twisting or touching the hair.

It is correct to reach for anything on the table provided you
do not stretch across your neighbor. When something is out of
reach, simply ask the person nearest to it, "Would you please
pass the jelly, Mrs. Betts?"

THE NAPKIN

As soon as you are seated, you put your napkin in your lap, unfolding it as much as necessary with both hands—avoid giving it a violent shake.

When using the napkin, blot or pat the lips.

When the meal is finished, or if you leave the table during the meal, put the napkin on the right side of your place, or if the plates have been removed, in the center. Do not refold it or crumple it; just lay it on the table in loose folds so that it does not spread itself out. At a dinner party, the hostess lays her napkin on the table as a signal that the meal is over; the guests then lay their napkins on the table—not before.

SERVING ONESELF AND BEING SERVED

Anything served on a piece of toast is lifted from the dish on it, unless you don't want the toast, in which case you help yourself to the asparagus and leave the toast. For sweetbreads, mushrooms on toast—foods that seem to be an arrangement— take the toast and all on the spoon and hold it in place with the fork.

When declining a dish offered by a waiter, you say, "No, thank you," in a low voice.

Gravy is put *on* the meat or potatoes, and the condiments, pickles, and jelly *at the side* of whatever they accompany. Olives, radishes or celery are put on the bread-and-butter plate if there is one; otherwise on the edge of the plate from which one is eating. Salted nuts are put on the tablecloth or place mat.

When passing your plate to the head of the table for a second helping, always leave the knife and fork close together across the center of the plate with the handles far enough on not to topple off.

It is good manners to take a little of every dish that is offered, but if it is a food you especially dislike and you are among friends, you may refuse with a polite "No, thank you." You need not give your reason for refusing a dish, but if it is an allergy or a diet, you might quietly tell your hostess so, without drawing the attention of the entire table.

WHEN TO START EATING

At a small table of two, four or even six people, it is certainly polite to wait to start eating until all have been served. Then the hostess picks up her implement and the others follow suit. If the group is larger, it is *not* necessary to wait until all have been served. The hostess, as soon as the first two or three guests have their food, says, "Please start—your dinner will only get cold if you wait"; the guests take her at her word and start immediately. If the hostess says nothing, it is perfectly correct to pick up your spoon or fork after five or six people have been served; the others will soon follow your lead. At family meals, as Mother or Father fills and passes the plates, the children say, "May I please begin?" if they are not old enough to be expected to wait.

As to which silver to use: *You always start with the implement farthest from the plate.* Starting at the outside, you work your way with each course toward the center.

USING THE KNIFE AND FORK

The proper way to use the knife and fork can best be explained by the accompanying illustrations. The American custom of "zigzag" eating (changing the fork from left to right hand after cutting meat) is perfectly correct, but unnecessarily complicated. The simpler method is to leave the fork in your

left hand, raise the meat to your mouth, after cutting it, with the fork tines down, still in the same hand, rather than turning the fork over and switching it to your right.

Dessert may be eaten with spoon or fork or both. Stewed fruit is held in place with the fork and cut and eaten with the spoon. Peaches or other very juicy fruits are peeled, then eaten with knife and fork, but dry fruits, such as apples, may be cut and then eaten with the fingers. *Never* wipe hands that have fruit juice on them on a cloth napkin without first using a fingerbowl, because fruit juices leave injurious stains.

Fingers or forks:

All juicy or soft fruit and all cake is best eaten with a fork. If you can eat a peach or ripe pear in your fingers and not let juice run down your chin or make a sucking noise, do so. But if you cannot eat something—no matter what it is—without getting it all over your fingers, use a fork and, when necessary, a spoon or a knife also.

Pushers:

A piece of dry crust is an excellent pusher. Lacking this, the knife is also correct—if properly used. Held in the left hand in the same position as it is when held in the right hand, the tip of the blade helping to guide each mouthful for the fork to lift, it is a quite acceptable pusher.

OTHER THAN THE MAIN COURSE
Soups:

Either clear soup or thick soup may be served in a cup with one handle or with handles on both sides. After taking a spoonful or two, you may pick up the cup, using both hands if it has two handles.

Clear soups are often served in a soup plate. When the level of the soup gets low, lift the near edge in your left hand and tip the plate away from you. Then the soup may be spooned away from you or toward you.

Croutons are either put on the soup or else passed separately in a dish with a small serving spoon. Oyster crackers and any others are put on the bread-and-butter plate or the tablecloth —and dropped two or three pieces at a time into the soup.

Bread and butter:

Bread is broken into moderate-sized,—not bite-sized—pieces with the fingers before being eaten. To butter it, hold a piece on the edge of the bread-and-butter plate, or the place plate, and spread enough butter on it for a mouthful or two at a time, with a butter knife—lacking a butter knife, use any other knife available. Never hold bread flat on the palm and butter it with the hand held in the air. Jellies and jams are spread on bread with a knife, never with a fork, though you do put butter on vegetables and jelly on meat with a fork.

Bread and gravy:

Certainly you may sop bread into gravy by putting a small piece down in the gravy and then eating it with a knife and fork.

Salad:

To cut one's salad in small pieces is eminently proper and practical, but avoid cutting up a whole plateful at a time. Anything more difficult than managing leafy salad with a fork alone is difficult to imagine. Beware of rolling the fork and wrapping springy leaves around the tines in a spiral. Since the advent of stainless steel knife blades, there has been no reason to refrain from using a knife to cut your salad.

Salt:

If there is no spoon in the saltcellar, use the tip of a clean knife. If the saltcellar is for you alone, use your knife or take a pinch of salt with your fingers. Putting salt on the tablecloth and then pinching it between the fingers to put on food is permissible. But salt that is to be dipped into—for example, with celery or radishes—is put on the bread-and-butter plate or on the rim of whatever plate is before you.

Fruit at table:

The equipment for eating fruit at the table consists of a sharp-bladed fruit knife and fork, a fingerbowl and a napkin that fruit juice will not permanently stain. In a restaurant, when no knife is given you, ask for one.

Raw apples and pears. These are quartered with a knife, the core cut away from each quarter, and the fruit eaten in the fingers. Those who do not like the skin pare each quarter separately.

Bananas. Although it is permissible to peel the skin halfway down and eat the fruit bite by bite, it is better to peel the skin all the way off, lay the fruit on your plate, cut it in slices and eat it with a fork.

Berries. Strawberries and other berries are usually hulled ahead of time, served with cream and sugar, and eaten with a spoon. They are also served with their hulls on and sugar placed at one side of each person's plate—hold the hull of each berry in your fingers, dip the fruit in the sugar and eat it.

Cantaloupes and melons. These are served in halves or quarters and eaten with a spoon. A honeydew is cut into new-moon-shaped quarters or eighths and eaten with either spoon or knife and fork, as are Persian or Casaba melons. Watermelon is cut into large-size pieces or slices and is usually eaten in the fingers. If eaten with a fork, remove the seeds with the tines, then cut a piece with the side of the fork.

Raw cherries and plums. These are eaten in the fingers. The pit of the cherry is made as dry as possible in your mouth and dropped into your almost-closed cupped hand and thence to your plate. The plum is held in your fingers and eaten as close to the pit as possible. When you remove a pit in your fingers, do it with your thumb underneath and your first two fingers across your mouth, not with your fingertips pointing into your mouth.

Grapes. Hothouse grapes are eaten two ways: one, lay a grape on its side, hold it with the fingers of the left hand, cut into the center with the point of a knife, and remove the seeds; then put the grape in your mouth with the left hand. Or put a whole grape in your mouth, chew it, swallow the pulp and juice and drop the bare seeds into your almost-closed fist, and convey them to the plate.

Oranges. Slice the two ends of the rind off first; then stand it on the plate with the fingers of the left hand, cut the peel off in vertical strips with the knife, and cut the peeled orange in half at its equator. After this, each half is easily cut and eaten mouthful by mouthful with knife and fork together. They can also be halved, the sections loosened with a curved grapefruit knife, and then eaten with an orange spoon or teaspoon.

Peaches. A freestone peach or a nectarine is cut into the pit, then broken in half and eaten. If you mind the fuzz of a cling-stone, which won't come off the pit easily, peel the peach whole and then eat it with knife and fork.

DIFFICULT FOODS

Artichoke. The leaves are eaten with the fingers. A leaf at a time is pulled off, the edible portion dipped in the sauce, then bitten off. At the center scrape the thistlelike part away with a knife and eat the heart with a knife and fork.

Asparagus. Fastidious people invariably eat it—at least in part—with the fork. Cut the stalks with the fork at the point at which they become harder, then pick up the ends in your fingers if you choose. But don't squeeze the stalks. All hard ends should be cut off asparagus before serving it at a dinner party.

Baked potato. If not otherwise prepared before serving, it is eaten by breaking it in half with the fingers, scooping all the inside of the potato onto the plate with a fork and then mixing butter, salt and pepper in it with a fork. Or you may break it in half with the fingers and lay both halves, skin down on the plate. Mix a little butter in a small part of one half with a fork and eat that, then mix a little more, and so on, eating it out of the skin.

For those who like to eat the skin as well as the inside, cut the baked potato into two halves with the knife and fork, then again into pieces, a few at a time, of eatable size. Butter the pieces with the fork alone and eat with the fork held tines up. The skins may be eaten separately, exactly as you would bread and butter.

Bacon. Breakfast bacon is eaten, if possible, with a fork. If it is very crisp so that it scatters into fragments when broken by the fork, fingers are permitted.

Cheese. Cheese may be spread with either a knife or a fork. If eaten with a salad, with which one is using no knife, one may break off a piece of cheese and put it on lettuce or a cracker with one's fork. Runny or soft cheeses, such as Brie, Camembert or Liederkranz are always spread with a salad knife or butter knife.

Corn on the cob. Hold the ear, either broken in half or whole, by its own ends or by special little handles. Spread the butter across half the length, about two rows at a time. If the ear is not too long, spread it across the whole length of two rows, add salt and pepper, hold the ends in both hands, and eat those two rows. Repeat the buttering and eating until all is finished. When corn is served for a dinner party, it should be cut off the cobs in the kitchen and creamed or buttered.

Chicken (roast or broiled), squab, game hen. At a formal dinner, no part of a bird is picked up in the fingers. Among family and friends, however, it is permissible to eat as follows: You cut off as much meat as you can and eat it with your knife and fork. If you know how to manage very small bones, such as the joint or wing of a squab, put the piece of bone with meat on it in your mouth, eat it clean, and remove the bare bones between forefinger and thumb. Larger joints, such as the drumstick of a chicken, may be picked up after the first few easily-cut-off pieces have been eaten.

French-fried potatoes. When they are accompanying a hamburger, hot dog or other sandwich, they may be eaten in the fingers. Otherwise they are cut into reasonable lengths and eaten with a fork.

Lamb chops. At a dinner party or in a restaurant, lamb chops are eaten with knife and fork. At the family table or among an informal group of friends, the center may be cut out and eaten with the fork, and the bone picked up and eaten clean with the teeth. (This is permissible with veal or pork chops provided they are broiled without gravy or sauce.)

Lobster, broiled. Pick up the claw in its shell and pry out the meat with a lobster fork; then put the meat (and that from the main body) on your plate, cut it with a knife and eat it with the fork. (An extra napkin and a fingerbowl with hot water and lemon slices should be put at the side of each place at the table as soon as people are served and taken away when the plates are removed.)

Olives. Eat them with your fingers; don't nibble too avidly around the stone. Bite a stuffed one in half—put only a very small one in your mouth whole. (When a small olive, cherry or onion is in a cocktail: after the glass is drained, tip it and drop the olive, etc., into your mouth. Lift out a large olive with the fingers and eat it in two or three bites.)

Sandwiches. All ordinary sandwiches are eaten with the fingers. Club sandwiches are best cut in smaller portions before being picked up and held tightly in the fingers of both hands; if literally dripping with mayonnaise they should be served on a plate and eaten with a knife and fork.

Shrimp. If not too impossibly large, each shrimp in a cup should be eaten in one bite. The jumbo size is cut with the edge of the fork. Or arrange the shrimp attractively on a small plate, where they can be cut easily with knife or fork.

Spaghetti. Winding spaghetti on a fork held against a spoon is incorrect both here and in Italy. A few pieces are held against the plate with the end of the fork, which is twisted to wrap the spaghetti around the tines and then conveyed to the mouth. An extra amount of grated Parmesan cheese makes the strands less slippery.

EMBARRASSING DIFFICULTIES

If food is too hot, quickly take a swallow of water. Never, NEVER spit it out! Once food has been taken into your mouth, you must swallow it. It is offensive to take anything out of your mouth that has been put in it except dry fish bones and equally dry fruit pits or seeds. If you choke on a fish bone, cover your mouth with your napkin and leave the table quickly. If you get a bad clam or something similar, take it from your mouth in your fingers—thumb underneath and the other four fingers forming a screen over it—and wipe your fingertips on your napkin. Pits of stewed prunes or cherries that are eaten with a spoon are made as clean and dry as possible in the mouth with the tongue and teeth, then dropped into the spoon with which you are eating and conveyed to the edge of the plate. Fish bones are taken between finger and thumb and removed between compressed lips.

Spills:

If you spill jelly or other solid food on the table, pick up as much as you can with a clean spoon or the blade of your knife. If it has caused a stain, apologize to your hostess, who should assure you that "No harm was done—the cloth will be washed tomorrow in any case." If you spill wine or water at the family table or informal dinner, offer to get a cloth or sponge to mop up the liquid and help the hostess clean up in any way you can.

SOME TABLE DON'TS

Don't encircle a plate with the left arm while eating with the right hand. Don't push back your plate when finished. It remains exactly where it is until whoever is waiting on you removes it. If you wait on yourself, get up and carry it to the kitchen.

Don't lean back and announce, "I'm through"—just put your fork or spoon down.

Don't *ever* put liquid into your mouth if it is already filled with food.

Don't dunk, except in the privacy of your home.

Don't apologize if you have to blow your nose at the table. The only thing to do is to end it as quickly as possible.

Don't wipe off the tableware in a restaurant. If you find a dirty piece of silver at your place, call a waiter and ask for a clean one.

Don't, if you are a woman, wear an excessive amount of lipstick to the table (out of consideration for your hostess's napkin—it is also unattractive on the rim of a glass or on the silver).

Don't spread jelly or jam directly onto a piece of bread from the dish in which it is served. Put a small portion on your butter plate (or the rim of your dinner plate), using the spoon provided to serve the condiment. If there is no spoon with the jelly, use a clean knife to put a little on your plate.

Don't crook your finger when picking up your cup. It's an affected mannerism.

Don't—ever—leave your spoon in your cup.

Don't leave half the food on your spoon or fork to be waved about during conversation. This is often done with ice cream, but the coldness is no excuse—put less on the spoon.

Don't cut up your entire meal before you start to eat; it makes a mess on your plate.

Don't bend your head so low over the plate that you seem to be bobbing up and down for each bite like a robin for a worm. Lean forward slightly to avoid spilling on your lap.

WHEN CHILDREN COME TO THE TABLE

No child under five can be expected to use a napkin instead of a bib, but he may be given a napkin in addition to the bib to become accustomed to using it. It is much easier to supply him with a clean bib for the next meal than to change his clothes for the next moment, so do not force the issue unduly.

Very little children usually have warming plates—a double plate with a hot water space in between—on which the food is cut up and the vegetables "fixed" in the kitchen. It is brought to them before other people at the table are served as it is hard for them to wait, and they naturally eat slowly and deliberately. As soon as they are old enough to eat everything on the table, they are served, not last, but in the regular rotation in which they come at table.

The left-handed child:

To the many who ask whether it is best to set the place at the table in reverse of usual order for a left-handed child who has to "cross over" for every implement, the answer is definitely "No!"

Nothing could turn out to be a greater handicap than letting him become accustomed to reversed place-setting. It is only by being obliged to make this maneuver at every meal at home that he becomes adept at it. If his place is set especially for him at home, he will be conspicuously as well as helplessly awkward at every meal he ever eats away from home where his place will not be so set.

Table tricks that must be corrected:

To pile mashed potato and other vegetables on top of meat on the convex side of the fork for two inches or more of its length is an ungainly habit dear to the hearts of schoolboys and sometimes of their fathers—a habit that is more easily prevented in the beginning than corrected later. Taking a big mouthful (next to smearing the face and chewing with the mouth open) is perhaps the worst offense at the table.

To sit up straight and keep their hands in their laps when not occupied with eating is hard for children, but it should be insisted upon in order to forestall careless habits of flopping this way and that and fingering whatever is in reach. Never allow the child to drum on the table, screw his napkin into a rope or make marks on the tablecloth. If he shows talent as an artist, give him pencils or modeling wax in his playroom but do not let him bite his slice of bread into the silhouette of an animal and model figures in butter at the table. And do not allow him to construct a tent out of two forks or tie the corners of his napkin into bunny-rabbit ears. Food and table implements are not playthings, nor is the dining-room table a playground.

Teach children from the time they are little not to talk at the table about what foods they like and don't like. A child who is not allowed to say anything but "No, thank you," when offered something he doesn't want at home, will not mortify his mother in public by screaming, "I *hate* spinach. I *won't* eat potato. I want ice cream and cookies!"

A child, once his feet reach the floor, should sit down in the center of his chair and draw it up to the table by holding the seat in either hand while momentarily lifting himself on his feet. Do not let him jump or rock his chair into place. In getting up from the table, he must push his chair back quietly, using his hands on either side of the chair seat, and *not* by holding onto the table edge and giving himself, chair and all, a sudden shove.

56

In business

In the well-run business office, the more important the executive, the greater courtesy he shows to those who come to see him. If, for example, an unknown person asks to see the president of a large industry, an assistant goes out to find out what the visitor's business is. Instead of telling him bluntly that the executive can't see him and to write a letter, he not only says, "Mr. Prominent is in conference just now," but adds, "I know he wouldn't like you to be kept waiting. Can I be of service to you? I am his assistant."

The president has a courteous manner that makes every visitor feel there is nothing in the day's work half so important as what he, the client, has come to see him about. Should he be due at an appointment, his secretary comes in, a few minutes before the hour, and reminds him, "I'm sorry, Mr. Prominent, but your appointment with the traffic committee is due." Mr. Prominent uses these few minutes in an unhurried close of the conversation, showing undiminished interest until the end. This is neither sincerity nor insincerity, but merely bringing social knowledge into business dealing. A less experienced man might show his eagerness to be rid of his visitor and possibly still be late for his own appointment!

Fundamental knowledge of etiquette is no less an asset in business or public life than it is in society. An expert at a machine bench gives an impression of such ease as to make his accomplishment seem to require no skill. A bungler makes himself and everyone watching him uneasy. Inexpertness is quite as irritating in personal as in mechanical matters. Wash-

ington was completely a gentleman—and so was Abraham
Lincoln. Though Lincoln's etiquette was self-taught, it was
no less mastered for that!

WOMEN IN BUSINESS

The ideal business woman is accurate, orderly, quick and
impersonal, whether she is a typist or the top executive of a
great concern. "Impersonal" means exactly that. Her point of
view is focused on the work in hand, not on her own reactions
to it or on anyone's reactions to her. At the top of the list of
women's business shortcomings is the inability of many of
them to achieve this impersonality. Mood, temper, jealousy,
these are the chief flaws of the woman in business. The greatest handicap to woman's advancement in business is her inability to leave her personal feelings and affairs at home.

A woman who goes into an office because she thinks herself pretty and hopes to meet romance in the form of her employer, or at least to rise quickly because of her physical
charm, has clerkship and chorus work mixed up. A man naturally likes a girl who is attractive, but business personality
and leisure personality are two different things. Every time the
prospect of romance intrudes into a business situation, think
twice before allowing an office relationship to become a personal one.

THE PERFECT SECRETARY

The function of the perfect secretary is to complement her
employer's endeavor and not make any intrusions that would
be more likely to impede than help. A good secretary never
betrays the secrets of her employer. His business dealings must
be regarded as professional secrets no matter how inconsequen-
tial they may seem to her.

Business training teaches every secretary to know everything she can that will be of service to her employer, but to
know as little as possible about the things that are not her
concern. When sorting his mail, she leaves unopened obviously private letters—envelopes written by hand on stationery
not suggestive of business—and having opened his other letters and clipped them in whatever order he likes to have them,
she then clips a sheet of blank paper on the top of each pile,

or puts the mail in a manila folder so that visitors or others who have access to his office will not inadvertently see them.

When a secretary enters a man's office in response to his summons, she takes a chair and places it near enough to hear him easily. He need not get up and offer her a chair or show her the sort of personal attention that a man in social life shows to a woman.

In unconventional situations:

The young woman who is a confidential secretary to an executive may be required to stay late into the evening, working with him alone, or to go with him on business trips of investigation or conference with firms in distant cities. Every professional or business woman must write her own code of propriety. She knows exactly how necessary she is or is not to the work her employer must do, his attitude toward her, hers toward him and whether she must or need not go with him.

In making business trips, it is true the business woman is free from criticism, but there are qualifying exactions that the critical world expects her to follow. In preparation for the journey, she orders whatever accommodations her employer always expects. On trains, she engages a drawing room or a roomette for him, and a roomette for herself in the same car; but in hotels she engages a suite for him, and a room and bath on another floor for herself. This is not prudishness since everyone knows that the relationship between Mr. Employer and herself is one of professional necessity. But such carefulness insures that there can never be any possible distortion of the truth about their relationship.

It is almost certain that she will lunch with him or have dinner with him—especially on trains or boats or in hotels or restaurants. On rushed days, she may have to eat in his rooms where they are working. In other words, she takes eating alone or eating with him as incidental to convenience. The danger point appears when the pleasure of dining becomes social.

Greeting visitors:

Should a secretary rise when visitors enter the office? Unless the visitors are persons of importance to her employer, it would not be expected of her, or even proper, to greet them in such a way as to encourage their talking to her at length.

If she is the private secretary of an executive and part of her job is to make a pleasant impression, she would naturally leave her desk to greet a stranger or an important customer but not to greet one who comes into the office constantly. A secretary's duties do not include helping a visitor off and on with his coat, unless he actually needs help.

THE WELL-RUN OFFICE

You should take as much pride in helping to keep up the tone of the office you work in as you take pride in your own efficiency.

Do not bring your personal problems to the office. Leave them at home, or, if you must, discuss them with a friend during lunch.

In the office of a large company, the executives usually call their employees "Miss [or Mrs.] Jones" rather than "Mary," and they, in turn, call him "Mr. Smith." There are, however, varying degrees of formality in business organizations. Offices today tend to be more casual than formerly. Many employers feel that in a more relaxed atmosphere employees will be more efficient, more reliable and more loyal. The ranking executive determines the degree of formality in his office. He may, for instance, prefer to be on a first-name basis with his staff and the informality does not itself imply a too-familiar relationship. This is invariably true in a small office.

A young woman in a subordinate position does not go out to lunch with her superior or employer. If she holds a responsible position and has matters of business to discuss, she may quite properly lunch with him, provided their going out together does not become a habit.

Though a man does not rise when a woman employee comes into his office, he stands to receive a woman visitor and remains standing until she is seated. He stands again when she prepares to leave and usually goes with her to the door, opens it for her and "bows her out."

Personal messages over the telephone are at times unavoidable, but personal calls that interfere with the routine of office procedure, either incoming or outgoing, are inexcusable except in genuine emergencies.

Discourage visits from your family and friends at the office. Your baby brother may be a most enchanting child, but his place is not in the office in which you work.

Gifts from a firm to its employees are usually in the form
of a bonus or a proportion of one's salary. At Christmas a
man may give his personal secretary a present. (Wearing apparel is NOT suitable.) A private secretary known well to a
man's wife is occasionally remembered by the wife at Christmas. Employees may give presents to their employers, but it
is not common. There are exceptions: If there is a wedding
in the employer's family, or if a baby is born, then the employees may all contribute and send a gift. As a group they
may also send flowers to a funeral. A committee usually collects contributions and makes an appropriate selection.

STORE ETIQUETTE

The technical aspects of salesmanship are much too special-
ized for such a book as this, but aspects that depend for their
success upon tactful and pleasing manners do belong here, as
well as the good manners expected of all customers who make
any pretense to being well-bred.

The successful saleswoman:

Really great saleswomen have cultivated not only an expert
knowledge of the commodities they sell, but an equally expert
ability to appraise each of the customers to whom they sell:
whether a customer likes to be "dearied" or "madamed" or
chatted to about every topic under the sun, whether she likes
to have her mind made up for her or whether she prefers to
have her questions answered intelligently without any unasked-
for advice. The saleswoman whom an intelligent customer is
certain to like best—and return to—is one who listens to what
she says and tries to give her what she wants, instead of trying
to sell her what the store seems eager to be rid of.

For example, when you ask for something she can't supply,
the ideal saleswoman answers, "I am sorry we have nothing
like that in the color you want; but I could give you something in a small pattern of yellow"; then with certain eagerness she asks, "Have you time to let me show it to you?"
When she brings it, you are inclined to be pleased because,
though you know it is not just what you want, you are sure it
is not going to be thrust upon you. Even if you do not want
it, you will certainly come back to that saleswoman another
time when you are looking for something else.

The poorest saleswoman is the one who brushes aside what

you say you want and blandly spreads before you something that you do NOT want, extolling its beauties or its bargain values and capping the climax by telling you that Mrs. Uppity thinks this is exquisite. High-pressure salesmanship never pays in the long run and sends a customer out of the store determined not to return.

The inconsiderate customer:

An inconsiderate customer can be at her worst and cause the greatest strain on a saleswoman's good temper in the ready-to-wear clothing department. A careless customer often smears the dresses with lipstick as she pulls them on or off, tears them in her haste or sheer carelessness. And in the end she orders none, or perhaps she buys several and then returns everything looking still more shopworn the next day.

Another lack of consideration is shown by those who go shopping ten minutes before closing time. The salespeople have had a long day and have routine chores to do before they can leave.

And finally there are women who, with no thought of buying anything, will go into a dress department solely to pass an hour or so before a lunch date, and waste the time of a saleswoman who is paid at least in part by commissions on the dresses she sells—and not on the ones she shows.

57

With the handicapped

There are certain rules that apply to your behavior in regard to all handicapped people and the most important by far is this: NEVER stare or indicate that you are conscious that the person is different from others in any way. People who are getting themselves about in wheelchairs or have mastered the use of crutch or brace or can manipulate a mechanical hand dexterously take great pride in their independence and approach to normalcy. An offer to help a man in a wheelchair seeking to navigate a steep curb or an arm proffered to a lady with a cane and a leg brace trying to maneuver steps is, of course, in order. But before grabbing the wheelchair or seizing her arm, ask if, and in what way, you can be of assistance.

Never make personal remarks or ask personal questions of one with an obvious disability. Let him introduce the subject, if he wishes, but never pry into his feelings or his clinical symptoms.

Deafness and blindness are the two disabilities with which the greatest number of people come into frequent contact. Here are suggestions for those meeting deaf or blind people, and for those so handicapped.

DEAFNESS

In the case of total hearing loss, where the deaf person must depend on lip reading, speak distinctly and reasonably slowly. Don't use exaggerated mouth movements that may confuse him, as he has been taught to read normal lip movement. If he is not facing you, tap him gently on the arm or shoulder to attract his attention. Be willing to repeat or make your statement in words that are easier for him to understand.

Here are rules in conversing with someone who is partially deaf:

If you know a friend is deaf in only one ear, sit on the side of his good ear in movies, restaurants or any place where you may not be face to face.

Don't raise your voice or shout—his hearing aid is probably adjusted for a normal voice. Call him by name to attract his attention. If you must repeat, don't shout or appear annoyed. This will only embarrass him. Don't exclude him from conversation, but try to place him so that he may see you or the group. Even normal people read lips unconsciously, and being able to read another's lip movements is a great help to one handicapped by partial deafness.

If you are handicapped by deafness the following suggestions may add to your comfort and that of your friends:

DO wear a hearing aid—loss of hearing is no different than loss of sight, and few people refuse to wear glasses. Keep your aid turned on. Listen attentively and concentrate on what people are saying. (Look at the people talking to you—their expression and their lips will help you to "hear" them.)

BLINDNESS

The most important thing to remember when coming in contact with someone who is blind is that in every other respect he is exactly like you. He has a problem, but it is a problem with which one can learn to live, and most blind people have done so with considerable success. Therefore treat the blind man as you would any other person. Talk to him about the same subjects that would interest your other friends. Don't avoid the use of the word "see." Blind people use it as much as anyone else. Don't show surprise that he can dial telephone numbers, light a cigarette, dress himself or perform the daily chores that we all do. He has simply made a little more effort to learn to do them by touch or sound.

When you are with, or pass by, a blind person on a street corner, you are perfectly correct in asking if you may help him to cross, but never grasp his arm or try to give assistance without first asking whether he wishes it or not. If he does, let *him* take *your* arm. If he asks you for directions, be sure to use left and right from his viewpoint—the direction he is facing.

If you go to a restaurant with a blind person, read him the menu, including the prices if the occasion demands. Tell him quietly where the salt and pepper are and help him to the sugar and cream if he wishes. You may tell him how the items on his plate are arranged and help him cut his meat if necessary.

When he visits your home, lead him to a chair and then just place his hand on the arm or back. If he is staying with you for any length of time, tell him where the furniture is, mention it if anything is rearranged, and keep doors open or closed—never halfway.

When taking him to a strange place, tell him where the furniture is located and who is present. Before you leave him alone, be sure that he has someone to talk to with whom you feel he would be congenial.

When there is a blind person in a room you have just entered, make your presence known and tell him, if he does not recognize your voice, who you are. Tell him also when you leave.

If the blind person has a Seeing Eye dog, do not attempt to play with or distract the dog in any way. His attention must remain fully on his master, whose safety and well-being depend on his strict adherence to his training.

58

At public beaches and parks

At the beach:

When there are children to be watched, choose places near the spot where they are going to wade in and out of the water and dig canals and build sand castles. Not only is it dangerous to have little children paddling in the water far away, but when a child runs back and forth he is apt to kick sand and splash water over those sitting in his path.

Before letting Johnny make himself one of a group of strangers sitting nearby, be sure to notice whether the strangers respond to his interest. If not, call him back immediately.

When dogs are allowed in an area where there are other people, they must be kept on leash so as not to alarm anyone. If your dog is to be free to run and swim, find a more deserted part of the beach, being sure to leash him again if a stranger approaches.

Groups of athletic young men throwing a ball over, around and between the sunbathers are an all too common annoyance. Another one is an obvious display of affection, such as languid back-rubs, heads resting on stomachs, kissing and caressing. These breaches of good manners can make neighbors thoroughly uncomfortable.

The public park:

Don't crowd others if you can help it. Don't spread your picnic baskets and personal belongings over two or three tables when your share is one. Picnic tables do not grant children the privilege of eating like little savages to the distress of those nearby who cannot help but see them.

Where there is playground equipment, teach your child to take turns and be satisfied with his own share of time with the slides, swings, seesaws and any other pleasures offered to all children.

Always leave public grounds as clean or cleaner than you find them. Papers, cans, trash and broken bottles completely destroy the beauty of the loveliest landscapes.

59

For pets and people

DOGS

I could quote instances by the dozen of pleasant neighborhood friendships that have become strained and even broken by the Smith dog that barks all night, or the Pope dog that runs through flower beds and digs in them. Other dogs are brought by their owners into friends' houses and allowed to jump up on the furniture with muddy paws or sharp claws.

The behavior of a dog—like the rest of us—is seldom better out in company than it is at home. If Kiltie (bright little

Scottie though he is) is allowed to run around the dinner table at home and beg, he will do the same in every other house. It is always safest in a friend's house to keep him on a short leash. He can, with patience and love, be trained to obey certain fundamental commands. On the street, he pays no attention to another dog unless his master releases him with a "Go run." At the command "Heel!" he takes his place at his master's side. He sits and stays when told to and never jumps up on a friend unless encouraged to.

If you are invited to stay with those who do not welcome four-footed visitors, you must stay home unless you have someone with whom you can leave the dog or a good kennel at which you can board him. On the other hand, no absolutely obedient dog has ever—as far as I know—been objected to by anyone, even as a house guest. Unless, of course, your prospective host has a pet who resents four-footed intruders.

If you cannot train your dog, there are excellent "obedience schools" who will do it for you for a modest fee.

CATS

Cats are taken visiting far less often. When your cat has the run of the neighborhood, you may have to take steps to see that he does not become an inadvertent but regular visitor at a neighbor's house. It is perfectly proper to ask your neighbors not to feed your pet, as the bad habit is hard to break and can easily become a neighborhood problem.

In your own house, you may be quite accustomed to having your cat jump into your lap without warning, but remember that your guest probably isn't. Until you know your visitor likes and is not allergic to cats, it is far safer to put Fluffy securely in another room. This also avoids a suit or dress covered with hairs and possibly snagged.

OTHER PEOPLE'S PETS

If you are one of those who have an allergy or an aversion to dogs, cats, hamsters, white mice or any of the other pets you are likely to encounter, it is only polite to tell your host or hostess so, quietly and unobtrusively. No one will wish you to suffer as a guest in his house, and a few words can usually prevent much discomfort and possibly an unpleasant misunderstanding.

If you are fond of household animals, be careful to respect their training and encourage their good habits. Don't, for example, thump the sofa beside you and invite Kiltie to jump up until you have asked whether he is allowed to sit on the furniture. Your thoughtless actions may undo months of careful training. Finally, don't ever feed an animal without his owner's permission.

PART TWELVE

ON HOW TO DRESS

60

Women's clothes and fashions

THE WOMAN WHO IS CHIC

The woman who is chic is always a little different. Not different in being behind fashion, but always slightly apart from it. Chic (pronounced *sheek*) is a combination of sophistication and fastidious taste, and the woman who is chic adapts fashion to her own personality. This is in contrast to the woman who will merely buy the latest hat or dress and adapt herself to it, whether the fashion is suited to her or not. When it conspicuously is not, it is likely to be chi-chi (pronounced *she-she*), or a flashy imitation of chic.

ACCESSORIES

Accessories provide the accents that can vary the costume, giving it versatility as well as adding to its beauty. In planning your wardrobe, stick to a narrow range of colors, so that the same accessories may be used with a number of outfits. A simple black dress may be perfect for lunch at a restaurant when it is worn with a gold circle pin, single-pearl earrings and a daytime watch or wide gold bracelet and accompanied by black kid pumps and a plain leather pocketbook. But change these accessories to a diamond or zircon clip, a double strand of pearls, diamond (or pearl drop) earrings, a bracelet, perhaps, or a ring of glittering stones, suede pumps and a small suede purse, and you may appear at any but the most formal party that night.

Jewelry:

It has always been the rule of the well-dressed not to wear too many jewels in public places because such a display is considered ostentatious and in poor taste. But with the rise in popularity of costume jewelry, smart women all over have increased the amount of jewelry they wear in public as well as at home. Cultured pearls and semiprecious stones such as zircons, garnets or jade come in an infinite variety of colors. With the lower cost of these substitutes for expensive gems, many more women than ever before are able to wear beautiful jewelry.

Jewelry should be chosen and worn with an eye to suitability rather than to fad. A woman with stubby hands, for example, should not draw attention to them with a large flashing ring. When engaging in an active sport, jewelry of any kind is out of place. In the daytime, a gold or silver bracelet, a string of pearls and earrings unadorned by large stones are more suitable than the brilliant gems that go well with evening clothes. A pretty pin or clip to set off a dress or suit is lovely at any hour. In short, the choice of jewelry is limited only by the good taste and the budget of the wearer.

Gloves:

Gloves are worn on city streets, to luncheons, dinner parties and other social gatherings, to churches, restaurants, theaters and other public places of entertainment. At a restaurant, theater or the like, they may be removed on arrival, but they are generally left on in church except during communion or when it is very warm.

A lady never takes off her gloves to shake hands, no matter when or where, and *never* apologizes for not doing so. But she *always* removes them for dining. On formal occasions, the hostess wears gloves to shake hands with her guests—and keeps them on until food is served. Gloves are *always* worn when standing in a receiving line. When long gloves are an intrinsic part of your costume at a ball, they may be left on for dancing—otherwise they are taken off. A bracelet may be worn outside a long glove, but never a ring.

Hats:

If you look well in hats—wear them! If well chosen, a hat may add a dash and distinction to your outfit that a bare head can't possibly achieve. You must wear a hat to all Roman Catholic church ceremonies, and it is always correct at churches of every faith. At official luncheons and receptions, they are almost a requirement. A small hat or veil is appropriate, but not necessary, with a cocktail dress. Except for the necessary head covering at an evening wedding, a hat, even the smallest veil, is never worn with an evening dress.

Shoes:

The first thing to consider in buying shoes—and this cannot be stressed too strongly—is comfort. The most beautiful pair of shoes in the world will destroy the appearance of the wearer if the height of the heel causes her to teeter or the tightness of the toes causes her to stand painfully, first on one foot and then the other.

When picking out shoes, try to find colors and styles that will go with more than one dress. Red is an excellent choice for spring and summer, as it goes well with black, navy, white and many of the light summer shades.

If you are more comfortable in "flats" or low heels, stick to them.

The business girl who is on her feet much of the day should sacrifice some smartness for comfort and choose a shoe that has a thick soft sole and gives her foot some support. A good suggestion is to keep an extra pair of shoes at your place of business, as a change in the middle of the day is very restful to the feet.

Shoes worn with more formal clothes should match or blend with the costume in color and be appropriate in material and style. Generally speaking, leather shoes such as alligator or kid, in dark colors, are correct for daytime in the winter. Black shoes go well with almost every winter costume. Suede or satin shoes in a color matching your dress are worn for more formal occasions or in the evening. Pumps or sandals in gold or silver are worn with a formal evening dress, but they are in very bad taste for daytime wear with street costumes. "Spectators" (white pumps trimmed with black, brown or navy) for daylight occasions and white linen or cotton pumps for after dark go happily with almost any summer ensemble. High heels worn with sport slacks look—and are—ridiculous.

Handbags:

Bags can now be found in a literally unlimited variety of colors, styles and materials. Decide on whatever color blends best with all of your costumes. A good quality black leather one, large enough to contain all the items you may need for a whole day, will last for years and pay for itself many times over in usefulness, durability and beauty. A straw handbag for daytime use in the summer goes wtih all cottons and sport clothes.

Bags with changeable covers are not inexpensive, but the cost is more than made up for by the versatility. For a winter bag of this type, the basic purse might be black leather and the covers (designed to snap on so that the result appears to be an ordinary purse) might be of brown kid, black lizard or suede. The summer bags have covers of cotton or linen and are washable!

For evening, gold metallic bags are popular or, for older people, black velvet, silk or satin. Small suede or satin bags come in pretty colors and are a good choice for cocktail time.

Corsages:

There is no rule in existence about how a woman wears a corsage. She simply stands in front of a mirror and holds the flowers against her dress in various places until she finds the spot that pleases her most. If the dress is so designed that a corsage does not go well on it, or if the wearer is afraid of crushing the flowers while dancing, they may also be pinned on a cloth evening bag. If the flower has a stem, wear it upright as the flower grows—if not, place it whichever way it looks best.

CLOTHES FOR THE BUSINESS WOMAN

The unfailing directions for clothes worn in an office are that they be neat, tailored, smart, in good taste, but in no way conspicuous. Avoid everything that interferes or catches or keeps getting out of place. Also wear clothes that properly cover you.

One important accessory for beautiful business clothes is a pair of plain sensible shoes of best quality. High-heeled, fancy sandals and heel-less slippers are inappropriate. A well-shod foot is much to be prized—and noticed.

YOUR TRAVELING WARDROBE

When you plan a wardrobe for a trip, whether it be by airplane, car, train or boat, there are two considerations— space and weight. Nothing takes up more space or weighs more than handbags and shoes. If you can plan your costumes so that one pair of the most comfortable, sturdy shoes available for sightseeing can be exchanged in the evening for a pump of the same color, your packing and overweight problems will be almost solved. The handbags with changeable covers mentioned earlier in this chapter are ideal for traveling. You may carry the bag itself onto the boat or plane and pack only the light-weight covers. For evening, pack a small flat silk or satin bag.

Dresses of wrinkleproof material are a "must." Take along a little package of cleaning powders, put up specially for travelers—a spot on a dress that forms an important part of your clothing scheme can be a disaster.

Think of the versatility of your clothes. Sweaters should go well with *all* your skirts, shorts and dresses. A skirt with a matching coat makes a stunning costume for cruise or country wear because with a change of blouses, the skirt can give the appearance of several outfits. One rarely needs an evening dress when traveling, but a sleeveless cocktail dress with a jacket may be worn in any restaurant or theater or at any party to which you are invited.

Shorts and slacks, incidentally, are never worn by women abroad except at resorts, and therefore American women should "in Rome, do as the Romans." So if you are traveling on the Continent rather than on a cruise ship, save space by taking only those shorts needed for your day or two on the Riviera. Don't forget a bathing suit—even a wayside stream can provide a refreshing relief from the heat of southern France, Italy or Spain in summer; swimming pools and lakes are found near resort hotels all over the world.

(For clothes appropriate to special occasions, please consult the Index.)

61

Men's clothes

FORMAL DAYTIME WEAR

When it is necessary to dress formally, the cutaway or a black sack coat and striped trousers are worn at any affair that takes place before six o'clock in the evening. They are often worn at government or diplomatic receptions, but they appear most frequently on the principals in a formal afternoon wedding or when they are worn by pallbearers in a large funeral.

The Cutaway:

The cutaway is the most formal afternoon attire and is rarely seen except on participants in large afternoon weddings or at official teas or receptions. For this reason, few men not in the diplomatic corps have cutaways, but they can always be rented. Make your arrangements well ahead of the date it is to be worn, so that it may be fitted to you.

The cutaway (sometimes called the morning coat)—Black or oxford gray worsted or cheviot, with peaked lapels. Edges may be bound, but plain edges are preferred. Buttons are bone or self-covered.

Waistcoat—Double-breasted. In winter, black wool to match the coat or pearl-gray fine wool. In summer, white or fawn linen or white piqué.

Trousers—Black and gray striped worsted or cheviot. Cuffless.

Shirt—White, with starched bosom and starched cuffs.

Collar—Detachable wing or starched fold collar.

Tie—For weddings, ascot, in gray, silver-gray or black silk,

plain, figured or striped. Worn with wing collar. For
funerals, black four-in-hand, worn with fold collar. Other
occasions, a four-in-hand or bow tie with either wing or fold
collar.

Socks—Black or dark gray. Any material except very heavy
wool.

Shoes—Black calf oxfords.

Hat—Black silk hat. Less appropriate, a black homburg.

Topcoat—Black, dark gray or dark blue.

Gloves—Gray, any material of good quality.

Accessories—Jewelry; pearl pin with ascot, gold cuff links.
With stiff shirt with bow tie, gold single stud. Boutonniere,
white or red carnation. At a wedding, the groom may wear a
small sprig from his bride's bouquet. Handkerchief (white
linen) and white or gray silk scarf. Handkerchief initialed
in white, with all initials, or that of last name only, is folded
square and shows no more than ½ to 1 inch above the
pocket.

The sack coat:

The sack coat, a less formal version of the cutaway, is worn
by the participants in morning or afternoon weddings, large
funerals, and on any daytime occasion when the formality of
the cutaway is not essential.

Sack coat—Black or oxford gray worsted, single breasted.

Waistcoat—Double-breasted. Black or oxford gray, same as
the sack coat, or pearl-gray fine wool.

Trousers—Same as for cutaway.

Shirt—White, soft bosom, starched French cuffs. Starched
fold collar.

Tie—Black or gray and black pattern, silk. Four-in-hand style.

Hat—Black homburg or soft black felt.

All other clothing and accessories are the same as for a
cutaway.

EVENING CLOTHES

For all informal evening wear, the dark (preferably blue)
suit, with white shirt, dark tie and dark socks, is the accepted
outfit. For formal evenings, either full evening dress, called
"white tie" or "tails" (sometimes "white tie and tails") or a
dinner jacket, called "black tie" or "tuxedo," is worn. If in

doubt as to what to wear, err on the side of informality. Thus, if you are not sure whether to put on your full-dress suit or your tuxedo, wear the latter. When an occasion is important, it is entirely proper for a man to call his host or his hostess on the telephone and ask, "Do I wear a black tie tonight, or a white one?" or the question may be: "Day clothes or tuxedos?"

Black tie:

To go out for the evening dressed in "black tie" means that you are wearing a dinner jacket or tuxedo. Nowadays, black tie is accepted as correct on almost every formal occasion. Therefore, while it is more practical for most to rent a "set of tails" when the occasion demands, a good quality, well-fitted tuxedo is an excellent investment. It consists of:

Jacket—In winter or summer, black or midnight blue; the material is usually tropical worsted or, if it is not shiny, one of the new blended materials. The lapels are faced with satin. In hot weather, white linen is worn for formal affairs, but for less formal parties, plaid (madras) or a solid-color cotton, Dacron or other blend is appropriate, attractive and gay. On all jackets the lapels are rolled or peaked and of whatever width current fashion demands. Dinner jackets are usually single-breasted, but a few men still prefer the double-breasted form, which requires neither waistcoat nor cummerbund.

Trousers—When a dark jacket (black or midnight blue) is worn, the trousers are always of the same material. If a colored jacket is worn, they are of good-quality black material, usually the same pair that is worn with a black jacket. In either case, they do not have cuffs and do have a single stripe of black braid or satin.

Waistcoat or Cummerbund—The waistcoat is of white piqué or plain or patterned black silk. Nowadays, instead of a waistcoat, a cummerbund, usually (and most formally) of black or maroon silk, is frequently worn; it may also be plaid or figured, especially in the summertime.

Shirt—A daytime white shirt with fold collar; for a formal occasion, a piqué or pleated bosom.

Tie—Black silk bow with waistcoat or black cummerbund. If cummerbund is other than black, the tie should be of matching color and material.

Socks—Black silk or lisle.

Shoes—Black patent leather.

Hat—A black homburg or black or gray soft-brimmed fedora in the winter, gray fedora in the spring or fall, and a panama in the summer. Many men prefer no hat.

Gloves—Gray chamois or buck.

Topcoat—Black, dark gray or navy, with or without velvet collar.

Accessories—Jewelry; pearl or mother-of-pearl or black onyx studs. Cuff links may be gold or mother-of-pearl to match the studs. White linen handkerchief, with or without initials. White silk scarf. Boutonniere, white or red carnation.

White tie:

The great majority of men rent their "tails" for the occasion. This is perfectly correct, provided the rental establishment has excellent tailors to do alterations.

A tailcoat *must* be worn by the fathers and escorts of debutantes at their coming-out parties and to any affair when the invitation reads "white tie." Otherwise, it *may* be worn to formal dinners or balls, to official or diplomatic parties or when sitting in a box at the opera or by those in charge of benefits or charity affairs.

Tailcoat—Black worsted or tropical worsted; lapels are peaked and faced in grosgrain or satin. The tails should hang to the break at the back of the knees.

Waistcoat—White piqué. Usually single-breasted, but may be double-breasted.

Trousers—Match the coat. Single stripe of satin or braid; no cuffs.

Shirt—White, made to wear with detachable wing collar. Piqué or plain linen bosom, stiffly starched. Cuffs are single, starched. Shirt may have either one or two buttonholes for studs.

Tie—White piqué bow. Current fashion favors straight ends rather than "butterfly" shape.

Socks—Black silk or nylon.

Shoes—Black patent leather pumps or oxfords.

Hat—High silk or opera hat is most formal, but a black homburg is more frequently worn. Many men prefer not to wear a hat with tails.

Topcoat—Black or dark gray or blue.

Gloves—White chamois or doeskin.

Accessories—Jewelry; pearl or mother-of-pearl studs for shirt, mother-of-pearl or platinum or white gold for the waistcoat and cuff links. White linen handkerchief and white silk scarf. Boutonniere, white carnation or small white gardenia.

COATS AND HATS

For the man who frequently wears evening clothes, a solid black, navy or dark gray coat is a necessity. For daytime wear he also requires a less formal coat in the color that goes best with his suits. The dress coat may or may not be double-breasted—the daytime sports coat, never.

For men whose wardrobe is limited, a gray felt fedora is the best choice. It can be worn with any color and in any circumstance except with full evening dress. Those who wear white tie frequently should have a black homburg or silk hat to go with it. Derbies, which used to be worn with business suits, are rarely seen and the high silk hat has almost disappeared.

Lifting or tipping the hat:

Lifting or tipping the hat means merely lifting it slightly off the forehead—by the brim of a stiff hat or by the crown of a soft one.

A gentleman does this: (1) When walking with a friend who greets a woman who is a stranger to him. (2) When a lady who is a stranger drops a glove or other article and he retrieves it for her. (3) When he passes a lady in a narrow space so that he blocks her way or in any manner obstructs her. (4) If he gets on a bus and the bus gives a lurch and throws him against a woman. (5) If an older woman or a young one carrying a baby or heavy packages enters the bus, and he rises and offers his seat (also when she thanks him). (If he is seated when a young woman enters a bus, he may keep his seat.)

If he is in the company of a woman anywhere in public, he lifts his hat to a man who offers her a seat or who picks up something she has dropped or shows her any other civility. He lifts his hat if he asks a woman a question and always if, when walking on the street with a lady, she greets another person. In short, he tips his hat to say "Excuse me," or "Thank you."

When to remove a hat and gloves:

A gentleman takes off his hat and holds it in his hand when a lady enters the elevator in an apartment house or hotel—any building which can be classified as a dwelling. He puts it on again in the corridor—an elevator in a hotel or apartment house has the character of a room in a house and there a man does not keep his hat on in the presence of women. But in public buildings such as offices or stores or buildings that contain neither apartments nor assembly rooms, the elevator is considered as public a place as a bus or train.

When a man stops on a city street to speak to a woman of his acquaintance, should he be smoking, he transfers the cigarette or pipe to his left hand before he removes his hat. Then he pulls off his right glove and offers his hand to the lady. If they walk on together, he puts his hat on. While standing in the street talking to her, he remains hatless unless, in cold weather, she thoughtfully says, "Please put your hat on." At a formal ball or wedding, a gentleman need not remove his glove to shake hands.

An American citizen always stands with his hat off at the passing of the flag and when the national anthem is played—indoors or out-of-doors. He also takes his hat off in the presence of a funeral and in all Christian churches.

Men's jewelry:

The best rule for buying men's jewelry is to choose the simplest that can be found.

Cuff links should be of moderate size. Flashing stones in tie pins or rings in the daytime are in poor taste.

The most appropriate rings are those of gold, with initials or crest, worn on the little finger, or a seal ring of one's school or military service, which are worn on the fourth finger of either hand. Wedding rings should be of plain gold, or with the very simplest of patterns.

PART THIRTEEN

THE WELL-APPOINTED HOUSE

62

The employer-servant relationship

THE NEW EMPLOYER

If you have never kept house before and do not know what a maid should be able to do, go to a reliable employment office where the personnel will be glad to tell you about hours and wages and an average working plan. Or you may ask a friend who has a maid to help you.

When an applicant comes to you for an interview, she brings with her written references from her last employer. If she has several, she shows you the last two or three. A good reference says that she is honest, sober, capable, trustworthy and of good disposition. If one of these items is missing in each of the references shown you, take this possible shortcoming into consideration. References also give the telephone number and addresses, so that you may talk to or write the previous employer if you wish to.

If the references are good, the wages you can pay meet her expectations, and you find her personality pleasing, you describe to her the schedule of both working and time-off hours. Be accurate. Misrepresentation of facts or intentions is unfair. If she is going to care for the baby, say so quite honestly. Don't say you are always prompt when you are not or that your meals will be simple if you expect her to be an expert chef. Don't say that the house is easy to take care of if it isn't. At the other extreme, don't exaggerate whatever inconveniences there may perhaps be.

HOW MUCH WORK?

Out of every twenty-four hours, every normal human being should have at least nine hours for sleeping, dressing and undressing, in addition to plenty of time for eating three meals. During the rest of the day, she must find the time for rest and recreation as well as for work, and this additional time off must be adjusted to the household routine. The maid's days off should be stated clearly and respected. If it is absolutely necessary to change a day off, she must be given ample warning so that she may change her own plans.

The maid's food and lodging, her uniforms and aprons are part of her pay so that her hours for housework would naturally on occasion run longer than ordinary business hours.

MAY SERVANTS ENTERTAIN FRIENDS?

Certainly! In every large house, there is always a sitting room furnished with comfortable chairs, a sofa, a radio, a television set and good light to read by. In a smaller house where no sitting room is possible, the kitchen table has an attractive cover put on it and a droplight and a few restful chairs are provided if there is space. Or the maid's room, especially one on the ground floor, may be furnished as a sitting room.

In homes with one servant, the use of the living room is sometimes offered the maid when the family is not at home. The man of the house may even suggest that her caller will find a soft drink in the refrigerator.

UNIFORMS

All maids' uniforms as well as aprons and collars and cuffs are furnished by the employer, with the exception of the dresses worn by a lady's maid and those worn by a cook, for whom the employer furnishes only the aprons.

AN ATTRACTIVE ROOM

Make her room as attractive as possible with a comfortable bed, attractively painted furniture and a little gay chintz. Smooth-flowing paints or enamels in beautiful colors can be applied even by an amateur. The kitchen should be equally attractive, for this is where she will spend much of her time.

COURTESY ON BOTH SIDES

In a formal household servants are addressed as James, Margaret or Katherine, rather than Jim, Maisie or Katie. A butler is called by his last name. The Worldlys' butler, for instance, is called Hastings, not John; the housekeeper is Mrs. Jones and the nurse is called by her name or a nickname such as "Nanny." In a less formal household, the maid may be called by a nickname, or if she is an older woman, she may be called Mrs. Helper.

Every courteous person says "please" in asking that something be brought her or him. "Would you mail these letters, please" or "Some bread, please." So, too, in refusing a dish at the table one says, "No, thank you."

The well-trained servant is faultlessly neat in appearance, reticent in manner, speaks in a low voice and moves silently. In answering a bell, she asks, "Did you ring, madam?" A courteous maid answers her employer, "Yes, madam," "Very good, sir," or "Yes, sir," but never "Yes," "No," "All right," or "Sure."

In a formal house, grown sons and daughters are called "Miss Katherine" or "Mr. Oliver"; half-grown children are generally called by their familiar names with the prefix of Miss or Mr. (Miss Kitty, Mr. Ollie), but never by the nurse, who calls them by their first names until they are grown—always.

In the smaller house with one maid, all the young children are called by their first names or nicknames.

SUCCESS IN HOUSEHOLD MANAGEMENT

Justice is the foundation upon which every tranquil household is constructed. It is not right to be too lenient, any more than it is right to be unreasonably demanding. There is no greater example of injustice than to reprimand those about you because you happen to be in a bad humor and overlook greater offenses because you are in an amiable mood. There is also no excuse ever for correcting an employee in front of anyone else. If the lady of the house and the other members of the family show human understanding and fairness in what they exact, they are very unlikely ever to have any housekeeping difficulties.

63

Household assistants

THE CHILDREN'S NURSE

A children's nurse is either the comfort or the torment of the house. Innumerable young mothers put up with inexcusable crankiness from a crotchety middle-aged woman because she is "so wonderful" to the baby. In ninety-nine cases out of a hundred, the sooner a domineering nurse—old or young—is let go, the better. When the right sort of kindly and humane person takes the tyrant's place, the mother usually finds that the child is as relieved as the rest of the family. A young child is inescapably imprisoned in the atmosphere created by the disposition of the person in charge of him and sunlight is not more essential to a plant than an atmosphere of sympathetic lightheartedness is to a child.

A nurse's references should *always* be checked by talking on the telephone with the woman who employed her last. Her moral character is of utmost concern, for she is to be the constant and inseparable companion of children whose whole lives are influenced by her example, especially if busy parents can give only a small portion of time to their children.

The nurse dresses in white in the home—the wonderful wash-and-wear fabrics available today make this entirely practical. On the street she wears a simple suit or dress and hat (the cloak and cap of the English nurse is suitable only if she actually is British).

THE REGISTERED NURSE

The social position of a registered hospital nurse is that of a deputy physician and, when on a long case, the closest of the family's friends. She always eats her meals with the family or has them served to her on a tray in a sitting room. When on duty in her patient's room or anywhere in a private house, she wears her uniform. But when going into the street, going downstairs in a hotel or traveling with her patient, she dresses as does any other lady.

THE BABY-SITTER

A baby-sitter's age may range from the early teens up to that of an elderly lady. The customary rate of the community should be observed and the sitter paid at the end of the evening. The sitter should be told that after the children are asleep he or she may use the television set or play the radio, read or do homework; in other words, what he is expected to do and what he may not do. It is thoughtful to leave a snack in the refrigerator. Be specific about where you are going—leave address and telephone number, as well as the name, address and telephone number of the children's doctor. Always tell the sitter when you expect to be back—and try to be on time. Adequate transportation must be provided for her safe return home, and this applies for sitters of any age.

PART-TIME HELP

The maid, or "cleaning woman," who comes by the hour or day, is treated with the same courtesy as the permanent servant. She is paid promptly—daily, weekly or any other way agreed upon. In the country, if the house is far from public transportation, the employer sees that she is transported to bus or train or, if she is not, that her pay is augmented to cover taxi fare. In the city, the employer pays all carfares involved. If the employer wishes her to wear uniforms, she naturally provides them for her.

The maid's duties should be carefully outlined in advance. Will there be cooking to do? Are washing and ironing expected, and what about heavy cleaning like waxing floors and washing windows? For any unusual work, to help with a dinner party, for example, the hourly rate for this extra service should be agreed upon beforehand.

64

Serving the family meals

THE TABLE

In many of today's houses and apartments, the pressures of space and expense have caused the large, formal dining room to disappear. The dining table appears in an ell or an alcove off the living room, in the end of the living room nearest the kitchen, or at one end of the kitchen itself. Whatever the location, the table should be thought of as a pleasant center of family gatherings. It should be large enough to accommodate the entire family comfortably, for young children especially need plenty of room to eat properly and crowding only encourages jostling.

A pretty cloth or attractive place mats lend an air of graciousness to even the simplest meal; a centerpiece is also pleasing. With a little help, children can pick and arrange a few flowers or make a simple table decoration. Such contributions help children recognize the importance of household appointments.

Most often, when there is no maid, mother sits nearest the

kitchen door with the youngest, who may still need help from time to time, next to her. Father sits opposite her.

If there is a maid in the house, the family always eats at the dining table, where they are served simply, in whatever way best fits their preference and the capabilities of the maid.

Kitchen dining:

If possible have an end or corner of the kitchen set apart, furnished and decorated in such a way that children growing up in the home feel the importance of good manners at the table, just as they would if they were being served in a beautifully appointed dining room. Even a kitchen table should be charmingly set for dinner with place mats (paper doilies will do), spotless utensils and pretty plates and glasses, attractive in color and pattern.

General Electric

THE PLACE SETTINGS

The main difference in setting a table for guests and setting a table for the family is that a minimum number of utensils is put at each place—only those absolutely necessary for each course. There may be no more than a fork, a knife, and a spoon or fork for dessert. At a family dinner, a separate fork for salad is not necessary, but a salad plate is, so that gravy and salad dressings do not become mixed. Bread and butter are often placed on the edge of the dinner plate, but with the convenience of an electric dishwasher, it is nicer to have a separate butter plate.

The table settings described below indicate the correct position of the articles that will be needed. No china or silver that will not actually be used needs to be put on the table —no salad forks if you are not serving salad, no bread-and-butter plate if you have no bread.

Breakfast:

There is a wide difference in the tastes of breakfast-eaters. If your daughter only eats toast and coffee, omit the fork. If your son doesn't drink coffee, you need only give him a glass for his milk.

In the informal household, a variety of cold cereals, milk, cream, sugar, salt and pepper, and jams or jellies are in the center of the table or on a convenient side table; whoever does the cooking serves the hot food directly onto the plates and places them in front of those sitting at the table. If your table is large enough, a "lazy susan" or turntable is most convenient.

Individual places are set with as many of the following articles as will be necessary: Fork at the left of the plate, knife at the right of the plate, spoon for cereal at the right of the knife, teaspoon for fruit (but not for coffee) at the right of the cereal spoon.

Butter knife across the bread-and-butter plate, which is to the left and above the fork. Napkins at the left of the plates if fruit or fruit juice is at the places; otherwise, napkins at the center of each place.

Coffee cups have spoons lying at right of, or on, the saucers, at the right of each plate. Glasses for milk or water are to the right and above the spoons.

Lunch:

For the busy woman of today, lunch usually consists of a sandwich, a bowl of soup or a salad served at the dining-room table, if there is a maid. Otherwise, it is often brought to the living room or patio on a tray. When children are home for lunch, it can be served either at the dining table or in the kitchen, according to the preference of the family. No more than three courses are ever served for lunch; even that number is most unusual. The setting is as follows:

Salad fork at the left, next to the plate, if salad is to be served after the meat. The meat fork is at the left of the salad fork. On the right, a meat knife; and at the right of this knife, a bouillon or fruit spoon, if necessary.

The butter plate and knife are above the forks at the left.

Because dessert, if served, is brought in after the main course, the dessert fork or spoon may be brought in with the dessert plate.

Dinner:

If the food is to be passed, the dinner plates are at each place on the table when the family sits down, or in front of the head of the household if he is to serve. Many women prefer to serve the plates directly from the stove. If there is a maid in the home, she may pass the plates around as they are served by the man of the house, or, if the family is small, she may pass the

dishes to each person. The table setting for dinner is similar to that for lunch with the implements necessary for each course arranged in order of their use: the one to be used first goes on the outside; that to be used last is put nearest the plate.

Next to the plate and at the left is the salad fork, then the dinner fork. (If salad is to be served first, the salad fork is farthest from the plate.) At the right, the dinner knife is next to the plate, then the soup spoon or the oyster fork or fruit spoon on the outside (if necessary).

The glass or goblet for the beverage is at the right above the knife. The butter plate is at the left with the butter knife laid on it diagonally from upper left to lower right. The dessert spoon and fork may be brought in on the dessert plate after the table is cleared; otherwise the fork goes next to the plate on the left, and the spoon immediately to the right of the knife.

THE MEALTIME TRAY

When a member of the family is ill and must remain in bed for his meals, an attractive tray with a flower in a little vase or a gay napkin and tray cloth can aid a lagging appetite. Always use a tray cloth or a doily of any sort. The setting is the same as the individual place setting at the table. The dessert plate and the coffee cup and saucer are usually brought when the main meal is finished because of lack of room. The dinner plate should be heated and covered, if the meal is hot, to keep it warm. If you do not have a regular domed plate cover, a piece of foil laid over the food will keep it warm for several minutes.

PART FOURTEEN

FAMILY LIFE

65

The young child

Etiquette applies to everyone, old or young, and the best way to teach etiquette to children is by consistency, firmness and example.

Children can scarcely be too young to be taught the rudiments of etiquette. Any child can be taught to be well behaved with patience and perseverance, whereas to break bad habits once they are acquired is a herculean task.

FAIR PLAY

Children should be taught, even before they go to school, to "play fair," to respect each other's property and rights, to give credit to others and not to take too much credit to themselves, to share their playthings and to take good care of toys that belong to other children. A bright, observing child should never be encouraged to brag about his own achievements or to tell his or her mother how inferior other children are.

"BECAUSE EVERYONE ELSE DOES"

All young people feel a need for conformity with the activities of others of their age. This they express in their speech, their play, their choice of clothing and their relationships to each other. This conformity is quite normal and is to be respected as part of the development of individual personality as well as social responsibility.

Children should be permitted to follow the customs of their community, so as not to differ too radically from the other children in the neighborhood, but there are necessary qualifications to this advice. Parents sometimes must make a decision at the risk of having their children a little different in some particular from their friends. There are times when children should be required to set an example for others to follow, rather than be just like all the rest. There is a certain element of risk involved in this position, but there is also an element of discipline that is far more important. Precepts and lectures are never a substitute for understanding and sympathetic guidance.

EATING HABITS

When children are a year and a half to two years old, they begin to learn to feed themselves. From the very first, they can be encouraged to keep the food on the plate, taught how to hold a cup so that it will not spill, and shown the use of a bib or napkin. These skills do not come naturally, but with patient repetition and gentle insistence, they can be acquired.

As soon as the child has learned to eat well enough so that his presence at the table is not offensive, he should be allowed to eat with adults, occasionally at first, and more often as his manners improve. As a member of the family group at meals, there are more advanced lessons to be learned.

He must be clean and neat when he comes to the table, chew quietly, with his mouth closed, not overload his spoon or fork, or fidget or play with his food or the implements at his place.

He must not interrupt the adults, but he should be included in the conversation, and his mother or father from time to time should introduce a subject within his range of interests.

If he finishes before the others, he asks, "May I please be excused?" and waits for permission before leaving the table. Very young children should be given this privilege, because when their food is gone, they resort to wriggling and noise-making to pass the time.

If he refuses to be good, say nothing, but lead him quietly from the table. The child quickly learns to be well-behaved when he understands that good behavior is the price of admission to grown-up society.

The little one's mother can help by bringing his plate to the table with the food ready for him to eat—the portions of small or moderate size, the meat and vegetables cut in small bite-size pieces. His glass or cup should have a broad base and be of plastic or pottery. If he is very small, his fork and spoon should be of appropriate size. A bib large enough so that an accidental spill will not ruin his clothes is mandatory. Let him have a high chair or put cushions on a regular chair to raise him to the proper height. If you think this is unimportant, try sometime to eat neatly while kneeling at a table that comes approximately to the level of your chin!

The child who sees his family enjoying their food and enjoying each others' company follows their example. Constant nagging and correction are as detrimental as a total lack of instruction. If older children are allowed to complain about the food and if there are continuous arguments at the table, unhappy associations will result in antagonism to food and to good manners in eating.

MONEY MATTERS

When a child is old enough to buy a candy bar or an ice cream cone for himself, he should be given a small, regular allowance in return for helping with the dishes or keeping his room neat. Extra duties—washing the dog or running an errand—deserve special consideration and are paid for separately if the parents feel that they merit a reward. Children should be permitted to use an allowance as they wish. The amount should be about the same as that given to his small friends. Some parents give the child more allowance but insist that a part be set aside for the weekly church contribution or saved for birthday presents or a special hobby or treat. This seems a wise system, as the child acquires a sense of the value of money.

As the child grows, so must his allowance and the expenses he is expected to pay for himself. As he approaches his teens, he pays for movies, cosmetics, presents or extra pieces of clothing or jewelry that are not actually necessary. To pay for such

items, he has to plan ahead and give up other pleasures until
he has saved a sufficient sum. This is excellent training. If he
is working toward something worthwhile that he really cares
about, his parents may encourage him by giving him extra
chores paid for at an hourly rate and by adding to his fund
with a small check for Christmas or birthday.

A CHILD'S APPEARANCE

As soon as a child shows any interest in what he is wearing,
he should be allowed a voice in choosing his clothes, though
naturally his mother must make the final decision. But he will
thus absorb some principles of dressing well and he will also
be happy to wear the clothes that are bought for him.

Don't overdress your child. If he or she is invited to a party,
ask the mother of the host or hostess what type of clothing
will be appropriate. Even school clothes should conform to
those of the other children. If wearing ties is not required of
the small boys, let your son go in a sport shirt, and if the girls
all wear brown loafers, don't insist on patent-leather slippers.

Never dress your child in clothes that are too old for him.
The three-year-old dressed in long gray flannels and a sport
jacket looks as inappropriate as his father would going to
business in shorts and an Eton jacket. Little girls should never
wear even moderately high heels before they reach their teens.
Nor should they wear makeup or dress their hair elaborately.
Let them play at being grown up in the privacy of their rooms
but never in public.

CHILDREN'S PARTIES

The span of attention of tiny children is limited, and they
tire quickly, so parties for very young children, under six,
let us say, should be no more than two hours long. The refreshments should be very simple. To avoid confusion and
permit better organization, the guest list should be short—five
or six guests for a second birthday party, and ten or twelve
for a six- to eight-year-old. The formula for a successful party
for the very young is as follows:

Guests arrive at four. One half hour is allowed for opening
presents and letting off steam. One hour of organized games
or entertainment follows. A magician is always popular; so
are comedy movies. Treasure hunts, "pin-the-tail-on-the-don-

key," musical chairs for the littlest children, and guessing games, a "three-legged" race for older ones are always good. At five thirty refreshments are served: sandwich (peanut butter and jelly cannot be surpassed for popularity), ice cream and the birthday cake. In warm weather a fruit punch, soda or ice-cold milk are popular; in winter, hot chocolate is welcome.

Parties for older children may run to two and a half or three hours if enough entertainment is planned. Games are more complicated, and a short feature movie takes the place of "shorts." A scavenger hunt or a swimming pool makes a summer party successful. At the age of ten or eleven or even older, hay rides, sleigh rides, trips to baseball or football games, or circuses or rodeos become more fun than the "game party" at home. When a group is taken to this sort of entertainment, be sure the invitation makes it clear whether or not lunch or supper will be provided.

Whether they are three or ten, the essential manners for party guests are identical. They say "Hello" to their host and the host's mother when they arrive, and they shake hands and say "Good-bye, and thank you for a wonderful time" when they leave. The young host or hostess greets them when they come and, in answer to their farewell, says "Good-bye, and thanks again for the present" or "Good-bye. Thank you for coming."

PARENTS AND CHILDREN

The first outward sign of respect you can show your toddler is not to talk *down* to him. "Baby-talk" is an insult to the intelligence of a normal child.

I have found that most children are far more capable than their elders believe. If you assume that your child will react to a situation in a reasonable way, you will generally find that he will live up to your expectations. One word of warning, however: nothing frustrates Johnny more than being required to do things that he simply is not capable of handling. To scold him for not being able to do up his snaps or buttons causes him to rebel against all attempts to teach him to dress himself.

Study your child as an interesting person, increase his responsibilities as he seems able to cope with them, reprove him when he falls short, and praise him when he takes a step forward. Teach him new words, and share as many family activities with him as you can. Laugh *with* him—not at him or his mistakes. Encouragement, appreciation and lots of love are essential in a baby's happy environment.

OBEYING THE RULES

Teach your children from their earliest years that certain rules have to be obeyed, particularly those that govern the relationship between themselves and other people. Delinquency is often the result of overly permissive parents, who either think that they should not ("Oh, I wouldn't want to stunt Harvey's independent development") or are afraid to discipline their children ("But Sally won't love me if I don't let her eat her ice cream before dinner"). Young people, no matter what they may say aloud, want and need direction and correction and the more honest ones will even admit it.

The single most important thing about disciplining a child is to make your point and stick to it. If you say "No" to an extra half hour at bedtime, and then say "Yes" when Susie says "But Mommy, this is my favorite TV program," how will Susie ever know whether or not you mean what you say?

The severity of the punishment should be directly related to the seriousness of the misdeed. A minor infraction should not result in a major penalty, or the child will have no way of differentiating between an important and an unimportant offense. If possible, the punishment should be related to the error. If Johnny refuses to remove his muddy rubbers time after time, he might be forbidden to go out and play in the mud puddles the next time his best friend calls him.

Unless you can hold to them, don't make threats. When you have not followed up on a threat once, your child will pay little attention when you make another. A simple one, such as "Bobby, stop throwing the wrappers on the floor, or I will take away the rest of your chewing gum," is all right. But to say, "Karen, if you don't go to bed at once, you can't go to kindergarten for a week," when you know (as does Karen) that she will be there the next morning, only makes you appear ridiculous.

When a child has committed a serious misdeed, such as lighting matches, take the time and trouble to explain the reason for the rule. Show him, with paper or kerosene or however you can make it the most impressive, how quickly a fire can spread and explain the consequences from his point of view—his favorite toy would be burned up, his dog might be killed, etc. And then decide on the punishment: deprivation of certain privileges like watching television, or the cancellation of a longed-for treat. In extreme cases, where repeated admonitions and punishments have not brought any results, there is no substitute for a good hard spanking with the palm of Daddy's or Mother's hand.

RESPECT

If you as parents lead your youngsters to believe that your experience, your education and your attitudes are worth emulating, respect, that quality most lacking today between parents and their children, will follow of its own accord. This, in turn, will be expanded, as your children grow up, to include relatives, friends and finally, more mature people of every sort.

66

The teen-ager

THE EARLY TEENS

If parents have had a loving, intelligent relationship with their sons and daughters during childhood, with confidence and respect growing on both sides, the problems of adolescence will be greatly modified. This book is not designed to discuss the psychological aspects of the young, but rather to discuss their manners and what they should or should not do. Remember, when making a rule or saying "No" to a teen-ager, to consider the importance of the decision to him (does it really *matter* if Bob stays out a half-hour longer?), the customs of his friends and classmates, and whether it will actually help him, either from his own point of view or in the eyes of others. The last reason in the world for making a regulation is "Well, I always had to wash the dishes when I was your age!"

APPEARANCE

It sometimes seems that teen-agers *like* to be sloppy. This applies not only to themselves but to their rooms and possessions. My feeling about this general attitude is that they be allowed to dress as sloppily as they please when they are not "in public" or with adults. But at school, at meals, on any excursion with adults, on all public conveyances, and at all social functions, they must be properly and neatly dressed. This does not mean that they can't go to an informal gathering without a tie and jacket. Of course they may wear a sport shirt, shorts and sweater, or whatever the favorite local costume is, but the sweater and shirt should be clean, the hair combed and shoes ON.

Young boys must constantly be reminded to wash and to shave. Many boys who are not accustomed to regular shaving do not realize that their beard is becoming heavier each year. Parents have to keep after them day in and day out until it becomes a habit.

Teen-age girls fix their hair interminably, but they need guidance as to style, length, becomingness and good hygiene. The simplest hairdo currently popular is generally the most becoming. As they get older and begin to experiment, the only restriction should be that they refrain from becoming too extreme, lest they look "cheap." A thirteen- or fourteen-year-old may wear a little light lipstick to a party. As she gets older, she uses a more vivid shade, and by the time she is sixteen or seventeen, she may choose any shade that goes well with her complexion, as well as powder, a *very light* rouge if she is pale, and inconspicuous eye makeup. Heavily made-up eyes belong only on the stage. As to style in clothing, avoid extremes: the lowest neckline, the barest bathing suit, the tightest trousers. People, young or old, who have the most delightful manners and the greatest charm are those who do not go out of their way to attract attention.

TABLE MANNERS

Slouching, tipping the chair back and fiddling all seem to be within the special province of the teen-ager. In many cases, it is not willful disregard of directions—they simply do not absorb them. Their minds are on a thousand other more interesting matters—girls, boys, parties, school, sports, ad infinitum, and the only hope of penetrating the screen is repetition in the hope that eventually your words will "sink in." By the tone of your voice and the way you say it, repeated correction can avoid the undesirable effect of "nagging."

ALLOWANCES

The question of a "clothes allowance" usually arises in the middle teens. Some youngsters can't wait to be given enough money to dress themselves and pay all their own expenses, while others cling to the security of letting their parents pay for their clothes and receiving a small weekly or monthly "daily expenses" allowance. As a general rule, the year a boy or girl enters college, or becomes of college age, is the time to give him or her financial independence.

But there is no set rule—the time might come a year or two earlier for a boy who is responsible and understands the value of money and the danger of wasting it, while the girl who has had little experience in shopping or managing a checking account might better wait longer.

A system that seems to me to be excellent is practiced by one of my neighbors. Her fourteen-year-old daughter, a sensible, intelligent girl wanted a clothes allowance. The parents started her out with a monthly sum to cover school clothes—blouses, skirts, shoes, socks, underwear, etc.—but no expensive ones such as party dresses or overcoats. In this way she is learning to understand the handling of money, but she does not have a large sum at her disposal which might prove to be a temptation to irresponsible spending. They are increasing the sum and the variety of clothing she is expected to buy each year; by the time she finishes high school, she will be completely responsible for her clothes and incidental expenses.

If paying all their children's tuition at school and college is too severe a strain on the family budget, teen-agers should certainly help by applying for scholarships, working part-time (in the cafeteria, dormitories or library) or taking an evening job, preferably one like baby-sitting that allows the student to study during those hours. Parents should never be ashamed to discuss the need for financial assistance of this sort with their children. Young men and women, brought up with love and respect for their families, will understand and take pride in doing what they can to help.

As to the amounts for suitable allowances, it is difficult to say, because requirements vary so widely. A city child needs more—bus or subway rides cost him money; his country cousin rides the same distance on a bicycle. Movies, food and entertainment also cost more than in the country.

A possible scale for a weekly allowance, necessarily subject to change to fit the circumstances, might run something like this:

13–14 years	$1.00–2.00
15–17 years	4.00–5.00

When the teen-ager is older and it seems advisable to add a clothing allowance to his pocket money, he might receive a monthly amount something like this:

16–18 years	$25.00– 35.00
18 and over	75.00–100.00

A boy or girl receiving one hundred dollars a month would be expected to pay all expenses such as school books, cleaning bills, etc.—everything, in other words, except tuition and doctors' bills.

67

College years

PERSONAL POPULARITY

Attending college is a serious business. Good marks are of primary importance. But of almost equal importance is the ability to make people like you, to get on easily with others and to make friends. The best way to do this is to become interested in what interests them and to be outgoing and friendly. Most of us go through life thinking of what *we* are going to do, what we hope or fear is going to happen to *us,* instead of thinking or caring about what happens to those about us. Sensitive awareness of the reactions of others is a priceless gift. If you would be liked by those with whom you come in contact, cultivate sensitiveness of perception. Attractive looks are an asset, certainly, but a bright, responsive personality is far more friend-making than great beauty or a handsome face.

THE FRESHMAN ARRIVES AT COLLEGE

Your first days in college will be harried and hurried but also a lot of fun: learning new things, meeting new people. Orientation or Welcome Week at many colleges is devoted exclusively to the freshman, helping the new student feel at home. Group meetings explain study programs, registration routine, the faculty-advisor system and other facts of campus life, including extracurricular activities. Faculty members meet and talk with the new students. If you will welcome the Welcoming Committee with interest and cordiality, you will acquire many first-of-the-year friends that will be yours for four years and possibly for life.

DORMITORY LIFE

Consideration is the key to successful dormitory living. The facilities of the dormitory are yours and your roommate's. This means sharing your quarters, keeping "your side" in order, and being considerate of your roommate's sleeping and studying habits as well as observing the quiet hours that the dormitory imposes. Obeying the regulations of the dormitory will not make you a "square." It will merely make the lives of many strangers living together run more smoothly.

Avoid borrowing like the plague, but respond graciously when asked to lend an article of yours, whether you accept or refuse the request. Take better care of borrowed property than of your own, and return it to the owner promptly.

Treat the house mother in a girl's dormitory with respect and friendliness. Drop into her apartment now and then with a few friends for a chat before dinner; this gesture will be appreciated for its thoughtfulness. Christmas gifts to the house mother and tips to the staff are in order. Usually a box is passed, with a sum being collected for those on the household staff, and a gift from all presented to the house mother; otherwise, a small remembrance can be given individually.

IN CLASS AND AFTER

The student encounters faculty members in the classroom, at joint student-faculty committee meetings, departmental teas, extracurricular activities and on the campus. A professor is never addressed as "Doc" or "Prof." If a graduate assistant himself requests it, it is all right to call him by his first name.

You will miss a lot if you don't join some of the many extracurricular activities the college offers: history or foreign-affairs clubs, religious organizations, student government and any kind of athletic club. Some of them are educational; in all you will make valuable friendships. But don't overdo it to the point where you have no time left for your studies.

Fraternities and sororities are an integral feature of many campuses but are not essential to a collegiate social life. Follow your own individual tastes and needs in deciding whether to affiliate with one or remain an Independent.

THE BIG COLLEGE WEEKEND

One of the most important events of the year at college is the special annual weekend that takes place in the fall or in the spring. There may be a Friday-night informal party at the fraternity house, on Saturday, a picnic or a game to watch or perhaps a ski excursion in midwinter. Saturday night is the formal dance, often preceded by a sit-down dinner. Sunday, students and their dates may go to church together and organize an excursion or informal party. After Sunday dinner, the weekend closes.

When a girl is invited to such a weekend, she pays for her own transportation to and from the campus. As soon as she has accepted her host's written invitation, he informs her of the bus, train or plane schedules. If it is impossible for him to meet her, he arranges for a friend to be there or sees that a taxi is available.

The girl may stay in the college's chapter house of her sorority, in a dormitory made ready for the visitors, or at a local hotel, perhaps sharing a room with another "import." The man makes all the arrangements and far enough in advance to get comfortable and convenient accommodations, and to let her know where she will be staying. He assumes the financial obligations, pays for all her meals and for all transportation after she arrives at the local railroad depot.

Don'ts for girls as house party visitors:

DON'T wait until the last moment to be sure your bag is in perfect condition. Don't arrive with a shabby, down-at-the-heels suitcase with the handle half off, the lock broken and straps carelessly hanging out. Neat, compact, goodlooking luggage pleases a man more than you might suspect.

DON'T forget to dress mentally as you pack. Stockings? Shoes? Slip? Dress? What goes with it? Belt, clips or other accessories, bag, etc.

DON'T make your luggage one inch bigger or one ounce heavier than necessary, unless you are driving your own car. On holiday occasions in small college towns there may not be taxis or cars for more than about one out of ten. Therefore DON'T count on being that one.

DON'T show an alive and interested manner toward the

boys and total indifference toward the girls. When you are shown to the room which you are to share with another girl, DON'T claim the bed you like best by throwing your bag on it. At least make the gesture of asking the other girl if she cares which she takes. DON'T take up more than exactly your share of the closet space and drawer space. If you have brought too many things for the space that is yours, leave some of them packed in your bag and leave the bag neatly closed.

DON'T monopolize the bathroom. DON'T leave your personal belongings around on all the bedroom furniture. When you pack to leave, DON'T leave powder, smears of lipstick or bobby pins in the bureau drawer. Be sure you have not left panties or other personal items in dresser drawers. DON'T forget throughout your stay to respect the wishes of the house mother and other chaperons and to say good-bye to her and to the others and thank them for their kindness.

On the evening of your arrival you will probably all congregate before dinner when introductions are made. They are likely to be not only by first names but by nicknames: "Sally, this is Slim," or "Babs," and so on. DON'T, however, wait for introductions under the house roof. If you are shy or afraid you won't make friends, remember that nearly every other girl is feeling exactly the same!

If you don't know anything about the boy seated beside you at dinner, ask your own date, who should be seated at your left, about him first so as to know what to talk to him about. A man is rarely bored if you talk—but with some intelligence —about him. DON'T lay flattery on with a trowel.

At the dances, greet the chaperons as though you liked them. DON'T refuse to dance with anyone who cuts in, unless he is drunk or objectionable.

Throughout the days of your visit, DON'T think only of what you like to do; do whatever the majority suggest—unless what is suggested is something you think is wrong. For instance, there is no obligation to drink anywhere at any time —unless you choose to.

DON'T be jealous of every attention your date pays to another girl. DON'T show that you hate to be teased or you'll be a target for it. DON'T show chagrin or disappointment. Be blind, deaf and insensible to annoyance or disappointment. DON'T do anything that can seem unappreciative of the efforts made for your pleasure by the man who is your host. DON'T try to impress him with your powers by attracting one of his classmates; your lack of loyalty will be resented by every member of his crowd.

Above all, DON'T forget that the friendship of other girls is the crown of your own success. Trying to take their boy friends will end in ostracism. The really popular girl is popular with girls as well as boys.

68

Chaperons and dates

MODERN CHAPERONAGE

From an ethical standpoint, the only chaperon worth having in the present day is a young girl's own efficiency in chaperoning herself. She must develop expertness in handling situations herself, be able to gauge the reactions of various types of persons, particularly men, in varying circumstances, which man has the instincts of a gentleman and which does not and will try to take advantage of her.

Apart, however, from the consideration of ethics, which is concerned with what the girl herself thinks or feels or the motives behind what she says or does, there still remain the appearances to be considered. Many young people today are foolishly inclined to ignore appearances; they feel they can act independently of public opinion. But gossip still influences a world that seldom takes the trouble to sift appearance from fact.

The necessary proprieties:

If on her return from a party, a young girl finds her family is not at home, she does not invite any man to "come in for a while." If he persists, she answers casually but firmly, "Sorry, another time," and bids him good night.

Some families insist on a sensible practice. Just before leaving a dance their daughter telephones home if she plans to go on to someone's house or bring friends to her own. The daughter finds this reasonable, making her practice of telephoning a mark of respect for her mother which no one questions. As for the mother herself, she must find the middle road between too great permissiveness and overprotectiveness which hampers the child's development of responsibility.

An unmarried girl should not go on overnight trips with any young man, even with her fiancé, because convention still decrees that she may not stop in a hotel with a young man unchaperoned. However, a girl of eighteen may perfectly well go on a weekend trip with several couples to a ski resort or a beach resort without giving any cause for gossip.

The chaperon at the school dance:

Chaperons for a school dance may be recruited from among the faculty, the parents of the students, or other townspeople. They may be single persons or married couples. Chaperons are the ringside participants at the dance, responsible for the general discipline and order of those dancing without putting a damper on the fun.

A committee of one or a few may be in charge of securing the chaperons for the gala evening, chaperons who will be congenial to one another. Single persons are always invited to bring escorts. And, of course, everyone bids the chaperons good night and thanks them for having come to the dance. After the dance, the same committee writes thank-you notes to each chaperon.

The house mother as resident chaperon:

The most usual chaperon today is the house mother in preparatory boarding schools, college dormitories or metropolitan women's residence hotels. She is neither inquisitive nor interfering, except for seriously considered, valid reasons. Charm is a necessary quality, because she meets and greets the parents, girl friends, and beaux of her charges, and serves at teas or presides at luncheons, dinners and other social occasions. A house mother offers friendship to all the girls under her wing and never shows favoritism.

A young girl in her parents' home:

Whether a girl of college age or her little sister of thirteen invites friends to a party, no chaperonage is necessary other than that of her parents' presence in the house; however, they arrange to be present at some time during the party, perhaps to say "Hello" when their daughter's guests arrive. Then they leave the young people alone, returning to serve the refreshments or, at the younger girl's party, bid the guests good-bye.

A girl of sixteen may invite a boy she knows well to have dinner with her in her parents' home on an evening when they are dining out as long as they are returning shortly after dinner. She may also invite a group in under the same circumstances, provided she sees that the kitchen is left clean and her mother does not have to return to a stack of dirty dishes in the sink.

When a bachelor entertains:

The bachelor-about-town may occasionally entertain in his apartment. On such occasions, four is a better number than two for a small dinner party. A young woman visiting a man's apartment alone is still subject to criticism and a wise girl avoids a tête-à-tête in a bachelor's apartment.

Young men who live out of the metropolitan area or who have a country house may give weekend house parties to which both men and women are invited. The bachelor host should make sure that sleeping accommodations are adequate and comfortable and, if bathroom facilities are limited, that his women guests have precedence. He should also arrange for transportation into town for any guests who may wish to go to church.

DATES

The age at which a girl may go out alone with a boy in the evening, and how late she may stay out varies according to the responsibility of the girl herself and the custom of the community. Only a parent can make the exact decision. A girl of fourteen might go out with a boy as part of a group of four or more to an early movie, dinner, sports event or some other special occasion. Most of the parties she goes to will be those at the homes of friends or dances organized by her school. Her parents should at all times know where and with whom she is and at what time she will be home.

Homecoming hours:

During the early teen years, when children do not have the wisdom to recognize their own needs, the parents must set time limits on dates and see that they are kept, even though it may mean waiting up to greet the returning son or daughter. This is a simple matter of good health, as well as setting a high standard of behavior. It is wise to discuss homecoming hours with other parents and arrive at an hour on which everyone, including the children, agree.

Dates should be restricted to weekends and vacations. Even high school students who are "going steady" should not be permitted to date during the week, even to study together. Exceptions might be made if a boy were given theater tickets to an excellent difficult-to-see show or a league-winning game.

As a general rule, ten thirty or eleven is a reasonable time for a thirteen- or fourteen-year-old to be home; or twelve o'clock for a school or club dance or other special party; a sixteen- or seventeen-year-old might stay at parties until twelve thirty or one o'clock, but for an ordinary movie date, this group should still return by eleven o'clock or thereabouts. If they plan to go to a friend's house or a snack bar afterward, their parents should know in advance or be called on the telephone, so that they may know the whereabouts of the child and re-adjust the hour when he must be home. When a youngster reaches his late teens, his hours are regulated only by his or her own need for sleep or, if he is away at college, the rules of the university. Parents of a child living at home should realize that, were he away at college, he would be making his own rules as to hours, and allow him the same privilege. Many eighteen-year-olds live away from home, they work, they are in the armed forces and they are even married, so it seems a little ridiculous for parents, simply because they are fortunate enough to have their youngster at home, to attempt to treat him as a child, rather than an intelligent, if young, adult.

Asking for a date:

A young man may properly ask any girl to whom he has been introduced for a date, at any time. Usually he uses the telephone, but there is no reason why he should not ask her in person when he sees her.

When telephoning, make sure your identity is established immediately and definitely: "This is Jim Brown. We met at Mrs. Worldly's." A minute or two of "small talk"—"How are you? Hasn't it been a freezing week?"—then state your purpose. Be specific; never say, "What are you doing Saturday night?" but rather, "I have two tickets for *Romeo and Juliet* for Saturday night. I hope you can come with me." You may ask, "How about dinner first?" Decide on the time, say something like, "I'm looking forward to seeing you," and end the conversation. When you can, give her two or three days' notice so she can make her plans.

Dates should not be made at the last minute. A man should call three or four days ahead for a weekend date, ten days or two weeks for a formal dance.

Refusing a date:

If she is busy, the young woman refuses in such a way that the man will be encouraged to try again. She keeps her apology brief, general and sincere—"I'm so sorry. I've already made other plans"—is better than going into detail. She may encourage him to call again by suggesting another night ("I'm so sorry I can't make it Friday. I wish you'd call again"), or ask for a "raincheck."

The man who is refused may try again. However, if he receives three refusals in a row, he may assume she's not interested and forget her and her telephone number.

Breaking a date:

Illness, business, family ties—these are legitimate reasons for breaking a date, but the receipt of a more desirable invitation is *not*. Notify the person concerned immediately, explaining briefly why you cannot keep the appointment and perhaps trying at that time to make another. The practice of willfully not keeping an appointment, known as "standing up," is inexcusable.

During the date:

The man calls for his date at her home. If he knows her well and there is good and sufficient reason, he may meet her at some other convenient place. The man plans and pays for everything they do that evening—transportation, entertainment and food.

If the man's financial situation is somewhat strained and the woman knows that an invitation to the movies is all he can afford, she may suggest, "How about having dinner at our apartment first?" In a restaurant she should not order the most expensive item on the menu, unless the man indicates what he expects her to order by saying, "Their sirloin steak is wonderful. Would you like some?"

When the young man arrives, the girl introduces him to her parents or roommates. The man who takes a few minutes to chat with her parents makes a good impression. She should join in the conversation briefly before saying, "Shall we go now?" then get her coat and handbag and bid her parents good night.

At the end of the evening it is she who suggests that it is time to go home. At her door, he thanks her for the pleasure of her company; she thanks him for an enjoyable evening.

THE BLIND DATE

The "blind date" is sometimes arranged by a third person such as Mrs. Towne, who thinks that Gloria Gorgeous and Harry Handsome would enjoy each other's company. She first makes sure that Harry would be interested in calling Gloria; then she asks Gloria if she would like to meet an attractive man. Only after both parties have indicated that they are willing to be so introduced should Mrs. Towne give Gloria's telephone number to Harry.

The date may also be arranged by a girl who is asked for a date by a boy she does not know well or does not wish to go out with alone. She might say, "Jane Ratsey is spending the night with me, so I would love to go out with you if you have a friend who would like to take her out, and we'll make it a foursome."

Another type of blind date occurs when a host or hostess arranges a date for his or her overnight guest. A girl calls a good friend and says, "Tom, Sally, who is my roommate at college, is spending the weekend with me, and I think you would like her, so how about taking her to a movie with Jim and me on Saturday night?"

A blind date may turn out to be great fun, but if not, make the best of it and act as if you were enjoying every minute. After all, you may meet other attractive people through your new acquaintance.

"GOING STEADY" and "PINNING"

"Going steady" has become a fact of American teen-age life. When a boy and girl date each other consistently, they are considered by their contemporaries to be "going steady." Usually they agree that neither is to date anyone else and this may even be formalized by an exchange of friendship rings or identification bracelets.

This is an unfortunate practice. Only by meeting many other young people of varied backgrounds and interests can a boy or girl broaden his or her own experience and gain enough insight to be capable of making a good choice of a marriage partner when the time comes.

The presentation of a fraternity badge by a college man to his girl, known as "pinning," may be merely another type of "going steady," or it may mean that the couple are "engaged to be engaged," depending on the customs of that particular college. This relationship allows them to examine their compatibility without committing themselves formally to an engagement. If the "pinned" couple "breaks up," the girl returns the pin to the young man.

69

A happy marriage

HINTS FOR THE NEWLYWEDS

I don't know why people should feel that because they have married, they may give up all pretense of good manners and treat their partner as an "old shoe." Many a marriage has failed because one or both of the partners allowed their attitude toward the other to become careless, ill-mannered or just plain bored. It takes effort to keep a good marriage going and the constant presence of good manners is more important than in any relationship with those outside the family.

The wife's part:

It's curious how the habit of careless manners and the habit of old clothes go together. And how many lovely women commit esthetic suicide by letting themselves slide down to where they feel natural in an old housecoat, not only physically but mentally. The very fact of *looking* attractive makes one feel less tired and therefore more charming and better company.

She who complains incessantly that this is wrong or that hurts or that some other thing worries or vexes her, very decidedly is getting into an old housecoat! If something is seriously wrong, if she is really ill, that is different. But of the petty things that are only remembered in order to be told to gain sympathy—beware!

The wife who smears her face with cream and rolls her hair in curlers before going to bed is not a sight that many husbands can endure. With a handy portable drier, there is no reason that hair cannot be dried while doing chores, feeding the baby, paying the bills or during any other household duties in the morning. And the wife who sees her husband off to work in a dirty bathrobe, with hair uncombed and face unwashed, sends him off with a thoroughly unflattering picture of her in his mind. He may find his neat, efficient, pretty secretary more appealing than his unkempt, uncaring wife!

The intelligent woman listens interestedly to her husband's problems at the office. She doesn't interrupt with "Oh really? Come and see Junior's new tooth—and then please repair the stopper in the sink."

Even though a girl loathes cooking, she makes an effort to cater to her husband's likes and dislikes and to make meals appetizing and interesting. If she is on a diet, she must not feed her husband a dinner of one lamb chop and a small green salad. A little surprise now and then—something he especially likes, such as a homemade apple pie or a special cut of steak ordinarily beyond her budget—will do wonders toward making her seem a marvelous cook and clever wife.

A considerate wife always consults her husband before accepting an invitation for them both unless she knows it is something he will enjoy. If he is working very hard, it is thoughtless of her to plan a dinner party for Friday, to accept an invitation for a dance on Saturday, and to organize an all-day picnic with the children on Sunday.

If her husband enjoys an evening of poker with his friends, the smart wife cheers him on his way and even offers to provide refreshments for his gang at home when it is his turn to invite them there. She leaves everything in readiness and disappears—completely! When he brings a business acquaintance home, she is a gracious hostess. After dinner, she excuses herself, washes up quietly and goes to her room to leave them to their business discussion. (A considerate husband never, if he can avoid it, brings home unexpected guests without giving his wife some warning.)

The husband's part:

The bride generally has to make more effort to achieve a successful marriage than the groom, but it is certainly a two-sided partnership, and she cannot do it alone. The man who rushed to open the car door or hold her coat for her when they were engaged, unfortunately too often drops these little politenesses as soon as they are married.

The worst of evenings begins when the husband—whose

wife has had no one but the baby to talk to all day long—grunts and buries his nose in the newspaper when she tries to carry on a conversation.

He may have been accustomed to living alone or in a bachelor apartment where no one cared, but the new husband must learn that trousers dropped in the middle of the floor, a sink spattered with shaving soap and soggy towels on the bathroom rug can be an unpleasant shock to his bride.

Many men do not care too much for babies until they are old enough to respond or even to show interest in things about which Daddy cares. But this can be a very sore point with a young mother to whom her husband's lack of interest seems callous. If Daddy will take the time really to observe and play with his infant son or daughter, he will find himself more interested in the babies than he thought possible.

The husband who keeps his wife company in the kitchen while she is finishing the dinner preparations and gives a helping hand with the dishes after dinner, rather than retiring to the TV set or his newspaper, will find himself more than repaid by his appreciative wife.

It is important to women that their husbands remember special occasions. If the budget is limited, the remembrance need only be a card for Mother's Day, a single rose for an anniversary or a simple little gift for a birthday. It is the thought that counts, and women, generally more sentimental than men, attach tremendous importance to these little gestures.

Unless he has come to an agreement with his wife, it is selfish and stupid of a man to spend all his free time pursuing a sport or hobby that does not interest her. A Saturday golf game with his friends, and a Sunday picnic with his family, plus, perhaps, an hour's workout at the driving range one evening or two during the week can be a happy solution for the whole family.

One of the most pleasing things a man can do is to plan occasional entertainments that will appeal to her—especially a dinner at a restaurant or a trip to the theater, an overnight jaunt to some favorite spot or even an evening at the movies can be a wonderful treat to a girl who spends much of her time at home. Or he may offer to plan and cook the dinner occasionally or take her on a picnic at a beach or lake or to a free concert or museum or lecture.

AIRING THE PROBLEMS

Lesser bones of contention in many marriages are: interrupting each other, making fun of idiosyncracies, not laughing at his or her jokes, never being on time, the wife using the husband's razor—these can build up a wall of resentment. Greater ones are: basic differences of opinion on bringing up children, how to spend vacations, watching television in the bedroom, and so on—these can undermine an otherwise sound marriage. The only way to handle these problems is by bringing them into the open and keeping the lines of communication free between husband and wife. The moment that one or the other feels he cannot discuss a problem and it is left to fester and grow inside is the moment the marriage begins to dissolve. The couple who agrees not only to listen to each other's problems, but to make an effort to see the other side and to DO something to correct the situation is one hundred percent certain to stay out of the divorce courts.

IN-LAW SITUATIONS

The two most difficult situations to meet happily and successfully are those between the husband and his father-in-law and between the wife and her mother-in-law. The other relationships are easy and there is little reason for failure. In any case, the very first rule that every father-in-law—and especially every mother-in-law—must learn is DON'T INTERFERE. Never mind what small blunders your daughter or daughter-in-law or your son or son-in-law may make; remember that is their right to live and do and think as they please. If you are asked what you think, answer truthfully, of course, but don't pour good advice upon them.

When a young wife, for any one of many reasons, goes to live with her husband's people, she must in this difficult situation adapt herself not only to their mode of living, but also to the dispositions of the various members of the family. In this way alone can she herself be happy.

When a mother or father must live with a married child, the situation demands the wisdom of a Solomon and the self-control of a stoic. She or he must conscientiously practice the art of "invisibility" at frequent and lengthy intervals. The mother should have or make occupations of her own—particularly when special friends of her daughter-in-law or even old friends of her son are present. If her room is equipped with radio and television she is always free to enjoy her own favorite programs. She assists with household chores or cares for the children as much as she easily can, but she should never be made to feel like a built-in baby-sitter.

If it is physically possible, it is far better for parents to live apart from their married children. The young people should, if necessary, help to support the older ones, especially a widow, but the parents should be allowed to feel that they are handling their own affairs. Love and affection will flourish in an atmosphere of independence, supplemented by close family ties.

SEPARATION AND DIVORCE

Divorce is always painful and all too prevalent in this country. But there are cases, of course, where divorce is the best—sometimes the only—solution for everyone concerned. If two persons are truly mismated, they and perhaps their children are better off if they part. The only consideration of vital importance is that they shall not part because of a love-for-another attack that might prove to be transient.

Sometimes a period of separation can solve the problem of too-hasty divorce. A separation may be legal or it may simply be arranged by unwritten consent of both parties. It may be either a "trial" separation, or viewed from the beginning as permanent, particularly if the faith of the couple forbids divorce, as does Catholicism.

In a trial separation two people have found it increasingly difficult to live together and decide to live apart. But they want time to consider before taking the final steps toward divorce. If they find they are better off apart, and do not intend to remarry, they make the separation legal. Papers making property settlements, arrangements for children, financial support and so on are drawn up by their lawyers.

When a couple separates, there is no public announcement. Because they are still legally married, the woman continues to use her husband's name and wears her wedding ring. He quietly moves out of their home, possibly on an extended "business trip," or she may take her children for a "visit" to her family. Friends respect the situation and never invite them both to the same party without their knowledge and consent.

If they decide that life together was better than life apart, they simply move back together. For this reason, it is wise for the wife, or husband, whichever has remained there, to keep the home and other property intact, rather than selling or renting in a moment of bitterness.

When a divorce is finally and irrevocably decided upon, there is no public announcement. The woman discards her wedding ring and substitutes her maiden name for her husband's first name (Mrs. McCallum Ford). Both parties must accept the fact that their marriage no longer exists. The husband who insists on "dropping in" to see the children or the wife who keeps calling his office to ask his advice on this or that is only prolonging the agony. They must start to make new lives for themselves and leave their ex-partner to do the same.

In the happy event that the couple resolve their difficulties after the divorce is final, they remarry quietly, with only their families or closest friends as witnesses.

In the thousands of cases where children are involved, it is far better that divorced parents make every effort to remain friendly. There can be no argument with the fact that maintaining a civil relationship is desirable not only for the couple, but especially for their children.

INDEX

Index

A

B

C

D

E

F

G

H

I

J

K

L

M

N

O

P

Q

R

S

T

U

V

W

BOXED SETS

New and exciting—permanent additions to the reader's home library and ideal year-round gifts.

GREAT RELIGIONS OF MAN

Concise histories of the growth of the major faiths, with analyses of their ideas, beliefs, rituals, dogmas, and world role, as well as extensive selections from ancient and modern writings, introductions, and interpretations.

BUDDHISM—Richard A. Gard, ed.
CATHOLICISM—George E. Brantl, ed.
HINDUISM—Louis Renou, ed.
ISLAM—John Alden Williams, ed.
JUDAISM—Arthur Hertzberg, ed.
PROTESTANTISM—J. L. Dunstan, ed.

6 volumes	59353	$3.60

HELOISE

America's champion homemaker offers hundreds of hints and how-to's to make life in the kitchen and at home more enjoyable, more economical, and more efficient.

Heloise's HOUSEKEEPING HINTS
Heloise's KITCHEN HINTS
Heloise ALL AROUND THE HOUSE

3 volumes	59356	$1.75

THE DECLINE AND FALL OF THE ROMAN EMPIRE
by Edward Gibbon
Edited by D. M. Low

An edition abridged by the leading authority on Gibbon and the Roman Empire, presenting major chapters intact, and with an epilogue tracing Rome to the dawn of the Renaissance.

3 volumes	W 9701	$2.95

U. S. A.
by John Dos Passos

The turmoil of American life before, during, and after World War I as seen through a major work of modern American fiction.

THE 42nd PARALLEL
1919
THE BIG MONEY

3 volumes	59354	$1.80

THE CENTENNIAL HISTORY OF THE CIVIL WAR
by Bruce Catton

A stunning history of the Civil War.

THE COMING FURY
TERRIBLE SWIFT SWORD
NEVER CALL RETREAT

3 volumes	59361	$2.85

THE COMPLETE SHORT STORIES OF W. SOMERSET MAUGHAM

The stories of one of the most versatile and popular authors of the twentieth century, including the Ashenden stories, the model of the genre of espionage fiction.

Book I
RAIN and other stories
Book II
THE LETTER and other stories
Book III
THE BOOK BAG and other stories
Book IV
THE HUMAN ELEMENT
and other stories

4 volumes	59355	$3.00

THE WORLD'S GREAT THINKERS
Edited by Saxe Cummins and Robert N. Linscott

Major works and selections by the most significant contributors to the history and development of world thought.

MAN AND THE UNIVERSE:
The Philosophers of Science
MAN AND SPIRIT:
The Speculative Philosophers
MAN AND THE STATE:
The Political Philosophers
MAN AND MAN:
The Social Philosophers

4 volumes	59352	$3.00

THE ALEXANDRIA QUARTET
by Lawrence Durrell

Major works of fiction focusing on the theme of love viewed from every aspect, explored on every level in the setting of modern Alexandria—a perfumed city of fleshly delights and moral decadence.

JUSTINE
BALTHAZAR
MOUNTOLIVE
CLEA

4 volumes	59362	$3.00

AMERICAN LITERATURE
Edited by Carl Bode, Leon Howard, and Louis B. Wright

An anthology of American writing—with critical comment — ranging from the early colonial period to the late nineteenth century.

Volume 1
THE 17th AND 18th CENTURIES
Volume 2
THE FIRST PART OF THE 19th CENTURY
Volume 3
THE LAST PART OF THE 19th CENTURY

3 volumes	59351	$2.70

POCKET HOUSEHOLD LIBRARY

Basic books for the well-run home.

Heloise's HOUSEKEEPING HINTS
Heloise's KITCHEN HINTS
THE HOUSEHOLD ENCYCLOPEDIA
FIRST AID FOR THE AILING HOUSE
Schifferes' FAMILY
MEDICAL ENCYCLOPEDIA
THE LEGAL ENCYCLOPEDIA

6 volumes	98099	$3.95

DR. LYNCH'S
HOLISTIC
SELF-
HEALTH
PROGRAM

DR. LYNCH'S HOLISTIC SELF-HEALTH PROGRAM

Three Months to Total Well-Being

JAMES P. B. LYNCH, D.C.
WITH ANITA WEIL BELL

A DUTTON BOOK

DUTTON
Published by the Penguin Group
Penguin Books USA Inc., 375 Hudson Street,
New York, New York 10014, U.S.A.
Penguin Books Ltd, 27 Wrights Lane,
London W8 5TZ, England
Penguin Books Australia Ltd, Ringwood,
Victoria, Australia
Penguin Books Canada Ltd, 10 Alcorn Avenue,
Toronto, Ontario, Canada M4V 3B2
Penguin Books (N.Z.) Ltd, 182–190 Wairau Road,
Auckland 10, New Zealand

Penguin Books Ltd, Registered Offices:
Harmondsworth, Middlesex, England

First published by Dutton, an imprint of Dutton Signet, a division
of Penguin Books USA Inc.
Distributed in Canada by McClelland & Stewart Inc.

First Printing, March, 1994
10 9 8 7 6 5 4 3 2 1

 REGISTERED TRADEMARK—MARCA REGISTRADA

LIBRARY OF CONGRESS CATALOGING-IN-PUBLICATION DATA:
Lynch, James P. B.
   [Holistic self-health program]
   Dr. Lynch's holistic self-health program: three months to total well-being / James P. B.
Lynch with Anita Weil Bell.
   p.   cm.
   Includes bibliographical references.
   ISBN 0-525-93760-9
   1. Holistic medicine.   2. Self-care, Health.   3. Health.
I. Bell, Anita Weil.   II. Title.   III. Title: Holistic self-health program.
R733.L95   1994
613—dc20   93–33558
                                                                                          CIP

Printed in the United States of America
Set in Century Book
Designed by Leonard Telesca

Contents

PART THREE
SELF-HEALTH RESOURCES

Acknowledgments

This book would not have been possible without the driving force that motivated me to become a holistic doctor: the premature deaths of my beloved parents, James and Johanna Lynch. After experiencing the health care system, and how it contributed to their deaths, I was determined to help change health care for the better.

I would also like to acknowledge the loving support of my family and my wife, Ann.

Appreciation to Dr. William Holub and the other physicians and healers who taught me to rely on the natural healing power of the body; and to the late Dr. Robert Mendelsohn for his honest, inspiring work. Many thanks to the patients of the Holistic Health Force, from whom I have learned a great deal.

Thanks to Anita Bell, for her hard work and dedication. Much gratitude to our literary agent, Faith Hamlin, for her enthusiasm; and our editor, Carole DeSanti, for her guidance and expertise.

Anita Bell thanks her parents, Shirley and Gilbert Weil, for their love, interest, and support. And a heart full of gratitude to her husband, Jonathan Bell, for his positive attitude, creative spirit, and unconditional love.

Finally, we wish to acknowledge the inner healing force that is the natural order of the Universe and the power of love.

Introduction

Would you like to meet the greatest healer in the world? Look in the mirror. *You* are your own best doctor.

Every person possesses an innate healing force. This book will teach you how to use this powerful healing force to love and nurture yourself into optimal health.

Good health is your natural birthright; it's not a commodity you need to pay for with frequent visits to overpriced M.D.'s. The power to create good health and enjoy life to the fullest lies within *you*. Your own knowledge, faith, love, and actions are far more powerful and effective than any pill or scientific "advance."

The purpose of the Three-Month Holistic Self-Health Program is self-empowerment: to help you learn to help yourself. As a holistic doctor I consider myself first and foremost a teacher. I am a partner in healing with my patients, and now I hope to be your partner.

Since you're reading this book, you're probably interested in alternatives to traditional medical care. Perhaps, like millions of other people, you're dissatisfied with the inflated costs and market mentality of orthodox medicine. You may be sick and tired of doctors who patronize you and don't take the time to consider your unique needs. Perhaps you've suffered side effects from prescription drugs or have endured unnecessary or unsuccessful surgery.

Your motivation to explore holistic health might have been prompted by a serious illness, a nagging complaint, or concern about your future. Whatever your current state of mind and body, you will be healthier and stronger when you finish the Natural Self-Health Program. You'll take greater responsibility for your own health and enjoy the fruits of independence. You'll be part of the holistic health revolution.

The holistic health revolution is as necessary as our American Revolution of 1776. The medical establishment has evolved into an empire, primarily concerned with its own power and riches rather than the well-being of its "subjects." Of course, there are many sincere and dedicated physicians, and there's a place for the techniques of conventional medicine. But there is also an urgent need for a massive overhaul of the system. It's crucial that we begin to focus on prevention and natural remedies instead of drugs and surgery.

The holistic health revolution involves a growing number of individuals who make health care choices based on solid, scientifically tested knowledge. They visit alternative health care professionals such as nutritionists, chiropractors, massage therapists, herbalists, homeopaths, acupuncturists, and others. They adopt more healthful diets and utilize supplements and herbs. *Instead of waiting for symptoms to happen, they take steps to balance their bodies and minds so that ailments are less likely to occur.*

The term "holistic" stems from "wholistic." It means consideration of the whole person: body, mind, and spirit. It's interesting that the word "health" finds its roots in the Anglo-Saxon word *hal*, or "whole." Yet the term "medical care" derives from "medicine," something given as a remedy for disease. In truth, medical care is generally *disease* care rather than *health* care.

Consider *Webster's New World Dictionary's* first definition of health: "physical *and* mental well-being." If you think about it, you'll realize that a system that recognizes the integral connection between the body and mind is truly *health* care, while a system that concentrates solely on the physical is *disease* care.

The basic difference between the medical approach and the holistic approach is that medicine treats the *symptom* while holistic health care treats the *whole person* and the *root* of the symptom. For example, if you have migraine headaches, instead of prescribing a drug that temporarily blocks the pain, a holistic practitioner will investigate dietary, emotional, and physical factors until the cause of the pain is discovered and addressed.

Medical care often involves smothering the symptom with drugs or, when the situation worsens, surgically altering the body. Holistic practitioners *respect* the symptom. We search for the root cause and try to correct the imbalance without insulting your body any further. It sounds like simple common sense, doesn't it? Yet this basic approach is unknown to modern medicine.

Medical science tends to make disease sound too complicated for laypeople to understand. Yet the truth about disease is actually simple.

The basis of all disease is the same: toxemia, or poisoning, and/or imbalance of the body. The body is in a state of health when all the organs and systems are in balance and harmony and free of toxins. And this can be achieved only when you take responsibility and proactive steps to maintain your own well-being. Holistic healers can help, but no one can do it for you. Ultimately your health is in your own hands.

I first became aware of the powerful connection between the mind and body when I studied martial arts as a teenager. By the time I gained my black belt, I knew on a deep level that the mental, spiritual, and physical components of a human being were interconnected and interdependent. I sought a way to integrate this knowledge with my goal to become a doctor.

My desire to become a doctor had been triggered when my mother died of heart disease and my father died of cancer, both at relatively young ages. It was clear their deaths were brought on by poor dietary habits, stress, and exposure to toxins. I wanted to help other people avoid our family's tragedy by becoming a doctor who teaches people how to take care of themselves.

Modern chiropractic training, with its emphasis on healing the whole person and teaching prevention, was the path I chose. I was also attracted to the intensive study of nutrition included in the curriculum of chiropractic college.

Once I established my own practice, I was determined to help patients learn how to stay balanced and well instead of merely providing them with temporary relief. However, I found that most people could understand the principles of holistic health intellectually but were unable to apply these ideas to their own lives. They were well intentioned but found it difficult to nurture all aspects of their body/mind without a structure.

To help my patients apply the principles of holistic health and prevention more effectively, I developed the Holistic Triangle. This approach has proved to be extremely successful. During my fifteen years of practice, hundreds of people have not only overcome persistent ailments but learned to live healthier lives using this model.

The Holistic Triangle is a teaching tool, a healing tool, and a means of helping you direct your thoughts and actions. The Holistic Triangle puts your health in your own hands. There are three sides to the Holistic Triangle: the mental/spiritual base, the physical side, and the chemical side.

In this book we will explore in depth what each side of the Triangle represents. You'll learn about the strengths and weaknesses of each side of your Triangle and how they influence your life. You'll discover how the three sides of your Triangle—mental/spiritual, physical, and chemical—interact.

Here are some basic examples: What you eat (the chemical side) affects your mood (the mental/spiritual side) and your energy level (the physical side). Exercising (the physical side) affects your metabolism (the chemical side) and makes you more positive and alert (the mental/spiritual side).

Most important, knowledge and self-love (the mental/spiritual side) give you the inner strength to eliminate toxins (the chemical side) and stay with an exercise regimen (the physical side). The mental/spiritual base *supports* the other sides of the Triangle and enables you to take healthy action.

The foundation of health is nourishing your mental/spiritual side with love. *Love is the most powerful healing force.* Unconditional love for yourself is the basis of health and the most essential nutrient.

This is not narcissism but the true self-love that enables you to do right by yourself and by others. Loving yourself actually reduces selfish behavior by enhancing your ability to love others and have a positive influence on the world.

You may be worried that you don't love yourself enough and don't have the mental/spiritual strength to take healthy action. I ask you from my heart: Have an open mind and give yourself a chance. *You can learn to love yourself.* There are practices and ways of thinking that can help you relax into the self-love and good health that are your natural state.

Then you can continue on to the next steps of nourishment. You can detoxify your body and adopt a wholesome, individualized diet with appropriate supplements. You can nourish your physical side with oxygen by committing yourself to an exercise program specially designed for your abilities and needs. You can learn which holistic practitioners complement your self-care. It's all part of the Three-Month Holistic Self-Health Program.

This program is a step-by-step plan to improve every aspect of your well-being by nourishing your Holistic Triangle. It's a user-friendly program designed for real people, not saints. Everyone has lapses, and part of the program is learning to forgive yourself and get back on the right track.

The program begins with Self-Health Evaluation questionnaires to help you learn about the state of your Holistic Triangle. You'll gain motivation to start the program and the commitment to stay with it.

The first month of the program focuses on developing your mental/spiritual side with practices and self-education. Once your mental/spiritual side is reinforced, you'll be ready to build and limber up your body by starting an exercise program.

The second month emphasizes detoxification and replacing

low-nutrient foods with fresh, energy-giving foods. You'll eliminate toxins, develop healthier eating habits, and enjoy a variety of nature's food. You'll benefit from raw-juice fasting—that is, refraining from all food and drink except raw juices—during this period, as you continue your exercise and mental/spiritual practices.

The goal of the final month of the program is to reach a higher level of physical fitness by revving up your exercise program. You'll probably find yourself feeling and looking leaner, younger, and stronger this month. And by the end of the program you'll be remarkably rejuvenated and energized.

This may sound overly optimistic, but it's based on many years of experience. In my practice, which is called the Holistic Health Force, patients are guided through their own Self-Health Programs. My primary goal is to help my patients become self-sufficient so they don't need me anymore!

My patients' programs include office treatments, but these are often secondary in importance. It's what people do when they are on their own that counts most. The results of this approach are astonishing and inspiring. People not only overcome health problems but transform their lives in many ways.

I don't mean to give the impression that it will be a breeze for you to attain excellent health and create a better life for yourself. In fact, I can promise the opposite: the Holistic Self-Health Program is not a magical panacea; it's hard work. Accomplishment is directly proportional to the amount of attention you put into your Triangle. However, it's enjoyable work. You'll have fun during the process and see a lot of improvement along the way. The more steps you take to love yourself to health, the more satisfaction you'll feel, which in turn will increase your self-esteem. Instead of the infamous downward spiral, the program will take you on an upward trajectory.

As you shift to a holistic lifestyle, you'll be enlivened by your increased knowledge, your spirituality, your exercise activities, and your nourishing diet. You won't live forever, but you'll probably live longer, and the quality of your life will be enhanced. You'll be a positive influence on those around you and on society, instead of being a victim of civilization.

The major diseases in our society—heart disease, cancer, diabetes, obesity, and addictions—all are natural consequences of an artificial environment that we call civilization. We're not winning the war against these killers because our resources are being misdirected.

Nourishing your Holistic Triangle will help you live in better harmony with the forces of the natural world and activate your innate healing force. It will enable you to create a sanctuary for yourself in the midst of the modern world. It will give you the energy and love you need to live a joyous, healthy life.

PART ONE

YOUR HOLISTIC TRIANGLE

CHAPTER 1

Getting to Know
Your Holistic Triangle

Is there a nagging health problem you want to eliminate? Are there aches or pains you wish to erase? Perhaps you want to have more energy and a higher level of fitness.

Do you need to relax and let go of tension? Do you want to be more optimistic and positive? Do you want to free yourself from guilt and fear? Would you like to develop your spiritual side?

All these changes, and more, are possible. The innate healing force is within you, and the power to change is in your hands. You can begin the process by learning about your Holistic Triangle, which you form with your hands.

Holistic Triangle

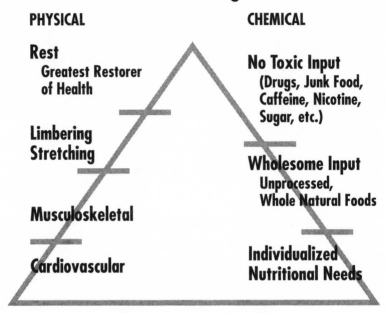

PHYSICAL

Rest
  Greatest Restorer
  of Health

Limbering
Stretching

Musculoskeletal

Cardiovascular

CHEMICAL

No Toxic Input
  (Drugs, Junk Food,
  Caffeine, Nicotine,
  Sugar, etc.)

Wholesome Input
  Unprocessed,
  Whole Natural Foods

Individualized
Nutritional Needs

Mental + Spiritual
Worst Mental Enemies: Fear and Guilt
Worst Spiritual Enemies: Rejection and Lack of Faith

HOW THE HOLISTIC TRIANGLE WAS BORN

In the early years of my practice I often discovered that patients wanted to consider their health in a holistic way, but they found it confusing or overwhelming to accomplish this without a road map. So I began to imagine a symbol that would bring holistic principles to life and enable them to be practically applied. It had to be a symbol that connected as well as delineated the components of holistic health.

The classical holistic trilogy or triangle is: Mind-Body-Spirit. Although this is a beautiful and profound trilogy, I found many patients couldn't relate to it, and it wasn't always workable in a practical sense. Many people thought the Mind-Body-Spirit trilogy sounded too mystical and far-out. Others thought having "Body" in one massive category was confusing.

My biggest problem with Mind-Body-Spirit trilogy was the separation of mind and spirit. In my experience it's *putting together* mind and spirit that works. Knowledge and faith need to support each other to instill the will to action. Therefore, the mental/spiritual side became the base of the Holistic Triangle I developed. I also found that defining the physical and chemical components of the body helped people identify their weaknesses and strengths and learn to nourish every aspect.

To form the Triangle, use your thumbs and forefingers. Stretch out your thumbs horizontally, one thumb resting on top of the other. Lift up your forefingers diagonally so your fingertips touch at the apex of the Triangle.

Your thumbs represent your mental/spiritual side, which is the foundation of health. The mental and spiritual elements, like your thumbs, overlap and support each other. The right side of the Triangle, formed by your right forefinger, represents the chemical side. The left side of the Triangle represents your physical side.

You can remember these sides easily with this association: The physical side is on the left because your heart is on the left, and your heart is the major cardiovascular organ. The right denotes the chemical side since the liver, the primary detoxifying organ, is on the right side.

Although the mental/spiritual, chemical, and physical sides each have unique qualities, they are interdependent and interactive. The three sides work together to create your total health picture. Nourishing one side of your Triangle supports and strengthens the other sides.

The Holistic Triangle is a symbol of your health. The Triangle is a teaching tool, a learning device, and, I hope, a source of inspiration. This may sound dramatic, but symbols can have tremendous power if you believe in what they represent. The more you learn and think about your Triangle, the more it will influence your decisions and your life.

In the following chapters, you'll learn many practical ways to nourish your Holistic Triangle. But first let's get acquainted with each side.

YOUR MENTAL/SPIRITUAL SIDE

Do you know the ABC's of self-health? Attitude, Belief, and Consistency. The mental/spiritual side of your Triangle is the support system for the ABC's and the foundation of well-being.

The mental side is about understanding the basic truths about health. The concepts that follow are some of the major principles:

- Good health is not merely the absence of symptoms; it is the state in which all your organs and systems are in balance and harmony.
- Diseases or symptoms are natural communications from your body and it's vital to discover their message. Smothering symptoms with drugs deprives you of valuable information about yourself.
- Lasting good health comes from discerning and correcting the root causes of symptoms and taking steps to prevent recurrence.
- Good health comes from healthful practices.

The two worst enemies on the mental side are fear and guilt. Conventional medical practice can instill fear when it assumes a superior, patronizing stance. And patients who don't swallow their doctors' prescriptions are sometimes made to feel guilty.

Holistic practitioners strive to eliminate the fear that springs from the unknown and promote understanding, awareness, and responsibility. You might think that being responsible for your own health will make you feel guiltier than ever. But the truly holistic approach is to understand how your actions and thoughts may be affecting your health and to be motivated to change because you love yourself, not because you feel guilty.

The mental side of the Triangle involves *knowing* what makes you truly well. But in order to put what you know into practice, you need to develop the spiritual aspect: faith in the innate healing force with which you were born.

Perhaps you'd like to believe in your self-healing force, but you're skeptical. Since most of us were trained to trust outside authority and not ourselves when it comes to our health, it's no wonder you have doubts. Don't worry if you don't start off with faith in your natural healing power; you can cultivate it.

There are three main ways to gain faith:

1. The intellectual approach: reading about holistic principles, case histories, and research studies.
2. Practices: prayer, meditation, Healing Moments, relaxation, and visualization. These practices help you *feel* the truth on a deep level.
3. Personal experience: perhaps the most powerful way to cultivate faith in natural healing. When you go through the Natural Self-Health Program, you'll see for yourself the power of your inner healing force.

The fundamental nourishment on the spiritual side is love. I can't repeat this too often: *Love is the most powerful healing force in the Universe.* When you love yourself, you treat yourself with care and respect. You take action to activate your self-healing and preventive measures to maintain well-being. The foundation of good health and happiness is unconditional, nonjudgmental self-love.

Think for a moment about whether or not you give yourself unconditional love. Do you treat your body with consideration and respect? Do you accept yourself or berate yourself for shortcomings? Do you take time out for the nourishment and relaxation you deserve? Do you encourage and forgive yourself? Do you treat yourself as well as you treat your best friend?

If the honest answer to some of these questions is no, don't feel defeated or inadequate. Most of us have negative programming we need to overcome. You don't have to remain stuck in any mental state. You can lose emotional baggage just as you can lose weight. You can transform the way you think just as you can change the contours of your body. You can actually *learn to love yourself.*

Of course, all human beings are fallible, and there will be times when you don't love yourself. But instead of continuing on a downward spiral, you can learn to nourish your Triangle and get back on the upward track of self-love. In this book you'll learn practices and ways of adjusting your thinking that can help you achieve self-forgiveness, overcome the effect of negative parenting, and relax into the nourishment of self-love.

Mental/spiritual strength can make all the difference in the healing process. Two patients, John and Bill, each came to my office complaining of lower back pain. John was thirty-five years old, about forty pounds overweight, strong but heavy. Bill was thirty-two years old, about twenty-five pounds overweight, and out of condition. John had played football in high school and then steadily acquired his beer belly throughout college and his working years. Bill had been naturally slim until after college, when he started eating out a lot and gaining weight. Both men had sedentary jobs and no regular exercise regimens.

John and Bill had each been to their medical doctors and had gone through courses of painkillers and rest that afforded only temporary relief. When they went back to work and off the drugs, the pain returned.

Their examinations yielded similar findings: Both men had discogenic sciatica, commonly known as slipped disk. In the office I gave John and Bill similar treatments: spinal adjustments, traction, and diathermy (electrical induction of heat into the tissues below the skin). I also explained that they needed to lose weight, take early-morning baths, and commit themselves to following a gentle exercise program to strengthen their spines and decompress their vertebrae. Their participation was the most vital aspect of their treatment programs.

John was enthusiastic about the prospect of curing himself of back pain. He liked the idea of being in control instead of helpless under a doctor's care. His attitude was: "I *will* do it; I *can* do it." John worked out at the gym, did relaxation exercises, modified his diet, and lost weight. Within two months he no longer needed my professional services, except for a seasonal tune-up. Over the next six months he kept losing weight until he was back down to what he called "fighting trim."

Bill, on the other hand, kept coming back with excuses. He

was too rushed to bathe in the morning. He didn't have time to join a health club and go swimming. He didn't want to give up the lavish late-night dinners he enjoyed. His attitude was: "I would, *but*—" and "Can't *you* do something?"

Bill wanted to be free of pain, but he wanted someone else to do it for him. Predictably the office treatments weren't enough to cure his back problem without his own efforts. Bill became disenchanted with the holistic approach and decided to go to a "real expert." He ended up having spinal surgery: a discectomy and laminectomy (removal of the disk and spinal fusion).

The surgery gave Bill only temporary relief from pain, and he wound up with failed back syndrome, a medical term for people who have chronic back pain even after spinal surgery. (It's interesting that it's called failed back syndrome instead of failed back surgery.)

Two men with similar histories and diagnoses, yet one becomes pain-free, trim, and fit; the other ends up with chronic pain. The moral of this true story is obvious: It's imperative to have a sturdy mental/spiritual foundation, to have faith in the natural healing process, and to take action to help it along.

YOUR CHEMICAL SIDE

The right side of your Holistic Triangle represents the chemical component of health. This involves everything you take into your body: food, drink, drugs, and supplements.

Nowadays there is a great deal of concern about pollution on the planet. But many of us don't pay enough attention to how we pollute our own bodies. And our bodies are one environment over which we as individuals do have control.

By detoxifying your body through dietary changes and fasting, you can create an optimally healthy "in-vironment." Not only will you have immediate benefits, but you'll also be less likely to develop a serious disease. The American Heart Association, American Diabetes Association, and National Cancer Institute, among others, have recognized the link between diet and the major killers. And natural healers have known this for centuries.

The number one tool on the chemical side of the Triangle is detoxification, eliminating toxins and cleansing your body. The Top Ten Toxins you'll be working to eliminate are sugar, white flour and refined carbohydrates, dairy products, red meat, food additives (including extra salt), caffeine, nicotine, alcohol, drugs, and environmental toxins.

Please don't let the list of toxins stop you in your tracks. This will be a gradual process, and you'll be gaining far more than you give up. You'll be adding to your diet a variety of fruits, vegetables, and grains, natural foods that are energizing as well as delicious.

Yes, it can be difficult to give up your favorite poisons, but it's not as hard as you might think. This is where the interaction of the three sides of the Triangle comes into play. Empowering your mental/spiritual side will give you the information and inspiration you need for the task of detoxification.

Giving up toxins doesn't mean you'll end up feeling deprived. Sure, it's hard to break bad habits, but there are many delicious, nutritious alternatives you can enjoy. These "Garden of Eden" foods come from the original source of energy: the sun. High-energy natural foods can help you feel better and younger now than you did at twenty (especially if you were partying and eating junk food at that age). You'll also learn to nourish your holistic Triangle through appropriate vitamin, mineral, and herbal supplementation.

YOUR PHYSICAL SIDE

The physical side of your Triangle encompasses your genetic inheritance and structure and your level of fitness. This is the side of the Triangle where we deal with what we've been given and what we've done with it.

Since we can't change our genetic legacies, the focus here is on how we can improve our bodies through physical nourishment. The primary form of physical nourishment is exercise. A holistic exercise program consists of aerobic (cardiovascular) exercise, musculoskeletal development exercises, and stretching. The holistic approach is to concentrate on proper breathing, technique, and form instead of on competition.

Secondary forms of physical nourishment are those that are provided by practitioners, such as chiropractic care, massage, and other natural physical therapies. As part of developing your physical side, it's likely you'll want to have periodic treatments from a professional. An overview of the different options on page 109 can help you pick the practitioner who suits your needs.

This is not to say you should give up your medical doctor altogether. There is certainly a place for medical expertise, and physicians can be incomparable in cases of serious trauma. But you can also benefit from the different services of holistic or complementary practitioners. The idea is to learn about alternatives and make informed choices instead of remaining locked into traditional care.

INTERACTION

Each side of your Holistic Triangle influences and interacts with the other two sides. A simple example of this process is exercise. Exercise is the number one nutrient on the physical side, but it also has an immediate affect on the mental/spiritual side. Endorphins, chemicals naturally produced by the body during exercise, evoke "runner's high," a sense of euphoria. Even nonaerobic exercise can lift your mood, enhance concentration, and instill a feeling of confidence. On the chemical side, exercise can lower tension and raise awareness. Then you'll be inclined to make healthy food choices and be less likely to overeat.

You've probably experienced how exercise affects all three sides of the Triangle, and you've undoubtedly felt the opposite results after overeating. A heavy meal can cause you to feel sluggish and unable to do anything more taxing than watch TV or take a siesta. That's the chemical side influencing the physical and mental sides of your Triangle.

Take a minute to think of some examples of this interaction from your own life. If you've experienced constipation, consider not only your diet but also your mental state. Were you tense, preoccupied, or under pressure? What about the physical side? Were you exercising regularly?

If you have frequent neck or back pain ask yourself: Do I hold emotional stress (the mental/spiritual side) in my body? Does my diet leave me feeling lethargic, so I can't uphold good posture (the chemical and the physical sides)? Do I care for myself enough to devote time and money to seeking out natural treatment (the mental/spiritual and physical sides)?

Once you see how it works, you can apply the "Three Sides of the Triangle" test to any health problem you may have. It's amazing the solutions you'll discover when you begin to think this way.

When you're investigating a health issue, remember to look at the *whole* picture. This includes your environment, your relationships, and your job.

Jill, a patient who had chronic neck and shoulder pain, worked in cytology, examining Pap smears and identifying cancers. Regardless of what treatment I could offer, there was no way she could spend all day peering down a microscope and not have this recurring pain.

Another contributing factor was that she felt her work was depressing and stressful, a "downer." Jill realized that her Holistic Self-Health Program had to include a change of career. Once she had identified this, she took necessary steps to obtain credentials to be a nutritionist. Now Jill enjoys looking up at people instead of down at cells. And she no longer has chronic neck pain.

You probably won't have to do anything as drastic as change your career. But you do need to consider every element of your life when you plan to improve your health. Everything you do, everyone with whom you're involved are part of the whole picture of wellness. Creating total well-being can at times involve changing your lifestyle as well as your diet.

MOTIVATION

It can be difficult to accept that good health requires effort and persistence especially since our society encourages instant gratification and the quick fix.

When Tony, a middle-aged factory worker, came into my office complaining of back pain, he asked me to "crack" his vertebra into place. He wanted a quick adjustment that would give him relief without any effort on his part. He didn't want to hear that he would have to stop sleeping on his stomach and cut down on drinking to shed the extra pounds that were stressing his back. When he learned that to alleviate his back ailment permanently, he needed to get involved in a comprehensive program, Tony cut out and went elsewhere to look for his "crack."

Well, Tony was back four months later. Although he had found a chiropractor who was willing to give him adjustments without an accompanying program, his back pain kept recurring. Finally, he was fed up to the point where he was willing to do some work on his own.

In the long run *quick fixes don't work*. The painkiller that is potent today may no longer be effective in a few months or may induce harmful side effects. Even a natural treatment won't provide permanent relief unless the root cause of the problem is addressed and corrected. And then it will be necessary for you to take steps to prevent the ailment from recurring. Good health is a gift that only you can give yourself.

Why bother? First of all, so you can eliminate your symptoms and enjoy a pain-free, high-energy life right now. Secondly, so you can live a longer life, with better health in your later years. Changing to a more healthful lifestyle will give you great rewards *now* and may save your life *later*. A holistic lifestyle means living for the moment *and* the future.

Sometimes I need to play the devil's advocate and warn patients about ailments that might develop in the future to motivate them to take preventive steps in the present.

Kimberly, a twenty-five-year-old dancer, came to see me about an ankle problem. She went through our usual office procedure, which begins with filling out a comprehensive wellness assessment. This includes a clinical history and family health information; questions on diet, exercise, and daily habits; and mental/spiritual/emotional components. (You'll be taking similar Self-Health Evaluations as part of the program.)

After I reviewed Kimberly's questionnaire, we sat down for a consultation. I explained the concept of the Holistic Triangle and how a "do-it-yourself" Holistic Health Program would result in overall health enhancement as well as relief of her symptom.

Kimberly was enthusiastic when I outlined the physical treatments and therapeutic exercises that would alleviate her ankle pain. But she was defensive when I pointed out that her wellness assessment indicated she was addicted to sugar. Kimberly protested that she was slender and energetic enough to teach modern dance, so why shouldn't she enjoy her chocolate treats?

Then I explained to her the connection between sugar addiction, hypoglycemia, and diabetes (see details on page 50). Since Kimberly's grandmother had died of diabetes, this information struck home. Kimberly decided to kick her candy habit. Two months later she reported that she was less moody and had even more energy than before. More important, she was no longer setting the stage for adult-onset diabetes.

When you think about your health and the state of your Triangle, consider the future. If you're a twenty-six-year-old mother who doesn't have time for therapeutic exercise, you may feel okay now, but will you develop osteoarthritis in twenty years? If you're a husky young man with an active job, you may be able to wolf down steaks without gaining weight, but are you setting yourself up for heart disease? You need to consider the whole picture: your history, the way you feel now, and the consequences your present lifestyle will have in the future.

GETTING YOUNGER

By working on the three sides of your Triangle, you may be able to slow down the aging process. You may be able to look and feel younger than you did five or even ten years ago. If this sounds farfetched, consider the following:

Research at the U.S. Department of Agriculture's Human Nutrition Research Center on Aging (HNRCA) at Tufts University has shown that people can control the ten major factors associated with aging. These "biomarkers" are: lean body mass, strength, basal metabolic rate, body fat percentage, aerobic capacity, blood pressure, insulin sensitivity, cholesterol/HDL ratio, bone density, and body temperature regulation.

Through diet, exercise, and relaxation techniques, you can in effect lower your physiological age. You can also reduce or eliminate many of the symptoms associated with aging.

Frank, a sixty-five-year-old retired businessman, was slowed down by arthritis. His symptoms were early-morning stiffness, pain that worsened when he used his joints, and restricted mobility. His doctor had prescribed aspirin and NSAIDs (nonsteroidal anti-inflammatory drugs), but these medications gave him gastrointestinal distress and ulcers. Instead of enjoying the retirement for which he and his wife had saved and planned, Frank felt old and miserable.

On the mental/spiritual side Frank needed to rethink his belief that nothing could help his arthritis. Reading several books on natural approaches to alleviating arthritis helped convince him there was hope.

The chemical side of his program involved reducing his intake of acidic foods and meat and eating more fruits. He also started taking appropriate supplements and drinking raw juices. Frank was skeptical about these dietary efforts, but his wife insisted he give them a try.

To nourish the physical side of his Triangle, Frank started a daily exercise program of gentle isometrics and swimming. His secondary treatment included diathermy and physical therapy.

After three months Frank no longer had early-morning stiffness and pain. He had greater energy and flexibility and had lost ten pounds. He reported that he felt younger than he had for fifteen years.

As long as he doesn't overdo it, Frank rarely has pain from the arthritis or gastrointestinal distress. He and his wife frequently go on Elderhostel trips and occasionally even go out dancing.

You're never too old, or too young, to feel younger. Many people have reported that by getting rid of toxins, increasing exercise, and improving their mental/spiritual aspect, they feel better at forty than they did at thirty.

The yogis have a saying, "You're only as old as your spine." I'd like to amend that to: "You're only as old as your Triangle."

SELF-EMPOWERMENT

Traditional medical care often creates a feeling of helplessness. My goal as a holistic doctor is to help patients activate their own natural healing ability. Self-empowerment is the basis of the holistic approach.

Self-empowerment can have dramatic results. Jan, a British woman in her early twenties, suffered from ankylosing spondyitis, a disease that is thought to be genetic and causes calcification of the spine. Jan had been told by medical doctors there was nothing they could do about her condition, and she was receiving disability payments. She lived like an invalid, with low self-esteem and frequent depression.

When Jan came to the Holistic Health Force, we did a blood work-up and took X rays that showed she had a mild case of ankylosing spondyitis. I told her there was no reason she couldn't live an active, fulfilled life.

Her program consisted of a more healthful diet and supplements, chiropractic work to take the biomechanical stress off her spine, and a gentle exercise regimen. Except for biweekly office treatments for three months, the bulk of the program involved self-help steps.

For the first time Jan believed she had some control over her condition. Her outlook changed tremendously. The listless, self-effacing person who had first come to see me was transformed into a vibrant young woman brimming with plans and enthusiasm. She enrolled in college and started dating for the first time.

Even more than any of the physical improvements gained by her program, it was thinking about her health in a new way that changed Jan's life.

CREATE YOUR OWN GARDEN OF EDEN

Our "civilization" is rife with uncivilized behavior, hardship, and stress. One key to well-being is to create a sanctuary for yourself and simulate paradise as much as possible.

On the mental/spiritual side, creating a sanctuary means feeling close to the Higher Force, however you experience God, the Universe, or your personal spirituality. It's letting go of guilt and returning to a state of peace and love without fear.

On the chemical side of the Triangle, a return to the Garden of Eden means eating the foods that were available in paradise: fresh fruits and vegetables, whole grains, seeds, and nuts.

Imagine how free and physical you might be in a "Garden of Eden" in your imagination. You might swim, run, walk, climb, stretch, dance, and play. On the physical side we want to aim for bodies that are as flexible and strong as the days before "civilization" glued us to our seats.

Let's take a practical look at how a few people create their own sanctuaries:

As soon as Leslie gets home from work, before she listens to her answering machine or looks at her mail, she goes into her bedroom and turns on a blue light. She finds this light soothing and comforting. Then she changes into loose clothes, stretches out on a mat, and does an hour of relaxation and yoga exercises. This switches her out of her workday worry mode for the rest of her evening.

Jeffrey used to slam the snooze button on his alarm clock every weekday morning. Then he'd be running late and would have to rush out of the house and grab a Danish and coffee on the train to work. By 11:00 A.M. he was usually in a mental slump and had frequent tension headaches. Now he gets up a little earlier and spends a relaxing, contemplative time in the bath, then has a nourishing breakfast. He wakes up looking forward to his morning ritual, instead of being instantly thrust into rush-hour anxiety.

Karen could afford either a one-week winter vacation or a year-long membership to a health club. She chose the health club and decided to make it into a minivacation two or three times a week. At her club she pretends she's at a luxurious spa and pushes herself through a vigorous workout. Then she goes to the sauna, where she concentrates on relaxing every inch of her body. After a shower she massages herself with herbal body lotion. She feels rejuvenated several times a week instead of once a year.

A NEW WAY TO START YOUR DAY

How do you start your average day? Does an alarm clock jolt you out of bed, straight to the kitchen, where a cup of coffee gives you another jump start? Do you rush through your shower and grab a quick bite? Do you already feel exhausted and harried by the time you start work?

Try a different routine that can change your entire day. First, switch to a clock radio that awakens you to pleasant music. Then, when you first wake up, begin by stretching a little in bed and taking a few deep breaths.

Think about what you can do that day to nourish your Holistic Triangle. On the mental/spiritual side perhaps you'll plan to stop by a bookstore and pick out a self-help book. Or you'll be sure to sit down for a stretching session when you get home from work (see page 215). On the chemical side you might want to plan a fresh salad you'll have for lunch or a visit to a health food store. On the physical side you might determine to push a little harder in your exercise class and then reward yourself with a foot massage.

After you get out of bed, I recommend doing the Bathing Ritual (detailed on page 219). Then you can enjoy a nutritious breakfast and take your supplements.

You'll be amazed at the difference this new morning routine makes for the rest of your day. You'll be taking control of your environment instead of allowing it to control you. Your energy and concentration levels will be higher; your body will be more relaxed, and your outlook will be brighter.

Sounds great, you may be thinking, but you don't have time for all that on a weekday morning. Perhaps you barely make it to work on time even when you rush.

If this is your situation, you need to establish new priorities. If you want to change your life and enjoy a balanced body/mind, you need to prioritize time to work on your Triangle.

Setting new priorities may mean you swim after work instead of joining your friends at Happy Hour. You could meditate instead of going to the mall. You think about what will enable you to feel good later, instead of what is escapist fun at the moment. You give up a few "junk food" activities to make time to nurture your Triangle.

Visualize yourself in glowing good health, filled with love and optimism. Then remind yourself that this picture is obtainable. It's a matter of choice.

Start with one little choice. Start by changing your routine in one small way. When the snack cart rolls around, eschew the doughnuts and go to the rest room for a private stretching session instead, or go outside for a ten-minute walk. Read up on a new subject that interests you instead of succumbing to TV. Make a tofu stir-fry instead of a meat dinner for your family. Spend thirty dollars on a shiatsu massage instead of a fattening restaurant dinner. On Sunday afternoon take a long, brisk walk instead of loafing and watching a ball game. The possibilities for nourishing your Triangle are limitless, and the choice is yours.

Changing your routine, making a different and healthier choice in one little way, will get you started. You'll gain faith in your ability to change. You'll realize you can choose love instead of fear. You can choose natural remedies instead of drugs. You're gaining inner strength and faith. Your Holistic Triangle is already getting stronger.

CHAPTER 2

The Mental/Spiritual Side of Your Holistic Triangle

When you form the Holistic Triangle with your hands, your thumbs overlap to form the mental/spiritual base of your Triangle. This symbolizes that your mental and spiritual strengths support each other to create the basis of good health. You need a fortified mental/spiritual base for wellness just as a building needs a sturdy and balanced foundation.

NOURISHING YOUR MIND

The mental aspect of this side of the Triangle means knowing the truth about health and disease. First, you may need to free your mind of the clutter of propaganda and misinformation about medicine and disease you've probably accumulated over the years. Then you can look at health from a fresh perspective.

The mental foundation of the Triangle includes understanding the basic truths about health. To review these concepts:

- Love is the most powerful healing force. When we love ourselves, we take action to get and keep ourselves well.
- Good health comes from healthful practices.
- Good health is a gift only you can give yourself. You must take responsibility for your own health if you want long-term wellness.
- Good health is the state in which all the organs and systems are in balance and harmony and free of toxins.
- The body has its own innate wisdom and inner healing force. The most effective way to get well and stay well is to learn to stimulate and utilize your natural healing force.
- The basis of disease is toxemia and imbalance of the body, not germs.
- You must listen to your symptoms, not smother them with painkillers, if you want to achieve lasting wellness. Listening to your symptoms means focusing on how the quality of your life affects the quality of your health.

Once you have established these principles in your mind, you can expand your knowledge. It's useful to have basic books in your home library on vitamins, herbs, natural healing arts, meditation and visualization, massage, and alternative health care. Books on these topics can be found in well-stocked mainstream bookstores, New Age bookstores, and some health food stores, as well as libraries.

A list of recommended readings is on page 229. You may want to use this list as a starting point if you find the choices in the bookstores and libraries overwhelming. But you can also browse and make your own selections, or ask friends about books they've found helpful.

Instead of reading primarily about subjects with which you're already familiar, try to expand your knowledge base by delving into areas in which your Triangle is weak. For example, if you already practice visualization, instead of reading another book on this subject, perhaps you could benefit more from reading a book on vitamins or acupressure. Spiritual reading is nourishing on a deep level, but you also need practical, hands-on books that teach you how to boost your health.

If you have a specific ailment, see if you can find a book with an all-natural, drug-free approach toward healing this problem. Many books on nutrition, supplementation, and herbology also have special sections on various maladies.

You'll find yourself turning to your favorite books time and time again once you become your own best doctor. Although you'll still need professional guidance, research can give you insights that expensive visits to an M.D. might fail to provide. A few examples:

Eddie, in his mid-forties, had endured a painful problem with hemorrhoids for more than fifteen years. He went through tubes and tubes of hemorrhoid medications, which did nothing more than temporarily relieve symptoms. When his doctor finally recommended surgery, Eddie was nearly desperate enough to try it. But a friend lent him a book on natural remedies for common ailments, and Eddie read about rutin, a bioflavonoid supplement available in health food stores. He found that taking rutin regularly, along with increasing his intake of water and fiber foods, cured his hemorrhoids within a few weeks.

Pilar had suffered from severe headaches for five years. She had been to several experts who prescribed costly drugs, such as Demerol, which caused disturbing side effects: extreme fatigue, drowsiness, and slurred speech. When Pilar became pregnant, she realized that she would have to survive for nine months without any drugs for migraine relief. She picked up a book on natural headache relief and learned acupressure massage and relaxation techniques she could do herself. These methods afforded such relief she decided to stay off the headache pills even after her child was born.

Patricia had been vulnerable to cold sores, or herpes simplex, on her lips since she was a teenager. Sometimes these sores lingered for weeks, causing her embarrassment and discomfort. After Patricia became interested in holistic health, she read that lysine, an amino acid, was useful in treating cold sores. The next time this problem occurred, she used an ointment containing lysine on her lips and also took lysine capsules. This time the cold sores didn't spread, and after three days they had completely dried up.

People have been able to help themselves overcome a host of physical ailments simply by reading books and magazine articles. Another bonus of becoming informed is that you can share your knowledge and help your friends and family. You may learn information that saves a loved one from needless pain and illness.

Audio- and videotapes are another way to nourish your mental side. Audiotapes can be particularly effective in guiding you through meditations and spiritual work, while videotapes can lead you through yoga classes and other exercise sessions.

Seminars, workshops, and courses are another excellent way to strengthen your mental base. In some communities chiropractors, nutritionists, and other holistic healers give complimentary lectures and programs. There's also a wide variety of courses, workshops, lectures, and seminars available for a fee, which can range from five dollars for a brief lecture to thousands for an extensive program.

The amount of time and money you should spend on a course depends on your financial resources and your degree of interest. Don't be talked into investing a great deal if you're not sure you're interested or you can't afford it. Attend an introductory lecture or demonstration, or read something the teacher has written before you sign up. It's certainly worth spending money on your mental side, but you don't want to end up feeling cheated. Courses can change people's lives, but they can also be disappointing. You need to be sure the person leading the program is truly an expert and a compassionate teacher.

Embark on the course with an open mind and a positive attitude, but don't have unrealistic expectations. Remember, you can't put your health and happiness in anyone else's hands, including holistic teachers or practitioners. It's not just what you learn and what you know; it's what you *practice* with consistency that creates change.

This brings us to the most important truth about nourishing the mental side of your Triangle: *It's what you do with your knowledge that really counts.* You can read books on meditation from here to nirvana, but if you don't practice, you won't gain peace of mind. You can stuff yourself with information about nutrition, but if you keep eating the wrong foods, it won't help. Don't let reading about holistic health become mere escapism. It won't work unless you practice what you learn.

How do you gain the discipline, motivation, and tenacity to carry through on what you have learned? By strengthening the spiritual aspect of the mental/spiritual side of your Holistic Triangle. It's putting together the mental and the spiritual that provides the alchemical magic. Love and faith are the fuel that turn knowledge into action.

There are many ways to gain faith in the natural healing force. You can read about cases and research studies. You can talk to holistic professionals and their patients about their experiences. You can look at nature's incredible way of restoring balance and the spontaneous healing in all forms of life.

You can also gain faith by thinking about all the times you've experienced your own natural healing power. Remember all the colds, flus, and other illnesses from which you have recovered? You might have taken medicine to ease the symptoms, but it was your innate healing force that made you well. Think of all the aches and pains that vanished after a good night's sleep. Consider the way your skin heals after a scrape or bruise. The regenerative healing force is within you, and all around you, every day.

Faith in the innate healing force and knowledge about natural healing techniques will give you a good start on strengthening your mental/spiritual side. But in order to realize your full potential, you need the self-love to turn right thinking into action.

LOVE IS THE MOST POWERFUL HEALING FORCE

Now that you're a critical thinker about health, you may ask, *Why* is love the most powerful healing force? How does love create good health?

The answer is simple. If you love and accept yourself, you will nourish yourself with healthy actions. When you love yourself, you *care*, and you believe that you're worth taking care of. It's not enough to *know* what is right. You need the self-love, discipline, and faith to *act* on what you know.

When we talk about love's creating health, we are not talking about romantic love or even familial love. Love from other people is precious beyond words, as everyone knows. And receiving love has been found to help people have longer and healthier lives. Everyone acknowledges the importance of love between people. But we must also realize the tremendous power of self-love.

This kind of self-love is not narcissism. Self-love does not mean thinking that the world revolves around you or that you're the best tennis player, the wittiest wordsmith, or the most attractive person in your crowd. In fact, this type of egotism reflects insecurity, rather than genuine self-love.

Genuine self-love means self-acceptance. It means working to accept and love yourself more fully every moment, every day, in every way, despite any qualities you may view as shortcomings. Self-love means loving yourself just the way you are, without criticism, without comparison, without conditions or requirements. It means loving and accepting yourself with a round belly or wrinkles around your eyes or a low-paying job.

At first it might sound as if this degree of self-acceptance will stand in the way of self-improvement. You may wonder, If I accept myself totally as I am, why bother to change? But you'll find that self-love actually motivates change and removes blocks. When you stop criticizing and fighting yourself, you free up a great deal of energy that you can redirect more productively. Fear will no longer hold you back. You can break through the denial or fear that keeps you from making changes. You'll have more confidence that you're capable of change.

When you love yourself, you respect your body and treat it with more care. You take the time and effort to nourish yourself with healthy food and exercise. You feel closer to your spiritual center. You have a greater capacity to love others and attract fulfilling relationships. You forgive and let go of anger and guilt, which can undermine your health. Your life is uplifted with optimism and hope.

The Holistic Triangle is designed to help you nourish all aspects of your self. And the most important nutrient of all, the nutrient that is the catalyst for all self-nourishment, is love.

All infants are born with an incredible capacity for love. However, our upbringings and life experiences can either reinforce and cultivate this self-love or suppress it. Parents who did not have nurturing upbringings themselves are sometimes unable to love their children unconditionally. Many people have to deal with childhood legacies of verbal, physical or sexual abuse, neglect, or abandonment. There are also the more subtle underminings of critical, perfectionistic, withholding, or smothering parents.

The cycle continues when children grow up to re-create these unloving scenarios with spouses and within themselves. And so the legacy of low self-esteem and destructive behavior is carried on from generation to generation. Later life experiences, both societal and personal, can also have a devastating effect on innate self-love.

This is, of course, a simplification of a complex subject. Family dynamics and self-esteem are multifaceted issues and are explored in many excellent books. Reading on these topics can help you gain tremendous insight into your mental/spiritual side and can also be very comforting.

SEEKING PROFESSIONAL HELP

Psychotherapy is an option to consider if you feel you need professional guidance to break through the barriers to self-love. There's a great deal you can do on your own to build self-esteem and learn to love yourself more. But depending on your life experience, you may want help. No one can make the decision for you. You need to think through your situation quietly and look within your own heart.

If you decide to seek professional help, look for a therapist with whom you feel relaxed and trusting. Choose one who is a loving, positive influence. Therapists can be professional and appropriate and still exude feelings of care and love for their patients.

If your gut instinct tells you the therapist is the wrong person for you, trust it. It's not enough for the professional to have a wall of certificates. You must feel a genuine connection with the person.

You might seek a mental health professional who is in tune with the basic principles of holistic health and knowledgeable about the influence of diet and exercise on moods. It's helpful if he or she is supportive of self-help techniques as a complement to your work together.

Unless you have a serious, biochemically based mental disorder, such as severe depression, manic depression, or schizophrenia, be wary of mental health professionals who are quick to prescribe psychoactive drugs. This is an area in which you need to proceed with great care and become as informed as possible. The long-term effect of psychoactive drugs as well as the short-term results should be carefully considered. The ultimate goal should be strengthening your Holistic Triangle so that medication is no longer needed.

If you cannot afford private counseling but need help in dealing with serious issues, there are several options. One is to visit a community mental health center, which may have lower or sliding scale fees. You can also look into counseling with a religious leader.

Joining a self-help or peer support group is another option. Al-Anon is a wonderful program for adult children of alcoholics, and there are also support groups for incest survivors, substance abusers, and people with behavioral addictions. Even if the group you find in your area doesn't focus on your specific experience or issue, the love and support from peers can be valuable.

Whatever barriers and traumas you need to overcome, remember, *the capacity for self-love is always within all of us.* In fact, those who have to overcome hardships and work harder at self-love often end up to be the most loving, spiritual people. Negative experiences can ultimately turn out to be life-enhancing because they compel people to gain insight, forgive, and grow stronger.

All of us, even those with very loving and supportive parents, can benefit by making a conscious decision to love ourselves more. We will explore several techniques that can help us do so later in this chapter. But first let's review some simple ways to build self-love that are so obvious you may be missing them.

HEALTHY, LOVING LIVING

Sheila hated herself for being overweight and overstressed. She couldn't break out of the tension/food binge/remorse cycle that started when she was in college, more than twenty years ago.

When Sheila came for treatment, she had a number of related complaints: gastrointestinal distress, constipation, and lower back pain. I explained to Sheila that she needed much more than chiropractic treatment. She needed to start treating herself in a loving way by taking healthy action.

Sheila read a number of books on deep relaxation and positive thinking, as well as on diet and nutrition. She began to recognize stress buildup and turn to relaxation techniques, meditation, and exercise as stress busters.

It was difficult for her to break her old pattern of filling up with junk food to deal with her stress and unhappiness. There were days when she managed to lie down and practice deep breathing or go for a quick walk to relieve her anxiety, but there were also times when she lost herself in eating binges. But now she was conscious of why she was binging and aware that she had the power to break the pattern. I kept reminding her that even when she binged, she could still come out ahead if she refused to wallow in self-hatred afterward.

After several weeks of struggling through her Holistic Self-Health Program, Sheila found her efforts had a "reverse domino" effect. The more she nourished her Triangle, the more she loved herself and the better she was able to cope with stress. Her digestive problems were reduced as she stayed with a healthier diet and practiced relaxation techniques. Over a period of three months she gradually lost weight and gained self-confidence. Even when the old self-loathing and negative thinking crept up on her, Sheila tried to react by *doing* something positive: by nourishing one of the sides of her Triangle.

Taking healthy action is a primary way to love yourself and raise your self-esteem. When you feel stuck in your mind or your habits, *do something nourishing.* Put on a favorite record from your teenage years, and dance around your room like crazy. Make yourself a lavish fruit salad. Lie down on your floor and practice deep breathing. Do something that will sustain your Triangle, not deplete it. You can choose whatever it is, but do it *consciously.*

Act, don't react. Quick fixes—routines that you know are bad habits—leave you feeling worse. Stuffing yourself with ice cream provides only a brief rush of childish solace, but in the long run it's going to make you feel worse. A shopping binge may be a temporary distraction, but it may leave you feeling guilty and broke. Think about not only how your action causes you to feel while you're doing it but how you'll feel later.

Remember, truly nourishing actions have only positive side effects.

The habit of blaming others for your state of mind or body is a trap, one from which you must free yourself. Again, the theme of simultaneous freedom and responsibility is paramount. You are responsible for your mental health, as well as your physical well-being, and you need to show love for yourself by taking action.

One of my most inspiring patients is Jane, a thirty-one-year-old woman who developed multiple sclerosis when she was twenty-five. She had difficulty walking, and the left side of her body was spastic. She also had general muscle weakness, vertigo, and bladder problems. Her medical doctors had offered no substantial intervention and said all she could do was wait and see how her disease progressed.

Jane used what little energy she had to take care of her husband, whom she had married at a young age, and her ten-year-old son. She continued doing everything for others and nothing for herself, as she had done all her adult life.

When Jane became a holistic patient, she realized that she had to devote more energy and time to herself. Her Holistic Self-Health Program of supplementation, dietary changes, physical therapy, exercise, and mental/spiritual work would take up part of her day. To create time for the program, it was necessary to assert herself with her husband and ask him to share some of the household work.

Confronting her husband with the need for change and relinquishing some of her caregiving responsibilities was the most difficult step for Jane. But she realized she had to devote more love on and attention to herself to fight her disease, and she took action.

Jane was seriously motivated and went into her Self-Health Program with a lot of determination. Since she was shifting from an unhealthy lifestyle, the results of her program were dramatic. Within three months her multiple sclerosis had started to go into remission. Her friends noticed that her gait had improved and her energy level was much higher. She reported that her husband was now glad he had taken over some of her chores so that she could have time to help herself.

After years of feeling that she was helpless against her disease, Jane was deeply affected by the positive changes that came about through her program. She was committed to continuing the diet, supplementation, therapeutic exercises, and other elements. When I last saw her, about two years after she had started the program, her MS was still in remission and her energy level was high.

LOVING OTHERS

The more love you give, the more you receive. It's also true that the more love you give, the more love you'll feel for yourself.

Children are living proof of this truth about love. Parenthood is a naturally transformative experience and often causes people to realize new dimensions of love and strength within themselves. As one young woman said about being a mother, "It's not the love you *get*, it's the love you *give*, that changes you."

It's natural and easy for most people to extend love to their families and romantic partners. Showing love to your loved ones is, of course, one of the most joyous and human of all experiences. But extending love, in the form of a simple, caring gesture, perhaps, to someone outside your intimate circle is also part of living a whole life. Developing compassion and empathy for someone who is difficult for you to love can build self-esteem and strengthen the mental/spiritual side of your Triangle. This shift in thinking and feeling is profoundly strengthening.

Altruism can strengthen every side of your Triangle. Dr. George E. Vaillant conducted a forty-year study of Harvard graduates, which was reported in his book *Adaptation to Life*. He found that altruism was one of the qualities that helped the men in the study group cope well with stress. A survey of one thousand people conducted by the California Department of Mental Health in 1980 and 1981 found that those who cared most for themselves and others were mentally and physically healthier than those with low concern for themselves and their fellow human beings.

OVERCOMING FEAR AND GUILT

The two worst enemies on your mental side are fear and guilt, which sap your energy and sabotage all three sides of your Holistic Triangle.

Just as you need to realize the true meaning of disease, it's also critical to understand the reality of fear. There's a saying: FEAR = False Experience Appearing Real.

Fear is fantasy and negative projection about the future. Guilt is negative fantasy about the past and its consequences in the future. If you keep bringing yourself back into the present, you can free yourself of a tremendous burden.

Your mind belongs to you. Remember, you can truly *change* your mind. You don't have to be a slave to negative thoughts and fantasies. You can project the future with hope. And you can spend more time in the present. But it takes practice and discipline. Don't be frustrated if you can't "change your mind" at first; be gentle and loving with yourself and keep trying.

The next time you start getting fearful and anxious, stop and ask yourself: What is this fear actually about? Unless you're in an extremely rare position of immediate physical danger, the fear will be about the future. The fear will be a result of projecting a negative fantasy about a future event.

Instead of getting carried away with the fantasy, bring yourself back to the present. Look around and really see where you are; feel the position of your body; listen to what you're hearing. Feel the breath coming in and out of your body. Realize that you have absolutely nothing to fear in the present. Affirm that you can exercise your free will to project the future with hope instead of fear.

Remember, you don't need fear and guilt to be safe. The less fear in your life, the more energy you'll have available for healing, positive action, and love. Fear and guilt are vampiric emotions. You don't have to let them drain your life force.

When you feel fearful or guilty, respond to this feeling by doing something to nourish your Triangle and something to help someone else. React by doing the best you can.

You can make the choice to free your body of medicines and toxic foods, and you can make the choice to free your mind of toxic emotions. The first step is to bring consciousness into your actions and thoughts.

SPIRITUAL NOURISHMENT

As long as you respect the laws of nature and the rights of other people, you're free to follow your own vision. You don't have to be a prisoner of anyone else's expectations or rules of success. You don't have to live by fear and guilt. Listen to your higher self instead of your ego.

All too often we forget to nourish our spiritual sides in the rush to succeed in the material world. But to be truly healthy and whole, we need contact with the Higher Force.

There are many names for this spiritual force: God, the Lord, the Light, the Universe, the Creator, the Higher Self, the Higher Power, the Source, Cosmic Consciousness, and countless other terms that strive to communicate what is ultimately beyond words. The ways in which people name, visualize, and seek contact with this power are as diverse as human beings themselves.

What you believe is a sacred and personal choice. I would never presume to tell you what to think or how to worship. I only want to encourage you to take the time to foster your spirituality, in whatever form it takes.

Listen to what your own heart and spirit tell you is true. "To thine own self be true." Develop and trust your own interpretation and practice of God and love. As the Bible says, "The kingdom of God is within you." Take the time and care to get in touch with the riches of your spiritual kingdom.

The two worst enemies on the spiritual side are rejection and lack of faith. Don't close yourself off to the Higher Force because of negative associations you may have with organized religion. Your spirituality is a precious gift. Choose the form and practice that make you comfortable and come from your heart.

Love, faith, and health are inextricably linked. When you feel close to your Creator, you feel love. When you have faith in a Higher Force, you believe in your inner healing power. This is a truth that can never be fully expressed in words; it can only be felt. So let's set aside the words for a moment and try an exercise to nurture your love and faith.

HEALING MOMENTS

The best place to begin your spiritual exploration is in the bathtub. This may surprise you, but if you try the following practice, you'll experience why this works.

Fill the tub only about one quarter of the way so the warm water barely covers your abdomen. Slide down so your head and back are flat on the bottom of the tub, and put your feet up against the wall or edge of the tub. This is a way to re-create the feeling of being in the womb.

If this sounds too strange at the moment, or you don't have a bathtub, you can practice Healing Moments lying on a carpet or a pad on the floor. Turn off the phone, lower the lights, and try to block out any other distractions.

Begin by inhaling slowly through your nose. Fill up your abdomen with your breath, then your rib cage and then your chest. Now exhale slowly and completely. This is diaphragmatic breathing, and it is used in most meditation practices. Establish this pattern until it becomes comfortable.

As you inhale, feel your body becoming light, floating. Slowly lift up your hands. Feel the pure white light and love of the Universe entering through your fingertips. This is the light and love of the Creator and humanity. Feel it fill you up, and absorb the love into your body, your solar plexus, your heart.

If there is a place in your body with a pain or problem, send the light-love to that spot. See and feel the healing light-love soothe and balance that area.

As you exhale, send the love and energy back out, to the Creator and to all the people in the world. Direct some of your healing light-love to specific people who need it. Send it to people you need to forgive. Keep inhaling the love, filling yourself up with it, and exhaling, sending it back out to the Universe.

When you're ready to emerge from the Healing Moment, do so gently, slowly. First open your eyes and stretch a little. Then turn to one side, and rise to a sitting position slowly.

Try to follow the Healing Moment with another nourishing activity. If you're in the tub, you can continue with the Bathing Ritual on page 219. If you're on the floor, this is a good time to do yoga or to stretch. You can turn on the light and read a book on a spiritual topic. Your mind and body are open and relaxed; be careful what stimulus you give yourself.

Now that you've read through this section, please try it.

How did it go? If you are new to any form of meditation, you may have experienced some common blocks. Maybe you felt silly or uneasy. Perhaps you felt skeptical or insincere. Perhaps your thoughts kept darting all over, and you couldn't concentrate on the healing. These all are extremely common reactions. Don't berate yourself. Just keep at the practice.

The moment will come when you truly feel the light and love. As you become more and more adept with this practice, you'll be able to evoke the feeling in different circumstances. You'll be putting together the mental and spiritual in a very powerful way.

MEDITATION IS FOR EVERYONE

Meditation is not just for yogis sitting in lotus positions in India or those with exotic lifestyles. Meditation can benefit everyone everywhere. For many years holistic healers have recognized the ability of regular meditation to reduce mind/body stress, improve mental attitude, and enhance the immune response.

In the past decade medical science has finally started to give attention to the link between mind and immunity, and this has given rise to a new discipline called psychoneuroimmunology, or PNI. Dr. Bernie Siegel, author of *Love, Medicine and Miracles*, and Dr. Joan Borysenko, author of *Minding the Body, Mending the Mind*, are two leading lights in this field.

There are many different forms and philosophies of meditation. Basically meditation is a way to quiet the mind and give yourself a respite from the usual busy thoughts. Meditation is a way to focus your mind firmly in the present moment, without thought of the future or past. It's good practice for bringing yourself back into the present to eliminate fear.

There are various types of meditation that use mantras, prayers, or religious chants as focal points. Other people prefer to use a simple word such as "one" or to concentrate on their breathing. Whichever form you practice, meditation will help you get in touch with your spiritual self. See page 183 for instructions on how to meditate.

AFFIRMATIONS

Another way to nourish your mental/spiritual side is to use affirmations, which are a form of positive programming. Affirmations involve replacing negative thought patterns with positive statements that you repeat to yourself until they become part of your reality.

You can say your affirmations out loud, repeat them to yourself silently, or write them down. Some people like to have written affirmations greet them when they open their closets or drawers. Sitting quietly and repeating the affirmations has a powerful effect, but you can also sing them to yourself while you do housework or take a walk.

Affirmations can be any positive statement, stated in the present tense. Some basic examples, which may be familiar, are:

I enjoy vibrant good health.
I love and accept every part of myself.
I have loving, nourishing relationships.
I am filled with unconditional love.

Affirmations can also be more specific, about your career, relationships, or any other aspect of your life. However, affirmations are not to be used to manipulate other people or as a selfish "wish list." The idea is to state affirmations that establish basic patterns of positive thinking and leave you open to a variety of possibilities. You don't want to turn your affirmation practice into a goal-oriented task. Leave yourself open, and use affirmations for spiritual growth.

When you compose your affirmations, make them short, clear, and positive, and state them in the present tense. For example, instead of saying, "I am not nervous or tense," say, "I am calm and relaxed." Make your affirmations about yourself, not about others. "I attract loving relationships," is preferable to "Everyone falls madly in love with me."

As you repeat your affirmations, try to let go of your doubts and judgments. Try to believe in your affirmations even if they are not reflective of your present reality.

VISUALIZATION

Visualization or positive imagery is another way to nourish the mental/spiritual side of your Triangle. Visualization, like meditation, should be done in a quiet place and a comfortable position. You begin by relaxing your body and focusing on your breath. Then you imagine a scene that nourishes your mind/body.

Another way to use visualization is for specific goals. Once you have set the goal, you begin the visualization in the same way: Sit comfortably; close your eyes; concentrate on your breath. Now imagine or see the scene in your mind.

For example, if you want to give up caffeine, picture yourself starting the day with a glass of fruit juice instead of coffee, drinking lots of refreshing mineral water, and feeling energetic yet calm all morning. If you want to handle a difficult person with more patience, you can visualize yourself responding to the person's complaints in a more compassionate manner.

The goal is to imagine the scene in great detail, to create a vivid positive image in your mind in place of a negative projection. Of course, this doesn't mean everything will always go exactly as you visualize or affirm. But it can help tremendously to use the power of your mind and the natural habit of association to create positive expectations instead of fear.

Visualization can be a powerful healing tool. It may take time and patience before you can fully utilize imagery to evoke your natural healing force, but it is an exercise that is well worth practicing. Please see page 184 for guided healing visualizations.

EXPERIMENT

This chapter has introduced you to many ways in which you can nourish your mental/spiritual side. Try a variety of techniques, and see which ones work best for you. It doesn't mean you're a spiritual dilettante if you experiment with different ways to strengthen your mental/spiritual base. However, consistency is needed for true spiritual growth. After you find the practices that feel right, try to do them on a regular basis.

Everyone has different ways to express unconditional love and nurture her or his spirituality. Your individual temperament, your lifestyle, and your religious background and upbringing all will influence your choices.

The only absolute rule is that you need to nourish this mental/spiritual side of your Triangle to be holistically healthy. Mental/spiritual nourishment and love are as essential to good health as the food you eat. Take time to eliminate toxic fear and guilt from your mental diet and to feed yourself more love and faith.

CHAPTER 3

The Chemical Side of Your Holistic Triangle

When your body is free of toxins, an incredible healing force is released. You can think more clearly, you can take deeper breaths, and your body can gather all its energy to heal ailments that may have been plaguing you for years. It's an energizing, joyful state that you need to experience firsthand to appreciate fully.

The goal on the chemical side of the Holistic Triangle is to eliminate toxins and to increase your intake of natural, wholesome, unprocessed foods. Then you can experience for yourself the power and pleasure of detoxification.

Although nourishing all three sides of your Holistic Triangle is crucial to good health, the choices you make on the chemical side can be a matter of life and death. According to the *Surgeon General's Report on Nutrition and Health*, food can affect the risk of diseases that account for more than two thirds of all deaths in the United States: coronary heart disease, stroke, atherosclerosis, diabetes, and some types of cancer. One of the most important and life-affirming steps you can take is to improve your diet.

THE HOLISTIC FOOD GROUPS

In the spring of 1991 the U.S. Department of Agriculture was set to issue a pamphlet titled *U.S.D.A.'s Eating Right Pyramid.* The meat and dairy interests were upset that their products were given less space on the pyramid than grains, fruits, and vegetables were. In fact, meat and dairy products merited just slightly more space than fats and sweets. Pressure from meat and dairy industry groups held up the release of the food pyramid for another year.

The new food pyramid, which was finally released by the USDA is a step in the right direction since it suggests fewer servings of meat and eggs and more of vegetable and grain products. But it is a timid step that does not go nearly far enough in giving Americans optimal nutritional advice. The pyramid recommends two to three servings of milk, yogurt, or cheese, whereas eliminating dairy products altogether is a better idea for most people. And the pyramid fails to emphasize that the bread, cereal, rice, or pasta products should be whole grains and unrefined forms of these foods. The Holistic Food Pyramid on page 49 represents a better balance for optimal nourishment and detoxification.

HEALTHY ALTERNATIVES TO THE TOP TEN TOXINS

Strengthening the chemical side of your Holistic Triangle boils down to a simple formula: *Less toxic input; more wholesome input.*

The Top Ten Toxins are substances that weaken your Holistic Triangle: sugar, white flour and other refined carbohydrates, dairy products, meat, food additives, nicotine, caffeine, alcohol, drugs, and environmental toxins.

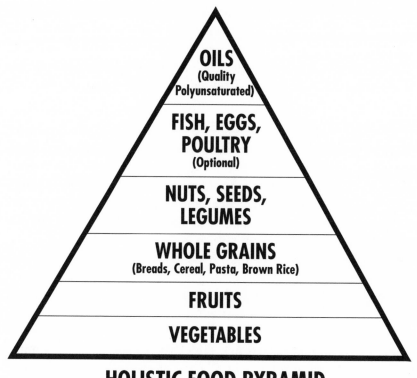

HOLISTIC FOOD PYRAMID

The goal is to eliminate these toxins from your *daily* diet. If you choose to have a cappuccino on a sunny day in Little Italy, eat roast beef on Christmas, or drink a glass of champagne during a romantic dinner, it's not going to do you a great deal of harm. It's the habits you indulge in day after day, year after year—the ones that your own body tells you it wants to dispense with—that you need to address.

Certain toxins, such as nicotine, you'll need to eliminate completely and forever. Other substances on this list, such as alcohol, sugar, and meat, you may want to indulge in occasionally. The choice is yours, but it's important you have enough knowledge to make intelligent decisions.

Entire books have been written to explain the hazards of many of these toxins. If you have an addiction to a particular substance, such as sugar, and have a hard time believing you need to give it up, you might do additional reading on your pet poison. Meanwhile, the information here will alert you to some of the dangers. The purpose of this section is not to scare you; it's to motivate you to make changes. I've provided healthy alternatives to each toxin to show you'll be gaining more than you give up.

Sugar

Understand that sugar is a drug. Large amounts of refined sugar have a profound physiological response and pharmacological effect. A "sweet tooth" is a euphemism for "sugar addiction."

It's well known that sugar is a major cause of tooth decay and causes overweight. Sugar provides virtually no vitamins, minerals, enzymes, or any other nutrients. Sugar actually *drains* the body of vitamins and minerals, while placing a tremendous strain on its systems.

Most of us are familiar with the sugar "buzz" and subsequent letdown. Sugar can produce an emotional roller coaster: anxiety, shakiness, and other metabolic responses culminating in the "sugar blues." These reactions reflect what refined sugar does to your blood sugar level.

Sugar consumption causes the blood sugar to rise rapidly. The pancreas responds by churning out insulin, which causes the blood sugar level to fall. These sharp fluctuations can lead to anxiety and depression. As with other addictions, the sugar "high" is followed by a crash.

Worse yet is the long-term effect: stress on the adrenals and endocrine system that can lead to hypoglycemia and diabetes. Studies by Dr. Thomas Cleve (the former surgeon captain of the Royal Navy and research director of the British Institute of Naval Medicine) found that increases in consumption of sugar and refined carbohydrates in residents of African nations were followed by precipitous rises in diabetes cases in these countries.

A warning is needed about products that are falsely presented as safe substitutes for sugar. Brown sugar is simply white sugar with a small amount of molasses added for coloring. Molasses is a by-product of sugar refining and is also nutritionally worthless.

The "sugar substitutes" cooked up in laboratories are far worse. In fact, you're probably better off consuming plain old white sugar than artificial sweeteners.

After a two-year investigation of aspartame, the Government Accounting Office (GAO) reported that 40 percent of the scientists surveyed called for further research, 32 percent suggested new warnings, and 15 percent favored a total ban of the sweetener. Studies reported in the *Tufts University School of Nutrition Guide to Total Nutrition* found that large amounts of saccharin cause bladder cancer in laboratory animals.

The data on artificial sweeteners are incomplete, and more carcinogenic effects may be found in the future. Remember that cyclamates were an approved sweetener for twenty-five years until they were found to cause bladder tumors in lab rats and finally banned in 1969.

Healthy Alternatives

There are some natural sweeteners that are safe if used sparingly. Raw, unheated, unfiltered honey and maple syrup in small amounts are acceptable. Barley malt syrup is a grain-based sweetener that has less impact on the body than refined sugar. Rice syrup is another gentle sweetener.

The healthiest sweetness comes from the sun, in all the wonderfully diverse forms of fruits. Fruit juices are versatile sweeteners to use in cooking and baking. Fruit itself is the healthiest sweet snack. Fruit juices are nutritious sweet beverages, but they should always be diluted with 50 percent water to reduce the fructose concentration. Fructose in other forms should be used sparingly.

White Flour and Refined Carbohydrates

Nature produces a miniature nutritional miracle in each tiny grain. Unfortunately, modern food processing strips away most of the nutrients and leaves empty calories.

Whole wheat contains essential amino acids, fiber, vitamins, minerals, and trace elements. But nearly all these nutrients are found in the germ and bran layers, which are removed to produce white flour. Processing also strips rice of its most nutritious layers to produce white rice.

White flour and polished rice, and foods made from their ingredients, are lacking in B vitamins and can exacerbate B deficiency. In addition, altering the form of complex carbohydrates through food processing affects the rate of digestion and absorption and can lead to blood sugar level problems.

Healthy Alternatives

Instead of nutritionally deficient white flour products, you can choose from a great variety of whole grain foods.

—Whole wheat flour is the most popular choice for cooking. You can also use buckwheat flour, rice flour, rye flour, and cornmeal for different recipes. Many prepared baked goods are now made with these whole grain flours. (A small amount of white flour may be included in these products.)

—Brown rice still has the germ and bran layers intact and is far more nutritious and satisfying than white rice. Wild rice, which is actually the seed of an aquatic grass, has a distinctive taste and texture.

—Dried pastas made from whole wheat flour are available, some with vegetables such as spinach, carrots, and tomatoes added. Japanese soba noodles, made from buckwheat and wheat flour, are a tasty option.

—A wide selection of hot and cold cereals is made from whole grains. Look for products sweetened with fruit juice instead of sugar.

You can also expand your grain repertoire far beyond rice. Bulgur, traditionally used in Middle Eastern cooking, is a precooked grain with a nutty flavor. Couscous made from whole wheat flour is another idea. Millet can be eaten as a breakfast cereal or used in other meals instead of rice. Amaranth and quinoa have been called supergrains because of their high nutrient content. A selection of fascinating health food cookbooks can teach you how to prepare these and other grains.

Dairy Products

The National Dairy Council does a tremendous job convincing Americans of two lies: Milk is essential for children, and dairy products are also healthy for adults. The milk myth is one of the most widespread examples of nutritional brainwashing. Even baby calves can't survive on homogenized milk, yet we feed our children cow's milk loaded with antibiotics, synthetic hormones, and pesticide and herbicide residues.

The consumption of milk, cheese, butter, and other dairy products has been found by researchers to be a factor in atherosclerosis, heart attacks, and strokes. One of the largest studies of diet and health ever undertaken was the China-Oxford-Cornell Project on Nutrition, Health, and the Environment (also known as the China Health Project), begun in 1983 and reported upon in 1990. This study found both dairy and meat consumption is unnecessary and can contribute to cancer, heart disease, obesity, and many other illnesses.

In addition to the problems caused by high-fat content, dairy products contain alarmingly high levels of pesticide residues and other environmental contaminants. Compounding this danger is the high level of antibiotics in cattle feed, which becomes concentrated in dairy products and meat.

Dairy products are also a leading cause of food allergies. At about the age of four many people begin to lose the ability to digest lactose, which is the carbohydrate found in milk. Lactose intolerance is particularly high in certain ethnic groups, including Asians, African Americans, and Jews. Allergies to milk caseinate, or protein, are also common. Symptoms of dairy allergy can include irritability, muscle pain, mental depression, abdominal pain, cramps, gas, diarrhea, constipation, nasal stuffiness, and sinusitis. For more on detecting dairy and other food allergies, see page 194.

Yogurt is promoted as a health food, but this is another illusion created by clever marketers. Most supermarket brands of yogurt contain sugar and milk from polluted American cattle and are a far different substance from the natural product that helps people live to be one hundred and five in the Caucasus Mountains.

If you want to eat yogurt, do so in moderation, and be sure to choose a type with active yogurt cultures and without added sugar. Or, if possible, make your own yogurt with milk from an organic farm.

Healthy Alternatives

The delicious, nutritious alternatives to cow's milk include soy beverage, almond beverage, and rice beverage. These can be used in cereal, for cooking, or as satisfying drinks.

Margarine is *not* a healthy substitute for butter since it is hydrogenated and can interfere with the body's ability to absorb calcium and magnesium. Alternatives include almond butter, filbert butter, cashew butter, pecan butter, and apple butter.

Health food stores now offer cholesterol-free "mayonnaise" made from tofu. Soy cheeses and yogurts are also available.

Despite what the Dairy Council would have us believe, human beings *do not* need cow's milk or cheese for calcium. Calcium comes from soil and is absorbed into the structure of plants. That's how cattle get calcium. Why not get the calcium directly from the source instead of filtered through a contaminated cow?

Foods with high levels of calcium include green vegetables, such as kale and spinach; fish, beans, and nuts; and soy beverages fortified with vitamins, minerals, and protein.

Meat

For decades, nutritionists and cardiologists have urged Americans to eat less meat to avoid heart attacks, strokes, and cancer. Thousands of articles have been published demonstrating that the less animal fat you take into your body, the healthier you will be. Even the usually conservative American Dietetic Association came out with a paper that stated people who do not consume meat are at a lower risk for colon cancer, heart disease, obesity, adult-onset diabetes, high blood pressure, osteoporosis, kidney stones, gallstones, breast cancer, and lung cancer.

In 1990 the *New England Journal of Medicine* reported the results of a survey of the health and diet histories of more than eighty-eight thousand women. This survey found that the more red meat and animal fat the women ate, the more likely they were to develop cancer of the colon. Cancers of the prostate, kidneys, testicles, uterus, lungs, and breasts and lymphomas are also higher in populations that consume diets high in fat.

Animal flesh contains high levels of environmental contaminants, which are ingested by animals and concentrated in their fatty tissues. Meat is further contaminated by hormones, stimulants, and antibiotics used to speed animal growth and combat infectious illness. Many of these contaminants have been found or are suspected of causing cancers, birth defects, and other severe effects.

Switching to a vegetarian diet can help save the planet as well as yourself. Beef production accounts for an enormous waste of land that could be more efficiently utilized for grain production. According to John Robbins, author of *Diet for a New America* and *May All Be Fed*, if Americans reduced their meat consumption by only 10 percent, it would free land and resources to grow more than twelve million tons of grain each year and feed forty to sixty million people. As the population of the planet continues to explode, we desperately need to shift to an agriculture that feeds people, not livestock.

If you are sincerely concerned about the destruction of the tropical rain forest, you'll want to give up beef since much of the rain forest is razed to give way to cattle-grazing land. Throughout the world more and more forests are being cut down to clear land for grazing or growing cattle feed. By reducing the demand for meat, we can help curb the destruction of the environment.

Healthy Alternatives

Nature provides a bounty of foods that contain high levels of protein without the side effects of meat and dairy products. The vegetable foods with the highest protein levels are legumes—that is, beans, peas, and lentils.

It is *not* necessary to combine foods to "create" complete proteins, as some early vegetarian books suggested. Legumes and other high-protein plant foods are sufficient sources of protein by themselves. However, several different types of plant protein should be consumed in the course of a week.

Tofu, made from soybeans, is a favorite with vegetarian cooks because it has a neutral taste that soaks up seasonings and sauces. It comes in firm and soft forms and can be baked, broiled, grilled, marinated, scrambled, or steamed for use in salads, dressings, soups, main dishes, and desserts. Tempeh, which is also made from soybeans, has a rich, meatlike taste when it is prepared with the right seasonings.

Nuts and seeds are also high in protein, but they need to be eaten in moderation because they are high in calories. Buy and eat nuts in their natural form—that is, unsalted and raw—rather than roasted. Roasted nuts have already been cooked, and the oils within the nuts hydrogenated, so your body cannot utilize the oils as effectively.

Other high- to medium-high-protein foods include potatoes, corn, oatmeal, onions, artichokes, asparagus, mushrooms, spinach, kale, lettuce (except iceberg), and oranges.

A Word About Fish, Chicken, and Eggs

A vegetarian diet with careful attention to eating enough protein foods is the purest and most nourishing plan for the chemical side of your Holistic Triangle. It also provides the steady energy you need for a vigorous physical side.

From the mental/spiritual standpoint, practitioners of spiritual disciplines usually advocate a vegetarian diet for two reasons. First of all, it's obviously more humane not to have any living creatures killed for your supper. Secondly, meat is dense food that requires a lot of energy in the gastrointestinal tract to break down. It tends to create a lethargic mental state that makes concentration more difficult.

However, sticking to a vegetarian diet may be too much of an adjustment for you at this time. If this is the case, it's recommended you give up red meat and consume fish, eggs, and chicken in moderation.

Fish would be a healthy food if we lived in a pristine world. Unfortunately our rivers, lakes, and oceans are highly polluted, and their poisons accumulate in the fish tissues. Shellfish carry particularly high levels of toxic lead, cadmium, arsenic, and other heavy metals, along with dangerous microbes and toxins. Shellfish are also a cause of frequent food allergies and should be avoided entirely. Stick with fish high in omega fatty acids, such as haddock, halibut, salmon, and swordfish. Always select the fish carefully, and eat it cooked, not raw.

If you choose to eat chicken, purchase only free-range chicken from health food stores or specialty markets. Commercial chickens are raised in appalling conditions and are often contaminated. Always cook your chicken thoroughly, and again, limit the amount you eat.

If you want to eat eggs, buy brown fertilized organic eggs from your health food store. Poach or soft-boil the eggs, and try to limit yourself to two to four per week.

Food Additives

According to *Fit for Life* nutrition experts Harvey and Marilyn Diamond, more than one billion pounds of chemicals are added to food consumed by Americans each year. These include colorings, preservatives, flavoring agents, and chemicals for texture, firmness, thickening, and emulsifying. Manufacturers also add artificially produced nutrients in an attempt to replace what was destroyed by food processing.

These food additives are a frequent source of food allergies and allergic reactions. Reactions can include hyperactivity in children, weakness and fatigue, swelling, asthma, shock, headaches, and nausea.

Table salt is perhaps the most common food additive. Many people paralyze their taste buds by adding salt to everything. Eliminating this excess salt is instrumental in controlling high blood pressure and water retention.

There is enough natural salt in wholesome foods that using the shaker shouldn't be necessary. But when healthy recipes do call for salt, use a dash of sea salt.

Healthy Alternatives

The alternative to food additives is simple: Eat fresh food in its natural state, and learn to use herbs and spices in creative ways in cooking. When you do want to eat a premade bread, cereal, or snack food, check the label. If salt is one of the first ingredients listed or there are chemical additives, leave it in the store. As you lose your taste for packaged and refined foods, you'll gain a greater appreciation of the taste of the flavor of raw food in its fresh original state.

Caffeine

Nearly half the adult population of the United States is addicted to this insidious drug, which is found in coffee, tea, and many carbonated beverages. Sodas contain the double whammy of caffeine with sugar or artificial sweeteners.

Although caffeine is accepted in society, it can have serious consequences. High levels of caffeine consumption can cause nervous symptoms, including insomnia, irritability, and trembling; irritation to the stomach and diarrhea; and aggravation of heart and artery disorders.

In addition, studies have found that eliminating caffeine can control or cure fibrocystic breast disease (painful breast lumps). Even in small or moderate doses, caffeine can prevent iron from being properly utilized and cause other vitamins to be pumped through the body before they are absorbed.

Caffeine is a stimulant, and what goes up must come down. The surge of mental energy is often followed by a letdown, leading to an urge for another dose. This creates the cycle of caffeine addiction.

Decaffeinated beverages are *not* recommended since the process of decaffeination is itself questionable. Methylene chloride, which is used to extract the caffeine from coffee beans by some companies, has been found to cause cancer when inhaled in large amounts by laboratory animals. Even when other decaf methods are used, you'll be making a more health-affirming choice by leaving the beverage behind altogether.

Healthy Alternatives

Maintaining a good energy level through good nutrition, adequate rest, and exercise is the best substitute for caffeine. Since caffeine is highly addictive, kicking it can be hard, with low-grade headaches and fatigue common during the first days of withdrawal. But after the withdrawal is complete, your energy level should be better than ever if you nourish your Holistic Triangle well.

Increasing your oxygen consumption through exercise is the ultimate natural stimulant. Yet we need balance to be healthy, and rest is equally important. Listen to your body's signals; don't keep forcing and stressing yourself beyond natural limits.

Healthy beverage substitutes for coffee include drinks made from roasted grains and seeds. Herbal teas generally don't contain caffeine and are available in an array of flavors. You can make your own caffeine- and sugar-free soft drinks with a mixture of seltzer and fruit juice. Fruit juice, especially the type you make yourself in your juicer, can provide a natural lift.

Nicotine

It is common knowledge that nicotine addiction is a lethal habit and a leading cause of heart disease and some types of cancer. If you smoke, you probably don't need to be convinced it's bad for you.

What you need to do is take a holistic approach to kicking the habit. This requires a quit-smoking program that addresses the mental/spiritual component of the habit as well as the chemical addiction.

Healthy Alternatives

There is no healthy alternative to nicotine except to quit smoking. Breathing pure oxygen is the only substitute. Oxygen is the most important nutrient on the chemical side; it is life itself. Don't inhale death instead of life.

There are many different ways to kick the nicotine habit. Some people swear by quitting cold turkey on their own, while others find support groups and smoking-cessation clinics to be the answer. Whatever approach you take, good nutrition, plenty of exercise, and practicing relaxation methods will help you maintain your resolve.

Raw-juice fasting can be an excellent tool when you want to quit smoking. Once the body has been cleansed of accumulated poisons, the craving for nicotine often disappears. Acupuncture is an excellent aid during the nicotine withdrawal process. Some people find hypnosis helpful.

You should also be careful of the dangers of secondhand smoke. If you live or work with smokers, assert your right to a smoke-free environment. If you can't escape the smoke, supplements of vitamins A, E, and C and beta-carotene may be somewhat protective.

Alcohol

Excessive drinking can lead to alcoholism and a host of potentially fatal health problems: brain deterioration, cirrhosis of the liver, malnutrition, and strokes, as well as automobile accidents.

Even in moderation, alcohol adds empty calories and causes weight gain while it depletes vitamins. Alcohol turns into acid aldehyde, a metabolic waste product, and travels through the entire systematic circulation, burning out brain cells and causing other damage along the way. Another complication is caused by the sugar in alcohol, which can lead to or aggravate hypoglycemia.

Healthy Alternatives

Alcoholism is a disease that needs to be fought on all levels: mental/spiritual, physical, and chemical. Alcoholics Anonymous has incredible impact with its meetings, which focus on the mental/spiritual side.

Recovering alcoholics also need to pay attention to the chemical sides of their Triangles. Studies have shown that alcoholics who consume nutritious food and multivitamin supplements have greater success in staying sober. Since many heavy drinkers are also hypoglycemic, avoiding sugar and caffeine and eating small, frequent meals are recommended. Alcohol drinkers need vitamin/ mineral supplementation to replace depleted nutrients. Some experts believe that supplements of L-glutamine lessen the urge to drink.

Learning to unwind without alcohol can reduce the desire to drink. Relaxation techniques, meditation, exercise, and enjoying the outdoors can take the edge off your day without the side effects of alcohol.

Many beverages can substitute for alcoholic drinks. Fruit juices mixed with carbonated water are refreshing spritzers. Sparkling cider can substitute for champagne. Punches made with blends of exotic juices and fresh fruits are festive drinks.

Drugs

The government and the media focus on the dangers of illegal drugs, such as heroin, cocaine, amphetamines, barbiturates, and hallucinogens, and most people are well aware it's wise to avoid these substances. But we need to raise our consciousness about the legal drugs that are sanctioned by the government and promoted by pharmaceutical companies.

According to Dr. Joseph Beasley, the director of Bard College's Institute of Health Policy and Practice and a leading expert in addiction, every year Americans consume more than *five billion* legal yet addictive "minor" tranquilizers for anxiety and sleeplessness.

These tranquilizers include the most popular brand names consumed by basically healthy people without severe psychological problems. Yet the side effects of these ubiquitous drugs can include drowsiness, fatigue, lack of muscle coordination, confusion, depression, headache, sleep disturbances, urinary difficulties, loss of balance, blurred vision, anxiety, and addiction.

The overuse of penicillin is another epidemic of drug abuse. Antibiotics wipe out the friendly germs in your body, especially in your digestive tract. This can allow yeasts, such as *Candida albicans*, to proliferate and put toxins into your system, leading to such potential problems as fatigue, headaches, depression, and fungal infections. The long-range effect of the frequent use of antibiotics is still in dispute, but overall lowered immune function may be the result in many cases.

Even such a "harmless" nonprescription drug as aspirin can upset the gastrointestinal tract, cause hemorrhage, stomach cramps, nausea, heartburn, and blood in the stool. Prolonged use or large doses of aspirin can result in reduced production of blood cells, kidney damage, and activation of peptic ulcer. Aspirin is a prostaglandin inhibitor, and studies have shown that long-term use can exacerbate arthritis. Decongestants, when overused, can increase blood pressure and affect circulation.

Virtually all drugs, legal or not, can have side effects, and we need to treat them as toxins that should be used only as last resorts, not as cure-alls that can be popped without concern.

Healthy Alternatives

The more you nourish the three sides of your Holistic Triangle, the less likely you are to feel the need for drugs of any kind: recreational, prescription, or over-the-counter.

On the mental/spiritual side, meditation, positive visualization and affirmation, and spiritual/religious practices can help reduce the craving for drugs.

On the chemical side, eating natural foods and avoiding toxins will help you maintain good health and reduce the need for drug remedies. Supplements also help maintain health independence from drugs. Herbal remedies can be used to treat some ailments, on a limited, short-term basis.

On the physical side of the Triangle, exercise lowers the desire for drugs by creating a natural high. Yoga and relaxation practices can reduce anxiety and create a more balanced state of mind.

Environmental Toxins

There are several categories of environmental toxins to consider: pesticides and herbicides in food, toxins in personal products, and chemicals in the home and workplace. While environmental toxins are difficult to avoid in today's world, there are many measures you can take to protect yourself and your family.

Healthy Alternatives to Pesticides and Herbicides

Fear of pesticides and herbicides should never keep you from eating plenty of fruits and vegetables since the benefits far outweigh the risks. And there are measures you can take to protect your health.

Try to purchase organic fruits and vegetables that are certified as having been grown without pesticides and herbicides. These are available in many health food stores, in special sections at some supermarkets, and at some farmers' markets (although you need to check with the growers).

If your local food store does not carry organic fruits and vegetables, speak to the manager about stocking an organic produce section, and have your friends and neighbors add their support for this idea. Another possibility is to start a health food co-op in your area.

Organic produce tends to be more expensive than the supermarket variety that is grown with pesticides and herbicides. However, in the long run organic produce supplies better value for your dollar since it has more nutrients and you don't have to discard outer layers to get rid of the poisons. You'll also save a great deal of money by switching from a meat-based to a primarily vegetarian diet.

If you are unable to obtain organic produce, choose seasonal fruits and vegetables. Avoid imported produce from countries where pesticides are not regulated stringently. If possible, buy from farmers' markets, where the produce often has less pesticides.

You can soak the produce in filtered water with vinegar and lemon juice added, or use a biodegradable vegetable rinse, available in health food stores. Always wash the produce carefully, and if it is not organic and the skin is going to be eaten, scrub it with a vegetable brush.

If you have the time, space, and inclination, growing your own fruits, vegetables, and herbs is a wonderful way to get pure produce and exercise at the same time. Gardening nourishes all three sides of your Triangle: It provides exercise on the physical side, contact with nature to nourish your mental/spiritual side, and fresh foods to strengthen your chemical side.

Avoid the use of chemical pesticides, herbicides, and fertilizers on your lawn as well as your garden. Organic gardening manuals explain natural alternatives to chemicals.

Healthy Alternatives to Toxins in the Home and Workplace

Although it is difficult to completely avoid the toxins that infiltrate our world, there are measures you can take to minimize exposure.

—Use natural cosmetics, bath products, moisturizers, soaps, deodorants, and toothpastes. These are available in health food stores, in some drugstores, and through catalogs.

—Use toxin-free household cleaners and laundry products.

—Test your home for radon. If necessary, seal cracks in foundations and floors, improve ventilation, and treat contaminated water from private wells.

—Remove existing lead paint from your home. Test tap water for lead.

—Use stainless steel instead of aluminum cookware.

—If you must use toxic chemicals for home renovations, crafts, or hobbies, work in a very well-ventilated area and limit exposure time.

—If you work in a large office building, insist on good ventilation and windows that can be opened. If you notice a number of similar sicknesses in your office, bring it to the attention of management. Band together with your coworkers, and demand an investigation into whether there is a "sick building" problem. Assert your right to have renovations done that will ensure a clean work environment.

—If you are an industrial worker, consult with your colleagues and union leaders about steps to reduce exposure to hazardous materials and toxins.

—If your job entails unavoidable exposure to toxins, you may need to consider looking for other work. Despite economic difficulties and other serious considerations, you must put your health first. Sticking with an unhealthy job can finally result in greater financial hardship from missing work as the result of illness and from large medical bills.

WATER

Water, after oxygen, is the most essential nutrient on the chemical side. Yet few of us drink enough water each day.

Drinking eight glasses of liquid each day is optimal. Some of this liquid can be diluted fruit juice, soy or nut milk, or herbal tea, but six glasses a day should be pure water. Try to have a glass of water with you throughout the day—except when you are eating.

No animal in nature eats and drinks at the same time, and neither should humans. Drinking water neutralizes the enzymatic ability of the gastric juices, hydrochloric acid and pepsin, in your stomach. Diluting your gastric juices interferes with efficient digestion and assimilation of nutrients. Therefore, it's recommended you drink most of your water between, not during, meals.

When you're drinking a lot of water, you want it to be pure. But water straight from the tap cannot be trusted in most cities and towns. Many people drink bottled water, which usually comes in a plastic rather than a glass container. The drawbacks to bottled water are the plastic residue and the impact on the environment from all those discarded plastic bottles and jugs. A better solution is to purchase a water filter to attach directly to your tap. Then you can use pure water for your cooking as well as straight drinking. Having a water cooler with delivery of fresh springwater in reusable jugs is another option.

A HEALTHFUL DIET

The sun is our original source of energy, and foods that thrive on sunlight and soil provide energy. When you eat more live foods, you feel more alive.

Revitalizing the chemical side of your Triangle is an opportunity to enjoy more of nature's bounty and reject civilization's poisons. This is part of creating your own paradise. You won't go hungry in the "Garden of Eden," but you will have to detoxify to get there.

When you're radically changing your nourishment on the chemical side of your Triangle, it helps to have reinforcement on the mental/spiritual side by reading books on nutrition and health food cooking. By educating yourself about natural food, you'll learn that the choices of healthy nourishment are varied and enticing. See page 187 for Healthful Meal Plan guidelines.

You'll notice this plan consists of six meals, not three. It's not just what you eat; it's what you *assimilate* that strengthens your Triangle. Eating small, frequent meals provides a steady stream of nutrients without overtaxing your digestive system. This eating plan facilitates the ability of digestive enzymes to break down complex molecules into simple ones your body can absorb.

It's important to chew all your food slowly and thoroughly to maximize assimilation of nutrients. Chewing does more than break up food so you can gulp it down; it stimulates the production of digestive juices.

You can create the right frame of mind to appreciate your food by taking a few seconds to calm down before you eat. Close your eyes, take a few deep breaths, and give thanks to the Universe for your nourishment.

INDIVIDUALIZED NEEDS

When designing a healthy diet for yourself, consider your ethnic background and your genetic predisposition. Everyone is different, and while there are general guidelines, it's best to adapt your diet to suit your individuality. To accomplish this, you need to consider both your ancestry and your present way of life.

For example, if you have a heavy manual job, you can utilize more calories and larger portions than if you sit at a desk. If you are very athletic, you can also increase your intake. Your body size, build, and metabolism are factors. You may need to experiment with the amount of food you eat to lose or maintain a desirable weight as you adapt your diet.

Many people find they lose weight on a natural-food six-small-meals-a-day plan. The trick is to eat smaller portions of a variety of high-energy foods. This helps prevent your craving high-calorie foods and keeps your metabolism going at a brisk pace. It's especially helpful to eat lightly after sundown.

You can also use food as a targeted therapeutic tool to heal specific diseases and ailments. Nutritionists specialize in designing customized diets to treat health problems. There are many fine books on using foods for healing, in which you can look up your ailment and get a food prescription. This is another example of how strengthening the mental side of the Triangle can heal the chemical and physical sides.

A DOZEN HEALTHY EATING HINTS

- Just because a product is sold in a health food store doesn't mean it's healthy. Watch out for products containing too much honey, fructose, corn syrup, and oil.
- Fill your shopping basket with organic fruits and vegetables.
- Buy grains, nuts, and seeds from bag-it-yourself bins in health food stores to save money.
- Find out if there is a health food store co-op, owned and operated by customers, in your area. Food co-ops can be very economical, and you might consider organizing one if you have the time and interest.
- Use only small amounts of high-quality, cold-pressed, poly-

unsaturated oils for cooking and salad dressings: flaxseed oil, olive oil, safflower oil, and sunflower oil.

- Eat fruits and vegetables in their raw state whenever possible. When you do cook vegetables, steam them instead of boiling or sautéing them.
- Prepare green salads shortly before mealtimes, and use leafy green types of lettuce but no iceberg lettuce. If you're eating salad with other foods, have it during or after the meal, not before.
- Increase fiber by choosing only whole grains cereals, pastas, and breads. Add bran to cereals and batters.
- Prepare your lunch and snacks to take to work, so you know you'll be eating nutritious, pure food.
- Make your food preferences known ahead of time when you are eating at a friend's or relative's house. If you think this is imposing, offer to bring your own meal.
- Share your reasons for eliminating toxins and eating natural foods with your family, but don't shove your choices down their throats or expect them to see the light overnight.
- In addition to natural food restaurants, ethnic restaurants often have many vegetable-based entrées. Assert yourself in restaurants, and ask them to prepare what you want, how you want it.

WHAT GOES IN MUST COME OUT

Frequent bowel movements are a vital element of your holistic health regimen since partially digested food builds up in the bowel and can cause toxicity and disease. You'll find that giving up toxins and eating more fruits, vegetables, and grains will result in easier elimination, although it may take time for your body to adjust.

You can add flaxseed or bran to juice or cereals for more help. A recipe for a special Fiber Broth to aid elimination is on page 193. Drinking eight glasses of water a day also alleviates constipation. Supplements of probiotic microorganisms (e.g. acidophilus) can provide healthy intestinal flora, which may be lacking.

Since eating stimulates the peristaltic action of a healthy bowel, the best time for a bowel movement is after a meal. Avoid reading and other distractions when you're on the toilet; relax and allow your mind/body to focus on its natural response.

The modern toilet bowl does us a great disservice. The bowls are too high up and removed from the natural squatting position. Squatting increases intra-abdominal pressure and creates more compression and force in the bowel to get rid of the stool. It also improves the tone of intestinal muscles. You can modify the toilet bowl by placing a small stool (pardon the pun) under your feet to elevate your knees.

RAW-JUICE FASTING

One of the most powerful tools on the chemical side of the Holistic Triangle is raw-juice fasting. Fasting has been used since antiquity as a healing method. It has a profound effect on the mental/spiritual side as well as the chemical side and is part of many spiritual traditions. People often associate fasting with deprivation and starvation. Raw-juice fasting, however, is quite the opposite and can supply more nutrients than the Standard American Diet.

Raw-juice fasting can have dramatic effects on chronic problems. Brenda, a woman in her mid-thirties, had frequent constipation and chronic cystitis. Three or four times a year the cystitis would flare up and her doctor would put her on antibiotics. By the time she came to the Holistic Health Force, she needed very strong antibiotics to get temporary relief. Taking these antibiotics on a regular basis weakened her immune system and made her vulnerable to yeast infections.

Brenda's Holistic Self-Health Program began with cutting out toxins, particularly red meat, which she ate frequently. Eliminating meat and refined foods and consuming more raw foods, juices, and water solved her problem with constipation.

Two months after eliminating toxins from her diet (except for occasional lapses), Brenda was ready to embark on a three-day raw-juice fast. The fast cleaned out the lingering toxins in her system, and she immediately felt lighter and more energetic. After the discipline of the juice fast, she had more resolution to begin eliminating other toxins. She also decided to go on a raw-juice fast once each season. Brenda hasn't had a single episode of cystitis in more than three years.

Even people who are in good health and have nutritious diets can benefit from raw-juice fasting. Danny, a graphic designer in his late twenties, was a healthy eater but liked to party and stay out late drinking with his friends. He had started to gain weight around the middle and sometimes lacked energy and had difficulty concentrating.

Danny found that during and after his raw-juice fast he was mentally stimulated and unusually creative. He also lost weight and was energized to get serious about exercise. Now Danny goes on a juice fast two or three times a year because he enjoys the enhanced clarity, vigor, and creativity.

For more information on raw-juice fasting and instructions on how to use this healing force, see page 188.

SUPPLEMENTS AND HERBS

If the planet were still fresh and unpolluted, it would be possible to get all the vitamins, minerals, and enzymes we need from food. Sadly much of the soil in which today's produce is grown is depleted, and modern farming methods cause further depletion. While it is vital to consume plenty of fresh fruits and vegetables, we also need to supplement our diets to have optimal nourishment. See page 196 for information on choosing supplements.

As well as provide a backbone of basic strength and strong immunity, supplements can be used for specific therapeutic purposes. The chart on page 197 provides details about the specific properties of different vitamins and minerals.

Herbs have been used since ancient times for healing, prevention, and health maintenance. Eastern systems of medicine and folk healers throughout the world have used herbs throughout the centuries, and now holistic doctors continue the tradition. See page 205 for a summary of herbs with special healing properties.

CHAPTER 4

The Physical Side of Your Holistic Triangle

Health is a consummation of a love affair with the organs of the body.

—PLATO

Your physical state is an outward reflection of the amount of love and nourishment you give the three sides of your Holistic Triangle. Genetics play an important role, but your actions are also instrumental on the physical side. And since you can't change your genetic legacy, there's no use "blaming" it for physical limitations. The healthiest response is to accept and love what you were given as you work to strengthen your physical side.

There are three basic forms of nourishment on the physical side:

- Primary physical nourishment, which you give to yourself. This is the most important form of nourishment and includes exercise, relaxation, and rest.
- Secondary physical nourishment, which is provided by holistic practitioners. This includes chiropractic care, massage, exercise instruction, and many other natural therapies.
- Tertiary physical care, which is given by medical doctors and includes surgical procedures.

Surgery can be lifesaving in cases of injury and severe degenerative conditions, and medical doctors should be applauded for the valuable work they perform. However, the holistic viewpoint is that surgery should be utilized selectively and carefully, in emergency situations and when limitations of matter inhibit natural healing.

We should not count on surgeons to "fix" our bodies as if they are repairmen and we are machines. We need to do everything we can to nurture and love our bodies into health before resorting to invasive procedures. The more we nourish the physical side of our Triangles, the less likely we are to end up on the operating table.

AEROBIC EXERCISE

There are three main categories of exercise: aerobic exercise, which works the cardiovascular system; musculoskeletal development, which builds the muscles; and stretching, which provides flexibility. A basic holistic exercise program consists of alternating at least three days of aerobics and three days of musculoskeletal development and of stretching every day. Adding days of aerobic exercise is fine, and you may find that some activities combine the aerobic and musculoskeletal workouts.

Aerobic exercise tones the muscles and conditions the heart to pump more blood with each stroke. This results in a lowered resting heart rate and better cardiovascular fitness, which can lower the risk of heart disease. A fifteen-year study at the Institute for Aerobics Research in Texas found definite links between physical activity and life expectancy.

One of the goals of aerobic exercise is to oxygenate your body by forcing a large volume of blood through your heart, lungs, and muscle groups. Your breath should flow with each repetition of the aerobic movement. Inhale through your nose, and exhale through your mouth or nose, and keep breathing steadily throughout the workout.

Exercising with a holistic attitude allows aerobics to nourish the mental/spiritual as well as the physical side of your Triangle. Although it's fine to set exercise goals, try not to be entirely goal-oriented. Enjoy the process, not just racing to the finish line. Wellness, not winning or making another mile, is the ultimate goal. Don't judge your performance; congratulate yourself for trying. Anything you do to nourish your physical side means you're winning!

With the right attitude, aerobic exercise can relieve tension and strengthen your stress-coping mechanisms. When you have a well-conditioned cardiovascular system, your heart rate still rises under stress, but not as high or as quickly as that of a person who is not fit. This "ceiling" on the heart rate can enable you to stay calmer during periods of stress and reduce the chance of sudden heart attack.

Regular exercise is likely to improve your self-image and boost your confidence. Many people report that during and after brisk exercise they feel more able to cope with the demands of their lives; they feel strong and "on top of the world." Studies have shown that people who exercise have more positive images of their bodies than people who don't. Of course, this improved self-image is grounded in reality since exercise helps you look better to the rest of your world as well as to yourself.

During aerobic exercise, increased blood flow to the brain can boost your thinking power. Studies have shown aerobic exercise can improve memory, verbal fluency, and creative problem solving. This effect is enhanced by the rhythmic nature of aerobics, which induces a tranquil yet lucid state of mind.

"Runner's high" is a misnomer since this sensation of euphoria is also enjoyed by swimmers, bikers, hikers, and dancers. "Exercise exhilaration," a more accurate term, is partially a result of the release of endorphins from the pituitary gland. Vigorous exercise can increase endorphin levels as much as five times.

Aerobic exercise can also help people overcome depression. One reason is the increase in the release of norepinephrine, a deficiency of which has been indicated in depression. Another factor is that the lack of exercise may itself contribute to depression.

Clearly, aerobic exercise works wonders on all three sides of the Holistic Triangle: On the mental/spiritual side it helps you love yourself and experience more joy; on the chemical side it burns calories and releases "feel-good" hormones, such as norepinephrine and endorphin; and on the physical side it builds muscular and cardiovascular fitness. There's no doubt aerobic exercise is an essential element of your Self-Health Program; now it's a matter of choosing which form of aerobics is best for you.

The type of aerobic activity you do, as well as the frequency and duration, initially depends on your current level of fitness. For this reason, four fitness categories are offered: level 1, level 2, level 3, and level 4. When you choose your level, be realistic and honest. Don't feel bad if you're in level 4; you can probably work your way up to level 2 at least by the end of the Self-Health Program. These levels are not meant to be judgmental; they're only to protect you against overdoing it.

These levels are designated for people within the approximate age range of twenty-two to sixty. If you are older, your level will depend on your health history and how often you exercise. If you have any doubts, choose a level with a higher number to be safe, and start your exercise program slowly and carefully.

Level 1: ideal weight and already involved in a rigorous exercise program on a regular basis

Level 2: ideal to moderate weight and intermittent exercise, fairly active, no major health problems

Level 3: moderate to heavy weight and/or no regular exercise, inactive lifestyle

Level 4: overweight and no exercise and/or preexisting physical condition such as severe arthritis, heart disease, or disabilities

Aerobic Activity Choices

Running: Level 1 only to start. Level 2 can build up to it.

Walking:	All levels; distance and speed will depend on capabilities. Not recommended for those with severe arthritis in hips or knees.
Swimming:	Recommended for all levels; distance and speed will depend on level.
Aerobic Dance/ Step Aerobics:	Levels 1 and 2. Level 3 can build up to it. Not recommended if arthritis or injuries exist.
Biking:	Levels 1 and 2. Level 3 can build up to it.
Racquet sports:	Levels 1 and 2. Level 3 needs to start slowly.

Warning Signs

Whatever your level of fitness, you should have a checkup with a doctor before starting or accelerating your exercise program. The reason for this precaution is that only a professional can determine if you have a hidden heart weakness or other condition. Some of the warning signs of a heart condition are:

—Rapid resting pulse
—Irregular pulse
—Shortness of breath
—Pain or discomfort in the chest, abdomen, back, neck, jaw, or arms (can be referred pain from heart)

Although we need to exercise to keep our hearts healthy, we must be careful not to put too much sudden strain on the cardiovascular system. Following are some of the warning signs to watch out for during exercise.

If you experience any of these signs, or any sharp pain, before or during exercise, stop and have a thorough medical examination before you continue:

• Extremely rapid heart rate
• Irregular heartbeat
• Shortness of breath
• Difficulty breathing
• Dizziness or fainting
• Sudden sharp pain or recurrent pain

Running

Running builds cardiovascular capacity efficiently, burns calories quickly, and is one of the best ways to release endorphins and enjoy the mental benefits of aerobic exercise. But there are some drawbacks to consider.

Running, particularly on asphalt, puts a tremendous strain on the joints. Knee injuries are very common among runners, as are muscle pains, tendinitis, and hip injuries. It's not called jogging for nothing; the movement actually jogs your entire body, over and over again.

Another problem is the stress running puts on your lungs, heart, and circulatory system. The level of exertion means that running is a highly beneficial form of exercise but is risky for people with heart conditions. Since heart conditions may be hidden, you should have a complete cardiovascular examination before you take up running. If you learn that you do have a cardiovascular weakness, walking or swimming is a safer aerobic pursuit.

Running is never an entirely risk-free pursuit, but there are precautions that can reduce the chance of injury:

—Purchase a good pair of running shoes from a store where the staff is knowledgeable about runners' needs.
—Warm up before running with a gentle stretching routine.
—Run on a running track or a dirt trail instead of asphalt.
—Cool down with walking after your run.
—Stretch and take a warm bath after the workout.

Walking

Walking is more than exercise; it is a basic human activity that is meant to be part of our lives. It clears the mind and calms the soul as it nourishes the physical side of the Holistic Triangle. Walking is one of the most natural, gentle, yet beneficial forms of exercise.

A study by the Institute for Aerobics Research found brisk

walking improves the body's oxygen uptake and cardiovascular strength. A minimum of twenty minutes of brisk walking at least three times a week will keep your heart healthier and can help control mildly high blood pressure. Start at half a mile per day, and build up distance and speed gradually.

Wear comfortable clothing and good sneakers or walking shoes for your walks. As you walk, breathe deeply through your nose. Try to think positive, relaxed thoughts; don't dwell on problems. If you let your worries go, you may find creative solutions arise during or after your walk.

Follow a natural stride, with flexibility in the hips and torso. Keep your neck and shoulders relaxed. Keep your arms bent at the elbows, swinging back and forth naturally. After your walk, do some gentle stretches.

Swimming

Swimming is the ultimate holistic exercise: It soothes the spirit, stretches the joints, tones the muscles, and works the cardiovascular system. It is also our only opportunity to escape completely from gravity and experience the natural wonder of buoyancy.

Swimming is the one aerobic exercise that can be recommended to almost anyone. It's a particularly good choice for people with arthritis or the elderly, who may not be able to participate in other aerobic activities.

Even with the gentle art of swimming it's wise to start off slowly if you are at fitness levels 3 or 4. You may want to spend a few sessions simply walking back and forth in the water and stretching in the shallow area. Stretching in the water before and after swimming is also therapeutic for advanced swimmers.

The precautions for swimmers are mostly common sense. First of all, be sure you can swim well if you're going in deep water. Wear goggles to avoid getting chlorine in your eyes. Don't swim underwater for a prolonged period of time. If you're swimming in a natural body of water, such as a lake or ocean, always have someone with you.

Many of us were taught to lift our heads only to one side when doing the crawl. A more symmetrical and balanced form is to alternate lifting your head to both sides. The best workout is provided when you do a variety of strokes, including the breaststroke and the backstroke.

As with running and walking, swimming both stimulates and relaxes the mental/spiritual side. Some people like to combine swimming and meditation by concentrating on a mantra or the rhythm of their breaths. Others simply "go with the flow" and find creative thinking is enhanced during and after the swim.

Dancing

Aerobic dancing enjoyed a great vogue, followed by a backlash because of a high rate of injuries. Most aerobic dancing classes and videos were then modified to reduce the impact and potential for injury.

If you are a fitness level 1 or 2, aerobic dancing can be a good workout, but you need to ascertain that your instructor is well educated about safety. Low-impact classes or videotapes with nonjumping movements are recommended.

Work out only on cushioned health club floors or wooden floors, and wear supportive aerobic sneakers. If you have arthritis or a history of joint injuries, aerobic dancing is not a safe exercise choice.

Many of the same precautions apply to aerobic step classes. Those with a high level of fitness can include step training in their regimen, but this should not be the only aerobic activity.

Social dancing, while it is not as cardiovascular-intensive as aerobic dancing, can be good exercise and very pleasurable. The trick to dancing as exercise is to go out to a dance venue where you can keep moving; a couple of slow dances between dinner and dessert isn't going to work.

Dancing in all its forms, from rock-and-rolling around your room to a Broadway jazz class, is a wonderful way to get exercise and express yourself at the same time. Dancing oxygenates the body, strengthens and limbers the muscles, and releases the emotions. Music provides inspiration and energy as the rhythm echoes the heartbeat.

If you've always wanted to be a dancer, you can be one now, as part of your Holistic Self-Health Program. Just be sure to warm up and stretch out before dancing, and don't do movements that feel forced or unnatural. Whether you dance on your own or in a class, keep breathing, don't judge yourself in the mirror, be playful, and enjoy. Keep moving, vary your motions, and revel in the natural expression of your body.

Trampolines are another fun form of aerobic exercise. Minitrampolines can be purchased for home use and are an excellent way to work out without the stress of impact aerobics.

Biking and Racquet Sports

Outdoor biking is a refreshing activity that allows you to appreciate nature while you strengthen your physical side. However, bike riding on a regular basis is not a safe activity for everybody. If you have arthritis, a history of knee injuries, or back pain, walking or swimming may be a better choice since bike riding can place pressure on the joints and compress the spine.

English racers, which are ridden with the torso almost parallel to the ground, relieve this spinal compression, but you need to be fairly slim and strong to be able to handle this type of bike. If you ride a regular or mountain bike in a sitting-up position, get a spring seat and high handlebars so you can sit with a good lumbar curve.

Stationary bikes can provide solid muscular and cardiovascular conditioning. Be sure to purchase a dual-action bike that works the upper body as well as the legs.

Racquet sports are exciting, social activities that also build cardiovascular fitness. The competition and fast pace of racquet sports can motivate people who get bored easily with other exercise.

The problem with racquet sports, and with golf, is that they work one side of the body more than the other. This can result in asymmetrical muscle development, spinal disk problems, and postural distortion.

If you play these sports, you can compensate by working your body through a range of motion in the other direction to create muscular and spinal balance. For instance, if you play tennis with your right arm, address the imbalance by swinging the racquet in your left arm repeatedly before or after your game.

If you find yourself spending more time picking up the ball rather than playing, consider adding another form of exercise for a more sustained cardiovascular workout.

MUSCULOSKELETAL DEVELOPMENT

The goal of musculoskeletal development is to increase the strength, endurance, and flexibility of the skeletal muscles of the body. Muscular strength is the force the muscle produces in one effort; endurance is the ability to perform repeated muscular contractions in quick succession, and flexibility is the full range of motion.

Everyone knows muscular development will make you stronger and more physically attractive. But you may not be aware of the deeper effects of muscular strength and why it is so necessary.

The "inherent tone of the muscle" is the tone the muscle has in a relaxed, steady state. This inherent tone exerts pressure on the bone, which stimulates the bone to absorb calcium, which maintains the strength of the bone itself. Good muscle tone is needed to exert sufficient pressure on the bones, to keep them strong and reduce the likelihood of osteoporosis.

Muscle tone also affects blood circulation. For example, when the calf muscles are flaccid, they don't exert enough pressure on the veins. This can lead to varicose veins and phlebitis and, in extreme cases, the formation of blood clots, which can result in strokes.

The abdominal muscles are the weakest muscle group for most people. The abdominal muscles are responsible for taking the weight off the upper body and into the pelvis. When the abdominals are weak, it puts the burden of support on the lower back and often leads to lower back pain. Most people with lower back pain need to strengthen their abs.

Healthy development of the chest muscles is a prerequisite for efficient chest expansion and oxygen intake. Back muscles, since they are constantly working against gravity, are usually too tight rather than too weak and need to be put through a range of motion. Otherwise the constriction can result in lumbago: being painfully stuck in a contracted position. Neck and shoulder muscles are also frequently tight, resulting in neck pain and tension headaches.

The goal of musculoskeletal exercise is to increase the size of the muscle so it becomes stronger and more capable of doing its job without strain. When a muscle is well developed, the burden is distributed and the muscle is under less stress. There is greater blood flow and less muscle contraction and chance of pain and imbalance.

Just as everyone's Holistic Triangle is different, so everyone has a different state of muscular development, depending on age, frequency of exercise, type of job, and genetics. You'll want to work all your muscle groups, but there are certain areas on which you may need to concentrate.

A self-examination of your muscles can give you guidance on which ones you need to develop. Start by flexing your right calf as strongly as you can, then pressing your index finger into the center of the muscle. If your finger sinks in only a quarter of an inch or less, the tone in the muscle is quite good. If your finger sinks in more than half an inch, the muscle is weak.

Try the same flexion and finger pressure test with your thigh, abdominal, back, chest and arm muscles. Take note of the results so you can emphasize exercises to build these muscles.

Another indicator of health involves the triceps muscles in the back of the arms. Most everyday work is done by the biceps (the front arm muscles), while the triceps are often neglected. But since the triceps are utilized in most aerobic exercises, they are a barometer of cardiovascular health. Weak, flaccid triceps indicate you're not doing enough for your heart.

Another aspect of muscular development to consider is symmetry. Most adults have asymmetrical muscles, which can lead to pressure on the spinal disks and joints and ensuing pain.

Ask a friend or your spouse, workout partner, or doctor to help you inspect your muscular symmetry. Lie flat on the floor, put your arms behind your head, and lift your chin and chest off the floor at a forty-five-degree angle. The person who is studying you can usually supply information about which side has greater muscular development. Then you can do repetitions of exercises on the underdeveloped side to improve symmetry.

When you start your musculoskeletal exercise program, begin slowly and gently. Consistency—doing the exercise three times each week—is more desirable than doing a great number of repetitions infrequently. The number of reps will vary greatly depending on the current state of the physical side of your Holistic Triangle. Keep a record of the number when you start, and gradually increase the repetitions as you strengthen your physical side.

See page 211 for a series of basic musculoskeletal development exercises.

STRETCHING

Stretching is essential for keeping the spine aligned, the muscles fluid, and the joints lubricated. Stretching should be done every day, by everybody.

Animals stretch; it's instinctive and natural. But since we human beings spend so much time in unnatural positions, we have to be careful not to overstretch or to stretch too suddenly.

As you stretch, breathe deeply into your diaphragm. Think of breathing into the stretch; don't pull, bounce, or force. Be very, very gentle and aware. We all have structural and age limitations and need to listen to our bodies.

Try to focus on relaxing, positive thoughts as you stretch. This can be a nice time to do affirmations or active meditation.

Do your stretching on a padded surface—an exercise mat or a thick carpet. If you have the opportunity to stretch on a picnic blanket on the grass or a towel on the beach, that's an added pleasure.

See page 215 for a stretching sequence which provides overall flexibility.

YOGA

Most stretching exercises are based on yoga movements. The deep breathing used in meditation and relaxation is also called yoga breathing. And the Total Body Relaxation on page 218 is often done in yoga classes.

Yoga is stretching, strengthening, breathing, relaxing, meditating, and much more. It is an ancient art and science with a profound spiritual base. Much of the theory and practice of modern holism is based on ancient yogic teachings.

Yoga, born in India thousands of years ago, is probably the original Self-Health Program. It offers a wealth of wisdom that is as valuable today as it was a millennium ago. Yoga encompasses an incredible variety of practices for development of the mind/body and is practiced all over the world, in a multitude of forms.

The term "yoga" is based on the Sanskrit word which means "union" or "joining." This refers to the joining of the physical, mental, and spiritual components and, on a higher level, the joining of human beings and God.

This section on yoga appears in the "Physical Side of Your Holistic Triangle" chapter because many Westerners focus on the poses and breathing practices of yoga. But yoga could also be included in the mental/spiritual chapter since spirituality is a primary element. Some forms of yoga, in fact, focus entirely on spiritual development, meditation, philosophy, moral living, and helping others.

Yoga also influences the chemical side of the Triangle since it advocates the basic health food principles: vegetarianism; sobriety; avoiding dairy products and caffeine; eating wholesome raw foods.

Hatha yoga is the most familiar form of yoga in the United

States. Ideally, hatha yoga is the path to a greater realization of God through mental and physical control. This is achieved through meditation, breathing exercises, and asanas (also called poses or postures).

The asanas move the body through a full range of motions and affect all the body systems: muscular, nervous, digestive, respiratory, elimination, and endocrine. The physical benefits of yoga, which may have been intuitive to its originators, have now been scientifically proved in many studies.

Yoga is open to all ages and levels of fitness, although the practice of asanas and breathing exercises will vary widely according to abilities. What's wonderful about yoga is that you can start at any time and continue practicing for the rest of your life. Many people, including one of the authors of this book, Anita Bell, find yoga a lifelong source of renewal, strength, comfort, and inspiration.

You can begin to learn about yoga through reading and videotapes at home, but at some point you'll want to seek out a teacher. Yoga is taught everywhere from yoga centers to Y's to health clubs.

Wherever you study, ask about the teacher's accreditation and experience. Look for a teacher who is compassionate, communicative, and inspiring. Some people prefer to learn from yogis and yoginis who live in ashrams and dedicate their lives to yoga. But there are also many excellent teachers who lead secular lives and can relate well to the needs of beginning students. Teachers should be flexible in mind and body, be careful to teach correctly and help students avoid injury, and exhibit love of yoga and love of their students.

DEEP BREATHING

Deep breathing (also called yoga breathing or diaphragmatic breathing) increases oxygen intake, a primary goal on the physical side of the Holistic Triangle. It is also useful as a tool for evoking relaxation, another essential nutrient on the physical side.

Look at a baby breathing, or watch someone in a relaxed state of sleep. His or her abdomen gently expands on the inhalation and contracts on the exhalation. This is deep breathing. It is the most revitalizing form of breathing because it increases blood flow to all the organs and stimulates peristaltic function.

This type of breathing is called diaphragmatic because the lungs rest on the diaphragm, the muscle that separates the chest cavity from the abdomen. To fill the lungs completely, the diaphragm needs to lower so that there will be space for lung expansion. In deep breathing, the abdomen expands with each breath, and the diaphragm lowers and allows the lower lung to fill up with oxygen.

If you are a shallow breather, deep breathing can initially result in hyperventilation, dizziness, anxiety, or nausea. You may have to begin by practicing only four or five deep breaths several times a day for a week or two to become accustomed to this greater oxygen supply.

To experience deep breathing, lie down on your bed or the floor. Put your hands on your abdomen. Remember this maxim: The nose is for breathing; the mouth is for eating.

Exhale completely. Close your mouth, and inhale slowly through your nose, filling your abdomen with breath. You should feel your belly rise under your fingers. Continue to inhale, filling up your rib cage, then your chest. Exhale through your nose as slowly and completely as possible. Practice this several more times.

There is a Sufi saying: "Breathing being the secret of all being, it is the most important of all things." Breath is considered the primary link between mind and body in yoga and other holistic traditions. Modern science confirms this ancient wisdom.

The rhythm of the breath affects the right vagus nerve, which controls the sympathetic nervous system. The sympathetic nervous system regulates the excretion of adrenaline and other hormones. Fear, anger, and sorrow all bring uneven patterns to the breath and arouse the sympathetic nervous system.

The best way to learn the effects of deep breathing is to try it out in different situations. When you are concentrating on complex work, check your breathing. Are you breathing deeply through your nose? It will give you greater concentration and more energy and release useless tension.

The next time you get agitated, notice how you're breathing. Then exhale completely, and begin slowly, very slowly, to fill up your abdomen, your rib cage, and then your chest. You'll find this is an amazing calming agent—nature's tranquilizer. It's nearly impossible to be a nervous wreck when you're doing deep abdominal breathing.

A very simple relaxation exercise utilizes deep breathing: Inhale for a count of eight; hold for a count of four; then exhale for a count of eight. When you are comfortable with this ratio, you can try another pattern: Inhale for eight; hold for four; exhale for twelve counts. You can also create your own rhythm, always exhaling at least as long as you inhale. Counting your breaths clears your mind and is a form of relaxation you can practice anywhere.

THE STRESS REACTION

In reaction to stress the body goes into a reactive state, readying itself for a survival response. This is called the fight or flight response and can include these changes:

- Heartbeat increases.
- Blood pressure goes up.
- Breathing becomes rapid and shallow.
- Blood sugar level rises.
- Senses are heightened.
- Muscles tense for movement or protective actions.
- Blood flow to the digestive organs is constricted.
- Blood flow to the brain and major muscles increases.
- Body perspires to cool itself.

These reactions were mandatory for survival in the days when people needed to fight or flee in response to a threat. They could club a wild boar or run from invading tribes and physically utilize those instinctual responses.

Nowadays, however, most of the threats we face are not of a physical nature, and there is no physical release for our stress response. When your boss is critical, you can't work off the muscle tension by beating him or her over the head with a large stick. When someone cuts in front of you on the freeway, you can't suddenly run through the woods to work off the increased heart rate and muscle tension. Instead the biochemical reaction continues for a prolonged period, resulting in wear and tear on the body's response systems.

Dr. Hans Selye, who was one of the world's leading researchers on the effects of stress, discovered that when the brain perceives stress, it automatically sends a message to the hypothalamus, which then sends impulses to the pituitary gland, which releases hormones to stimulate other glands, such as the adrenals. If this stress response continues, the presence of these stress-response hormones begins to wear down the immunological system, and the body becomes more susceptible to disease.

CONSCIOUS RELAXATION

By consciously evoking relaxation, you can counteract some of the effects of stress. *Conscious* relaxation is different from relaxing by watching TV, reading, or even napping. Conscious relaxation methods include meditation, progressive relaxation, deep breathing, yoga, and biofeedback. They decrease the activity of the sympathetic nervous system and release muscle tension, lower blood pressure, and slow the heart and breathing rates.

Dr. Herbert Benson, a cardiologist who is a leading researcher and writer in the field of psychoneuroimmunology, termed this phenomenon the relaxation response. His best-selling book of this name offers simple ways to elicit this response.

Research has proved that conscious relaxation has many dramatic physiological effects. A study of 150 employees of the New York Telephone Company revealed that those who practiced relaxation had less anxiety, high blood pressure, and insomnia five months after they started. Those who practiced relaxation techniques also had more success in overcoming smoking, drinking alcohol, and overeating habits. Other studies have indicated that relaxation is a major tool in alleviating chronic pain from backache, headache, or such diseases as cancer.

Healing Moments, meditation, and deep breathing are basic relaxation methods you can use. Page 218 offers a Total Body Relaxation sequence, which you can either memorize or read onto a cassette to create your own customized relaxation tape.

BATHING

Water is more than required nourishment on the chemical side of the Triangle; it is also a healing tool on the physical and mental/spiritual sides. Bathing has been used for soothing and healing as well as cleaning the body for thousands of years.

Using hot and cold water in combination can be highly therapeutic. Hot water increases surface circulation, dilates pores, increases elimination through the skin, and helps the muscles to relax. Cold water stimulates the circulation while it contracts the blood vessels and pores of the skin. Bathing is also one of our few opportunities to escape the weight of gravity and the burden it places on our muscles and bones.

On the mental/spiritual side, hydrotherapy gives us a chance to evoke the feeling of being inside the womb. Since we come from water and we're partly composed of water, being in this element relaxes the mind along with the muscles.

See page 219 for a hydrotherapeutic Bathing Ritual that provides spiritual as well as physical nourishment.

SLEEPING

Sufficient sleep is part of your fundamental nourishment on the physical side of your Holistic Triangle. Remember: *Rest* is the greatest *rest*orer of health. No matter how busy you are, try to show your love for yourself by getting enough sleep.

How much sleep is enough is highly personal. Six to eight hours' sleep is the normal range for optimal functioning, but it's variable. Listen to your body, and give it what it needs. However, if you feel you habitually need more than eight hours' sleep a night, this may indicate you need to eat a healthier diet, take more supplements, do more exercise, and/or address feelings of depression.

If you have insomnia, avoid taking sleeping pills, which can be addictive and lead to a host of serious side effects. Instead you can utilize these safe, natural techniques for overcoming sleeplessness:

—Eliminate caffeine, sugar, nicotine, and meat from your diet.
—Eat early, light dinners; then have a small snack two hours before bedtime.
—Get vigorous exercise during the day.
—Get out in the morning daylight (this does not have to be direct sunlight) to adjust your inner clock.
—Go to sleep and get up at approximately the same time every day of the week.
—Do gentle stretches, followed by the Total Body Relaxation sequence, directly before going to bed.
—If your thoughts keep you awake, try a simple meditation by focusing on the word "one" as you exhale. You can also do relaxation practices in bed.
—Reserve your bed for only sleeping (and sex); don't read, eat, or watch TV in bed. Let your mind associate bed with rest.
—Making love and masturbating can help you get to sleep if you are comfortable with your partner and your own sexuality.

How you sleep as well as how much is a consideration on the physical side of the Triangle. Use only one pillow, not too thick, to avoid neck compression. Sleep on your side or on your back, but never on your stomach. Stomach sleeping causes uneven twisting of the cervical vertebrae, which can put the whole spine out of alignment and add pressure to the lower back. When you rise out of bed, turn on your side first and use your hands to push up to a sitting position.

POSTURE

It's ironic that in elementary school, where we're supposed to learn good habits, we learn bad posture. Despite the admonitions of stern teachers to sit up straight, school desks and chairs promote poor postural habits. We learn to slouch in our uncomfortable chairs and look down at our reading and writing. These habits continue into adulthood and are exacerbated by the office environment. The result is frequent lower back pain, neck pain, and headaches.

Lisa, a thirty-two-year-old public relations writer, came to the Holistic Health Force complaining of neck pain and tension headaches. She had a very common distortion pattern: a developing dowager's hump and loss of cervical (neck) curve. Looking at Lisa, you probably wouldn't notice anything was wrong since a slightly forward curve of the neck is such a common trait. But it was enough to cause Lisa neck pain, reduced blood supply to her head, and recurrent headaches.

Lisa was given chiropractic adjustments in our office and muscle work to rehabilitate the supportive elements. However, the principal component of her treatment program was the work she did on her own.

Lisa learned to sleep on her back instead of her stomach and to use a cervical pillow. She started the day with the Bathing Ritual, which was a great relief for her neck. An exercise program of swimming, yoga, and musculoskeletal exercises gave her better alignment, greater strength, and more energy.

At the office Lisa adjusted her computer screen to eye level so she didn't have to look down. She invested in an ergonomic chair and had it delivered to her office. Coffee breaks became stretching breaks. She stopped cramming the phone between her ear and shoulder and held it in her hand, with her head up.

Paying attention to the physical side of her Triangle relieved

THE SKELETAL SYSTEM

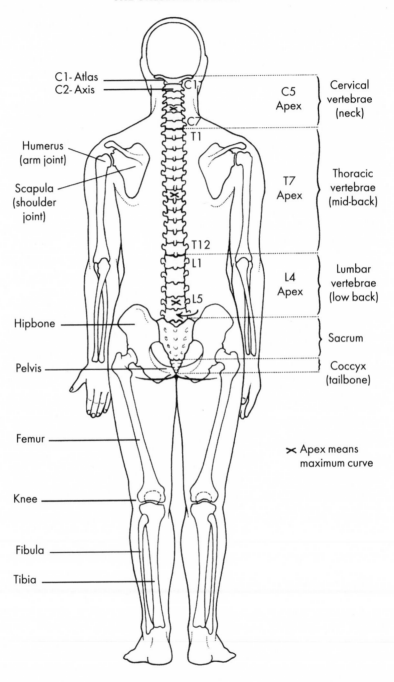

C1- Atlas
C2- Axis

C1

C5
Apex

Cervical
vertebrae
(neck)

C7

T1

Humerus
(arm joint)

Scapula
(shoulder
joint)

T7
Apex

Thoracic
vertebrae
(mid-back)

T12

L1

L4
Apex

Lumbar
vertebrae
(low back)

L5

Hipbone

Sacrum

Pelvis

Coccyx
(tailbone)

Femur

✕ Apex means
maximum curve

Knee

Fibula

Tibia

GOOD POSTURE REFLECTS GOOD HEALTH

Gravitational Forces

Gravitational Forces

UNHEALTHY POSTURE

a. Fatigue and negative thinking

b. Restricted neck, loss of normal curve*

c. Rounded, weak shoulders

d. Rigid low back, flattened curve*

e. Reduced pelvic angle with compressed organs

f. Flat feet and poor ankle alignment

*Results in compressed spinal disks

Note: Poor posture: Center of balance is off

HEALTHY POSTURE

a. Energy and positive thinking

b. Flexible neck with natural curve

c. Strong, erect shoulders, normal curve

d. Flexibility and normal forward curve

e. Normal pelvic angle with relaxed internal organs

f. Good arch (or arch support) and proper ankle alignment

Good posture: Body is balanced and well aligned

Lisa's neck pain and headaches. As a bonus, her improved posture and physical development made her look taller, trimmer, and more attractive.

When working on your posture, remember, a healthy spine is *not* a straight spine. The admonition "Sit up straight" is misleading. The correct goal is to support your spine with strong muscles and to sit or stand with the natural curvature of your spine in place. The illustration on page 93 will give you a visual sense of balanced curvature.

Here are some ways you can nurture your physical side by developing better postural habits:

- Sit tall. Maintain the natural curve in your lower back as you sit; don't slump. Imagine a puppet string pulling you up from the top of your head. Keep your spine long and your gaze ahead, not down.
- Don't cross your legs. Leg crossing causes poor circulation in the legs and vulnerability to varicose veins and phlebitis. It also reverses the normal lumbar lordosis (forward curve) of the lower back and compresses the spinal disks and lower back muscles.
- Work in a healthy chair, even if you need to buy it yourself and have it delivered to your workplace. Get an ergonomically designed desk chair or a kneeling chair that will facilitate good posture.
- Your seat height should allow you to keep your feet flat on the floor and your knees level with or slightly higher than your hips. If you're short, you may need to place something under your feet to achieve this posture. (This rule does not apply to kneeling chairs, which place the knees lower than the hips in a kneeling position.)
- Position your computer screen at eye level. Get a standing clipboard or reading stand so you don't need to peer down at papers. The idea is to look down as little as possible.
- Whenever you read, hold the material up to eye level or use a reading stand; don't look down. If you wear bifocals, hold the reading material slightly below eye level so you can read

through the bottom of your glasses while still maintaining your natural neck curve.

- Holding the telephone between your ear and your shoulder is a recipe for neck pain. Hold the phone with your hand, and keep your head erect. If you often write or type when you're on the phone, purchase a telephone headset to free your hands.
- Stand tall, with your head up, weight balanced on both legs, and spine lengthened. However, you don't want to hyperextend your lower back; maintain the natural curve.
- Look ahead when you walk, not down.
- When carrying heavy packages, hold them close to your body in both arms.
- Squat when you need to lift something; don't bend from the waist.
- If you carry a pocketbook, try to lighten it and take only what's necessary. Wear the strap diagonally across your chest rather than on your shoulder, and alternate sides. Consider using a lightweight backpack instead of a shoulder bag.
- Avoid high heels, which compress the lower back and torture the feet. If you stand tall and exercise frequently, you'll look terrific without heels. Remember, improving your posture results in instant figure enhancement.
- Even with excellent posture, remaining in one position for a long period of time is unnatural and unhealthy. Human beings are meant to be dynamic. Get up, stretch, and walk around the room as often as possible.

SECONDARY FORMS OF PHYSICAL NOURISHMENT

The secondary forms of nourishment on the physical side of the Holistic Triangle are those that are provided by natural health professionals, such as chiropractors, massage therapists, physical therapists, acupuncturists, naturopaths, nutritionists, homeo-pathic doctors, and others.

One of the ways you can show yourself love is to spend the time and money necessary to get appropriate professional care. Visits to holistic practitioners can be costly, but they serve as a form of health insurance. In many cases, reasonable natural health care has helped people avoid devastatingly expensive sur-gery.

David, a commercial artist, came to the Holistic Health Force in a last-ditch effort for a second opinion before undergoing back surgery. He had severe sciatica that was no longer relieved by the painkillers his doctor had prescribed. His doctor recommended disk surgery, but as a freelancer with no health insurance David was worried this would wipe him out financially.

A holistic rehabilitation program consisting of chiropractic care, therapeutic exercise, supplementation, and a change of pos-tural habits afforded David pain relief and corrected the imbal-ance that was causing him pain. He didn't have to submit to surgery, and he stopped taking painkillers. Best of all, he has been able to maintain a healthy back by following his own Holis-tic Self-Health Program rules and visiting the office only three or four times a year.

Mabel, an eighty-two-year-old woman, was depressed when her doctor told her she had to undergo surgery to remove her pain-fully inflamed varicose veins. She was afraid of hospitals and be-lieved surgery would be a strain she might not survive.

A holistic program of therapeutic exercise, physiotherapy to strengthen her calf muscles, and chiropractic treatment, com-bined with weight loss from a customized diet, rendered the sur-gery unnecessary. Mabel also elevated the foot of her bed and started wearing support panty hose to help her condition.

Within two months Mabel was able to resume her part-time cooking job and activities with her church group. Because of her age, she needs biweekly visits to our office to prevent her condi-tion from deteriorating. But this continuing care is certainly less expensive and invasive than surgery.

These case studies from the Holistic Health Force are a micro-cosm of the findings of many research studies. AV Med, the largest health maintenance organization (HMO) in the southwestern United States, sent one hundred of its medically unresponsive patients to a chiropractor. Within three weeks 86 percent of these patients had their ailments corrected, and the twelve who had been previously diagnosed as needing disk surgery had their conditions corrected. This saved AV Med approximately $250,000 in surgery costs.

A study of workers' compensation records of more than three thousand cases in Utah found that chiropractic outperformed medicine by a ten-to-one margin in compensation costs. Overseas a study by the Italian government of seventeen thousand patients showed that chiropractic care reduced hospitalization by 87.6 percent and work loss by 75.5 percent.

According to a Rand Corporation study, one fourth of all days spent in the hospital, one fourth of all procedures, and two fifths of medications are unnecessary. One way you can avoid becoming a statistic is to seek out drug-free, noninvasive health care treatments.

There are many different holistic healing therapies, each with its unique strengths. On page 222 you'll find a brief introduction to some of these alternatives. Please keep in mind that these therapies are multifaceted, and you can find whole books devoted to most of them. You may want to support your physical side with mental nourishment by reading in-depth studies of the modalities that interest you.

PART TWO

THE HOLISTIC SELF-HEALTH PROGRAM

CHAPTER 5

Ready, Set, Go: Starting Your Self-Health Program

The Three-Month Holistic Self-Health Program is a framework for nourishing the mental/spiritual, chemical, and physical sides of your Holistic Triangle. It will help you systematically utilize the techniques introduced in the previous chapters and mobilize your healing force and energy.

For thousands of years people have searched for the Fountain of Youth. If youth can be equated with feeling young, energetic, limber, strong, and full of hope and optimism, then the Holistic Self-Health Program is an attainable fountain. If you stay with the program, by the end of three months you'll find yourself revitalized, looking and feeling fresher. And if you adopt the principles of the program into your permanent lifestyle, it will help you maintain your vigor and health into your later years.

A three-month span is used for the program because this is the amount of time in which many conditions heal. Three months is a typical period for both the innate self-healing mechanisms of the body and professional treatment programs. In my clinical experience, three months is also the average time it takes many patients to make serious changes in their lifestyles and adopt holistic habits. Of course, the period in which people heal and change is as individual as their Holistic Triangles, and many patients respond in less time, while others take longer.

Before you embark on the Self-Health Program, please understand this is a process, not a pass/fail course. The program is a series of steps and goals, a journey toward health. The ultimate goal is to keep loving yourself to wellness by nourishing your Holistic Triangle as much as you can.

The greatest result you can achieve is to keep trying. If your resolve falters, respond with love and forgiveness instead of berating yourself. Pick yourself up and carry on with the program as best you can.

Like any other endeavor that yields a high-quality result, the Self-Health Program is not easy. Accomplishment is directly proportional to the amount of work you put into the program. However, you'll quickly realize this is the type of work that brings deep satisfaction and pleasure.

Think of gardening, which is hard work that millions of people love. Gardeners begin by preparing the soil and planting the seeds. They weed and water the garden, and with nature's help, it blossoms, bringing a great deal of joy to the cultivator. With the Self-Health Program your hard work and nature's assistance will result in the flowering of your body and spirit.

KEEP THE MOMENTUM GOING

Depending on the present state of your Holistic Triangle and your level of discipline and resolve, you may or may not be able to accomplish all the steps of the program in the three-month period. If this happens, it's critical not to get bogged down. Focus on another side of your Triangle until you've gained the strength to deal with the more difficult area.

For example, if you simply can't give up sugar, set that goal aside for a week, and do an activity on the physical side that will give you a sense of accomplishment: Swim ten extra laps or walk that extra mile. When you've achieved a new level on one side of your Triangle, you may find it gives you confidence and determination to get through the "stuck" area.

If you find it too difficult to accomplish the major goals during your first effort, you can start the process again and reembark on the Self-Health Program for a second or third time. During these repeat cycles of the program, goals that may have seemed too difficult the first time should become more manageable. The more obstacles you work through, the more self-empowerment you'll gain. Instead of the downward spiral, you'll be swept up in a current of positive change.

IT'S NEVER TOO LATE TO CHANGE

When I explain the Holistic Self-Health Program to patients, some of them voice this initial response: "But it's too late for me to change now, Doc."

If this is your attitude, you need to realize that you're going to change whether you want to or not. Life is a process of change; it's inevitable. You have a choice: You can take control of your health and change for the better, or you can avoid responsibility and change for the worse.

Douglas, age sixty, was fifty pounds overweight and had high blood pressure. For years his medical doctor and his wife had urged him to diet and exercise, but he preferred to take his hypertensive medication and continue with his unhealthy lifestyle. It wasn't until he started getting severe headaches as a side effect of the medication that he was motivated to change.

Douglas started by eliminating sugar from his diet and was encouraged by the benefits he felt in a few weeks. This provided the positive reinforcement he needed to start exercising and reducing his intake of other toxins.

Years of ingrained habits were difficult to change, however, and by the end of three months Douglas still consumed too much red meat and beer, was erratic in his exercise program, and hadn't managed a juice fast. He had lost fifteen pounds, and his blood pressure was lower, although not normal. But the progress he had made encouraged him to start on another round of his Self-Health Program.

During the next cycle Douglas finally broke his red meat habit and actually started to look forward to his daily health walks. His wife went on a juice fast at the same time he did, and that made it easier for him to get through it.

By the end of the second three months, Douglas had lost an additional twenty pounds and reduced his blood pressure to the point where medication was no longer required. He felt full of vim and vigor, and his family joked that he looked better than his thirty-eight-year-old son. Douglas was living proof that it's never too late to change.

MAKING TIME FOR YOURSELF

Another negative response I often hear from patients about the program is: "I'm too busy; I don't have time." This is certainly a valid concern. Lack of time is a major area of stress in today's world and is connected with the ever-present worry about money. But we need to find balance; we can't always put work ahead of health.

"Health is wealth" is a cliché because it happens to be true. Not only is it difficult to enjoy money if you're unhealthy, but it's also hard to earn it. If you don't take time out for now for self-nourishment, in the future your earning capacity may be disrupted by premature illness that prevents you from working at all.

No matter what your responsibilities, you deserve and require a certain amount of time for yourself. And this time, if it is limited, needs to be spent in the most positive way possible: nourishing your Holistic Triangle. The greatest gift you can give yourself is time.

Li, a forty-five-year-old teacher, came in complaining of neck and shoulder pain. An examination found that she had the beginnings of arthritis and a reversal of the normal neck curve (cervical lordosis). This is a common condition that results from neck stress, looking down, and using too many pillows.

After three weeks of chiropractic adjustments to align the vertebrae, ultrasound to break down scar tissue, and electrical therapy to reduce inflammation, her pain was gone. She then decided she didn't have time to go on the Holistic Self-Health Program; she was too busy with her high school teaching position and additional evening job teaching English as a second language to adults.

A few months later she returned to the office with a recurrence of neck and shoulder pain, this time more severe. Now she was ready to embark on the exercise part of the program, but she still didn't know why she should bother changing her diet if the pain was in her neck.

Then we discussed the results of a Nutriscan test of her blood. (Nutriscan tests are a comprehensive chemical analysis of the blood to determine the level of vitamins and minerals.) This test showed she lacked beta-carotene and other nutrients that were indicated for the prevention of cancer. Since Li had already had a melanoma removed from her back, she was very concerned about cancer, and this news motivated her to work on the chemical side of her Triangle as well as the physical side.

Li realized she needed to drop one of the night classes to make time to exercise regularly, practice relaxation, and prepare fresh meals for herself. Once she began to apply her high level of discipline and determination to loving herself, she made rapid progress in building up her Triangle.

HINTS FOR BUSY PEOPLE

When you first read through the program, it may sound like a lot to do, and you may worry that you won't find the time. Please realize that in most cases it's a matter of replacing present habits with more nourishing activities, and you will not need to "make" a lot of time.

Here are tips on how to manage the program in a "timely" fashion:

Mental/Spiritual Side

- Practice Healing Moments as a quick and effective way to nourish your spiritual side.
- Practice deep breathing in the car, while waiting on lines, and whenever else you can think of it.
- Affirmations can be done during any spare moments. Another idea: Every time you start worrying, try to replace the worrisome thoughts with affirmations.
- Do a relaxation or visualization session instead of watching a half hour sitcom.
- For the three months of the program consider giving up reading your daily newspaper and spend the time reading more uplifting material.
- Replace your daily shower with the Bathing Ritual. Set your alarm clock fifteen minutes earlier so you have time for the Healing Moments and exercises in the bathtub. The sense of well-being will more than compensate for a little less sleep.

Chemical Side

- Raw, natural foods are quicker and easier to prepare than many typical American meals. Instead of spending time on elaborate recipes, stick to simple, nourishing foods that give you strength for the rest of your activities.
- You can prepare raw juices on weekends and freeze them to use during the week. (They are most nourishing when fresh, but if you're extremely pressed for time on workdays, this is an alternative.)
- Set your supplements out in the kitchen, and establish a habit of taking them before meals; this takes very little time.

- Eliminating toxins—one of the most important steps in the program—will give you more energy and time for the rest.

Physical Side

- Exercise with friends, partners, or children so it can be a social as well as physical time.
- Cut down on shopping and watching TV during the three months of the program so you have more time for physically active pursuits.
- If you have a baby, use his or her nap time as your exercise time. Even when you're exhausted, this is likely to give you more energy for the rest of the day.

*A note of caution: It is *recommended that you do not go on the Self-Health Program during pregnancy.*

SHARE THE PROGRAM WITH IMPORTANT PEOPLE IN YOUR LIFE

Being involved in the program will mean certain changes in your eating habits, exercise routine, and other aspects of your lifestyle. It's helpful to explain to your family, partner, close friends, or relatives what you are trying to achieve so they won't stand in the way of your goals.

You may want to show them this book and have them leaf through it. Or you can describe in your own words your desire to enhance your well-being through the program. Present the information in whatever way you think is appropriate, but try not to preach or drown other people in ideas.

Most people are resistant to change, and you may encounter naysaying and skepticism. Even the people who love you dearly and wish you well may disappoint you with their lack of support. Try not to take it too personally. Everyone is at a different stage of mental/spiritual development, and many intelligent and well-meaning people are still not open to new ideas about health. You can inform people, but you can't force anyone to listen, and proselytizing tends to strengthen resistance.

The very best way you can convince other people of the validity of the Self-Health Program is to set an example. Let them see how it benefits you, and it may open their minds. Ultimately, however, you're responsible only for yourself; you cannot create total well-being for anyone else.

THE BUDDY SYSTEM

If your spouse, partner, friend, relative, or colleague is genuinely interested in the Holistic Self-Health Program, you may want to invite her or him to be your "buddy" throughout the process. The buddy system is often used in self-help programs and can be helpful and fun.

Let your potential buddy read this book and decide if he or she would like to go on the program with you. If you use the buddy system, these are some of the ways you can help each other:

—Share books on holistic topics and discuss ideas.
—Go to lectures, seminars, and workshops together to strengthen your mental/spiritual sides.
—Practice meditation and relaxation techniques together, and discuss which practices you find most nourishing.
—Share cookbooks and natural food recipes.
—Prepare and eat healthy meals together.
—Call on each other for verbal support when you are eliminating toxins.
—Go on a raw-juice fast at the same time.
—Embark on an exercise program together.
—Work out together on a regular basis to keep the momentum going.
—Openly discuss procrastination, resistance, and setbacks you encounter during the program.
—Give each other affirmation and recognition of your efforts and progress.

—Celebrate your progress with a special treat, such as a professional massage, a weekend in the country, or a party with lots of delicious natural food.

As delightful as it is to have a buddy during the Self-Health Program, it is not necessary. You can be your own buddy and give yourself encouragement and support through self-nourishing practices. The program is designed to be an independent effort, although you will need an initial checkup from a health care professional before starting.

CHOOSING A NATURAL DOCTOR

Before you begin the Self-Health Program, it is required, as mentioned earlier, that you have a doctor give you an examination to determine that there are no hidden conditions that you need to consider. I recommend a complete physical checkup that includes an assessment of health history, height, weight, blood pressure, a cardiovascular examination (including an EKG if you are over forty-five), a musculoskeletal examination, and a blood work-up.

The comprehensive chemical profile of your blood will test the size, type, and differentiation of red and white blood cells and help identify such underlying conditions as hypoglycemia, anemia, thyroid malfunctions, vascular disease, and deficiencies. These tests should be performed by a qualified doctor who will take the time to communicate with you about the results.

The Three-Month Holistic Self-Health program is primarily a series of self-help activities. However, in addition to the mandatory checkup before starting the program, it is helpful to maintain contact with a health care professional who can provide supervision and encouragement during the process. Before starting the program, you may want to seek out a holistic practitioner from one of the following disciplines:

Natural chiropractic physician (D.C.): This person should be knowledgeable about nutrition and exercise, as well as physiology, and believe in helping patients achieve independent good health.

Natural medical doctor or physician (M.D.): Some medical doctors are now embracing a more holistic approach. If you work with a holistic medical doctor, ascertain that he or she is committed to the natural approach and will not encourage drug therapy or surgical intervention.

Natural Doctor of Osteopathy (D.O.): Osteopathic physicians provide comprehensive medical care, with particular attention to joints, bones, muscles, and nerves. D.O.'s can prescribe drugs or surgery, so if you are working with one, you need to establish clearly if she or he is dedicated to natural healing. Also inquire about the D.O.'s experience with nutritional counseling.

Naturopathic physician: Naturopaths utilize a wide variety of holistic modalities that may complement the Self-Health Program. However, since they are licensed only in seven states at this time, qualified naturopaths can be difficult to locate.

Personal recommendations from friends, family, and colleagues are helpful in finding a new doctor. If you need to start from scratch, you can look for practitioners who advertise in natural health publications in your area, call professional associations, or even check the phone book. When you don't know anyone who has worked with the practitioner before, however, you need to be especially cautious.

Start with a phone call and ask to speak to the professional directly. He or she should be willing to answer basic questions about training, certification, scope of practice, methods of treatment, and use of tests. The doctor should have a friendly, enthusiastic manner and give you a positive first impression. If you have a gut feeling she or he is wrong for you, either on the phone or during the initial consultation, pay attention to your instincts and look for someone else.

During the initial consultation, assess whether the doctor's fees, insurance arrangements, location, and schedule fit your budget and lifestyle. Take note of the practitioner's human skills, her or his attitude toward holism, and his or her willingness to answer questions.

After the first examination, see if the doctor gives you sufficient information about your current state of health and explains recommendations. If treatment is needed, he or she should outline the timetable (although this can never be absolute), the approximate cost, and the pros and cons of different treatments.

Your health care provider should have excellent professional qualifications, but she or he also needs strong interpersonal skills and qualities. The doctor should be a teacher, who will take the time to talk with you about your present state of health, how your body works, and what you can do for yourself. You should feel his or her genuine interest and compassion. A sense of humor and natural warmth is a plus. Your doctor should treat you as an equal and a partner in your health and not have a condescending attitude.

As holistic health gains in popularity, some doctors may call themselves holistic though they are not truly committed to a natural approach. Therefore, it's necessary to determine that your doctor will not rely on drugs, surgery, or quick fixes but will emphasize and explore a variety of natural remedies. The professional should be dedicated to finding and correcting the root cause of problems, not just covering symptoms. To be considered sincerely holistic, he or she should have a deep belief in the integral connection of the mind, spirit, and body and view you as a whole person, not as a series of symptoms.

A holistic doctor should recognize the essential connection between nutrition and good health and have a background in nutrition. She or he should also be acquainted with therapeutic exercise and relaxation techniques.

It's helpful to have your doctor look at this book, and you should then explain that you would like her or his support during the Holistic Self-Health Program. After your initial comprehensive exam, the practitioner should review the program and let you know if your tests indicate any special precautions should be taken.

THE SELF-HEALTH EVALUATIONS

While clinical tests given by a health care professional are useful, they are limited in scope. Clinical tests are aimed at identifying deficiencies, illnesses, and weaknesses rather than strengths. The following Self-Health Evaluations are designed to clarify both your strong points and weaknesses on all three sides of your Holistic Triangle.

Take the tests now, review the results, and then save them. When you take the tests again at the end of the Three-Month Holistic Self-Health Program, you can chart your progress. This is, of course, just reinforcement since your progress will be evident from the way you feel, think, and look.

No test can define a human being, and the following evaluations cannot present a definitive picture of your infinitely complex self. The goal of these tests is to get you thinking about the state of your Holistic Triangle and what you can do to nourish it. The tests are a learning tool, not a judgment. For this reason, the scores are not separated into categories such as "good, mediocre, awful." The numerical scores are intended to help you compare the relative strengths of each side of your Holistic Triangle and to help you see how you are benefiting from the program when you retake the tests after three months.

Answer the questions to the best of your ability; circle your answers; then add up your score. The higher the score, the stronger you are on this particular side of your Triangle. The lower your score, the more attention you need to pay to nourishing this side.

The Mental/Spiritual Side Evaluation

1. Overall, would you say you give yourself enough unconditional love and acceptance?

   1-No   2-Sometimes, but not usually   3-Yes

2. Do you consider yourself a positive thinker?

   1-No   2-Somewhat   3-Yes

3. How do you rate your level of self-esteem?
   1-Low   2-Medium   3-High

4. How often do you feel fearful?
   1-Often   2-Occasionally   3-Rarely or never

5. How often do you feel guilty?
   1-Often   2-Occasionally   3-Rarely or never

6. How often do you feel depressed?
   1-Often   2-Occasionally   3-Rarely or never

7. How often do you feel anxious?
   1-Often   2-Occasionally   3-Rarely

8. Do you wake up looking forward to your day?
   1-Never or rarely   2-Sometimes   3-Most days

9. Do you enjoy your work?
   1-No or very little   2-Somewhat   3-Very much

10. Do you feel satisfied with spouse or partner?
    1-No or don't have one   2-Somewhat   3-Very much

11. Do you feel satisfied with the quality of your friendships?
    1-No   2-Somewhat   3-Very much

12. Do you do volunteer work, or otherwise help people outside your own family?
    1-Never or rarely   2-Occasionally   3-On a regular basis

13. Do you consider yourself a spiritual person?
    1-No   2-Somewhat   3-Yes

14. Do you engage in religious/spiritual practices?
    1-Never or rarely   2-Occasionally   3-Frequently

15. Do you meditate, do affirmations and visualizations, and/or practice relaxation techniques?
    1-Never or rarely   2-Occasionally   3-Frequently

16. Do you read books on spiritual and/or holistic health topics?
    1-Rarely   2-Occasionally   3-Frequently

17. Do you believe in your innate healing force?

    1-No   2-Not sure   3-Yes

18. Do you believe your mental/spiritual state has a profound effect on your health?

    1-No   2-Not sure   3-Yes

19. What is your level of discipline when it comes to making healthy choices?

    1-Low   2-Medium   3-High

20. Do you believe you have the power substantially to improve your mental and physical well-being?

    1-No   2-Not sure   3-Yes

The Chemical Side Evaluation

Note: Since eating habits vary, try to answer the questions according to your general pattern.

1. How often do you consume sugar?

    1-More than twice a week   2-Once or twice a week   3-Rarely or never

2. How often do you eat white flour products and other refined carbohydrates?

    1-More than twice a week   2-Once or twice a week   3-Rarely or never

3. How often do you eat dairy products?

    1-More than twice a week   2-Once or twice a week   3-Rarely or never

4. How often do you eat meat?

    1-More than twice a week   2-Once or twice a week   3-Rarely or never

5. How often do you consume foods with additives (or added salt)?

    1-More than twice a week   2-Once or twice a week   3-Rarely or never

6. How often do you smoke?

   1-Daily or often   2-Rarely   3-Never

7. How often do you consume caffeine?

   1-Daily or often   2-Rarely   3-Never

8. How many glasses of alcohol, wine, or beer do you have per week?

   1-More than seven   2-Three to five   3-Two or less

9. How often do you take drugs, including recreational drugs, prescriptions, and over-the-counter medications?

   1-One to seven times per week   2-Once a month to several times a year   3-Rarely or never

10. How would you rate your exposure to environmental toxins?

    1-High   2-Average   3-Low

11. How often do you eat vegetables and salads?

    1-A few times a week or less   2-Three to six times a week   3-Every day

12. How often do you eat fruits or drink raw-fruit juices?

    1-A few times a week or less   2-Three to six times a week   3-Every day

13. How often do you eat legumes, nuts, and seeds?

    1-A few times a week or less   2-Three to five times a week   3-Six or more times a week

14. How often do you eat whole grains?

    1-A few times a week or less   2-Three to six times a week   3-Six or more times a week

16. How frequently do you go on a raw-juice fast?

    1-Never   2-Once or twice a year   3-More than twice a year

17. How many glasses of pure water do you drink each day?

    1-Zero to three glasses   2-Four to five glasses   3-More than five glasses

18. Do you have regular bowel movements without straining?
    1-Rarely or never   2-Sometimes   3-Usually

19. Do you eat six small meals, with the largest portion at lunch-time?
    1-Rarely or never   2-Sometimes   3-Usually

20. Do you take vitamin and mineral supplements?
    1-Rarely or never   2-Sometimes   3-Habitually

The Physical Side Evaluation

1. How often do you do aerobic (cardiovascular) exercise?
   1-Less than once a week   2-Once or twice a week   3-Three or more times a week

2. What is the average duration of your aerobic workout?
   1-Less than fifteen minutes   2-Fifteen to thirty minutes   3-Over thirty minutes

3. How long can you do aerobic activity without becoming short of breath?
   1-Don't know, or less than fifteen minutes   2-Fifteen to thirty minutes   3-Over thirty minutes

4. How often do you do musculoskeletal exercise?
   1-Less than once a week   2-Once or twice a week   3-Three or more times a week

5. How many sit-ups (as described in Chapter 5) can you do without feeling neck strain?
   1-Less than five   2-Five to twenty   3-Over twenty

6. How many push-ups can you do while maintaining form? (Women can test with modified push-ups.)
   1-Less than five   2-Five to twenty   3-Over twenty

7. How often do you do limbering and stretching exercises or yoga?
   1-Less than once a week   2-One to four times week   3-More than four times a week

8. Can you touch your toes, keeping your legs straight?
   1-No   2-Yes, with effort   3-Can place palms on floor

9. Can you reach your arms over your shoulders and touch your back between your shoulder blades?
   1-No   2-Yes, with effort   3-Easily

10. According to the criteria on page 75, what is your level of fitness?
    1-Level 3 or 4   2-Level 2   3-Level 1

11. How close is your current weight to your ideal weight?
    1-Want to lose over twenty pounds   2-Want to lose three to twenty pounds   3-Close to or at ideal weight

12. How would you rate your level of energy?
    1-Low   2-Medium   3-High

13. How often do you practice deep breathing?
    1-Rarely or never   2-Occasionally   3-Often

14. How often do you practice a technique to evoke conscious relaxation?
    1-Rarely or never   2-Occasionally   3-Often

15. How often do you do the Bathing Ritual?
    1-Rarely or never   2-Occasionally   3-Often

16. In what position do you usually sleep?
    1-On stomach   2-Various positions with two pillows   3-On back or side with one pillow

17. How would you rate your sleep generally?
    1-Poor, not enough, and/or insomnia   2-Adequate, sometimes not enough, or insomnia   3-Good

18. How is your posture while you are working?
    1-Poor   2-Fair   3-Good

19. Do you sit with your legs crossed?
    1-Often   2-Occasionally   3-Rarely or never

20. How often do you see a holistic health practitioner?

1-Rarely or never   2-Occasionally, usually when in pain
3-On a regular basis

Your Family Health History

In a notebook or journal, write down the names of your maternal and paternal grandparents, parents, brothers, and sisters. Next to each name, write down any major illnesses the relative had and the cause of death if he or she is deceased.

The purpose of this evaluation is to see what diseases "run in the family." Then you can take extra preventive measures to reduce your chances of developing these illnesses.

Family history does not have to be destiny; it can be a useful tool in loving yourself to health. Although genetics create a predisposition, you can build up immunity by nourishing your Triangle and, in many cases, avoid the illnesses of your ancestors. Continue to note down your own health history.

Your Health History

1. List any diseases you've had in the past.
2. List any injuries and operations you've had.
3. List any episodes of chronic pain or complaints.
4. List all the messages your body has given you recently. Messages can be in the form of pain, discomfort, conditions, diseases, allergies, breathing problems, digestive disorders, and weaknesses. (The term "messages" is used instead of "symptoms" to remind you to pay attention to what they have to say.)

   Next to each message, make a note of the frequency of occurrence and degree of severity.

Message   *Frequency*   *Severity*

Take some time to study the messages your body has given you in the past and the present. It is likely that if you follow through with the Holistic Self-Health Program, in three months you will see a significant change.

SET YOUR STARTING DATE

The final step in preparing for the program is to pick a date to begin it. Try to choose a period when you will not be under any extraordinary demands at work or at home. However, don't wait until a time when you have no stress at all, or you may never get to the program. Remember, you can fit the program into your life by replacing many present activities and habits with more beneficial ones.

Once this date is set, it should be a firm commitment and a top priority. Don't procrastinate or invent rationalizations as to why you should postpone beginning the program. The sooner you start, the sooner you can begin your progress toward total well-being.

CHECKLIST FOR STARTING YOUR HOLISTIC SELF-HEALTH PROGRAM

❑ Make a commitment to create positive change and spend time on more nourishing activities.

❑ Explain to your family and close friends that you will be on a special program. Enlist a buddy for support if you wish.

❑ Select a holistic doctor who communicates well and treats you as a partner.

❑ Have a comprehensive professional examination to determine if you have any underlying conditions. Discuss adapting the steps of the Self-Health Program with your doctor, if indicated by your condition.

❑ Take the Self-Health Evaluations, and record your health history. Review your familial and personal health histories.

❑ Set a firm date to start the program. Once you establish the date, don't let any excuses postpone your progress.

CHAPTER 6

The Momentum Month: Month One of the Holistic Self-Health Program

The first month is the time to establish your commitment to the program. You need to begin gently and slowly, but with strong and steady resolve. Consistency and determination are keys to building self-health and achieving the goals of the program. Keep your eyes on the prize: a renewed sense of energy, purpose, and well-being that awaits you.

During each biweekly period you'll be starting new activities but also continuing with those you've already initiated. Once these healthful patterns are incorporated into your life, it's important to continue them for the duration of the program (and, we hope, much longer). First you put down the foundation; then you build on your progress.

When you're ready to start the program, read through this chapter once for an overall picture of the first month. Then review the steps, and plan how you will accomplish them.

Congratulations on starting your new life!

WEEKS ONE AND TWO

Evaluate Your Triangle and Decide Where to Focus

All of us need to nourish all three sides of our Holistic Triangles constantly in order to achieve balance and total well-being. But during the program we should also be aware of what needs extra attention.

During the first few days set aside some time to look at the results of your Self-Health Evaluations. This will give you an indication of which sides are strong and which need more work.

You can also evaluate your Triangle by reviewing the health problems you've had in the past and any messages your body is giving you now. All the sides are connected and affect the way we feel, but certain maladies indicate weaknesses on certain sides of the Triangle:

- Weakness on the physical side may be indicated by frequent injuries, aches and pains, bodily tension, low energy level, and feeling out of shape.
- Diseases, gastrointestinal distress, fluctuating levels of energy, and headaches are signals of weakness on the chemical side.
- Anxiety, confusion, poor concentration, lack of faith, low self-esteem, and depression indicate lack of nourishment on the mental/spiritual side but often also have a strong chemical component.

If the majority of your problems are on one or another of these sides, this signals where to give extra nourishment. Restoring optimum nourishment will help your body heal itself.

You can also contemplate which sides of your Triangle are already powerful and receiving plenty of nourishment. If you're very strong on one side, focus attention on nourishing the less developed areas of your Triangle.

This doesn't mean you'll neglect a side if it is already strong; it means the program will take you even further. If you're in good shape now, you can get closer to your physical peak. If you're a healthy eater, you can go on an extended juice fast (see page 188). Whatever side is strong can be taken to a higher level, and whatever side is undernourished can be given special attention.

The tendency is to do more work on the side that is already powerful and to resist confronting the weak areas. You'll need to make a plan to avoid this common pitfall, and remember: Where there is resistance there is tremendous potential.

At this point you should establish a Self-Health Notebook to chart your progress during the program. You can put your Self-Health Evaluation questionnaires inside this notebook, and use it to plan and record your Self-Health activities.

List "Mental/Spiritual Side," "Chemical Side," and "Physical Side" on each page. Referring to the results of your Self-Health Evaluations, and your own thoughts, write an assessment of each side of your Triangle. Include a determination assessment of which sides you think are stronger and weaker and need special care. This written evaluation allows you to be your own doctor, recording your condition on your own health chart.

Create a Weekly Nourishment Plan

A Weekly Nourishment Plan is a written plan on which you list all the ways you will nourish each side of your Triangle that week. Here is an example of a plan:

Weekly Nourishment Plan

Mental/spiritual side:

Do Bathing Ritual, including Healing Moment, every day.
Practice deep breathing in spare moments.
Go to bookstore, and buy books on visualization and massage.
Try healing visualization for that annoying lower back pain.

Chemical side:

Have soy milk and whole grain cereal instead of my usual breakfast.

Bring a banana or plum to work for morning munchies.

Make chili with beans instead of meat for dinner.

Cut out the afternoon cup of coffee. Later in week, put half the usual amount in filter for morning cup.

Get the cookies out of the house so I won't be tempted.

Keep up my Daily Diet Report (see page 134).

Physical side:

Try to stop crossing my legs.

Stretch when I get home from work.

Go for a brisk twenty-minute walk at least three times a week.

Look into joining the Y for swimming.

At the end of the week review your Weekly Nourishment Plan, and check off how many of your planned activities you accomplished. Then create a plan for the following week.

It's also helpful to record your activities on the Physical and and Mental/Spiritual Nourishment forms on page 133. You can make copies of these forms, three-hole-punch the pages, and include them in your Self-Health Notebook. This offers a quick and efficient way to chart your progress.

These written exercises are very helpful for most people; they provide a structure that makes the Self-Health Program more manageable. However, if you hate making lists or keeping records, don't let this aspect of the program stop you from progressing. You can plan your activities and keep a list in your head, if necessary. Don't let technicalities slow you down; be creative and adapt the program to suit your personality.

Luxuriate in the Bathing Ritual

The Bathing Ritual is the ideal preparation for the other activities of the program. Try to do it as many days of the week as you can.

Please review the Bathing Ritual instructions on page 219.

While you are in the bath, picture the current state of your Holistic Triangle, and visualize exactly what you'll do to nurture each side today. Ask yourself these questions:

Am I going to let my environment and work control me, or am I going to control my environment and take steps to nourish myself?

How am I going to nourish the mental/spiritual side of my Triangle today? The chemical side? The physical side?

What obstacles and difficulties might I encounter when working on my program? How will I overcome them and continue to make progress?

Nourish Your Mental/Spiritual Side

To build your commitment to the program and your faith in the innate healing force, you need to have a thorough knowledge of the truth about health. Continue to educate yourself and nourish your mental side throughout the three months of the program.

The books you choose may be about spiritual topics, religion, affirmations and visualizations, self-healing, yoga, meditation, relaxation, nutrition, vegetarianism, vitamins, herbology, raw juicing, fasting, the history of health care, alternative health care modalities, massage, exercise, or any other topic that builds your mental/spiritual side. Suggestions are on pages 229–232.

It's also vital to nurture your spirituality during the program. Take some time to review the methods of developing faith and nourishing your spiritual side in Chapter 2. Then decide which practices you will include in your program. Try to spend some time on your spiritual self, at least a few Healing Moments, every day during the program.

Practice Positive Thinking

The number one goal during the first month of the program is to build your foundation of self-love, self-esteem, and faith in your innate healing force. Throughout the month, try continually to affirm in your thoughts and actions that you deserve unconditional love. Promise to show your self-love by nourishing your Triangle and staying with the Self-Health Program.

You can use affirmations and visualizations to confirm your commitment to the program, enhance your self-esteem and self-love, and work toward healing specific problems. These techniques can help positive thinking become a natural reflex. See details on page 44.

Start Your Daily Diet Report

The purpose of the Daily Diet Report is to give you a clear picture of your toxic input and your healthy input. Even if you choose not to do the other written exercises, try to do this report. If you resist writing down the truth about what you consume, it probably means there's something you don't want to see.

The Daily Diet Report should include everything you eat and drink and the number of servings. Use the form on page 134 or create your own. Fill in the report at the end of each day or the following morning. Don't let it go longer than the next morning, or you may forget what you had.

At the end of the week make a list of all the toxins you consumed, referring to the list of the Top Ten Toxins in Chapter 3. It will give you guidance when you start to reduce your intake of toxins.

Increase Healthy Intake

It's vital that you consume plenty of healthy food and drink to supply fuel for the activities of the Self-Health Program and reduce the craving for toxins. During the first month increase your consumption of raw fruits and vegetables, whole grains, and nonmeat protein, such as legumes, nuts, and seeds. Reviewing the suggestions in Chapter 3 can give you some ideas on wholesome nourishment. Vegetarian cookbooks are also full of ideas.

Try to follow the pattern of eating six small meals a day rather than three large ones. Lunch should be the largest meal, while dinner is light.

Start a new habit of keeping a glass of pure water at your side throughout the day. Try to drink at least six glasses a day of water during the first month of the program. You may find it helpful to carry a plastic pint or quart bottle of water with you.

It's also recommended you take high-quality multivitamin/ mineral supplements made from natural food sources throughout the program. These will address any deficiencies you may have and fortify your chemical side.

Do Aerobic Exercise Three Times a Week

Start your aerobic exercise program gently with an activity you know you can do and you think you'll enjoy. Don't be intimidated by the term "aerobics," which can bring to mind impossibly fit people jumping up and down for an hour. Remember, walking and swimming are also highly beneficial aerobic activities.

Even if you've been neglecting your physical side for years, you can make a determination to walk three times a week. If walking is not enough of a challenge, choose a more dynamic aerobic activity. Refer to the Aerobic Choices for Fitness Levels 1–4 on pages 75–76 for guidance.

Chapter 4 can also give you an idea of the pros and cons of different exercises. You may want to try a variety of forms and then stick with what you like best, or you may choose to do several different aerobic workouts each week. You can swim one day, walk one day, and dance one day—whatever gets you going and keeps you moving.

Exercise researchers have found twenty minutes to be the minimal amount of time to gain the full benefits of aerobic activity. If your physical side is weak, you may need to work up to this time by doing ten minutes twice a day, with rest periods in between, for the first week or two. Then try to do fifteen minutes straight the next week. The goal by the end of the first month of the program is twenty minutes of aerobic exercise at least three times a week.

Before starting any aerobic exercise, review the danger signs on page 76. If you experience any of these problems, consult your health professional. Whenever you work out, be highly aware of your breathing. If you become out of breath or have difficulty speaking while you are exercising, slow down. A comfortable respiratory rate should be maintained, with your inhalations and exhalations in sync with the exercise. Monitor your pulse according to the formula on page 210.

Keep in mind that the law of inertia may make it difficult to get started, but once you get moving, aerobic exercise is *fun*. Your endorphins will be stimulated, and you'll feel a natural "high." You'll gain confidence, feel more energetic, and have a stronger heart as a result of your workouts.

Begin Musculoskeletal Exercises

Another goal on the physical side is to begin the practice of muscular development exercises three times each week, alternating with aerobic exercise. If you have been neglecting your physical side, the musculoskeletal workout can be gentle and modified. Consistency is the primary concern; in later months of the program you can build up duration and intensity.

The musculoskeletal exercise sequence on page 211 provides a basic workout. Depending on your condition, you may need to start with only the leg raises the first week, add the sit-up sequence the second week, and then include the push-ups and jumping jacks.

For every action there is a reaction, and once you start exercising, weaknesses and problems you did not realize were present may surface. Pay attention to the messages your body sends you. Don't give up, but modify your exercise program until you've built up your physical side. Consult with a professional if you experience anything worse than minor body aches.

Challenge your body, but respect it. Don't push too hard or you may have a backlash in the form of injury or giving up on the program. You need to find your own delicate balance between being lazy and pressing yourself too hard.

You can keep a detailed record of your exercise activities on the Physical Nourishment form. This will help you see how your endurance builds during the program and will give you positive reinforcement.

Include Stretching and Deep Breathing in Your Daily Routine

The stretching exercises in the bathtub will get you started on your flexibility program, but you should also do stretches before and after your aerobic and musculoskeletal sessions. If you limber up conscientiously, you'll be less vulnerable to injury and pain.

It's suggested you do a complete stretching session, as outlined on page 215, or practice yoga once or twice a week. You may want to do this on your own or join a class.

The stretching session is an excellent time to practice deep breathing and increase your oxygen intake. You can also practice deep breathing while you're driving, waiting, or taking a "breather" at work. Stretching is one of the perks of the Self-Health Program, and you should enjoy it whenever possible.

Rest and Relaxation

One of the ways to show self-love is to give yourself enough time to sleep. Throughout the program you'll probably need seven to eight hours of solid sleep each night. Try not to over-sleep, for this can make you lethargic and interfere with your progress.

Since so much of your life is spent sleeping, it pays to invest in a good, quality firm mattress to give your body the support it needs. If you're a stomach sleeper, begin training yourself to sleep on your side or your back to reduce strain on your lower back, spine, and neck. If you sleep with two pillows, try sleeping with one to reduce stress on your cervical vertebrae.

Since you'll be challenging the physical side of your body during the program, it's beneficial to practice Total Body Relaxation at least twice a week. This will enhance your body awareness and reduce aches and pains from exercise.

One day a week can be your vacation from all exercise except stretching. On this day of rest you might treat yourself to extra physical nourishment, such as a sauna or Jacuzzi, a self-massage or a professional massage, or a longer session in the bathtub.

THE THIRD AND FOURTH WEEKS

Reminder: During these weeks, in addition to the new activities detailed below, continue with all the healthy actions of the first two weeks:

- Weekly Nourishment Plans
- Mental/spiritual nourishment through reading and spiritual practices
- Bathing Ritual
- Daily Diet Reports
- Increase in natural food and water intake
- Aerobic exercise, musculoskeletal exercise, and stretching on a regular basis
- Rest and relaxation

Keep the momentum going!

Reduce Toxic Intake

The third week of the program is the time to start reducing the amount of toxins you consume. Refer to your list of toxins from your Daily Diet Report. Write down in your Weekly Nourishment Plan what toxins you plan to reduce or eliminate each day.

You are not expected to eliminate completely all toxins during the first month of the program; the major focus is on building up your mental/spiritual side so you have the commitment and knowledge to detoxify in the second month. But you should aim to *reduce* toxic input during the first month. The degree of reduction will depend on the current state of your chemical side. A reduction of 50 percent is a general goal, but if you find yourself doing better, more power to your Triangle!

When you begin reducing your intake of "everyday" toxins, such as sugar, white bread, dairy products, or meat, expect to encounter a lot of resistance within yourself. It helps to read more about these particular toxins so as to reinforce the reasons why you need to eliminate them. Also keep in mind that your tastes will evolve, and by the end of the second month you'll find yourself less attracted to toxins you now crave. You can educate the chemical side of your Triangle as well as the mental side.

Seek Support to Overcome Addictions, If Necessary

If you are addicted to nicotine, alcohol, or drugs, it's crucial to seek out support for the withdrawal process.

If you have a drug or alcohol addiction, you can find out about local meetings of Alcoholics Anonymous and other twelve-step groups, or look into professional treatment programs. A trusted holistic health care professional can also be a resource for the rehabilitation process. If you have a nicotine addiction, consider joining one of the quit-smoking groups that are run by many state lung associations. Look into hypnotherapy or acupuncture for additional support.

Learn what meetings, programs, and professional help are available in your area, and the schedules, locations, and costs. Try to visit the group or meet with the health practitioner to determine if this is the right source of support for you.

By the end of the first month of the program set a firm date to go to the meeting, enter the program, or consult the health professional within the next ten days. Make a vow to do whatever is necessary to overcome your addiction, and strengthen your resolve with prayer, Healing Moments, and affirmations.

Become Aware of Your Posture

During the first month set aside time to become aware of your posture when sitting and standing. Study yourself in a mirror, or have a friend take a few front and side photographs to get a clear view of your standing posture. See if your neck is craning forward, if you are slumping, if you are hyperextended or swaying to one side. Then you can make a mental note to work on pulling up and aligning yourself.

When sitting, notice if you habitually cross your legs. If you do, you may need to put up written reminders near your chairs for the first month to undo the leg-crossing habit.

See if your chairs allow you to keep your feet flat on the floor and your knees level to or slightly higher than your hips. Are you sitting up tall or rounding your lower back? Determine if you need to get an ergonomically designed chair for your workplace or better chairs for home.

Good posture takes muscular strength as well as awareness, and it may be some time before you can maintain it throughout the day. But during the first month you can start being conscious of your posture and making the effort to improve it. Soon you'll have more strength to maintain good posture, and doing so will give you more energy and power.

CHECKLIST FOR THE MOMENTUM MONTH

❑ Evaluate your Holistic Triangle and start your Self-Health Notebook.

❑ Write out your Daily Nourishment Plan each week.

❑ Start your day the holistic way with the Bathing Ritual.

❑ Nourish your mental/spiritual side with reading, spiritual practices, affirmations, and visualizations.

❑ Keep a Daily Diet Report, and list all toxins.

❑ Eat more fruits, vegetables, grains, and nonmeat protein. Drink at least six glasses of water a day.

❑ Take high-quality multivitamin/mineral supplements.

❑ Sleep seven to eight hours a day.

❑ Do the Total Body Relaxation and breathing exercises frequently.

❑ Stretch every day.

❑ Do aerobic exercise three times a week, gradually building up duration and intensity.

❑ Do musculoskeletal exercise three times a week, gradually building up repetitions.

❑ Start to reduce your intake of toxins.

❑ Plan to join a support group or seek professional help to overcome addictions, if necessary.

❑ Become aware of your posture and work to improve it.

❑ Think about how much you've done at the end of the month, and give yourself a heartfelt pat on the back!

Physical Nourishment Report

Physical Side

Date: From _____ To _____

	1st Day	2nd Day	3rd Day	4th Day	5th Day	6th Day	7th Day
Cardiovascular (Aerobic)							
Time							
Musculoskeletal							
Time							
Stretching/ Limbering							
Time							
Rest (Sleep)							
Time							

Approximate time per seven days

Mental/Spiritual Nourishment

Mental/Spiritual Foundation Side

Daily Diet Report

Date: From _____ To _____

Chemical Side

Meals	1st Day	2nd Day	3rd Day	4th Day	5th Day	6th Day	7th Day
Breakfast							
Time							
Snack							
Time							
Lunch							
Time							
Snack							
Time							
Dinner							
Time							
Snack							
Time							

CHAPTER 7

The Cleansing Month: Month Two of the Holistic Self-Health Program

The primary goal of the second month is to detoxify your entire system by eliminating toxins and through raw-juice fasting. You'll also continue to build your physical side with a balanced exercise program and get plenty of mental/spiritual nourishment.

This is a cleansing month, when you'll get rid of chemical toxins *and* negative thoughts and habits. If you are overweight, it's likely that you'll lose fat and gain muscle. You'll emerge feeling leaner and cleaner, both mentally and physically.

The second month of the program requires sharp focus and organization. Your Weekly Nourishment Plan should include a specific timetable for giving up each toxin. Even if you decided not to write the plan during the first month, it's recommended you write down a timetable for giving up each toxin. Otherwise you may fall into the "I'll start tomorrow" trap. Put your detoxification schedule in writing, and sign it, as a contract with yourself.

For some people with some toxins, it's easier to go cold turkey, while for others, a gradual withdrawal is more feasible. You don't want to make it too gradual, however. *Aim to eliminate all toxins by the end of the second week of this month.*

If you don't succeed with this schedule, you can still continue with the program and make progress. But if you set your mind on this goal, you may surprise yourself with your success. You can do it!

You also need to plan ahead for two major events during this month: a one-day juice fast, preferably at the beginning of the third week, and a three-day juice fast at the end of the month. Try to schedule these fasts on weekends or at times when you won't be under particular stress at work. Circle your fast dates in red on your calendar, and promise yourself you'll stick to your plan.

If you do not already own a raw juicer, you'll need to purchase one for the Cleansing Month. This is an essential health appliance that will allow you to enjoy the benefits of raw juices throughout the month as well as during fast days.

WEEKS FIVE AND SIX

During the first month it was recommended you seek appropriate support if you needed to overcome an addiction to alcohol, drugs, or nicotine. The first week of the second month is the time to start going to meetings, support groups, treatment programs, or the health practitioner who will help you through withdrawal.

Even if the toxins you need to eliminate are socially sanctioned substances, such as caffeine, sugar, dairy products, or meat, it's helpful to have support. If possible, enlist the assistance of your spouse or a trusted friend or relative. Be sure to pick a person who believes in detoxification and understands the dangers of the Top Ten Toxins. If there's no one in your personal life who understands, you can ask your holistic health care provider to be your support person.

Often it's easier to lie to ourselves than to people we respect. Having someone who cares check on the progress of your program can be a motivation for good behavior. Tell your support person exactly what toxin you plan to eliminate and when. Ask her or him to inquire how you're doing with your plan every few days and to encourage you to stick with the detoxification program. Ultimately it's up to you, but a caring support person can help you stay the course when the going gets rough.

Review Healthy Alternatives to the Top Ten Toxins

As you eliminate toxins, you can replace many of them with nourishing substitutes. After a transition period, you'll probably find these replacements much more appetizing than the toxins. Here is a refresher on Healthy Alternatives.

1. Toxin: Sugar and Sugar Products

   Alternatives

   Small amounts of raw, unfiltered honey, maple syrup, barley malt syrup, rice syrup, and diluted fruit juice

   Six small meals a day, with a variety of wholesome foods, to maintain blood sugar level and reduce craving

Note: During sugar withdrawal, limit consumption of fruit juices, and avoid white flour products and white potatoes.

2. Toxin: White Flour and Refined Carbohydrates

   Alternatives

   Foods made with whole wheat flour, buckwheat flour, rice flour, rye flour, and cornmeal

   Pastas, breads, and cereals made from whole grains (be sure they do not contain sugar)

   Brown rice and wild rice

   Couscous, millet, bulgur wheat, buckwheat, quinoa, amaranth, and other whole grains

3. Toxin: Dairy Products

   Alternatives

   Soy beverage, almond beverage, and rice beverage

Almond butter, filbert butter, cashew butter, pecan butter, and apple butter

Cheeses, yogurt, and mayonnaise made from soy

For calcium: greens, beans, and seeds

4. Toxin: Meat

Alternatives

Legumes (beans, peas and lentils)

Tofu and other soybean products

Nuts in moderation

High- to medium-protein plant foods

Limited amounts of fish, organic poultry, and eggs (no more than one serving per day)

5. Toxin: Food Additives (Including Salt)

Alternatives

Fresh food with its natural flavor

Prepared food bought only in health food stores with labels checked carefully to see there are no additives

Foods seasoned with a variety of herb and spices instead of added salt

6. Toxin: Caffeine

Alternatives

Small, frequent, nourishing meals to keep up energy levels

Oxygen boosters—exercise and deep breathing—to increase energy

Fruit juices (diluted), herbal teas, and beverages made from roasted grains and seeds

7. Toxin: Nicotine

Alternatives

Quitting smoking with support of groups, clinics, acupuncture, and raw-juice fasting

Increased oxygen intake with deep breathing and exercise

8. Toxin: Alcohol

Alternatives

Sobriety with support of Alcoholics Anonymous, treatment programs, and holistic health care

Development of spirituality; practice of meditation and relaxation techniques

Wholesome foods and increased vitamin/mineral supplementation for nutritional support

Diluted fruit juices with carbonated water, fruit punches, and sparkling cider

9. Toxin: Drugs

Alternatives

Maintenance of health by nourishing Holistic Triangle

Meditation and spiritual practices

Exercise for release of endorphins

Prevention of need for prescription drugs through proper diet, exercise, and positive thinking

Natural health care, such as chiropractic, nutritional counseling, acupuncture, and massage

Limited use of healing herbs and homeopathic remedies

10. Toxin: Environmental Toxins

Alternatives

Organic fruits and vegetables

Natural, chemical-free personal products

Chemical-free cleaning products

Checking for toxins in home, such as radon and lead paint, with removal if necessary

Assessment of health hazards in workplace, and steps taken to correct problems

Review the list of toxins you made during the first month of the program. Be sure to add any you missed, such as environmental poisons, prescription drugs, cigarettes, and other nonfood toxins. This is your hit list: the enemies standing between you and well-being. It may sound melodramatic to call a piece of apple pie or a beer an "enemy." But during the program you need to view even sociably acceptable toxins as enemies of your health.

After the program, if you choose to indulge in toxins occasionally, that's up to you. It won't do you any good, but it probably won't do you much harm. But for these three months you're committed to completely detoxifying and filling yourself with love and healthy input. *If you want to maximize results and awake your full healing force, you need to give your body a complete cleansing.*

Take a blank page in your Self-Health Notebook and draw a line down the center. On one side write "Toxin," and on the other side, "Healthy Alternatives." Write down all your toxins on one side of the page and the healthier options on the opposite side. In addition to the choices listed here, be inventive and write down your own ideas.

As you give up each toxin, cross it off in your notebook. The other side of the page will remind you to reward yourself with healthy nourishment.

HALT Your Toxic Habits

In addiction therapy there is an acronym: HALT. Four triggers for substance abuse are: **H**unger **A**nger **L**oneliness **T**iredness. These triggers represent lack of nourishment on the different sides of the Triangle: hunger—chemical side; anger and loneliness—mental/spiritual side; tiredness—physical side. Boredom and tension are two other triggers of which you should be aware.

When you have the desire to indulge in a toxin, reflect on whether you are experiencing one of these feelings. Then, before you reflexively give in to the urge, think of how you can overcome your discomfort in a healthy, loving way. Here are some ideas:

Hunger

Eat small portions of healthy foods six times a day. Concentrate on your meals while you are eating. Chew slowly and thoroughly to make the food last. Drink eight glasses of water between meals.

Anger

Anger usually comes from fear. Work on your mental/spiritual foundation to reduce fear and learn to be more forgiving. Remember we're all imperfect, yet we're all deserving of unconditional love. For immediate alleviation of fear and anger, try deep breathing. Above all, don't consume a toxin that will make you angry at yourself. Do something truly nourishing that will help you be strong enough to rise above anger.

Loneliness

The more you love yourself, the greater opportunity you have to attract loving people into your life. However, loneliness is a complex problem with societal as well as personal factors, and there may be times when you lack fulfilling companionship. Try to develop healthy coping mechanisms for loneliness instead of seeking comfort in toxins. For example, join a spiritual or religious group where you may find kindred spirits, go to an exercise class where you may make friends, or do volunteer work with people who need your help.

Tiredness

People often turn to toxins to give them temporary lifts and then are left lower than before when their blood sugar levels crash. A diet of six nutritious minimeals a day can lift you out of this cycle and help you avoid using toxins to overcome fatigue. Deep breathing, yoga, and exercise can also boost your energy level naturally.

Boredom

During the program it's unlikely you'll have time to be bored since you'll be busy with activities that stimulate your mind and body. These nourishing activities can become lifelong habits to keep you from becoming bored and turning to toxins to fill your leisure hours.

If you often get bored at your job, try to become more engaged in your work and create new challenges. If your job does not have any room for growth, change, or intellectual stimulation, you may need a career change. The month after you finish the program, when you'll be in peak mental and physical condition, may be a smart time to make a move.

Tension

Keep in mind that the very toxin you are reaching for to relieve tension may have a rebound effect and actually increase anxiety. Try to react with a healthy coping mechanism instead of a toxic crutch.

The more you love yourself and nourish your mental/spiritual side, the less power tension and anxiety will have over your life. However, you also need balanced nourishment on the physical side to relieve tension. Exercise is a potent tension reliever, and deep breathing is also effective.

Whenever you reach for a toxin, HALT! Reflect on whether you are hungry, angry, lonely, tired, bored, or tense. Think of a way you can alleviate your condition in a healthy, self-loving way. Then do it. Gradually, healthy actions will become habitual, and you won't need toxins as coping mechanisms.

Drink Raw Juices Throughout the Month

If you do not already own a juicer, purchase one at the beginning of the second month of the program. Later in the month you'll be accelerating your detoxification with raw-juice fasts. But throughout the month you should drink three glasses of raw juice each day: two vegetable juices and one fruit juice. The enzymes in the raw juices will fortify your entire Holistic Triangle and give you the energy to detoxify.

During this month of detoxification it's highly recommended that you buy organic produce and avoid the pesticides and herbicides in most supermarket produce.

Fruit juices should always be distilled with 50 percent water. If you are withdrawing from a heavy sugar habit, avoid the juices of the sweeter fruits and have no more than six ounces of fruit juice each day, in the morning. Also, be aware that citrus juices can cause skin problems and acne for allergic people. If you have a history of citrus allergies or find yourself with skin symptoms after drinking citrus juices, select other produce.

Green juices made from spinach, kale, parsley, alfalfa, and other green vegetables contain chlorophyll, which is effective in the cleansing process. One of the most potent green drinks is wheatgrass juice, which requires special equipment to produce. Your home juicer may not work to supply this, but you can buy wheatgrass juice fresh in some health food stores or in frozen or powdered form. One ounce of this strong detoxifier is enough to produce an effect.

Raw juices made from vegetables help remove wastes from the body and supply precious antioxidants, amino acids, vitamins, and minerals. Sprouts are highly nutritious and can be added to any of your vegetable drinks.

It's best to drink your raw juices immediately, but if you want to bring them to work, you can store them in an airtight container in a refrigerator or a thermos for up to twelve hours. If necessary, you can prepare them on weekends and store in the freezer.

You can try some of the raw-juice suggestions in Chapter 3 and experiment with your own combinations. We recommend highly that you drink at least one of the detoxification recipes on page 191 each day. These special combinations are designed to nourish and cleanse the lungs, liver, skin, immune system, and vascular system.

Support Cleansing with Energy Foods, Water, and Supplements

During withdrawal from such toxins as sugar and caffeine, it's crucial to maintain a steady stream of nutrients to reduce cravings. Eating six small meals spaced throughout the day will help keep your blood sugar and energy levels steady. Raw-juice drinks can constitute two of these meals, especially if you want to lose weight. Be sure to include a hearty green salad on a daily basis and a whole grain dish every day.

Be adventurous during this month. Try new grains and fruits and vegetables. Eat for the health of it, not just the taste of it.

Imagine your body being nourished on a deeper level; focus on the energy and sustenance from the food.

Drink at least six glasses of filtered water throughout the day to promote cleansing and reduce the tendency to overeat.

Supplements can also support withdrawal from toxins and detoxification. Your holistic health care provider can give you specific guidance on vitamins, minerals, herbs, and amino acids that benefit your particular condition. You can also refer to page 208 for guidelines on supplements and herbs for detoxification.

Eliminate or Reduce Medications

This is the month to stop leaning on quick fixes and commit yourself to the hard work of looking for long-term solutions to health problems without drugs.

Holistic health books organized according to ailment can teach you about alternatives to medications. It's worthwhile including such books in your home library and learning how to utilize natural remedies and prevention. You can refer to page 207 for natural alternatives to several common nonprescription drugs.

The Cleansing Month is the time to eliminate or reduce dependency on prescription drugs as well as over-the-counter items. Schedule a consultation with your doctor to discuss the possibility of reducing or eliminating medications if you take them regularly. Whether or not you can do this will depend on the severity and chronicity of your condition and how long you have been on the medication. But the majority of people can eventually improve their health to a point where drugs are no longer required.

It may take much longer than three months of the program to strengthen your Holistic Triangle sufficiently so that medication is no longer needed, and in rare cases it may never be possible. But it is your right to have your health care practitioner explain the reasons for your medication and carefully consider if you can reduce or discontinue it.

In many cases medication is freely dispensed because it seems an easier solution than major lifestyle changes. Since nearly all drugs have side effects, it's critical to examine every possible natural alternative instead of blindly continuing to swallow your medicine.

Be Prepared for a Healing Crisis

As you withdraw from toxins and your body begins to cleanse itself, you may undergo a healing crisis. Common symptoms include headaches, coughing and clogged sinuses, skin eruptions, gastrointestinal distress, diarrhea, fatigue, irritability, and depression. These messages show the powerful physiological power the toxin is exerting on your mind/body. The more extreme the healing crisis, the more necessary the detoxification.

Symptoms during a healing crisis need to be monitored by your health care professional. But they are not a signal that you should stop the program and turn back to your old habits. Call on your mental/spiritual stamina to keep going. Let the symptoms serve as motivation and a reminder of how much you need to detoxify.

Keep in mind that with most addictions the first three days are the worst, and after this period the physical symptoms usually subside. Take one day at a time, and give yourself plenty of support on all three sides of your Holistic Triangle.

When you give up caffeine, even if your habit is as little as one or two cups of coffee a day, you may experience a withdrawal headache, fatigue, and irritability. These symptoms indicate the serious nature of the ubiquitous caffeine addiction. Don't take aspirin or any other type of pain reliever to relieve your discomfort; this will only prolong your dependency. Instead you can turn to holistic treatments:

- Massage of acupressure points
- Alternating hot and cold compresses (see page 228)
- Exercise, particularly swimming
- Chiropractic care
- Acupuncture

Acupuncture is also recommended if you are overcoming an addiction to drugs, alcohol, or nicotine. It is often effective in easing withdrawal symptoms and is utilized in some progressive rehabilitation programs.

Chiropractic adjustments to maximize the flow of energy through your nerves is another therapeutic alternative during withdrawal. Professional Swedish massage, lymphatic massage, and reflexology can help move waste material through the system and facilitate lymphatic drainage.

Plenty of sleep is required during the detoxification process. Your liver and other organs are working hard to eliminate years of accumulated debris, and you may need extra hours of sleep or quiet, restful time by yourself.

Be sure you have a supply of fresh air when you are indoors: an open window, not just an air conditioner. And try to get outside for short walks whenever possible. You may need to slow down your exercise program during a health crisis, but continue to stretch and do some movement.

Drink eight glasses of filtered water during a detoxification process to help flush through the toxins. Eat steadily but lightly, mostly raw fruits and vegetables.

If You Relapse, Try Again

Toxins have a powerful effect on our mental/spiritual base and often sabotage our decisions and resolve. It's very common to be unable to give up a toxin during the first attempt or to give it up for a short time and then relapse.

If you fail to eliminate the toxin or have a relapse, don't let this throw you off the Self-Health Program.

Be a loving, understanding friend to yourself. Forgive yourself, and reaffirm your unconditional self-love. Don't let a setback make you feel like a complete failure; review the progress you've made in the program and the steps you've accomplished. Focus on your successes as a reminder that you *can* change.

Next, consider why you couldn't give up the toxin or started taking it again. What stood in your way? Was it a physical craving? A psychological need? An escape? Plan how you can keep these pitfalls from sabotaging your progress. What extra nourishment on every side of your Triangle can give you the strength to free yourself of the toxin?

Plan extra nourishment and support during your next attempt to give up the toxin. Call on the powerful healing force of love and the Creator to give you support. Reaffirm your commitment to the program and your faith in your innate healing power. Set a firm date and try again.

Nourish Your Physical Side

The Holistic Self-Health Program is a progressive plan; each month you add to the previous month's accomplishments. During the second month you should continue to nurture your physical side with these activities:

- Bathing Ritual and bathtub exercises nearly every day
- Additional stretching before and after musculoskeletal and aerobic sessions
- Musculoskeletal exercise three times a week
- Aerobic exercise at least three times a week, for at least twenty minutes each session

If you want to do more exercise than this schedule indicates, go for it. Vary your exercise program if you're starting to get bored. Increase the intensity of your aerobic exercise if you feel ready. Add weight training to your musculoskeletal workout if you want to build up.

Listen to your body, and don't overdo it. "No pain no gain" is a fallacy. A pain-free, fun, and natural exercise program is more likely to become a permanent part of your life. By this second month of exercising, you should be seeing and feeling the benefits, and these will inspire you to keep moving.

WEEKS SEVEN AND EIGHT

During the last two weeks of the Cleansing Month continue to nourish your mental/spiritual side with stimulating reading material, spiritual practices, and positive thinking. You should also carry on with your aerobic and musculoskeletal exercises, with the exception of the fast days, when you can reduce activity. The highlight of this period will be the three-day raw-juice fast, which will shift your inner healing force into high gear.

Go on a One-Day Raw-Juice Fast

The best time to schedule your one-day fast is at the beginning of the third week of the second month. By this date you should have reduced or eliminated most of your toxins. Even if you have not, however, it's likely you can still go on a one-day juice fast, provided you consult your holistic doctor first. The fast may well be the day you finally learn you can live without toxins.

Remember, *raw-juice fasting is not starvation.* In fact, drinking raw juices throughout the day can provide more nourishment than the Standard American Diet.

Juice fasting is a powerful healing tool that will help you cleanse your body of years of toxic buildup and also benefit your mental/spiritual side. On your first fast day you'll gain confidence and learn you don't have to be a slave to your habits. You'll also learn to disassociate a certain degree of hunger from punishment and realize that cutting back on food is actually a *reward* for your body.

Try to schedule the fast for a day when you'll be home so you'll have easy access to your juicer. The day before your fast, eat only raw fruits and vegetables, and drink several fresh juices and the Fiber Broth to start the cleansing process.

A one-day juice fast lasts for twenty-four hours—from the first morning when you wake up to the second morning. It is not effective to fast all day and then eat dinner; you need to give your body a rest for a full day and night.

On the day of the fast drink six to ten ounces of a freshly made raw juice every two hours, until a few hours before bedtime. This should be seven glasses of juice: four or five primarily vegetable juices and two or three fruit juices. Start with a fruit juice for your first drink of the morning. Include at least three of the special detoxification recipes in your juice menu.

While raw-juice fasting, you won't need to drink as much water as usual, but still drink one or two glasses a day. It is not necessary to take your vitamin and mineral supplements while you are juice fasting, since you'll be getting high concentrations of nutrients in the juices. Don't chew gum or anything else while fasting.

Start with the Bathing Ritual and bathtub exercises in the morning. Stretching, yoga, walking, or other light exercise are fine while juice fasting, but strenuous aerobics and musculoskeletal workouts are not recommended. Healing Moments, relaxation practices, meditation, and communion with nature are ideal activities.

You may want to keep a diary of your one-day fast in your Self-Help Notebook. Record how you feel, what cravings you experience, the good and bad moments. This will help you identify possible stumbling blocks for the grand finale of your detoxification month: the three-day juice fast.

Go on a Three-Day Juice Fast

Your three-day juice fast should be scheduled at the end of the second month of the program. By this point you've eliminated most toxins from your diet. You've had a month of sun foods, raw juices, and supplements. You've learned you can gain control of your appetite by completing the one-day juice fast. You're ready to activate your inner healing potential with the three-day juice fast.

Before embarking on this fast, check again with your doctor to be sure you have no conditions that preclude juice fasting. If you have a history of diabetes, kidney disease, or another major illness or are on medication, you need to consult with your doctor and find out if fasting is safe and what special precautions you may need to take. Even if you are in the best of health, have a holistic health professional on call in case you experience any unusual symptoms during the fast.

Have a serving of the Fiber Broth each day between your one-day and three-day juice fast. For two days before the second fast, eat only raw fruits, vegetables, nuts, and seeds; drink plenty of water; and take supplements. Once you are on the juice fast, you don't need supplements and can drink less water than usual.

Each day of the fast drink a raw juice every two hours, starting with a fruit juice in the morning. Include at least three of the detoxification juice recipes each day. Add a teaspoon of spirulina powder to two or three of your juice drinks daily.

Each day of the fast, drink one or two cups of healing teas, such as pau d'arco and echinacea, and at least one glass of distilled water.

It's important to have a bowel movement during each day of the juice fast to continue the inner cleansing process. But since the peristaltic response will not be stimulated by any food, you'll probably need an enema on the second morning.

Use distilled lukewarm water in the enema bag, with a little lemon juice added (unless you have a citrus allergy). Insert the tube with your head down and bottom up. After the fluid insertion, lie on your right side and gently massage the right side of your abdomen. Turn on your back, and massage the center of your abdomen; then turn to the left, and massage the left side.

Be sure to place a small stool or a couple of telephone books under your feet when you are on the toilet bowl to simulate the squatting position. If there is any blood or excess mucus in your feces, notify your health care provider. These signs do not necessarily mean your fast needs to be discontinued, but you may require special therapeutic juices.

After the enema you can relax in the bath, perhaps adding some soothing oils.

On fast days you need to brush your tongue as thoroughly as your teeth. Buildup of white mucus on your tongue while fasting is to be expected; it's a sign your body is cleaning itself out. Brush your tongue with a natural toothpaste; then wipe it from the back to the front with a terry-cloth washcloth until it's clean.

Fasting is used as a spiritual tradition in many cultures, and juice fast days are an excellent time to give extra attention to your mental/spiritual side. Meditation, relaxation, affirmations, visualization, Healing Moments, and prayer may reach deeper levels than usual. You may find yourself with creative insights and a heightened sense of spirituality and enlightenment.

Breaking the juice fast correctly is imperative. On the morning of the fourth day have a juice as your first meal. Midmorning eat an apple. At lunchtime have a detoxifying vegetable juice. Midafternoon have a small bowl of a cooked grain. At dinnertime, have another juice. Then, in the early evening, you can have a small green salad.

The following day you can resume normal eating, but lightly and no toxins. After the three-day fast, refraining from toxins may be much easier than you ever dreamed possible. You'll probably find yourself repelled by toxins and attracted to natural nourishment from the earth and sun.

CHECKLIST FOR THE CLEANSING MONTH

❑ Set up your support system: groups, holistic practitioners, and personal support people.

❑ Review the list of Top Ten Toxins and healthy alternatives. Make a list of your personal toxins and healthier options.

❑ Write down a firm schedule for giving up toxins and a date for juice fasts.

❑ Don't turn to toxins when you're hungry, angry, lonely, tired (HALT), bored, or tense; react with conscious actions and nourishment.

❑ Drink raw juices, including special detoxification juices, throughout the month.

❑ Eat six light meals a day. Drink six to eight glasses of pure water each day.

❑ Take supplements for support on the chemical side. Use herbs, if needed, to facilitate detoxification.

❑ Work with your doctor to reduce or eliminate medications.

❑ If you're unable to give up a toxin on the first attempt or have a relapse, try again.

❑ Go on a one-day raw-juice fast for initial cleansing.

❑ Go on a three-day raw-juice fast to activate your inner healing force.

Good work!

CHAPTER 8

Feel the Force Month: Month Three of the Holistic Self-Health Program

The third month of the program is the time to consolidate your gains and bring all three sides of your Holistic Triangle to new heights of well-being. This month you'll feel the power of your inner healing force and experience higher levels of energy, stamina, and strength.

You'll work and play hard to get closer to your physical ideal and support your evolving body with the healing arts. You'll eat a variety of foods to maximize your energy level and go on a final cleansing fast. You'll experience the synergistic effect of the Holistic Triangle and tap into your innate healing force to overcome lingering ailments.

You'll be revitalized and rejuvenated, generating strength from your empowered Triangle. It's going to be an exciting month!

WEEKS NINE AND TEN

Work Toward Reaching Peak Physical Condition

Lie down, close your eyes, and relax. Visualize how you looked and felt when you were in peak physical condition. Perhaps this was when you were in high school and had all the natural gifts of youth, or maybe it was later, in a period of intense involvement in a sport or exercise program. If you've never been in the best possible shape, imagine how you would look and feel in top condition, and create a clear picture in your mind.

This vision of your optimal physical state is the goal toward which you will be working, both this month and after the program, as you continue your holistic lifestyle.

Take a few minutes to start a new list in your Self-Health Notebook: "Action Plan for Physical Conditioning." Write down all the possible ways you can nourish your physical side to build toward your ideal.

Also, continue to write your Physical and Mental/Spiritual Nourishment reports each day. You should see a rewarding upsurge in your activity and endurance.

Of course, everyone has physical limitations, and you're not expected to become an Olympic swimmer, a prima ballerina, or a basketball star. The holistic goal is to be the best *you* can be; you're not competing against or being compared with anyone else. The emphasis in holistic exercise is always on personal goals, breathing, consistency, and form, not on competition.

Increase the Challenge of Your Exercise Program

During the third month of the program, aerobic exercise should be done at least three times a week, preferably more often, in sessions of at least thirty minutes' duration. The intensity of the workouts can be increased so your exercise pulse is in the high end of your target zone.

Please note: This schedule is based on the assumption you've been following the program up to this point and have been doing aerobic exercise for two months. *If you have not been exercising regularly, you need to go more slowly.* And no matter how high your fitness level, always be conscious of the warning signs of danger during exercise (see page 76). Stop and consult your doctor if you experience any of these signs.

Another goal this month is to increase your stamina and recovery time. How long does it take you to stop feeling exhausted after an aerobic workout? As you get in prime condition, aim to be able to do a specific aerobic exercise for thirty minutes, rest for an hour or two, and then have the energy for a recreational activity, such as a racquet sport or bike riding.

The third month is a terrific time to add variety and challenge to your aerobic program. For example, if you enjoy running, you might want to train for a marathon. If walking is your main exercise, you can try racewalking, walking backward, walking in water, or walking up and down hills.

Your new physical challenge might be an activity you enjoyed in your youth, such as ice skating, jumping rope, ballet classes, or playing on a basketball team. Or it might be a sport that you found appealing but intimidating before: in-line roller skating, skiing, backpacking, snorkeling, or long-distance biking.

Perhaps you'd like to study martial arts, an intense discipline for both the physical and mental/spiritual sides. Iyengar or kundalini yoga classes are also dynamic ways to strengthen the mind/body.

Aerobic dance classes are offered in diverse styles, such as salsa, gospel, Motown, hip-hop, and Broadway jazz. Aqua-aerobic classes, which are given in pools, are great fun and offer the beneficial resistance of water without the impact of gravity.

Step aerobics can be invigorating, provided you don't have a history of knee pain. If you do have weak knees, you may be able to do special therapeutic exercises to strengthen the quadriceps muscles so they support your knees more efficiently. Once you've built these up, you may be able to participate in step classes safely.

Try to get hooked on a form of exercise you thoroughly enjoy. Adults need to have the fun of physicality as part of their lives as much as children do. Find an activity you *want* to do, not one you think you *should* do. Your exercise activity should be a perk, not a chore.

Once you're committed to regular exercise, you may decide to invest in home workout equipment, such as a minitrampoline, treadmill, rowing machine, skiing machine, stair climber, or dual-action exercise bicycle. To get maximum aerobic benefit from exercise bikes and rowing and skiing machines, keep the resistance low so you can go fast, and keep moving for about twenty minutes. Low resistance also reduces the chance of spinal compression and injury. During the last ten minutes of the workout you can increase the resistance to enhance the musculoskeletal benefit.

This is the month to add intensity to your musculoskeletal workout as well as to aerobics. You can increase the number of repetitions of exercises you have been doing steadily, and use small hand weights during your workouts. You might want to work the Nautilus circuit at a gym or purchase weight equipment to use at home. Once you've developed your muscles sufficiently, you might find a sport or exercise class that combines a musculoskeletal and aerobic workout.

Get Expert Support for Your Exercise Program

A book, such as this one, can take you to only a certain point on the physical side. There is no substitute for hands-on training, one-on-one attention, and the personal touch.

This month consider joining a health club where you'll have available the expertise of a personal trainer and a variety of classes. Even if you've joined health clubs before and ended up a dropout, your new strength on the mental/spiritual side might keep you going this time.

If a health club is too expensive or doesn't appeal to you, there are other ways you can learn from the experts without making a major financial investment. Adult schools, community centers, and Y's often have lower-cost programs. Some dance, yoga, and exercise centers allow students to pay on a per-class basis.

Exercise videotapes have the advantage of being relatively inexpensive and accessible at home, but they have two drawbacks.

First, you can develop bad habits and faulty techniques without anyone there to make corrections. Secondly, since there's no one to urge you on, it's easy to quit mid-tape or sit out the harder exercises. For these reasons, exercise videos are best used as a complement to other activities rather than the sole means of fitness.

If you have a program buddy, you can cheer each other on to accomplish your exercise goals this month. If you take a class, you might meet a new exercise friend with whom you can discuss your Self-Health Program and how you're nourishing your physical side. You can also discuss the program with teachers or trainers and ask for their support with your physical goals.

As you rev up your exercise program and transform your physical state, you may experience "growing pains." You may become aware of imbalances, limitations, and conditions that lay dormant when you were less active, and you may suffer joint or muscle soreness or pain.

When your body sends you these messages, it's best to consult a holistic professional, who can tell you if you need to adapt your exercise regimen, who can teach you specific rehabilitative exercises and provide therapeutic treatments. Many holistic chiropractors are experienced in these areas and familiar with sports injuries. Massage therapists can also be skilled in alleviating exercise-related pain.

Give Yourself Extra Physical Nourishment and Care

If possible, treat yourself to at least one professional deep-muscle, full-body massage during the final month of the program. Massage therapy improves circulation and helps disperse fatigue and pain-causing by-products of exercise, such as lactic acid, from the muscles and surrounding tissues.

A session with a talented massage therapist can put you in touch with different areas of your body and let you know where you're holding tension and tightness. This provides insight into how you can warm up more thoroughly before working out and what parts of your body might need continued therapy.

In addition to professional massage, you can exchange massages with your program buddy, friend, spouse, or companion. It's worthwhile reading books on massage or taking a course to learn techniques that are truly therapeutic and not just pleasant. Learning massage together may be a way you can bring your partner into your Self-Health Program and enhance your relationship at the same time. If the best things in life are free, exchanging massages is certainly one of them. You can also use the self-massage techniques on page 226.

The Bathing Ritual in the morning will release muscular tension and start you off in a relaxed mode. But since you're increasing your level of fitness this month, you might need additional hydrotherapy. As you're building muscle, you can use hot and cold compresses to relieve aches and pains and reduce the chance of injury. See page 228 for directions on compress therapy.

If you have an area of achiness resulting from exercise, but no severe pain or injury, you might use a gentle support "sleeve" in the area. Common sleeves include knee supports, elbow supports, ankle supports, wrist supports, or light "corsets" to pull up the abdomen and support the lower back. Use the support only as a temporary measure, until you can build up the weak spot. Continued need for a support indicates you need to learn a healthier technique, reduce the intensity of your activity, or seek professional care.

You can also use natural liniments, such as tiger balm or mineral ice, to relieve achiness and pain. Again, this should be done only on a temporary basis as your body adapts to new demands and growth. If you continue to need any pain relief, consult your holistic doctor.

Stretch, Relax, and Rest

Stretching each day is extremely important when you're doing aggressive aerobics and musculoskeletal exercise. It's vital to keep the joints lubricated, the structure balanced, and the muscles as relaxed as possible.

The bathtub stretches in the morning are a good start, but

don't neglect stretching before and after working out. Too many people are injured because they don't take the time to warm up, cool down, and stay loose. Give yourself the precious gift of ample time for a safe and loving exercise program.

It's beneficial to perform the Total Body Relaxation several times a week this month, especially after cooling down from a strenuous exercise session. Continue practicing deep breathing to increase oxygen intake and stimulate circulation.

A healthy amount of solid sleep is required during this active third month of the program. The additional exercise is likely to help you sleep soundly, but if you do have bouts of insomnia, use the natural techniques on page 90.

Increase Mental/Spiritual Nourishment

Many athletes instinctively use positive visualization to achieve their success. They also channel their belief in their abilities into the discipline and hard practice required for physical excellence. Although you're not expected to become a world-class gymnast or play in the Super Bowl, you can still use the secrets of the stars to attain your personal goals on the physical side of the Triangle.

To use visualization to support your physical development, start by deciding on a specific goal. This may be completing fifty sit-ups and twenty push-ups, keeping up with an advanced aerobics class, or simply swimming continually for thirty minutes—whatever is appropriate for your fitness level and exercise choices.

When you're ready to do the visualization, lie down in a quiet place, close your eyes, breathe deeply, and relax your body. Then see yourself preparing for the physical challenge: putting on your workout clothes, doing a series of stretches, and warming up. Imagine starting the activity, overcoming fatigue and hurdles, and completing what you set out to do. Picture every possible detail: what you're seeing, how your heart is beating, how your body feels, what you hear and smell. Then visualize yourself cooling down, stretching, and feeling triumphant. Keep this feeling in your mind, and try to evoke it several times a day.

Another technique is to lie down and do the Total Body Relaxation exercise. When you are in this receptive state, imagine the sun with all its energy over your head. Feel the energy entering through the top of your head, moving down your face and into your neck. Experience the sun energy filling up your heart and your lungs and being carried by your arteries into your arms and legs. As you breathe, feel vitality flowing in with the oxygen. Focus on the solar energy and oxygen empowering every cell of your body.

When you're fully charged and energized, begin a series of stretches to prepare for your workout. As you stretch, feel the sun energy flowing through your veins. Inhale more power and vitality with every breath. When you're finished with your preliminary stretches, bring this stored energy and power to your aerobic exercise.

While you are exercising, use your mind to maximize the benefits. If you run or walk, visualize yourself moving smoothly and quickly, feeling light and streamlined, taking great strides as if moving on air. If you swim, imagine yourself gliding through the water like a beautiful sailboat on a clear river. When you stretch or do yoga, concentrate on your limbs lengthening, your joints opening up, your body becoming limber and young.

Explore New Varieties of Healthy Foods

This month continue with your Daily Diet Report and healthy eating basics:

- No toxins
- Six small meals a day
- Six to eight glasses of water a day
- Multivitamin/mineral supplements
- At least two raw-juice drinks a day
- A one-day raw-juice fast once during the first two weeks of this month

You may still need to discipline yourself to stay with this nutritional program, but it will probably be much easier than last month. You can make your holistic diet more palatable by trying new varieties of fruits, vegetables, and legumes. Here are some ideas:

—For interesting salads, use arugula, endive, radicchio, mesclun, maché, bibb lettuce, or dandelion greens.
—Add sprouts, lemon grass, chopped nuts, and exotic mushrooms, such as chanterelle or porcini, to salads and other dishes.
—Explore Latin markets for hearty vegetables, such as yuca, plantains, malanga, and boniatos.
—Asian markets are a source of delightful ingredients that can be used in stir-frys and salads: bok choy, Chinese celery, cabbage, water chestnuts, snow peas, wood ears, and fresh tofu.
—Many varieties of squash, including buttercup, calabaza, chayote, delicato, golden nugget, and "spaghetti" squash, can be used for soups and entrées.
—Treat yourself to exotic fruits, such as mangoes, papayas, guavas, kiwis, passion fruit, pomegranates, and star fruit.

This month you might also explore different restaurants where you can stay on your program but enjoy unusual cuisine. Find out if there are any health food or macrobiotic restaurants in your area. Asian, Latin, and nouvelle cuisine restaurants may also have dishes that allow you to stay on the program while experiencing new taste sensations. Just be sure to inquire about ingredients, avoid dishes with too much oil, and ascertain there are no additives, such as MSG.

THE ELEVENTH AND TWELFTH WEEKS

In the final weeks of the program continue with the healthy, high-energy eating pattern, supplements, and lots of raw juices and water for cleansing.

You'll also want to keep up the momentum of your exercise program, with the exception of the fast days. By this time you're likely to be experiencing rewarding improvements on the physical side and a resultant uplift on the mental/spiritual side. Keep going. You're doing great!

Address the Causes of Lingering Maladies

By the last two weeks of the program, many of the conditions and symptoms you had before embarking on the Self-Health journey are likely to be alleviated. If, however, you still have recurrent pain or ailments, this is the time to address these messages.

Write each remaining health problem on the top of a page in your Self-Health Notebook. Research what you can do to correct the root cause of the ailment and prevent it from recurring in the future. Consult books on herbal remedies, foods that heal, vitamin therapy, and body work techniques.

Write down under the symptom all the steps you can take to correct the problem permanently. Also, consult with your holistic doctor to learn what treatment he or she suggests. If you have come across anything interesting in your research, tell your doctor. Remember, you are equal partners, and you may have information your doctor doesn't know.

Once you have written down all the possible solutions, create an action plan. The timetable for this plan may well extend beyond the third month of the program since you may have to counteract years of neglect. But even if you can't overcome your health problems by the end of three months, you can take the primary step: Create a game plan for recovery, and resolve to see it through.

One step you can complete this month is to identify any remaining food intolerances or allergies (see page 194). Most of the common food triggers are eliminated when you give up the Top Ten Toxins; however, it's possible to be allergic to normally healthy foods, and you may need a blood test to track down the culprit.

Allergies to pollen, house-dust mites, animal dander, mold, household chemicals, secondhand smoke, ingredients in cosmetics, and work-related chemicals should also be considered during testing. Once the allergen has been identified, you can take steps to reduce or limit your exposure.

Develop Healthy Posture and Daily Habits

As part of your physical transformation during the final weeks of the program, work on establishing good posture as a permanent habit. Here are some questions that will show you the way to healthy posture:

—When you examine your posture from the side and front while standing:

Is your neck long without being tight (following normal curvature of spine)?
Are your shoulders back instead of rounded?
Is your chest upheld or caved in?
Does your lower back follow the natural spinal curve, or is it flattened or hyperextended (swayback)?
Do you stand tall or lean to one side?

—When sitting:

Do you sit tall, without crossing your legs?
Do you elevate your knees to your hip level or higher (except in a kneeling chair)?

—When sleeping:

Do you have a good, supportive mattress?
Do you sleep with one pillow instead of two?
Do you sleep on your back or side, not your stomach?
Do you keep the window cracked open for ventilation?
Do you rise from bed by turning on your side first rather than using your neck?

—When relaxing:

Do you hold your reading material up to eye level? (If you use bifocals, adjust position so you can maintain posture.)

Do you watch TV from a supportive chair or couch, rather than being propped up with pillows in bed?

Do you frequently get up, stretch, and move around during your leisure time?

—When working:

Do you have an ergonomically designed chair or kneeling chair for work?

Is your keyboard at a comfortable level? Is your computer screen at eye level rather than lower?

Do you hold the phone up with your hand or use a headset instead of jamming the phone between your ear and shoulder?

Do you have fresh air in your office environment?

Do you take stretching breaks at work?

—When walking:

Do you wear comfortable, low-heeled shoes instead of high heels?

Do you look ahead, not down?

—When carrying:

Do you bend your knees and squat before lifting a heavy object?

Do you shift the sides on which you carry objects (or your baby, if you're a parent)?

Do you carry as light a pocketbook as possible and wear the strap diagonally across your chest, or use a lightweight backpack?

You can explore these questions to discover areas of posture and daily habits in which you need improvement. Then write a list of related goals in your Self-Health Notebook. Reading the list several times a day can serve as a reminder. You can also post little notes by your desk, such as "Don't cross your legs!"

As you begin to change your posture, you may experience difficulty or discomfort, since different muscle groups are working. It will take some persistence, but in time your improved postural habits will make you less vulnerable to pain and tension and more confident and attractive.

Continue with Raw-Juice Fasts for Inner Cleansing

During the first two weeks of the final month of the program, it's recommended you go on a one-day juice fast. This will continue the cleansing process and prepare you mentally and physically for a longer fast.

The final raw-juice fast of the program should be planned for the third or fourth week of the month. You can go on a three-day juice fast at this time or a five-day fast. The five-day juice fast is preferable since it allows deeper cleansing of the lymph tissues, liver, and kidneys.

Consult your holistic doctor before going on either fast. Once you have the go-ahead, set your date. Spend two days before the fast eating only fruits and vegetables and drinking juices, herbal teas, and water.

During the three- or five-day juice fast follow all the guidelines beginning on page 188.

There's probably no reason why you can't go to work during the first days of the fast, unless your job is very physically demanding. You just need to plan ahead to have your raw juices available during the workday. If you're lucky enough to have a refrigerator and a relaxed work environment, you can bring your juicer and produce along. Otherwise, prepare the juices in the morning and pack them in thermoses and an insulated picnic bag.

If you're going on a five-day fast, try to have the last two days fall on a weekend.

Be sure to follow carefully the guidelines on page 151 when you break the fast. If you fast for five days, eat lightly for at least forty-eight hours afterward.

Give yourself special treatment during the juice fast. Refrain from strenuous aerobic and musculoskeletal exercise, and concentrate on limbering, deep breathing, and relaxation. If possible, schedule a massage or another therapeutic treatment.

Spend extra time nourishing the mental/spiritual side of your Triangle to get in touch with your higher self during this sensitive period. Take time to listen to your heart, and open yourself up to the endless, infinite love.

Celebrate!

When you've finished the Three-Month Holistic Self-Health Program, plan a celebration. The program has been hard work, and you deserve congratulations and a special treat.

You might want to have a party, as if it were your birthday, only this time you're celebrating feeling younger instead of getting older. The party can be an intimate dinner for you and your love, a small get-together, or a big bash, whatever you please. To mark the occasion with the right spirit, serve natural sun foods and drinks, no toxins. Let your guests know that you're celebrating your self-renewal.

Another way to celebrate completing the program is to take a healthy vacation. This could be a visit to a spa, a spiritual retreat, or a sports-oriented resort. If your funds are limited, take a day trip to a beautiful outdoor spot where you can take a walk, appreciate nature, and refresh your spirit.

You can also celebrate by treating yourself to a professional massage or other body work. You can sign up for a class or buy a piece of exercise equipment to use at home. You can get a new outfit to show off your toned, leaner figure.

For a low-cost celebration, you can give yourself a home spa day. Start with a vigorous workout session, followed by stretching and Total Body Relaxation. Then have a light meal of spa cuisine with a fruit ambrosia drink. You might give yourself a facial with ingredients from your own kitchen and a self-massage with natural lotion. In the evening take a long, hot bath with scented oil and candlelight. Relax and reflect on how much you've achieved during these three months.

CHECKLIST FOR FEEL THE FORCE MONTH

❑ Visualize your peak physical condition, and plan how you can achieve it.

❑ Continue doing aerobic and muscoloskeletal exercise at least three times a week each. Increase the intensity of your workouts.

❑ Try exciting and challenging new forms of exercise.

❑ Seek support and guidance from fitness experts. Consult a holistic health professional to address pain and imbalances, if needed.

❑ Do stretching exercises every day. Do the Total Body Relaxation several times a week.

❑ Support your physical side with creative visualization and affirmations.

❑ Enjoy the benefits of massage. Give yourself compress therapy, if needed.

❑ Eat a light, high-energy diet, drink plenty of water and raw juices, and take supplements. Explore new varieties of wholesome foods. Continue with your Daily Diet Reports.

❑ List all remaining symptoms, and research how to correct and prevent them. Write an action plan for overcoming each problem. Have an allergy test done, if necessary.

❑ Establish healthy posture and daily habits.

❑ Go on a final cleansing juice fast during the third week, for three to five days.

❑ Celebrate the completion of your Holistic Self-Health Program with a special treat.

Congratulations!

CHAPTER 9

Your Healthy Future

The real purpose of attaining better physical health and longer life is not just the enjoyment of a pain- and disease-free existence, but a higher divine purpose for which life was given to us.
—Dr. Paavo Airola

The end of the Three-Month Holistic Self-Health Program is a beginning of your healthy future. The program gave you an opportunity to establish a solid mental/spiritual foundation, detoxify and fortify yourself with healthy foods, and build up your physical side with exercise. Now you have the rest of your life to continue to nourish your Holistic Triangle and love yourself to total well-being.

The primary objective is to incorporate the activities of the program into your permanent lifestyle. It's also desirable to remain in touch with the ever-changing condition and needs of your Holistic Triangle. Nourishing your Triangle is an ongoing, lifelong process, constant yet always changing. The basic forms of nourishment remain the same, but there are different demands and goals as you progress through the years.

EVALUATE YOUR PROGRESS AND ESTABLISH NEW GOALS

A week or two after you have completed the program, retake the evaluation tests in Chapter 5. Compare your scores in each section with the figures from your initial evaluations, taken more than three months ago. It's likely you'll see a dramatic increase in your scores, an upswing that reflects the renewal of your Holistic Triangle.

Of course, the way you *feel* is a more potent reminder of your achievements than any tests can be. The evaluations are only a form of measurement. The reality is your renewed energy, vigor, flexibility, strength, optimism, and empowerment.

However, the tests can help you locate areas of your Triangle that may still need attention and nourishment. Now that you're invigorated, you can tackle these difficult aspects and establish fresh goals.

Write down in your Self-Help Notebook any remaining weaknesses indicated by the evaluations and your own observations. Create a plan for taking healthy action to heal, love, and restore these undernourished areas. Include all the primary and secondary nourishment you can think of that might strengthen these weak links in your Triangle.

You can continue to utilize the evaluations on a yearly basis. Asking yourself these questions each year provides a framework for reflecting on all aspects of your Holistic Triangle. It can help you chart which areas you have been nourishing and which you may have been neglecting. You can use this information to design updated nourishment plans and goals for yourself each year.

EXTEND YOUR MENTAL/SPIRITUAL STRENGTH

Now that you've learned the art of loving yourself to health, it's an excellent time to share the wealth. Extend your love, energy, and knowledge to people who need your help.

You might want to introduce the ideas of holistic health to your family and friends, in a loving, nonjudgmental way. Once they've seen your transformation, they may be more open to the concepts than they were initially.

If you're eager to have your family make healthy changes, such as giving up toxins or exercising more often, take a positive approach, rather than a negative judgmental stance. Let them know how much healthier you are now that you've detoxified, how much happier you feel now that you're in touch with your spirituality, how much you enjoy being fit. Present holistic activities as being fun and rewarding, rather than as something they *should* do.

If the people you love are not ready to make major changes, encourage them to take small steps in the right direction. But if they are completely resistant and unwilling to change, you may have to accept their attitude. No one can be responsible for another person's Triangle. All you can do is set a good example and keep on loving others unconditionally.

If anyone you know is inspired by your example to go on the program, you can volunteer to be her or his buddy and support throughout the three months. You can offer to refer the person to holistic health professionals, share your books and information, and be his or her exercise partner. But be sure you *offer* rather than *force* your advice and participation. The Self-Health Program is a personal journey, and everyone has her or his own way.

You can also share your mental/spiritual energy by doing volunteer work. Pick a group of people for whom you feel genuine compassion, and volunteer to assist on a regular basis, whether it's once a month or once a week.

When you can care for people who are very different in circumstances, yet understand they are basically the same inside, your spiritual side grows enlightened. You learn the meaning of unconditional love on a spiritual, rather than merely intellectual, level. And the more you reach out, the more you tap into the infinite love in the Universe.

When you're helping less fortunate people, remember, we all have the same basic needs. Not everyone is ready to understand or accept the concept of the Holistic Triangle, but every person on the planet needs to nourish his or her mental/spiritual, chemical, and physical sides. And we all need more unconditional love and acceptance. Now that you've been consciously nurturing these qualities within yourself, you are in a powerful position to share your love with others.

Another way to share your mental/spiritual empowerment is to become active in your community or in a national group. For example, you might organize a health food co-op in your town or work toward creating a new park. On a national or global level, you can volunteer for an environmental group or lobby the government to reform the health care system. There are so many ways in which you can make a difference in the world, with faith and action.

LIFESTYLE CHANGES

The period of peak condition after the program can be an optimal time to undertake necessary lifestyle changes involving your relationships, home, or career. These may be changes you have wanted to make for a long time, or they may be an outgrowth of your higher level of awareness.

Remember, however, that any change is stressful, and it's best not to undertake too much at once. Pace your progression realistically, with patience, acceptance, and self-consideration. Don't initiate so many sudden changes that you find yourself unable to keep nourishing your Triangle.

Loving Relationships

The first part of your lifestyle you may want to consider concerns intimate relationships. If you are involved with a person who is abusive, self-destructive, highly critical, negative, or withholding, this will inevitably undermine your mental/spiritual base. This erosion is likely to lead to weakness on the chemical and physical sides and eventually harm your health.

The period following completion of the Self-Health Program, when you feel empowered and capable of change, may be a good time to deal with an unhappy relationship. This may mean seeking help from a psychotherapist, family counselor, spiritual leader, substance abuse program, or support group.

Ultimately, if your partner refuses to seek help or change behavior that is hurting you both, you may need to leave the relationship. A crucial part of loving yourself is the ability to disengage from a person who is unable to receive and reciprocate your love.

Your Holistic Triangle can give you precious support when you're dealing with a painful relationship. Your mental/spiritual foundation of unconditional self-love provides the strength to take action. Faith and spirituality offer profound comfort. Wholesome, balanced nourishment on the chemical side supplies energy and helps prevent stress-related illness. On the physical side, exercise releases uplifting hormones, releases tension, and feeds self-esteem. The Bathing Ritual, Healing Moments, and relaxation sessions are also soothing support when you are dealing with stressful personal issues.

Nourishing Work

Work is another aspect of your lifestyle to examine after the program, when you are feeling confident and clear.

It's natural for human beings to have a degree of resistance to hard work, but it's not healthy to dread your job every day. A certain amount of pressure is unavoidable in the workplace, but a high level of stress on a long-standing basis will wear down your Triangle.

Perhaps you need to work on changing your *attitude* toward work. We can't always control what happens to us, but we can usually control how we react. Control doesn't mean repression; the goal is to maintain a sense of perspective and balance in your reactions and to avoid the physical effects of stress.

Affirmations, visualizations, deep breathing, and meditation can help you learn not to overreact to the demands of your job. Biofeedback training, meditation, relaxation practices, and yoga can reduce the stress response. There are also books and courses offering stress reduction techniques specifically for the workplace.

If an unfair boss or unpleasant coworker causes you to dislike your job, you may be able to use your mental/spiritual power to rise above that person's level and refuse to be provoked. Remind yourself that his or her negativity is a symptom of mental/spiritual weakness and lack of self-love. *Your* self-love is unconditional and does not depend on anyone's approval.

If you find your work boring or demeaning, try to find ways to make it more challenging. Many managers are impressed when employees offer to take on new responsibilities or carry the job a step farther than required, and this can lead to a more rewarding position.

If you try different approaches and still find your work extremely stressful, upsetting, boring, or unsatisfying, you may need to move on. Or you may be unwillingly forced into a period of unemployment at some point in your career.

Whatever the circumstances, your Holistic Triangle can help you during a job search. On the mental/spiritual side, faith, self-esteem, and such techniques as creative visualization and affirmation are supportive. On the chemical side, a nourishing diet provides stamina and reduces the chance of illness during a stressful job hunt. On the physical side, a toned, fit appearance fosters a positive first impression during interviews. You can rally all three sides of your Triangle to help you get the job you deserve.

A Healing Home

The third major aspect of your lifestyle to consider when you are planning a healthy future involves your home. Is it a sanctuary? Is it conducive to relaxing and replenishing your Triangle? If not, what can you do to make it a more peaceful, serene, comfortable place?

Some people are able to create sanctuaries for themselves in apartments in the middle of cities. They thrive on the diverse people, stimulating culture, and high-powered jobs in the urban environment. Other people find cities depleting and need daily contact with nature to stay sane and de-stressed.

Look into your heart and ask yourself what you need. Don't be afraid to ask if your environment is healthy for your spiritual as well as physical state. Do you have easy access to forms of exercise you enjoy? Do you feel safe and comfortable in your area? Do you have people you know and care about nearby?

When you've thought about these questions, you may discover that you're fine where you are or learn you would be happier in a different environment. Moving to a healthier location may be a long-range goal, requiring years of planning, saving, and hard work. But once you decide on a plan and make a commitment, you're on your way.

CONTINUE TO NOURISH YOUR MENTAL/ SPIRITUAL SIDE

Many people continue to work out and maintain healthy diets after the three months of the program but start to neglect the mental/spiritual sides. This is often the first part of the Triangle to be ignored, yet it is the most sustaining.

Many aspects of spirituality and holistic health have been touched upon in this book. Why don't you choose a practice or topic that piques your interest and delve into it more deeply?

For example, if you're attracted to meditation, you can read books by the masters, take classes, or practice with a spiritual group. If you found affirmation and visualization useful, you can read more, listen to tapes, go to seminars and workshops, and practice, practice, practice.

If you're intrigued by herbal healing, you can read up on the subject or study with an herbologist. Perhaps you'd enjoy a vegetarian cooking course or like to learn about the healing qualities of different foods.

These are just a few examples. The potential for learning and strengthening the mental/spiritual side is truly infinite. And you can expand this side for the rest of your life. Although a certain amount of decline on the physical side is inevitable, your mind can continue to flower.

CONTINUE TO NOURISH YOUR CHEMICAL SIDE

On the chemical side of the Triangle, the basic goal after the Self-Health Program is to adopt healthy eating as a way of life. As you get older, it becomes more and more crucial to eat light, wholesome food, avoid toxins, and take supplements. A young person's chemical side can take a lot of abuse, but as the years go by, you need to be careful.

You may be able to indulge in toxins occasionally if you're strong and well. But it's safer not to begin to think of these indulgences as "treats," or you may end up treating yourself to an early grave.

When you take a toxin, think about why you did it. Remember the triggers—hunger, anger, loneliness, tiredness, boredom, and tension—as well as societal influences. Refresh your knowledge of alternative ways to deal with these emotions as well as healthy substitutes for the toxin itself.

If you find yourself craving a certain toxin, reread the reasons why it is detrimental to your health. Remind yourself that you stopped before, during the program, and you can stop again. You don't have to be a slave to any food, drink, or chemical. You're free, and you love yourself enough to make healthy choices.

One of the healthiest choices you can make is to continue raw-juice fasting on a regular basis. Raw-juice fasting one day a week is highly beneficial for inner cleansing and rejuvenation. Think of the raw-juice fast as a weekly Sabbath for your body, a spiritual and chemical day of rest.

It's also an excellent practice to go on a three- to five-day juice fast four times a year. This will allow you to rest and renew your internal environment on a seasonal basis, as nature renews itself.

Drinking plenty of water each day and eating small frequent meals of plant foods are also healthy habits to maintain. Taking vitamin and mineral supplements each day will benefit your immune system and help keep you well.

CONTINUE TO NOURISH YOUR PHYSICAL SIDE

If you want to feel youthful and energetic, continuing your regular exercise program is a requirement. Exercise is a key to maintaining optimism, confidence, and a zest for life. It is also essential for reducing your chance of suffering from heart disease and other leading causes of early death.

Try to do some type of physical activity on a daily basis. Unless serious conditions interfere, you should be able to exercise for the rest of your life. The intensity of exercise does, however, need to be modified in later years. Stretching can continue to be a daily routine and can stave off the symptoms of aging.

Other forms of physical nourishment are also lifetime companions: plenty of sleep, deep breathing, relaxation practices, massage, and the Bathing Ritual. If you find yourself neglecting your physical side because you're "too busy," plan a day off to give yourself a home spa treatment.

Since we're all subject to the effects of gravity, stress, and aging, body work is recommended on an ongoing basis, not only when you have pain. Chiropractic adjustments can help prevent osteoarthritis, painful trigger points, and fibrous lesions from developing. Other secondary forms of physical nourishment, such as massage treatments, are also nourishing. Try to have some preventive, therapeutic body work at least once a season.

It's also a fine idea to stay in touch with your holistic doctor, even when you're feeling good. By having regular checkups, you can obtain an objective assessment of your condition and become aware of any developing problems. You can also discuss new research findings, family illnesses, and other concerns that crop up. Your holistic doctor can get to know you on a personal basis and have greater insight into what you need to do to keep your Triangle vital and balanced.

DEALING WITH SETBACKS

When most people finish the Three-Month Holistic Self-Health Program, they feel so terrific they plan to continue their healthy lifestyles forever. But as the weeks, months, or years pass, they find it easy to slip into old habits. A cup of coffee once in a while becomes a cup every morning, then two a day, until it's back to four cups a day. They figure dessert once in a while won't hurt and soon crave sugar after every meal. They decide to skip an aerobic walk because it's rainy one day, the next day they're tired, and soon exercise is no longer a habit.

The human ability to make excuses and rationalizations is limitless. You need to be careful not to fool yourself into believing you can neglect your Holistic Triangle and not suffer the consequences. If you're not totally honest with yourself, you can get trapped in a system of self-delusion and denial.

If you decide to have a nitrate-loaded hero sandwich, a cola, and a slice of cream pie for lunch, fine. Just be honest and tell yourself: I'm choosing to eat something that will weaken my Holistic Triangle, and I'm going to end up feeling worse. If you tell yourself it doesn't matter, today's special treat can easily become tomorrow's unhealthy habit.

Being a holistic person certainly doesn't mean you'll never taste a toxin again for the rest of your life. There are special occasions when it's appropriate to break the rules. If you've been nourishing your Triangle conscientiously, your body can handle the toxins, for a short time. But it's a fine line between "once in a while" and every day, a line that can creep up on you. You don't have to be fanatical, but you have to be vigilant. *You* are the only person who can guard your precious well-being.

The danger of relapses is they can be self-perpetuating. The most common pattern is the following: You start eating foods that cause blood sugar imbalance and don't supply wholesome nourishment. Your energy level drops, and you stop exercising regularly. You gain weight, and old symptoms return. You feel ashamed and stop loving yourself.

There are many other reasons why people turn away from a

holistic lifestyle. Unfortunate events or negative influences can undermine their mental/spiritual foundations, leading to neglect of the other sides of their Triangles. Illness or injury can cause people to lose faith in their innate healing power, and they stop making self-health efforts.

Life is a constant pull between dark and light, negative and positive. No one's perfect, and it's easy to fall into a downward slide. If you find this happening, it's time for drastic action. It's time to commit to three months of self-renewal and go on the Holistic Self-Health Program again.

The program is not meant to be a once-in-a-lifetime experience; it's meant to be a lifelong tool. Use it when you feel addiction creeping up on you; when you feel depressed, stressed, or fatigued; when you have persistent health problems; or whenever you need rejuvenation.

A LIFELONG COMMITMENT

In a way, loving yourself to health is like a happy marriage. You start off with the Self-Health Program, which, like a wedding, is a rite of passage. It takes a lot of preparation and effort, but you remember it for the rest of your life. After the ceremony you're full of hope and optimism. But as time passes, you learn it requires a lot of love, caring, attention, compromise, and effort to keep it going.

As the years go by, you have your ups and downs and plateaus. But if the commitment and faith and unconditional love are there, the holistic lifestyle will see you through.

No one is immune to the whims of fate, and no one lives forever. But you do have a great deal of control over the *quality* of your life. By nourishing each side of your Triangle, you can give yourself the ultimate gift: a positive, high-quality life.

CHECKLIST FOR YOUR HEALTHY FUTURE

❏ Retake the Self-Health Evaluations. Write down areas of weakness and an action plan for more nourishment. Continue using the evaluations as a learning tool periodically.

❏ Introduce friends and family to holistic health ideas. Help them make positive changes if they are ready.

❏ Do volunteer work on a regular basis.

❏ Undertake necessary lifestyle changes involving your relationships, your home, and your career. Pace yourself carefully; don't take on too many stressful changes at once.

❏ Continue to nourish your mental/spiritual side by delving more deeply into areas of interest.

❏ Continue to nourish your chemical side by avoiding toxins, enjoying plenty of wholesome foods, drinking water, and taking supplements. Continue raw-juice fasting on a regular basis.

❏ Make a holistic exercise routine a permanent part of your daily life.

❏ Continue to do the Bathing Ritual, and practice deep breathing and relaxation techniques. Replenish your Triangle with sufficient sleep.

❏ Have secondary forms of physical nourishment, such as chiropractic care and massage, on a regular basis.

❏ Be totally honest with yourself. Don't let rationalizations cause you to abandon healthy habits.

❏ If you find yourself in a downward cycle, embark on the Three-Month Holistic Self-Health Program again.

❏ Make a lifelong commitment to nourish your Triangle and give yourself plenty of love.

PART THREE

SELF-HEALTH
RESOURCES

CHAPTER 10

Self-Health Resources: The Mental/Spiritual Side

GUIDELINES FOR MEDITATION

1. Meditate in a quiet place where you won't be disturbed. Sit cross-legged on the floor if you're comfortable in this position, or sit upright in a chair. (You may want to do the Total Body Relaxation on page 218 or some stretching exercises to relax your body before meditating.)

2. Close your eyes. Establish a deep breathing pattern: Breathe slowly, through your nose if possible, into the abdomen, ribs, and chest. Exhale slowly and completely.

3. You can either focus on your breath or concentrate on a focal word. "Om" is an ancient and universal mantra. You may prefer "one," "peace," or "love"; a brief phrase such as "let go" or "good health"; or the Sanskrit mantra *om shanti* or *ham sah*. Repeat your mantra silently in sync with your

breathing as you inhale and exhale. Try to keep your thoughts only on the focus word and your breath.

4. When your mind wanders, quietly bring your thoughts back to your breath and your focus word. It will become easier to remain focused with practice. Try to practice once a day for ten to twenty minutes. You may want to set a timer when you start, so you aren't tempted to check the clock.

5. Allow yourself a few minutes after meditation to sit quietly and breathe; then rise slowly and stretch before resuming your activities.

NOTE: Meditation can cause anxiety initially since it can be disturbing to be left alone with your mind. Observe the anxiety, and carry on without judging or allowing fear to take control.

Meditation is a way to learn to observe your mind more objectively, without letting emotions take the upper hand. In a sense, it's paradoxical since meditation gives you more control over your mind and also teaches you to let go.

GUIDED HEALING VISUALIZATIONS

Basic Healing Session

Lie down on the floor, and begin slow, deep breathing. Relax each part of your body, starting with your feet, up through your calves, your buttocks, your abdomen. Relax your spine along the floor, all the way up through the back of your neck. Let your body sink into the floor, and relax.

Now focus on the part of your body where there is pain or illness. Look inside, and see what the malady is trying to tell you. What are you doing or not doing that may be causing the imbalance in your body? What organ or system has been neglected or abused and is now manifesting itself in a symptom? How can you give yourself more nourishment in that area?

Tell the part of your body that is in pain or dysfunction it is part of the whole and you love it. Even if you can get no message about what action to take to heal yourself, send your uncondi-tional love to the area that is symptomatic.

Tell the symptom that you are going to take action to heal it. Imagine yourself taking this action. Inhale the love and healing power of the Universe. Send it to the part of your body that is in pain. You can visualize this healing power as a warm white light. Feel it melt and dissolve the discomfort. Enjoy the soothing, healing nourishment you take in with every inhalation.

Picture yourself in glowing good health. Think of yourself get-ting up, going through your day, and the next, in superb condi-tion. Stay with these images until they are firmly established in your mind.

Before rising from this healing session, stretch your arms over-head, lengthening your body along the floor. Then slowly move to one side, and get up gently.

Immunity Visualization

Lie down, and begin with deep breathing and the body relaxa-tion, as in the previous visualization.

Picture your white blood cells, the janitors inside your body, which clean up toxins. Imagine these cells gobbling up toxins and harmful bacteria. See the white blood cells engulf and digest the debris, consuming it and rendering it harmless.

Visualize your bloodstream as being clean and clear, flowing freely, without obstruction or pollution. The white blood cells have swept away disease-causing poisons, and your system is strong and healthy.

Visualization to Alleviate Back Pain

(Before you do this visualization for the first time, it is helpful to look at the drawing of a spine on page 92 so you can picture the vertebrae in an aligned state.)

Begin by lying down and breathing deeply into your abdomen. The cleansing breath flows up your spine, nourishing and length-ening it. As you inhale, the breath brings energy up your spine. As you exhale, the vertebrae relax and elongate, relieving pressure on the nerves. Take time to focus on each area of your spine. Wherever there is tightness and constriction, send this area your breath until it releases the tension.

When your spine feels comfortable, focus on the muscles of your back, and pinpoint the painful area. Visualize these muscles as knotted, frayed rope. Slowly concentrate on unknotting the rope. Smooth and stretch it out. Then do the same to the parallel muscles on the other side of your spine. Feel the muscles unknot until they are long and smooth and your back is free.

CHAPTER 11

Self-Health Resources: The Chemical Side

HEALTHFUL MEAL PLAN GUIDELINES

1. Breakfast: When you first wake up, have a glass of water, warm water and lemon, or herbal tea. After your bath, enjoy one or two of the following:

   Fresh fruit
   Whole grain cereal with soy milk
   Whole grain pancake
   Whole grain toast with nut or fruit butter

2. Midmorning snack: A midmorning snack can help you avoid a slump and the urge for caffeine. Try one of these choices:

   Fruit

A small portion of nuts or seeds
A protein drink made with a natural supplement powder
Raw vegetable or fruit juice

3. Lunch: Lunch should be your biggest meal of the day since this is when your body is producing more enzymes and you have the most activity ahead. Some options:

Green salad
Raw or steamed vegetables
Cooked legumes and grains
Seeds and nuts
Fish

4. Midafternoon snack: Give yourself a treat:

Fruit, seed, and nut mix
Almond milk or soy beverage
Fresh fruit
Fruit-sweetened whole grain baked goods

5. Dinner: This meal is interchangeable with lunch, although it's best to eat smaller portions than earlier in the day. Also, it's recommended to eat dinner as early as possible:

Green salad
Raw or steamed vegetables
Cooked legumes and grains
Seeds and nuts
Fish

6. Evening snack: A light bite an hour or two after dinner:

Fruit
Crudité with healthy dip
Raw fruit or vegetable juice from your juicer

RAW-JUICE FASTING

To understand why raw-juice fasting is so effective, it helps to realize that the gastrointestinal (GI) tract, from the mouth to the anus, is actually one big juice extractor. The purpose and function of the GI tract are to break down complex foods into simple ones that can be assimilated.

Raw-juice fasting allows us to rest the often overworked GI tract. The juicer does much of the work the gastrointestinal tract normally does; it separates the liquid from the fiber and the nutrients from the pulp.

While juice fasting has dramatic effects, it is not a miracle cure or a quick fix. The primary step toward nourishing the chemical side of your Triangle is to decrease or eliminate toxic input and increase healthy input. After you have made some progress in reducing toxic input, you can consider a one-day juice fast.

Not only is raw-juice fasting a detoxification tool, but raw juices are a wonderful addition to your daily diet. The juices provide the essential nutrients of fruits and vegetables in a concentrated form that is easily absorbed.

Raw juices provide high levels of antioxidants, which can provide protection against cancer, heart disease, and the aging process. Antioxidants protect against free radicals (molecules containing a highly reactive unpaired electron) and pro-oxidants (molecules that promote oxidative damage). While these molecules are naturally produced in our bodies, environmental factors contribute to their proliferation. Free radicals can bind to and destroy other cellular components, and have been linked to the development of chronic degenerative diseases.

To counteract these degenerative disease-promoting agents, we need nutritional support. Our cells can protect us against free radical and oxidative damage with the help of antioxidants and enzymes such as carotenes, flavonoids, vitamins C and E, and sulfur-containing compounds.

Raw juice is far superior to canned, bottled, or frozen juice because it contains more of these vitamins and enzymes. Packaged juices are pasteurized, a process that causes the loss of many vitamins and minerals as well as the life force itself.

Raw juicers are an essential health appliance, since they separate the liquid from the pulp, while blenders merely liquefy everything. It pays to invest in a high-quality, high-performance juicer that will last.

If you purchase your juicer at a health food store, you can also get a book on juicing, with recipes and recommendations on which fruits and vegetables are helpful for specific conditions. Juicing can be used as targeted therapy as well as an overall preventive.

It also pays to buy organic produce to use for your raw-juice fasting. The Environmental Protection Agency has identified sixty-four pesticides as potential cancer-causing compounds, and you don't want to risk ingesting these chemicals in your raw juice, particularly when fasting. If you cannot obtain organic produce, clean your produce with a biodegradable rinse, available in health food stores. Even organic produce should be washed carefully before juicing, then cut into small pieces.

Follow the directions that come with your juicer, or obtain a guide to juicing for specific directions for all produce. Here are some of the fruits, vegetables, and combinations you can use:

- Apples, alone or with apricots, berries, grapes, lemons, pears, oranges, kiwis, papayas, peaches
- Bananas, alone or with cantaloupes, mangoes, oranges, papayas
- Berries, alone or with oranges, pears, apples
- Cherries, alone or with pears, peaches, pineapples
- Grapefruit, alone or with oranges, papayas, pineapples
- Grapes, alone or with lemons and apples
- Lemons and limes, in combination with sweet fruits
- Mangoes and papayas, alone or with oranges, pineapples, bananas
- Oranges, alone or with papayas, peaches, bananas
- Pineapples, mixed with berries or oranges
- Plums and prunes
- Watermelon, alone or with other melons

- Asparagus and green beans, added to carrots and apples
- Beets, with carrots, spinach, sweet potatoes, parsley, celery
- Broccoli, with carrots, celery, parsley
- Cabbage family vegetables (cabbage, broccoli, cauliflower, brussels sprouts, kale, collard, radishes, turnips), mixed with carrots, celery, parsley

- Carrots, alone or in combination with virtually all other vegetables
- Celery, alone or in combination with cucumbers, parsley, kale, spinach, fennel, lettuce
- Dandelion root, mixed with fennel
- Garlic and ginger, added to vegetable combinations
- Lettuce, added to carrots and celery
- Onions, added to carrots and parsley
- Parsley, added to carrots, cucumbers, other vegetables
- Peppers, with tomatoes
- Potatoes, added to carrots and other vegetable juices
- Spinach, with tomatoes, beets, carrots, parsley, cucumbers
- Tomatoes, alone or with cucumbers, parsley, watercress, spinach, peppers

DETOXIFICATION RECIPES

The following recipes are especially created to promote detoxification during the Self-Health Program. Drink the raw juices slowly, and stop when you are satisfied. Depending on your size, an adequate serving may be from six to twelve ounces.

Some of these concoctions don't taste delicious, but that doesn't mean you shouldn't drink them. As part of the program, you need to satisfy all the organs of your body, not just your taste buds. Instead of fixating on the flavor, concentrate on how the juices purify and strengthen your body. But if you simply can't bear the taste of a vegetable juice, add some apple or pineapple. All fruits and vegetables should be washed carefully and scrubbed, but do not peel unless specified.

Love Your Lungs Juice

6 carrots (with tops cut off)
Large handful of spinach
4 sprigs watercress
Large handful of parsley
¼ peeled potato

Love Your Liver Juice

3 apples* (chopped into quarters or wedges with seeds removed)
2 carrots (with tops removed)
1 beet
1 cucumber (waxed cucumbers only should be peeled)
People undergoing sugar withdrawal should use green apples.

Fresh Skin Tonic

2 apples (chopped into wedges with seeds removed)
1 cucumber (waxed cucumbers only should be peeled)
2 slices pineapple* (with skin removed)
½ lemon* (peeled)
People with citrus allergies or skin problems should substitute kale or parsley for lemon and pineapple.

Immune Booster Drink

4 carrots (with tops removed)
3 stalks celery (bottoms removed)
Handful of lettuce (any type except iceberg)
Small piece gingerroot (optional)

Vascular Rejuvenator

4 carrots (tops removed)
3 stalks celery (bottoms removed)
Handful of kale
Handful of spinach
Handful of alfalfa sprouts
Dash of cayenne pepper

Detoxification Special

3 carrots (tops removed)
2 beets
2 stalks celery (bottoms removed)
½ cabbage
½ white potato
¼ onion (peeled)
½ clove garlic (peeled)
Sprinkle of ginger

When you're in the mood for a warm beverage, try this vegetable broth, which is high in minerals and serves as an alkalizer:

Vegetable Broth

3 potatoes, chopped
3 carrots (tops removed)
3 stalks celery (bottoms removed)
1 beet
1 turnip
2 cloves garlic, chopped
½ onion, peeled & chopped
Seasoning to taste

Add all ingredients to two quarts of water. Bring to boil, lower heat, and simmer for ½ hour. Strain out vegetables, and let broth cool to warm temperature.

NOTE: To turn this into a *Fiber Broth* that relieves constipation, add 2 tablespoons flaxseed or bran. Refrigerate the broth overnight; then heat and drink it in the morning.

FOOD SENSITIVITIES

Food allergies and food intolerance can cause many different immunological and physiological responses and symptoms. These can include:

—Headache, migraine, fatigue, faintness, depression, anxiety, hyperactivity in children, blurred vision, dizziness, difficulty concentrating
—Sinusitis, rhinitis, earache, ear infection
—Cramps, vomiting, nausea, stomach ulcers, duodenal ulcers, diarrhea, irritable bowel syndrome, constipation, wind, bloating
—Water retention, vaginal discharge, frequent urination
—Joint pain, rheumatoid arthritis, muscle aches, weakness
—Rapid pulse
—Hives, eczema, swelling

While these symptoms *may* be caused by food sensitivities, they may also have other bases. It takes detective work to determine if a food is the allergen, and if so, which substance.

Many of the Top Ten Toxins are common culprits in food sensitivities. These include milk and other dairy products, chocolate, coffee, beef, and food additives. If you eliminate these toxins, you may automatically overcome food reactions.

However, a food sensitivity can also result from an inappropriate immunological response to a normally healthy substance. Healthy foods that cause reactions in some people include wheat, citrus fruits, corn, nuts, potatoes, soybeans, tomatoes, and spices.

There are several ways to track down food allergies:

Elimination diets: This involves avoiding suspected allergens for two weeks. Then you reintroduce the suspects one at a time, waiting several days to see if any symptoms arise. The problem with this method is it requires a great deal of patience and can be inexact and confusing.

The pulse test: This self-test is sometimes, but not always, effective for detecting food sensitivities. Find a place under your wrist where you can feel your pulse. Sit quietly, and relax for a minute. Count your pulse for sixty seconds to determine your resting pulse. Eat just one of the foods you suspect is an allergen, without eating anything else. Test your pulse thirty minutes later, then sixty minutes later, also while resting. If your pulse is twenty or more beats higher than the first resting pulse, this food may be an allergen. Stop eating the food for two weeks, and see if your symptoms are alleviated.

Direct blood test: The blood test for allergies involves an initial drawing of blood in a doctor's office. This is then sent to a laboratory for comprehensive allergy testing. This method is highly effective, although not foolproof.

The skin prick test: Also done in a doctor's office, this tests how the skin reacts to a range of common allergens. A prick or scratch is made in the skin, and a minute amount of an allergen extract is allowed to enter it. This can result in a reaction known as the weal-and-flare response. Skin prick tests are efficient for identifying inhaled allergies, but often fail to detect food allergies.

Once the allergen is identified, there are several treatment options. The treatments to avoid are allergy shots, which are based on the vaccination theory and consist of injections of small doses of the allergen. While this may give you temporary relief, it can lead to the development of an allergy to another substance or a worsened reaction when you discontinue the shots. Allergy shots insult the body's innate wisdom and, like most quick fixes, can backfire.

A safer option is simply to stop consuming the food to which you are allergic. In the case of many foods, after the initial withdrawal period you can easily do without it for the rest of your life.

If, however, the allergen is a healthy food, such as wheat, you can reintroduce it after you have been through the Self-Health

Program. Then watch yourself carefully to see if reactions occur. Some people overcome allergies to inherently healthy substances by ridding their bodies of accumulated toxins and building up their immune systems. Detoxification can also result in reduction or disappearance of allergies to inhalants such as pollen.

SUPPLEMENTS

The Food and Drug Administration has mandated that manufacturers cannot advertise the superiority of vitamins from natural food sources over synthetic vitamins. However, saying there is no difference between these two types is like saying there's no difference between coal and diamonds. They both derive from carbon, but one form is obviously superior.

Synthetic vitamins are artificially produced in laboratories. Natural vitamins are derived from living food sources. Which do you think would contain more easily assimilable nutrients?

The most important supplement for all of us is a high-quality multivitamin/mineral. When you're choosing your multisupplement, look for a natural product with a comprehensive range of vitamins and minerals. Unless this is a time-released product, it's recommended to take it several times a day, so there is a constant flow of nutrients into your system.

There are also special supplements that are useful to take on a periodic basis in addition to vitamins and minerals. These include kelp, brewer's yeast, spirulina, chlorella, acidophilus, rutin, lysine, and royal bee's jelly.

As well as provide a backbone of basic strength and strong immunity, supplements can be used for specific therapeutic purposes. The chart at the end of this chapter will give you more information about the specific properties of different vitamins and minerals.

The Required Daily Allowance (RDA) provides, in many cases, a minimal amount of supplementation. If you want to give the chemical side of your Holistic Triangle maximum nourishment, you can double the amount of many vitamins and minerals to provide the Optimum Daily Allowance (ODA).

VITAMINS

Vitamin	Function	Natural/Organic Source	Deficiency Condition	Excess Condition	Depleted by	Caution	RDA (ODA approx. twice RDA)
A carotenoids	Enhances immunity, antioxidant; aids in cancer prevention; needed for skin repair and maintenance plus bone and tooth formation; required for protein synthesis.	Alfalfa, apricots, asparagus, beets, broccoli, cantaloupes, carrots, fish liver oil, liver, garlic, kale, papayas, parsley, peaches, red peppers, sweet potatoes, spinach, yellow squash, turnip greens	Dry skin, itchy eyes, sensitivity to light, night blindness, influenza, and infections	Nausea, headaches, aching bones, hair loss, and irritability	Exposure to strong light, pollution, certain medications, drugs	Individuals with liver disease, diabetes, and hypothyroidism should consult a physician before taking large doses	5,000 IU 50,000 or more can be toxic
B₁ thiamine	Beneficial to circulation, blood formation, learning capacity, muscle tone for heart, intestines, and stomach muscles; aid to hydrochloric acid production and carbohydrate metabolism	Dried beans, brown rice, liver, peanuts, peas, rice bran, soybeans, wheat germ, brussels sprouts, oatmeal, plums, prunes, raisins, egg yolks, fish	Forgetfulness, fatigue, beriberi, insomnia, digestive problems, muscle tenderness, possible weight loss	Rapid or irregular heartbeat, restlessness, trembling, low blood pressure, cold sores, edema	Alcohol, tobacco, drugs, sugar, baking soda, overcooking food sources of B₁; also antibiotics and oral contraceptives	A diet high in carbohydrates increases the demand for thiamine	1.5 mg
B₂ riboflavin	Required for formation of red blood cells, cell respiration, growth, and metabolism of carbohydrates, fats, and proteins; facilitates oxygen use in skin, hair, and nails; vitamin A and B₆ maintain mucous membranes in digestive tract	Beans, cheese, eggs, fish, poultry, spinach, yogurt; also asparagus, avocados, broccoli, brussels sprouts, nuts	Eye fatigue, cracks and sores in the mouth, dandruff, carpal tunnel syndrome, purple tongue	Itching, tingling in arms and legs	Light, cooking, antibiotics, alcohol, drugs	Oral contraceptives and strenuous exercise increase the demand for riboflavin	1.8 mg
B₃ niacin, niacinamide, nicotinic acid	Supports nervous system, circulation, healthy skin; lowers cholesterol; also used to treat mental illnesses; helps prevent plaque formation in arteries	Beef, fish, broccoli, carrots, potatoes, tomatoes, corn flour, whole wheat, cheese, eggs; also tuna, halibut, and swordfish	Dermatitis, depression, diarrhea, pellagra, loss of appetite	Results in niacin flush; antidote: two large glasses of water	Emotional stress, drugs, cooking	High amounts contraindicated for pregnancy, diabetes, gout, liver disease, ulcers, glaucoma, hypertension	20 mg

Vitamin	Function	Natural/Organic Source	Deficiency Condition	Excess Condition	Depleted by	Caution	RDA (ODA approx. twice RDA)
B₅ pantothenic acid	Required by all cells of body, especially organs; aids in production of adrenal hormones and antibodies; necessary for steroid and cortisone production in the adrenal gland	Beans, beef, eggs, saltwater fish, mother's milk, whole wheat, fresh vegetables, yeast, wheat germ, peanuts	Depression, fatigue, poor coordination, heart trouble, headache, cramps	Not yet determined	Drugs and alcohol, stress	No known side effects	2 mg
B₆ pyridoxine	Affects physical and mental functions of body; helps maintain balance of sodium and potassium in body; required for normal brain function, nervous system, RNA and DNA synthesis; reduces symptoms of premenstrual syndrome; natural diuretic	Carrots, spinach, peas, eggs, fish, brewers' yeast, sunflower seeds, walnuts, wheat germ Less rich sources of pyridoxine; avocados, bananas, beans, blackstrap molasses, cabbage, cantaloupe, pears	Anemia, diarrhea, skin and mouth disorders, convulsions, blindness, loss of appetite	Not yet determined	Oral contraceptives, cooking and soaking food, drugs	Antidepressants, estrogen, and oral contraceptives deplete the body of pyridoxine	2 mg
B₁₂ cyanocobalamin	Required to prevent anemia, for digestion, absorption, protein synthesis, carbohydrate and fat metabolism; prevents nerve damage; maintains fertility; promotes normal growth	Mostly found in animal sources; lamb, beef, crabs, clams, herring, liver, mackerel, seafood; also eggs, almonds, cheese, tofu, most grains	Malabsorption, which is common in the elderly; blood disorders, hardening of the arteries, fatigue, pernicious anemia, memory loss, hallucinations, abnormal gait	High hemoglobin count	Drugs, stress, history of ulcers, gastritis	Vegetarians need to supplement their diet with B₁₂ since it is found mostly in animal products	3 mcg
Biotin also known as vitamin H for hair growth	Aids in cell growth, healthy hair, skin, sweat glands, nerve tissue, bone marrow; required for metabolism of carbohydrates, fats, and protein	Most foods, especially peanuts, beans, egg yolks, oyster, saltwater fish, poultry, soybeans	Deficiency is rare because biotin is produced naturally in intestines; absorption problems would cause fatigue and/or depression	Not yet determined	Antibiotics, sulfa drugs, which destroy intestinal flora that normally produce biotin	Raw egg whites contain a protein called ovadin that combines with biotin and depletes the body of this vitamin	Not yet established

Vitamin	Function	Natural/Organic Source	Deficiency Condition	Excess Condition	Depleted by	Caution	RDA (ODA approx. twice RDA)
Choline	Required for nerve transmission, gallbladder regulation, liver function; reduces buildup of excess fat in liver	Egg yolks, legumes, liver, meat, whole grains	Brain function and memory impairment; fatty acid buildup in the liver, cirrhosis of liver	Not yet determined	Drugs and alcohol, stress	Not established	Not established
Folic acid	Formation of red blood cells, DNA synthesis; cell division and reproduction of cells; regulates embryonic and fetal development of nerve cells	Barley, beans, lentils, navy beans, beef, bran, brewers' yeast, brown rice, cheese, chicken, dates, green leafy vegetables, split peas, root vegetables; salmon, tuna, wheat germ, whole grains	Abnormally red tongue, low white blood cell count; depression, brain damage, nervousness, anemia	Not yet determined	Drugs, oral contraceptives, stress	Avoid large dosages if you have experienced convulsions or have a hormone-related cancer	1–2 mg
Inositol	Hair growth, lecithin formation, fat and cholesterol metabolism; aids in prevention of hardening of arteries	Fruits, vegetables, whole grains, yeast	Not yet determined	Not yet determined	Large amounts of caffeine	Not established	Not established
PABA (para-aminobenzoic acid)	Protects against sunburn and skin cancer; is an antioxidant; assists in formation of red blood cells	Liver, yeast, brown rice, molasses, whole grains	Loss of hair color (graying of hair may be restored if caused by nutritional deficiency or stress), fatigue, depression, constipation, headaches	Suspected in topical skin disorders	Sulfa drugs	Not established	Not established
C ascorbic acid, mineral polyascorbate, (nonacidic buffered)	Beneficial as antioxidant especially when combined with vitamin E; promotes tissue growth, repair; enhances immunity; prevents bruising; heals wounds. Polyascorbate is more efficient form of C.	Citrus fruits, berries, green vegetables, asparagus, avocados, beet greens, broccoli, cantaloupe, mangoes, onions, papayas, parsley, green peas, sweet peppers, spinach, rose hips, tomatoes, turnip greens	Easy bruising; lowered resistance to infection, colds, and flu; tooth decay; gum disease; thyroid insufficiency; premature aging; anemia; deterioration of collagen	Diarrhea; lower dosage gradually until bowel can tolerate vitamin C level	Aspirin, alcohol, analgesics, oral contraceptives, steroids, antidepressants	Pregnant women should not use more than 5,000 mg per day	60 mg ODA 1–3g

Vitamin	Function	Natural/Organic Source	Deficiency Condition	Excess Condition	Depleted by	Caution	RDA (ODA approx. twice RDA)
D calciferol, ergosterol, viosterol Sunshine vitamin	Assimilates calcium, phosphorus, and other minerals within digestive tract; important for growth and development of bones and teeth in children	Fish-liver oils, fatty saltwater fish, eggs, sprouted seeds, mushrooms, sunflower seeds, sweet potatoes, vegetable oils; also sunlight when absorbed in the skin	Rickets, tooth decay, pyorrhea, osteomalacia, osteoporosis, poor bone and growth in children, premature aging	Excessive doses can can be toxic over a period of years; 65,000 IU or more synthetic D3 not recommended	Antacids, mineral oil, cortisone, and some cholesterol-lowering drugs	Vitamin D should not be taken without calcium; synthetic D may cause abnormal calcium deposits	5-10 mcg Sunshine is best source (not between 11:00 A.M.–1:00 P.M.; avoid burning)
E tocopherol	Effective antioxidant, preventing cancer and cardiovascular disease; promotes healing of wounds, normal blood clotting; aids in prevention of leg cramps and cataracts; required for healthy reproductive organs	Cold pressed vegetable oils, nuts, seeds, sprouted seeds, whole wheat, fresh wheat germ, green leafy vegetables, legumes, eggs, brown rice, cornmeal, oatmeal, sweet potatoes; Alpha is best (fat-soluble)	Heart disease, sexual impotency, reproductive disorders, miscarriages, muscular disorders	Not yet determined	Not yet determined	Diabetics and those suffering from rheumatic heart disease, an overactive thyroid, or hypertension should use small dosages	8-10 IU ODA 400 IU
F	Lowers blood cholesterol; required for healthy skin and mucous membranes; helps body utilize calcium and phosphorus	Cold pressed vegetable oils; most abundant in soybean, sunflower, safflower, and flaxseed oils	Skin disorders—eczema, dandruff—hair loss, prostate, menstrual, and kidney disorder	Not yet determined	Stress	No known problems; must have essential fatty acids	Not established
K	Necessary for normal blood clotting; converts glucose to glycogen, which affects liver	Kelp, alfalfa, broccoli, soybean oil, egg yolks; also brussels sprouts, blackstrap molasses	Hemorrhages, nosebleeds; premature aging	Flushing, sweating	Antibiotics hinder absorption; interferes with anticoagulants	Large doses can can be toxic to newborn; heart disease	Not established
Bioflavonoids citrin, hesperidin, quercitin, rutin	Not a true vitamin; assists in the absorption of vitamin C; strengthens capillary walls; acts as anticoagulant; promotes circulation; reduces cholesterol; helps treatment of cataracts	Fresh fruits, particularly pulp: grapes, apricots, strawberries, black currants; cherries; also prunes, buckwheat	Hemorrhoids, varicose veins, bleeding gums, eczema, psoriasis, hemorrhages, radiation sickness, coronary thrombosis, atherosclerosis	Diarrhea	Cooking	No known documentation	Not established

MINERALS

Mineral	Function	Natural/Organic Source	Deficiency Condition	Excess Condition	Depleted by	Caution	RDA (ODA approx. twice RDA)
Boron	Works with calcium to develop and maintain healthy bones	Green leafy vegetables, fruits, nuts, and grains	Few people deficient in boron	Not yet determined	Not yet determined	3 mg per day maximum	Not yet determined
Calcium	Required for development and maintenance of bones and teeth; beneficial to heart and nervous system; prevents cramps; aids in normal blood clotting	Dairy products, dark leafy vegetables, sesame seeds, sardines, seafood, almonds, dandelion greens, figs, filberts, tofu, turnip greens, organic nonpasteurized goat's milk, fortified nut milk	Osteomalacia, osteoporosis, depression, brittle cracked nails, muscle cramps and spasms, tooth decay, eczema, hypertension, sore joints	Hinders absorption of zinc	Antacid tablets taken as a source of calcium which interferes with absorption; heavy exercise, sugar, high-protein and fat diets	Do not take supplements if suffering from kidney disease or kidney stones	800–1,200 mg
Chlorine	Aids liver in detoxifying body; helps produce hydrochloric acid in stomach, required for protein and mineral assimilation	Kelp, seaweed, kale, saltwater fish, avocado, chard, tomatoes, cabbage, endive, celery, cucumber, asparagus, oats	Poor digestion; imbalance of fluid levels in the body	Not documented	Stress	Highly toxic in large doses; avoid heavily chlorinated pools	500 mg
Chromium	Removes glucose from blood to produce energy; maintains blood sugar levels; synthesizes heart protein	brewers' yeast, naturally mineralized water, corn and corn oil, whole grains, nonalcoholic beer	Diabetes, hypoglycemia, atherosclerosis, heart disease	Not yet determined	Refined white sugar	Not determined	Not established ODA 100 mcg
Cobalt	Required for synthesis of vitamin B12; also hemoglobin formation	Green leafy vegetables	Pernicious anemia	Not documented	Stress		Not established
Copper	Production of RNA facilitates healing; required for the absorption of iron; maintains natural color of hair and skin; benefits nervous system	Almonds, avocados, barley, beans, green leafy vegetables, mushrooms, pecans, soybeans	Anemia, loss of hair and hair color, heart damage	Depletes vitamin C and zinc	Excess amounts of zinc and vitamin C	Not determined	2–3 mg

Mineral	Function	Natural/Organic Source	Deficiency Condition	Excess Condition	Depleted by	Caution	RDA (ODA approx. twice RDA)
Fluorine	Utilized in development of healthy bones and teeth; acts as antiseptic; prevents infections	Sunflower seeds, cheese, garlic, beet tops, green vegetables, almonds	Not known	Can be toxic, stains teeth	Not known		Not established
Iodine	Highly beneficial to thyroid gland, physical and mental development	Kelp, seaweed, dulse, Swiss chard, saltwater fish, garlic, pears, pineapple, artichokes, egg yolks	Enlarged thyroid, fatigue, lethargy, loss of interest in sex, possible mental retardation and breast cancer	Metallic taste and sores in mouth	Raw and excessive amounts of cabbage, cauliflower, kale, which interfere with absorption	Limit iodine in the diet if a hypothyroid condition exists	0.15 mg
Iron	Most important is production of hemoglobin, which carries oxygen from lungs to red blood cells; beneficial to immune system and normal growth patterns	Eggs, fish, liver, blackstrap molasses, prunes, raisins, brewers' yeast, spinach, turnip greens, sesame seeds, beets and beet tops, sunflower seeds	Anemia, hair loss, brittle nails, fatigue, dizziness, lightheadedness, shortness of breath on exertion, headaches	Hemochromatosis, cirrhosis, diabetes, possible heart disorders; link to cancer	Coffee and tea interfere with absorption; excessive perspiration	Zinc and vitamin E inhibit absorption; excess amounts also produce free radicals	Males 10 mg Females 18 mg
Lithium	Metabolizes sodium beneficial to nervous system, particularly involuntary nerves	Kelp, seawater	Nervous and mental disorders	Not known	Stress	Used for bipolar mental disorders, must be monitored	Not established
Magnesium	Important in enzyme activity; required for healthy muscles and bones; acts as tranquilizer	Nuts, green leafy vegetables, fish, seafood, soybeans, kale, endive, figs, apples, blackstrap molasses, brown rice	Kidney damage, muscle cramps, nervousness, depression, twitching	Not known	Alcohol, caffeine, diarrhea, diuretics	Competes with calcium for absorption; use separately Balance 1:1 ratio	350–400 mg
Manganese	Protein and fat metabolism; fat digestion; benefits nervous and immune system; coordinates action and communication between brain, nerves, and muscles; aids in production of breast milk	Avocados, nuts, green leafy vegetables, spinach, beets, seaweed, kelp, apricots	Impeded growth, sterility, poor equilibrium, asthma, tinnitus	Not known	Stress	No known side effects	Not established

Mineral	Function	Natural/Organic Source	Deficiency Condition	Excess Condition	Depleted by	Caution	RDA (ODA approx. twice RDA)
Molybdenum	Nitrogen and carbohydrate metabolism	Whole grains, brown rice, millet, buckwheat, brewers' yeast, dark green leafy vegetables	Mouth and gum disease, gout, sexual disorders in male	Interferes with copper metabolism	Stress	Only small amounts needed	Not established
Phosphorus	Bone and teeth development healthy nervous system and mental activity; heart contraction	Most foods contain some phosphorus: whole grains, seeds, nuts, legumes, egg yolks, apricots, avocados	Poor nerve and brain function, poor sexual performance, lack of strength, lack of energy	Interferes with calcium absorption			Adults 800–1,200 mg Children 1,000–1,400 mg
Potassium	Required for proper muscle contraction, for maintaining proper acid-alkaline balance; maintains blood pressure and prevents stroke	Bananas, potatoes and potato peels, apricots, blackstrap molasses, brewers' yeast	Severe deficiency will allow salt to accumulate in the body; damage to heart; hypertension; disorders of nervous system		Stress, diuretics, diarrhea	Muscle weakness from high intake	1,875–5,625 mg
Selenium	Important antioxidant; protects immune system; works with vitamin E to produce antibodies; helps restore liver after damage	Brewers' yeast, Brazil nuts, broccoli, mushrooms, most vegetables depending on soil content they are grown in	Muscle deterioration, liver damage, premature aging, intestinal and colon cancer	Not known	Stress	Only small amounts needed	Not established
Silicon (silica)	Necessary for healthy hair, skin, and nails; forms collagen, which connects bones	Alfalfa, flaxseed, oats, apples, grapes, beets, onions	Brittle nails, hair loss, poor bone growth, Alzheimer's disease	Not established	Stress	Only small amounts needed	Not established
Sodium	Maintains proper body fluids, electrolyte balance; required for hydrochloric acid production in stomach	Kelp, seaweed, sea salt, celery, asparagus	Dehydration, heart palpitations, confusion, low blood sugar	High blood pressure, water retention, stomach ulcers and cancer, heart disease	Excessive perspiration, diarrhea	Excessive sodium is common in junk foods, lunch meats, antacids	200–600 mg

Mineral	Function	Natural/Organic Source	Deficiency Condition	Excess Condition	Depleted by	Caution	RDA (ODA approx. twice RDA)
Sulfur	Important for healthy hair, skin, and nails; disinfects blood; stimulates bile secretion; slows down aging process, synthesizes collagen, which keeps skin moist	Radish, turnips, onions, kale, cabbage, eggs, garlic, brussels sprouts	Poor skin tone, eczema, brittle nails, dull hair	Flatulence	Moisture and heat	Avoid hard-boiled eggs	Not established
Zinc	Has great importance to healthy prostate and reproductive organs; beneficial to immune system and formation of RNA and DNA; aids in elimination of toxic carbon dioxide	Fish, seafood, green leafy vegetables, pumpkin and sunflower seeds, brewers' yeast, egg yolks, lima beans	Birth defects, poor growth development, enlarged prostate, loss of sexual function	Daily doses of 100 mg or more inhibit the immune system	Diarrhea, diabetes, kidney disease, cirrhosis of liver	See excess condition	15 mg

HERBS

Herbs can be used in many ways, including:

—Compresses: Cloths soaked in herb solutions are applied to areas that need healing.

—Essential oils: Oils are distilled from herbs and used externally or in the form of inhalants or teas.

—Extracts: These very effective forms for healing are usually taken orally.

—Ointments and salves: Generally used for bruises, sores, and inflammations, these are applied externally.

—Poultices: Moistened, hot herbs are spread on cloths and applied to areas of body to relieve pain and inflammation.

—Powders: Herbs are ground into powders, often used in capsule or tablet form for specific disorders.

—Tinctures: Powdered herbs are added to a solution of alcohol and water.

The seeds, stems, roots, bark, leaves, and flowers of hundreds of different plants are used as herbal remedies. Here is an introduction to a dozen helpful herbs and some of their benefits.

Herbs	Uses
Alfalfa	Helps detoxify the body and promote pituitary gland function. Helpful for arthritis, anemia, colon disorders, diabetes, and ulcers.
Capsicum (Cayenne)	Improves circulation and aids digestion. Good for kidneys, lungs, pancreas, heart, and stomach.
Catnip	Aids digestion, helps relieve stress, and can control fever. Good for colic, colds, flu, inflammation, and pain.
Chamomile	Aids digestion and stimulates appetite; used as a nerve tonic and sleep aid. Helps relieve blad-

	der problems, colds, fever, headaches, colitis, hemorrhoids, muscle cramps, and pain.
Comfrey root	A blood cleanser; good for stomach, kidneys, bowels, and lungs. Helps coughs, ulcers, swelling, cramps, pain, and burns. CAUTION: Should be used only under the supervision of a health professional.
Echinacea	Has antibiotic, antiviral, and anti-inflammatory properties. Helps the immune system and lymphatic system and is used for colds, flu, and infections.
Garlic	Detoxifies the body and protects from infection; strengthens blood vessels and can lower blood pressure.
Goldenseal	A natural antibiotic that detoxifies the body and strengthens the immune system. Benefits the heart, liver, spleen, pancreas, and colon. Useful for colds, flu, diabetes, hypoglycemia, and inflammation.
Lobelia	Acts as a cough suppressant; can reduce fever and cold symptoms. Good for sore throats, laryngitis, bronchitis, and colds.
Parsley	Benefits thyroid, lung, stomach, bladder, liver, and kidney function. Helps goiter, obesity, fluid retention, indigestion, gas, and menstrual disorders.
Pau d'arco	A natural antibacterial agent; has a healing and blood-cleansing effect. Good for infection, diabetes, ulcers, allergies, candidiasis, and immune dysfunction diseases.
Peppermint	As a digestive aid helps control diarrhea, spasms, and indigestion. Can also relieve sinus problems and headaches.

NATURAL ALTERNATIVES TO COMMON NONPRESCRIPTION DRUGS

Painkillers

If you frequently take aspirin, acetominophen, or ibuprofen to overcome pain, you need to work with your health care professional to ascertain the root cause of the pain. Then you can decide on a treatment plan to correct the problem and prevent it from recurring.

This treatment may include dietary changes, therapeutic exercise, chiropractic care, physical therapy, massage, relaxation techniques, biofeedback, or acupuncture. Giving up toxins alone may alleviate your recurrent pain, but you may also need expert assistance.

Cold and Sinus Medicines

If you often resort to drugstore cold and sinus remedies, try the following alternatives.

- Eliminate toxins, especially dairy products.
- Drink powdered, buffered vitamin C in juice and water throughout the day.
- Drink eight glasses of water a day.
- Drink peppermint and other herbal teas, with lemon and a little honey.
- Take garlic in capsule form and in food.
- Take herbal supplements of echinacea and goldenseal.

Laxatives

If you take pharmaceutical laxatives, you can adopt healthier ways to avoid constipation.

- Eliminate dairy products, meat, white flour, and sugar, which contain no fiber.
- Drink eight glasses of water a day.
- Eat more high-fiber foods: beans, peas, fresh vegetables, fresh fruit, whole grains, and such dried fruit as figs and prunes.
- Add bran or flaxseed to cereal, juices, or the Fiber Broth recipe on page 193.
- Exercise is another way to relieve constipation without the artificial stimulation of laxatives.

SUPPLEMENTS TO AID DETOXIFICATION

During the Self-Health Program it is recommended that you work with a holistic professional to establish a vitamin/mineral/herbal supplementation program tailored to your particular condition and needs. However, if you are unable to set up a customized supplementation program, here are some general guidelines:

Take a high-quality, time-release multivitamin/mineral supplement after breakfast and after dinner.

Take a B complex supplement after your midmorning and your midafternoon snacks.

Take a buffered, esterized form of vitamin C three times daily as a detoxifier, for a total of one to three grams, depending on your size. If you experience diarrhea, cut down the dosage until you reach a tolerance level.

Take a multiplex amino acid blend after dinner.

Chromium, also called GTF (glucose tolerance factor), is a mineral that works with insulin in the metabolism of sugar and is required during withdrawal from hypoglycemic-related toxins, such as sugar, alcohol, and caffeine. Check your multivitamin/mineral supplement, and if it does not contain this mineral, purchase a chromium supplement and take one hundred micrograms daily.

Add a teaspoon of spirulina powder to two of your raw juice drinks each day, or take two spirulina tablets after two meals. Spirulina is high in protein, vitamins, and minerals and also has chlorophyll for cleansing.

Valerian, which is available in capsule form, can be used occasionally for its calming effect, particularly when overcoming an alcohol or drug addiction. *Do not use valerian for prolonged periods of time.*

Chamomile is a gentle sedative for the mind and body that also helps with indigestion that may arise during detoxification. You can prepare the flowers in tea form and drink a half cup at a time. Do not use chamomile if you are allergic to ragweed.

Catnip tea can also soothe the nerves. Alfalfa tea is rich in vitamins and minerals and acts as a cleanser. Pau d'arco tea and a mixture of echinacea and goldenseal tea are effective detoxifiers and may help strengthen the immune system. Other teas you can use intermittently include rose hips, dandelion, and red clover.

CHAPTER 12

Self-Health Resources: The Physical Side

MONITORING YOUR PULSE DURING WORKOUTS

During your aerobic workout you need to monitor your pulse rate. Here is the formula for establishing the target zone of your exercise pulse rate:

220 minus your age, multiplied by 0.60 = low end of target rate

220 minus your age, multiplied by 0.80 = high end of target rate

For example, if you are thirty-four years old, you would calculate this way: $220 - 34 = 186 \times 0.60 = 111.6$ low end

$$220 - 34 = 186 \times 0.80 = 148.8 \text{ high end}$$

Your target zone would be 111 to 148 heartbeats per minute during exercise.

If you have not been doing aerobic exercise on a regular basis before starting the Self-Health Program, the intensity of your workout should be in the low end of your target zone. For example, if you're thirty-four, during the first few weeks you should aim for an exercise pulse rate of 111 to 120 beats per minute. By the end of the program you might work up to an exercise pulse rate of 130 beats per minute.

You can take your pulse either in the soft area of the wrist, just under your thumb, or at the carotid artery at the neck. Unless you are elderly, the carotid pulse may be easier to count during exercise. You can take the carotid pulse on either side of your windpipe, to the right or left of the Adam's apple area.

About five minutes into the aerobic exercise session, place your finger (not thumb) gently on the pulse and count the beats for fifteen seconds, then multiply by four to get your exercise pulse rate. If it is too high up in your target zone or above the zone, you need to reduce the intensity of the exercise. Do this test again near the end of your aerobic sessions.

If all this pulse arithmetic sounds too complicated, there is an alternative. Sporting goods stores offer a device called the pulsemeter to wear on your wrist. You put in the parameters, and the meter beeps when your pulse is too high or too low. It's also a handy device for tracking your progress from workout to workout.

MUSCULOSKELETAL DEVELOPMENT EXERCISES

Here is a simple set of musculoskeletal development exercises that focuses on the muscle groups that are generally the weakest. You'll recognize some of the basic exercises of gym classes and calisthenics, but with an emphasis on proper form and breathing.

Breathing is primary in a holistic approach to exercise. The exercise rate should be directly connected to a comfortable respiratory rate. The rule is: Exhale on exertion; inhale on relaxation of movement.

These exercises should be done in comfortable, flexible clothing and supportive workout footwear. Work out on a carpet or, preferably, an exercise mat. An exercise mat is a good investment since you can also use it for your stretching exercises. *Always do some gentle stretches before the musculoskeletal sequence.*

Leg Raises

These are intended to strengthen the abdominal group of muscles. Leg raises also tone and strengthen the leg and buttocks muscles.

Lie on your back with your left knee bent and left foot flat on the floor; right leg stretched out. Place your hands under your lower back. You might also place a small folded towel under your lower back for more support.

IMPORTANT NOTE: Keep your lower back on the floor during all leg raises, and consciously use your abdominal muscles. If you let your lower back arch, you risk injury and are not properly working the abs.

1. Exhale as you lift your right leg about six inches off the ground. Breathe and hold the leg up until you feel fatigue. Inhale as you lower slowly. Repeat on the left side (with right leg bent and right foot on floor).
2. Exhale and raise your right leg slightly higher. Hold it up; breathe; lower slowly. Repeat on left side.
3. Exhale and raise your right leg to a forty-five-degree angle, parallel to the bent left leg. Hold it up; breathe; lower slowly. Repeat on the left.
4. Exhale and raise your right leg six inches off the floor *to the side.* Hold it up; breathe; lower slowly. Repeat on left.
5. Exhale and raise your right leg slightly higher, to the side. Hold it up; breathe; lower slowly. Repeat on left side.
6. Exhale and raise your right leg to a forty-five-degree angle, as high as the bent leg, to the side. Hold it up; breathe; lower slowly. Repeat to the left.

The goal is to do this six-part set three times on each side. However, if you haven't been training, start off with one set, and work your way up to more repetitions.

As you strengthen the abdominals, you can add clockwise and counterclockwise leg circles, always with the nonworking leg bent in and the foot on the floor. Later you can add ankle weights to the exercise.

Sit-ups

Sit-ups will strengthen the abdominal muscles, but remember, we want to do sit-ups, not "neck-ups." Concentrate on using your abdominal muscles and not straining your neck. Depending on your fitness level, you may be able to rise only an inch off the floor using just your abs. That is fine. When you're stronger, you can rise halfway up and increase the number of repetitions.

Bend both knees, feet on the floor. Place your feet under a piece of furniture or have someone hold them steady. Bend your elbows, and place your thumbs under your ears, index fingers on top of your ears. Keep your elbows to the side; don't use them to get up. You can also do sit-ups with your arms straight out in front of you.

Exhale and sit up, only as far as you can go using your abdominal muscles. Inhale through your nose as you lower your body to the floor. Repeat at least ten times to start. Add repetitions as you build up your abdominal muscles.

If you cannot rise at all with your hands in the suggested position, cross your arms diagonally across your chest. This reduces the body weight and makes sit-ups easier.

After you have worked out for a period of time and can do up to thirty sit-ups, rising halfway up, you can begin diagonal sit-ups, rotating toward the opposite knee. Be careful with rotation; don't rotate too far or rise up too high.

Push-ups

These develop the upper back, shoulder, and arm muscles as well as strengthen the abdominals.

Lie on your stomach, and place your hands slightly wider than your shoulders and your feet close together. Keep your legs and body in a straight line as you push up. Don't let your back arch or your pelvis drop; your body must be kept in a straight line to prevent injury and work the upper muscles.

Inhale deeply; then exhale as you push up, keeping your body straight. Inhale as you lower your chest to the floor; exhale as you push up. Repeat as many times as you can while maintaining proper form, without getting shaky.

Many women find they cannot do even one push-up when they begin training. If this is your situation, you can do modified push-ups, with your knees bent and lower legs on the floor. This reduces the weight you need to push up, until you can build up strength and do full push-ups. Be very careful not to flex your lower back in the modified push-up position, and place padding under your knees if needed.

Buttocks Exercises

These are often called doggie exercises since they're done on all fours, an undignified but effective position.

1. Position yourself on your hands and knees, back straight (except for the natural curve of the spine). Exhale and lift your leg to the side, keeping your knee slightly bent. Inhale and lower. Repeat ten times on each side. As your buttocks muscles get stronger, work up to three repetitions of ten on each side.
2. On all fours, inhale and bring your knee into your chest and your chin down, rounding your back. Exhale and bring your leg back, as you lift your head and slightly arch your back. Repeat ten times on each side. Move slowly, with attention to form and breathing. This exercise works the upper body muscles as well as the buttocks and provides a nice stretch for the neck.

Jumping Jacks

These are intended to build muscular and cardiovascular endurance. Jumping jacks work the muscles of the legs, arms, and chest, develop coordination, and are a good lead-in to aerobic exercise. If you do your jumping jacks in front of the mirror, you can check on the synchronicity of your arms and legs.

Supportive footwear is required for this exercise. If you have arthritis, lower back pain, or joint weaknesses or are elderly, jumping jacks are not recommended.

Start with your feet together, arms at your side. Inhale, then exhale as you bring your arms overhead and open your legs. Inhale as you bring your feet together and arms down. Repeat ten to fifty times.

As you develop endurance, you can do quadrant jumping jacks: Jump a quarter turn to the right side, then to the back, to the left side, and front.

STRETCHING SEQUENCE

Here is a stretching sequence that lasts about thirty minutes. It provides a good overall stretch that will relax you after a hard day of work or prepare you for aerobic exercise.

1. Lie down on your back, and breathe deeply into your abdomen.
2. Lift your arms over your head, and keep them on the floor. Slowly stretch your right arm and right leg, lengthening the whole right side; then release. Stretch and lengthen your left arm and leg; then release. Stretch and lengthen both arms and legs; then release. Repeat this sequence once.
3. Bend both knees, and place your feet flat on the floor, with your arms out to the sides. Lengthen your spine along the floor. Slowly drop your knees to the right side, looking left. Breathe in this position. Bring the knees center; then drop slowly to the left side, looking right. Return to center, and repeat.
4. Lie with your arms out to the sides, legs down. Bend in the right knee. Cross it over to the left side, looking and twisting your upper body to the right, to form a diagonal oppo-

sition stretch. Breathe in this position. Slowly return to center. Stretch your leg up in the air; then bring it down. Bend in your left knee. Cross it over to the right, while stretching your upper body and head to the left. Breathe; then return to center, stretch your leg up, and bring it down slowly.

5. Hug your knees into your chest, tuck in your head, and rock up to a sitting position. Sit in a comfortable cross-legged position. (If it's difficult for you to sit cross-legged, you can do these head and neck exercises from a standing position.) Be very gentle with the neck movements.

6. Slowly turn your head right to left, four times. Lower your chin to your chest. Then slowly raise your head into an arching position. Whenever you arch, think of lengthening your neck up, rather than back. (Don't drop your head all the way back and compress your neck.) Lift up and down four times. Then stretch your neck diagonally by dropping your ear toward your shoulder (although it won't touch), twice to each side. Do two slow head circles to the right; two slow circles to the left. Again, don't let your neck drop back.

7. After the head movements, if you have been sitting cross-legged, stretch your legs in front, and place the leg that was underneath before on top as you resume cross-legged position. Lift your shoulders up; then relax them, four times. Bring your shoulders into your chest; then stretch them toward the back, four times. Circle your shoulders to the back four times and to the front four times. Place your hands on your shoulders, and circle your elbows to the front four times and back four times.

8. With your knees bent, roll down slowly; then turn onto your stomach. Stretch your right leg up about six inches off the ground, hold for a few breaths, and lower. Stretch your left leg up, hold, lower. Stretch both legs up; hold while you breathe, and lower. Relax your legs.

9. Return to a sitting position, legs stretched out in front. Stretch your arms overhead; then reach forward over your legs. Keep your chin up and your back long as you grab

your legs and stretch forward. Don't pull or round your back; keep a slight arch in your lower back, and breathe into the stretch. Then roll up slowly, and shake your legs gently.

10. Bend in your knees so your feet are touching. Stretch forward between your legs, keeping your chin up and your back elongated. You can also stretch first toward one knee, then the other in this position. With your knees bent, roll down slowly.

11. Turn onto your stomach. Place your hands, elbows bent, about six inches outside your shoulders. Inhale and slowly lift your head, then slowly arch your spine. Use mainly your torso strength, not your hands, to rise. Keep your elbows slightly bent, and don't compress your lower back in the arch. Breathe for several counts; then lower slowly.

12. Staying on your stomach, bend your knees and clasp your ankles. Slowly lift your upper body and legs into a bow position. Hold for a few counts as you breathe, then lower slowly and relax. (You may need to exercise regularly for several weeks before you can do this "bow" exercise.)

13. Turn onto your side, and then rise to a standing position gently. Lift up tall through your spine. Keeping your hips front, slowly twist your upper body to the right and wrap your arms around your waist, looking right. Breathe in this position; then unwrap and shift to center. Repeat to the left side.

14. Place your feet a few feet apart. Keeping your hips forward, stretch your left arm overhead and tilt your body slightly to the right. Return to center. Stretch your right arm overhead and upper body to the left. Return to center.

15. Bring your feet back under your hips. Slowly roll down, starting with your head, rolling down one vertebra at a time, bending your knees slightly as you lower. Hang and relax; then roll up slowly, starting with the bottom of your spine and your head coming up last. Repeat the rolling up and down once.

16. Stand tall, feeling your posture and alignment. Imagine light and energy flowing all the way up your spine, up into

your head. Try to keep this feeling as you start your aerobic exercise or go about your day.

TOTAL BODY RELAXATION

Find a quiet, private room, and lower the lights. Lie down on a padded surface, but not a bed since you don't want to fall asleep.

Begin deep breathing. Fill up your abdomen, rib cage, and lungs with healing breath. Exhale slowly, and let your body sink into the floor. Feel the support of the earth. Let your body release and relax with every exhalation. Continue deep breathing as you focus your relaxation on the different parts of your body.

Relax your toes. Relax the soles of your feet. Let your heels sink into the ground and relax.

Relax your calves. Let them feel very loose and long. Relax your thighs. Let your thighs soften and relax. Your legs are long and relaxed.

Relax your hips. Feel them wide and relaxed. Let your buttocks sink into the ground and relax.

Relax your abdomen. Feel the breath relaxing and nourishing your organs. Your organs are relaxed and functioning smoothly.

Relax your rib cage and chest. Feel it open and relaxed.

Relax the base of your spine. Feel the relaxation flowing up your spine with your breath. Feel your lower back soften and relax. Let your middle back relax.

Feel your shoulder blades wide and relaxed on the floor. Let your upper back relax and release. Your spine is long; your muscles are released; your back is completely relaxed.

Feel the relaxing energy enter your fingertips. Relax your lower arms, your elbows, your upper arms. Let the relaxation flow into your shoulders. Relax the tops of your shoulders.

Let the relaxation flow up your neck. Let your head sink into the floor, supported by the earth. Your neck and your head are completely relaxed.

Relax your jaw. Relax your mouth. Relax your cheeks. Relax behind your ears. Relax your eyes. Relax your forehead. Your face is completely soft and relaxed.

Your entire body is relaxed, from your toes up through your legs, your organs, your back, your shoulders, your neck, your face.

Every breath you take is full of love. Feel the love flowing to all the open, relaxed parts of your body.

Meditate on the love flowing freely throughout your body.

When you are ready, open your eyes, and gently stretch. Roll onto one side, and rise slowly.

THE BATHING RITUAL

The following bathing sequence is called the Bathing Ritual because it provides spiritual as well as physical nourishment. If you do it regularly, it will become an integral part of your life and provide precious comfort and pleasure.

The best time to do the Bathing Ritual is in the morning, as a way to start your day by nourishing your Holistic Triangle. The bathing sequence takes only about fifteen minutes, and the benefits are well worth your getting up a little earlier. Try it and you'll see.

Set the scene by having a clean bathtub and natural light, if possible. You can use a scented candle, potpourri, or aromatherapy oils to enhance the atmosphere if you wish.

1. Fill the bathtub approximately one-quarter full with hot water, as hot as you can comfortably tolerate. The water level should be shallow enough so that you can lie with your back on the bottom of the tub, neck relaxed, and only your face above water.

2. Step in slowly, and sit down, feeling the heat relax each part of your body. Then slide down slowly until the back of your head is underwater (your head may rest on the bottom of the tub or float an inch or so). Bend your knees,

and rest your feet against the wall at the opposite end of the tub or up on the sides.

3. Breathe deeply through your nose, and say a positive affirmation to yourself, such as "My mind and body are calm and relaxed." Relax and let your body melt into the warmth.

4. With your arms alongside your body, tilt your right ear toward your right shoulder, keeping the left shoulder down, to stretch your neck laterally. Hold for five seconds; then return to center. Repeat toward the left side.

5. Bring your chin and your chest up slightly to arch your head back. Hold for five seconds; then shift your head slightly to the right and left in the arched position. Return to center.

6. Inhale, hold your nose, and turn your head to the right. Hold for five seconds; then center. Exhale, inhale, and repeat to the left.

7. Place your hands behind your head. Inhale and hyperextend (arch) your lower back. Hold for five seconds, stretching your lower back; then exhale and contract. Use your feet against the wall or sides as a stabilizing force during this movement. Repeat several times.

8. Place your arms alongside your body. Curve your right shoulder toward your right hip, forming a C with your torso, to stretch your left side. Hold for a count of five, and repeat to the other side.

9. Keeping your head and arms relaxed on the bottom of the tub, bend your knees and place your feet flat on the bottom. Bend both knees to the right side to form a spinal twist. Hold for a count of five, then return to center. Repeat to the left side. (You will need to adjust this movement depending on the size of your tub.)

10. Come up onto your side; then sit with your legs straight in front of you. Keep your chin up and your lower back slightly arched as you stretch forward. Grasp the outside of your calves, with your elbows bent and your thumbs on

top. Hold for a count of ten; then release and straighten up.

11. Slide back down to the original position (head on the bottom of the tub and feet elevated). This is a good time for a Healing Moment or your own personal form of prayer. Then visualize your ideal Holistic Triangle and what you are going to do to work toward your goal today. Picture how you'll nourish each side of your Triangle today.

12. Sit up gently, and kneel in the tub. Lather up your body with a fragrant natural soap, and rinse off. Shampoo your hair, if you wish, and lie back to rinse. (If you don't want wet hair, you can use a well-fitting bathing cap during the entire Bathing Ritual.)

13. Let the soapy water out of the tub. Stand up, and use the shower to rinse off with warm water.

14. Slowly adjust the faucets to change the temperature to cold water. At first this may be a shock, but after you're accustomed to the Bathing Ritual, you'll enjoy the cold. Stretch up to the ceiling a few times during this invigorating cold interlude.

15. Finish off with a rinse of warm, but not hot, water.

16. After you get out of the tub and dry off, massage yourself with moisturizer containing natural oils and vitamin E.

On days when you have extra time, you can perform the Bathing Ritual at night as well as in the morning. You can use incense, candlelight, scented bath oils, and music to make it even more sensual.

Although the Bathing Ritual is very pleasurable, remember it's not just a perk that can be sacrificed when you're busy: It has a therapeutic physiological effect. The hot water relaxes your muscles and allows dilation and expansion; the cold water causes contraction, and the warm water brings blood back to your muscles. The exercises are basic stretches to prepare you for the demands of the day. You may hear little cracks and crunches when you perform them; this is the sound of your body adjusting itself.

When you have the time and inclination, you can leave out the shower and perform the entire sequence in the bathtub, filling it up with hot water, then cold water, then warm water. This is also the way to do it if you have a tub but no shower.

If you do not have a bathtub, there is, unfortunately, no way to get the full benefit of weightlessness. To compensate, you can perform the exercises, both physical and mental/spiritual steps, on your exercise mat, then take a hot-cold-warm shower.

HOLISTIC HEALING THERAPIES

Acupressure refers to massage techniques that use manual pressure to stimulate energy points, based on the principles of acupuncture. The pressure serves to stimulate the body's recuperative powers by releasing and balancing the flow of chi.

Chi, which is called prana in India and ki in Japan, is considered the life force or inherent energy within each person. Chi flows through meridians, or energy pathways, and acupressure works to open and balance these meridians. Shiatsu, Jin Shin, do-in, and acu-yoga are some of the forms of acupressure.

Acupuncture involves stimulating the energy points through the insertion of fine needles, the application of heat produced by burning an herb, manual pressure, or a weak electrical current. As in acupressure, the goal is to facilitate the balanced flow of chi throughout the meridians.

The Alexander technique is a method of reducing physical and mental tension by improving habits of posture, balance, coordination, and movement. Alexander teachers offer hands-on guidance and verbal instruction to help their students relearn their innately healthy postures and ways of movement.

Aromatherapy uses aromatic essences extracted from plants. These essential oils are administered by massage, in baths, through skin preparations, compresses, and steam inhalation. Aromatherapists use particular oils for specific conditions, as well as for general beauty treatments and relaxation.

Ayurvedic medicine is the traditional system of healing in India. It is a complex holistic system that incorporates medicinal, psychological, and spiritual principles. Pulse diagnosis, energy points, herbal remedies, dietary counseling, and yoga are some of the modalities utilized in this comprehensive health care system.

Bach Flower Remedies are an outgrowth of homeopathy. Practitioners believe certain plants contain essences that can help reunite the body and soul, nature and spirit. Flower essences are used to strengthen the individual's innate healing power.

Biofeedback training is a technique for learning relaxation and control over automatic body functions. Clients monitor their metabolic changes with the biofeedback machine and learn to evoke relaxation using various techniques.

Body-oriented psychotherapies combine "talk therapy" with body work or movement techniques. Dance movement therapy, for example, uses expressive movement as a therapeutic tool. Bioenergetics, based on the work of Wilhelm Reich, explores the healing power of the body's sexual energy. These and other body-oriented psychotherapies help patients break through psychological barriers that are causing physical symptoms.

Chinese medicine is an ancient holistic system that continues to astound the Western world with its wisdom. Acupuncture, herbal medicine, moxibustion (heat therapy), massage, nutritional advice, and lifestyle counseling are among the techniques used by Chinese doctors.

Chiropractic is now the number one natural health care system in the Western world. As discussed in Chapter 1, traditional chiropractic is based on the principle that the basis of health is an optimally functioning nervous system. The nerve pathways can function properly only when the vertebral bones of the spinal cord are aligned. Misalignment of the vertebrae, called subluxation, puts pressure on the nerves, which can lead to pain, restricted blood supply, and susceptibility to disease. Modern chiropractic is based on the principle that disease is caused by a lack of innate nerve energy with or without subluxation.

"Straight" chiropractors work primarily on realigning the vertebrae through hands-on manipulation and adjustment. Holistic chiropractors utilize additional modalities, which may include massage, physical therapies, rehabilitative exercises, and nutritional counseling. Many of today's chiropractors are holistic physicians who give special attention to the nervous system, musculoskeletal system, spinal biomechanics, and nutrition.

Colonic hydrotherapy is the irrigation of the large intestine through a full enema to cleanse and detoxify. Fasting, saunas and hot tubs, deep breathing, and massage are sometimes used in conjunction with colonic therapy.

Deep tissue body work therapies release and "unstick" the body's connective tissues and muscles to allow them to function properly. The emotional component of posture, breathing, and physical conditions is addressed in some types of deep-tissue body work, such as Rolfing and Hellerwork.

The Feldenkrais method teaches awareness of the skeleton and its muscles and healthier ways to use the body. Teachers use movement training, gentle touch, and verbal dialogue to help students liberate their bodies and relearn the freer movements they had as children.

Herbal medicine, which uses plants in many forms, has been employed in every culture since ancient times to cleanse, heal, and nourish. Herbal medicines trigger biochemical responses in the body and can stimulate the natural healing response. Herbs are used for elimination and detoxification, prevention and health maintenance, toning the organs, nourishing the tissues and blood, and specific healing purposes.

In addition to herbalists, who specialize in prescribing herbal medicine, herbs are used by holistic chiropractors, naturopaths, nutritionists, traditional Chinese doctors, and many other natural healers.

Homeopathy is a system of medicine using preparations of natural essences. It is used for chronic problems, infections, physiological deficiencies, and preventive purposes. Classical homeopaths use homeopathy exclusively, while eclectic homeopaths may use other healing arts, such as vitamin therapy, nutrition, and massage.

Kinesiology is a diagnostic and therapeutic system that employs individual testing of muscles to learn about the patient's overall health. Nutritional counseling, manipulation and pressure point work, and exercise are often used as part of a treatment plan by kinesiologists.

Massage therapy is a system of kneading, stroking, and applying pressure to the body to promote healing, relaxation, cleansing, and general health. One of the most popular forms of massage is Swedish, which uses a series of kneading, friction, and stroking movements over the entire body. Swedish massage improves circulation and releases endorphins, among other effects.

Sports massage focuses on specific muscles and sports injuries. Many massage therapists learn a number of techniques and synthesize their own styles.

Naturopathy is a holistic system of health care based on the belief in the healing power of nature. Naturopaths, or naturopathic physicians, address the underlying cause of disease and use natural means to help restore the body to equilibrium. Herbal remedies, therapeutic diets, supplementation, homeopathic remedies, hydrotherapy, exercise, massage, manipulation, and relaxation training may be included in their practices.

Nutrition therapies use dietary changes and vitamins, minerals, and herbs to heal, promote health, and build immunity. There is a wide variety of nutritional therapies with different philosophies, including macrobiotics, clinical ecologists, and such programs as Pritikin and Atkins.

Physical therapy utilizes massage, exercise, electrical stimulation, ultrasound, and therapeutic exercise to help assist patients recover from disabling conditions and injuries. Physical therapy techniques are also employed by many holistic chiropractors.

Reflexology is a technique in which manual pressure is applied to one part of the body to promote healing in another area and stimulate the innate healing force. Reflexology traces its roots back to the Chinese theory of energy meridians and works to loosen tension and unblock energy flow. It is usually performed on the feet or hands, sometimes in combination with massage.

SELF-MASSAGE

Self-massage is another variation on the age-old healing art of the laying on of hands. While self-massage isn't as sybaritic or therapeutic as receiving a massage, it does have its advantages. It's free of charge and readily available and is a positive way to show your body love and acceptance. Self-massage can also help you become more skilled at massaging other people.

The face, neck, and shoulders are the areas most conducive to self-massage. When you massage your face, be sure it's well lubricated with a natural lotion and the skin is not dry. Keep your nails clipped, and use the flat part of your fingers.

Here is a self-massage sequence for the shoulders, neck, and face.

1. Dim the lights, and lie down on your exercise mat. Begin deep breathing. Let your body sink into the ground, and relax. Let your head feel very heavy and relaxed, your neck elongated.
2. Place your right hand on your left shoulder. Stroke across your left shoulder and up the side of your neck; then up and down behind your ear. Stroke back down to your shoulder. Knead the muscle of your shoulder between your fingers. Do this sequence three times on the left; then use your left hand to massage your right shoulder and the right side of your neck.
3. Place your right thumb in the hollow under your left collarbone and your other fingers under your armpit. Press into the hollow with your thumb in a circular movement. This is a center of lymph nodes and may feel sensitive. Use your left hand on your right side to massage the same area.
4. Relax your head and lengthen your neck. Using both hands, stroke up and down the sides of your neck. Lace your fingers behind your head, and lift your neck into a gentle arch. Hold for fifteen seconds, breathing deeply; then release.
5. Use your thumbs to find sensitive points on your skull.

These points are often at the base of the skull and top of the neck. When you find such a point, press into it with your thumb for ten seconds; then release. You can also massage these spots with a circular motion.

6. Place your fingertips in the center of your forehead. Slowly stroke down your forehead, down your nose, over your cheekbones, then up your temples and across your forehead. Complete five double circles with a slow, gentle movement.

7. Return to any spots that felt tense during the face circles, and massage these areas with minicircles or steady finger pressure.

8. Using all your fingertips, briskly massage your entire scalp with circular movements.

Although an upper body self-massage is most relaxing in a lying-down position, you can also use it as a quick pick-me-up when sitting at work.

1. Tilt your head to one side, and use the opposite hand to stroke up and down your shoulder and the side of your neck. Repeat on the other side.

2. Squeeze the muscles of your shoulders to relieve tightness.

3. Lace your fingers behind your neck, and use them as a cradle as you arch your head up.

To massage your legs, sit with them extended, and knead the muscles with your fingertips. To massage your arms, simply use the opposite hand. Always stroke your limbs toward your heart.

To massage your lower back, either stand or lie on your stomach and rub in a circular motion on the sides of the vertebrae. To relieve sciatic pain, you can massage your buttocks while standing or lying on your stomach.

To massage your own feet, sit in a chair and place one foot on the opposite thigh. Consult a book on reflexology if you want to learn which parts of the foot correspond to different areas of the body and internal organs.

Self-massage can be used as an adjunct to stretching or yoga exercises. As you stretch, you can massage different parts of your body to help them lengthen and relax. Experiment to find out what feels right for you.

HOT AND COLD COMPRESS THERAPY

You'll need two reusable hot and cold packs to use for your self-treatment of muscle pain. Remember, *never put a pack directly on your skin;* always use a towel underneath. Never massage the skin directly after using hot or cold packs; wait until it has returned to normal temperature. People with skin conditions, children, and elderly people should be particularly careful about compresses and seek the advice of a health professional before using them.

1. Place a towel warmed with hot water on the muscle or area where you are experiencing the most tension or pain. Then place the hot pack on the towel for fifteen to twenty minutes. This allows the muscle to relax and expand and increases blood circulation to the area.
2. Remove the hot pack and warm towel. Wait a few minutes for skin temperature to return to normal. Then place a cold, wet towel and an ice pack on the area. You can compress the muscle by lying on the pack if you wish. Be aware the cold may be uncomfortable and you may experience burning, pain, and numbness. Use the cold pack for no longer than ten minutes. The cold works by constricting the muscle, which removes the old blood and metabolic wastes.
3. Wait until the skin is normal temperature. Again, place a warm towel and a hot pack on the area for fifteen to twenty minutes. This allows the muscle to expand and fresh, oxygenated blood to enter.

Remove the hot pack and relax for a few minutes. Mentally send the muscle your healing energy. Rise gently, and avoid using the muscle strenuously for the next hour.

Bibliography/ Suggested Further Reading

HOLISTIC HEALTH

Bliss, Shepherd, ed. *The New Holistic Health Handbook.* Lexington, Mass.: Stephen Greene Press, 1985.

Melville, Arabella, and Colin Johnson. *Health Without Drugs: Alternatives to Prescriptions and Over-the-Counter Medicines.* New York: Simon & Schuster, 1990.

Mendelsohn, Robert S. *Confessions of a Medical Heretic.* Chicago: Contemporary Books, 1979.

Olsen, Kristin Gottschalk. *The Encyclopedia of Alternative Health Care.* New York: Simon & Schuster, 1990.

Pilkington, J. Maya, and the Diagram Group. *Alternative Healing and Your Health.* New York: Ballantine Books, 1991.

MENTAL/SPIRITUAL SIDE

Benson, Herbert, and Miriam Z. Klipper. *The Relaxation Response.* New York: Avon, 1976.

Borysenko, Joan, with Larry Rothstein. *Minding the Body, Mending the Mind.* New York: Bantam Books, 1988.

Chopra, Deepak. *Quantum Healing: Exploring the Frontiers of The Mind/Body Medicine.* New York: Bantam Books, 1989.

Gawain, Shakti. *Creative Visualization.* New York: Bantam, 1982.

Hay, Louise L. *You Can Heal Your Life.* Santa Monica, Calif.: Hay House, 1984.

LeShan, Lawrence. *How to Meditate.* New York: Bantam Books, 1974.

Miller, Ronald S. *As Above, So Below: Paths to Spiritual Renewal in Daily Life.* Los Angeles: Jeremy P. Tarcher, 1992.

Padmus, Emrika, and the Editors of *Prevention* Magazine. *The Complete Guide to Your Emotions and Your Health.* Emmaus, Pa.: Rodale Press, 1986.

Thich Nhat Han. *The Miracle of Mindfulness.* Boston: Beacon Press, 1987.

CHEMICAL SIDE

Airola, Paavo. *Hypoglycemia: A Better Approach.* Sherwood, Ore.: Health Plus, 1977.

Balch, James F. and Phyllis A. *Prescription for Nutritional Healing.* Garden City Park, N.Y.: Avery Publishing, 1990.

Blauer, Stephen. *Juicing for Life.* Garden City Park, N.Y.: Avery Publishing, 1989.

Buchman, Dian Dincin. *Herbal Medicine.* New York: Gramercy, 1980.

Diamond, Harvey and Marilyn. *Fit for Life II: Living Health.* New York: Warner Books, 1987.

Dunne, Lavon J. *Nutrition Almanac.* New York: McGraw-Hill, 1975.

Gershoff, Stanley, with Catherine Whitney. *The Tufts University Guide to Total Nutrition*. New York: HarperCollins, 1991.

Graedon, Joe. *The New People's Pharmacy*. New York: Bantam, 1985.

Long, James W. *Essential Guide to Prescription Drugs*. New York: HarperCollins, 1993.

Kloss, Jethro. *Back to Eden*. Loma Linda, Calif.: Back to Eden Publishing, 1939.

McDougall, John A. and Mary A. *The McDougall Plan*. Clinton, N.J.: New Win Publishing, 1983.

Mindell, Earl. *Earl Mindell's Herb Bible*. New York: Simon & Schuster, 1992.

———. *Earl Mindell's Vitamin Bible*. New York: Warner Books, 1979.

Muir, Murray, and Joseph Pizzorno. *Encyclopedia of Natural Medicine*. Rocklin, Calif.: Prima Publishing, 1991.

Murray, Michael T. *The Complete Book of Juicing*. Rocklin, Calif.: Prima Publishing, 1992.

Null, Gary. *Clearer, Cleaner, Safer, Greener: A Blueprint for Detoxifying Your Environment*. New York: Random House, 1990.

———. *No More Allergies*. New York: Villard, 1992.

Robbins, John. *Diet for a New America*. Walpole, N.H.: Stillpoint Publishing, 1987.

———. *May All Be Fed: Diet for a New World*. New York: William Morrow, 1992.

Wade, Carlson. *Immune Power Boosters: Your Key to Feeling Younger, Living Longer*. New York: Prentice Hall, 1990.

PHYSICAL SIDE

Anderson, Bob. *Stretching*. Bolinas, Calif.: Shelter, 1980.

Cooper, Kenneth H. *The Aerobics Program for Total Well-Being: Exercise, Diet, Emotional Balance*. New York: M. Evans, 1982.

Evans, William, and Irwin Rosenberg, with Jacqueline Thompson. *Biomarkers: The 10 Keys to Longevity*. New York: Simon & Schuster, 1992.

Glover, Bob, and Jack Shepherd. *Runner's Handbook*. New York: Penguin, 1985.

Hittleman, Richard. *Yoga: 28 Day Exercise Plan.* New York: Bantam Books, 1973.

Lidell, Lucinda. *The Book of Massage.* New York: Simon & Schuster, 1984.

Vishnu-devananda, Swami. *The Complete Illustrated Book of Yoga.* New York: Pocket Books, 1981.

FURTHER READING ON MAJOR DISEASES

Bennett, Cleaves M. *Control Your High Blood Pressure Without Drugs.* New York: Doubleday, 1984.

Dreher, Henry. *Your Defense Against Cancer.* New York: Harper & Row, 1989.

Heimlich, Jane. *What Your Doctor Won't Tell You.* New York: HarperCollins, 1990.

Matthews-Simonton, Stephanie, and O. Carl Simonton. *Getting Well Again.* New York: Bantam Books, 1979.

Null, Gary. *Healing Your Body Naturally: Alternative Treatments to Illness.* New York: Four Walls, Eight Windows, 1992.

Ornish, Dean. *Dr. Dean Ornish's Program for Reversing Heart Disease.* New York: Random House, 1990.

Siegel, Bernie S. *Love, Medicine and Miracles.* New York: Harper & Row, 1986.

———. *Peace, Love & Healing.* New York: Harper & Row, 1990.

Whitaker, Julian M. *Reversing Diabetes.* New York: Warner Books, 1990.

———. *Reversing Heart Disease.* New York: Warner Books, 1985.

Index

Entries in **boldface** refer to tables and illustrations.